The Social Acceptance of Inequality

The Social Acceptance of Inequality

On the Logics of a More Unequal World

Edited by
FRANCESCO DUINA
AND
LUCA STORTI

OXFORD
UNIVERSITY PRESS

OXFORD
UNIVERSITY PRESS

Oxford University Press is a department of the University of Oxford.
It furthers the University's objective of excellence in research, scholarship,
and education by publishing worldwide. Oxford is a registered trade mark of
Oxford University Press in the UK and in certain other countries.

Published in the United States of America by Oxford University Press
198 Madison Avenue, New York, NY 10016, United States of America.

CIP data is on file at the Library of Congress

ISBN 9780197814499

DOI: 10.1093/oso/9780197814499.001.0001

Printed by Sheridan Books, Inc., United States of America

The manufacturer's authorized representative in the EU for product safety is Oxford
University Press España S.A., Parque Empresarial San Fernando de Henares,
Avenida de Castilla, 2 – 28830 Madrid (www.oup.es/en).

Contents

List of Figures

List of Tables

List of Appendices

Acknowledgments

Edited volumes are somewhat akin to orchestral performances: Everyone must contribute, and everyone plays a necessary role in the delivery of the final product. A missing or out-of-tune instrument can undermine the entire effort. We—Francesco and Luca—as editors were very lucky to be joined by a remarkable set of scholars who proved deeply committed to the project. Throughout, all the authors took on dual roles as both orchestra players and conductors, creating a rare synergy. We are thankful to them for their interest and hard work. Their chapters constitute genuine research pieces offering valuable insights into the social acceptance of economic inequalities.

We held workshops in April 2024 with three external experts who commented on the first draft of the chapters: John Campbell (Dartmouth College), Elizabeth Sowers (California State University, Channel Islands), and Lynette Spillman (University of Notre Dame). Their observations helped elevate the quality of the chapters a great deal. They were the best guest-conductors we could have hoped for! Our authors listened, and the results were sharper and more cohesive chapters. The comments also helped us, the editors, refine the scope and intended contributions of the volume as a whole. We owe John, Elizabeth, and Lynette an enormous debt of gratitude.

At various points in the last two years, we discussed the project with additional colleagues. Each offered ideas that shaped the project in important ways. We are therefore thankful to Jonathan Eastwood, Liah Greenfeld, John A. Hall, Leslie McCall, and colleagues (as well as students) at our respective institutions for their ideas and suggestions. Ahead of publication, we had the opportunity to present the project at various venues. John Torpey hosted us in May 2024 for an episode of *International Horizons*, his podcast as Director of the Ralph Bunche Institute for International Studies at the Graduate Center, City University of New York. We are grateful for his interest. In August 2024, we presented the project at the American Sociological Association's annual conference in Montreal. Despite it being an early morning session, several scholars came and asked probing questions. An earlier virtual presentation at the annual conference of the Society for the

Advancement of Socio-Economics in spring served a similar function. The confluence of the resulting insights helped us in myriad ways, especially as we wrote the Introduction and Conclusion to the volume.

The idea of the project came to us in 2022. Soon after, we approached James Cook at Oxford University Press to test his interest. One of us had just published a volume with Oxford that also benefited from his support and insights. As with that volume, James proved to be a master at his craft: encouraging when needed, constructively critical where useful, and able to leverage his immense knowledge of our discipline—and his wisdom—to help us put forth what we think is an original and ambitious volume. To do this, he relied on the comments from three anonymous and extremely insightful readers. Simply put, the volume would have been very different without their involvement.

To ensure delivery of a well-prepared manuscript, we relied on the copyediting work of Anna Zuschlag. Academics are often perfectionists and tend to worry about all things small and big. Having worked with Anna before, we knew that we could trust her fully to work with our contributors and deliver the best-prepared manuscript possible. We are thankful to her for her excellent and hard work. Production at Oxford was handled by Sarah Ebel, who, from the start, proved organized, supportive, and helpful. We thank her for her work.

This was truly a collective effort. And throughout, we benefited from a grant from the Schmutz Fund for Faculty Support at Bates College. We are thankful to Bates for its support.

Francesco Duina and Luca Storti
Cumberland (Maine, US) and Torino (Italy), October 2024

Contributor Biographies

Lucy Barnes is Professor of Political Economy in the Department of Political Science at University College London. Her research focuses on the politics of economic policymaking in advanced industrialized societies, and in particular on the politics of economic inequality and redistribution, macroeconomic policy, and growth. Her interests range from understanding variation in policy and performance in these areas across countries and through time, to individual attitudes of both citizens and politicians.

Licia Bobzien is a Postdoctoral Researcher with the Chair of Inequality Research and Social Stratification Research at the University of Potsdam. Her research interests include (perceptions of) economic inequality, the formation of social and political attitudes, and comparative welfare state research. Her work has been published in journals such as *Social Indicators Research*, *European Societies*, *Journal of European Social Policy*, and *European Sociological Review*.

Priya Chacko is Associate Professor of International Politics at the University of Adelaide and Co-Editor-in-Chief of *South Asia: Journal of South Asian Studies*. Her research focuses on the political economy and geopolitics of India, Australia, and the Asia-Pacific region.

Marc Dixon is Professor of Sociology at Dartmouth College. He is the author of *Heartland Blues: Labor Rights in the Industrial Midwest* (2020). His papers have appeared in journals such as *Work and Occupations*, *American Sociological Review*, *American Journal of Sociology*, *Social Movement Studies*, *Social Forces*, *Sociological Perspectives*, *Elementa: Science of the Anthropocene*, *Mobilization*, *Social Science Research*, and *Social Problems*.

Francesco Duina is Charles A. Dana Professor of Sociology at Bates College, where he is also Chair of the Social Sciences Division. He has held appointments at Harvard University, Copenhagen Business School, and the University of British Columbia (where he was Professor and Head of Sociology from 2013 to 2015). His work lies at the intersections of economic and political sociology, international political economy, and cultural sociology. His articles have appeared in journals such as *Contexts*, *Journal of European Public Policy*, and the *Review of International Political Economy*. He is the author of seven books, including *Broke and Patriotic: Why Poor Americans Love Their Country* (2018). His most recent edited volume is *Standardizing the World: EU Trade Policy and the Road to Convergence* (2023).

Sam Friedman is Professor of Sociology at the London School of Economics. He is the author of *The Class Ceiling: Why It Pays to Be Privileged*, with Daniel Laurison (2019). His articles have appeared in numerous journals, such as the *British Journal of Sociology*, *American Sociological Review*, *American Behavioural Scientist*, *Sociology*, *Economy and Society*, *British Journal of Sociology of Education*, *Journal of Professions and Organization*, and *Poetics*.

Juan Diego García-Castro is Professor at the University of Costa Rica (San Ramón) and an Adjunct Researcher at COES (Centro de Estudios de Conflictos y Cohesión Social, Chile). His articles have appeared in journals such as the *Journal of Experimental Social Psychology*, *Social Science Journal*, *Journal of Social Psychology*, and *Social Psychological and Personality Science*.

Efraín García-Sánchez is an Economic Mobility Research Fellow at SPARQ, Department of Psychology, Stanford University, and Research Fellow in the Department of Social Psychology at the University of Granada. His research focuses on the effect of economic inequality on political attitudes and subjective well-being. His articles have appeared in journals such as *Perspectives on Psychological Science*, *British Journal of Social Psychology*, *Social Justice Research*, and *International Journal of Social Psychology*.

Robert C. Hauhart is Professor of Sociology, Humanities, and Legal Studies at Saint Martin's University. He is an editor and author of twelve books, including *Significant Food: Critical Readings to Nourish American Literature* (2024) and *Consuming the American Dream: Essays Celebrating the Intersection of Food, Literature, and Our National Myth* (forthcoming), both with Jeff Birkenstein. Professor Hauhart's other books in sociology include *The Routledge Handbook on the American Dream* (3 volumes), with Mitja Sardoč; *The Lonely Quest: Constructing the Self in the Twenty-First Century* (2018); and *Seeking the American Dream* (2016). Professor Hauhart was a Fulbright Scholar at the Research Center of the Slovenian Academy of Sciences and Arts in 2019.

Carola Hommerich is Professor of Sociology in the Faculty of Human Sciences at Sophia University, Tokyo. She has served as Associate Professor of Sociology at the Graduate School of Letters of Hokkaido University, Sapporo, and as Senior Research Fellow at the German Institute of Japanese Studies, Tokyo. She holds a PhD in Sociology from the University of Cologne. Her current research focuses on well-being and social inequality, particularly on the interrelation of experiences of precariousness, status anxiety, and feelings of exclusion, and their impact on behavioral outcomes. Her articles have appeared in journals such as the *Journal of Happiness Studies*, *Social Science Research*, *International Journal of Social Welfare*, and *Japanese Psychological Research*.

Joanna Kitsnik is a researcher at the Fondazione Eni Enrico Mattei in Italy. She previously held a JSPS-funded postdoctoral position at Sophia University in Tokyo and earned her PhD in Sociology from Kyoto University in 2022. Her research focuses on comparative perspectives on attitudes toward wealth, income inequality, and the environment. Her work has been published in journals such as *Comparative Sociology* and the *Japanese Journal of Sociology*.

Hanna Kuusela is Associate Professor of Sociology at the University of Jyväskylä. Her work concentrates on elite dynamics and cultures of inequalities. Her articles have appeared in journals such as *Socio-Economic Review*, *Sociology*, *Sociological Review*, *Governance*, *Journal of Education Policy*, *Economy and Society*, and *European Journal of Cultural Studies*.

Arvid Lindh is Associate Professor and Researcher at the Swedish Institute for Social Research at Stockholm University. His current research focuses on social class, politics of inequality, the welfare state, and climate policy. His work has appeared in journals such as the *Annual Review of Sociology*, *European Sociological Review*, and *Socio-Economic Review*.

Liz Moor is Senior Lecturer in Media and Communications at Goldsmiths, University of London. She is the author of *Communication and Economic Life* (2022). Her articles have appeared in journals such as *Consumption Markets and Culture*, *Journal of Cultural Economy*, *British Journal of Sociology*, *Sociological Review*, *Cultural Studies*, and *Economy and Society*.

Pía Riggirozzi is Professor of Global Politics, Department of Politics and International Relations, University of Southampton. Her research focuses on the political economy of development, human rights, and regional governance in Latin America. She is currently working on research projects regarding migration and gendered inequalities, and humanitarian responses addressing displacement in Latin America. Her publications include *Displacement, Human Rights, and Sexual and Reproductive Health* (2023), and her articles have appeared in journals such as the *Journal of Ethnic and Migration Studies*, *Development and Change*, *New Political Economy*, and *International Affairs*.

Rosa Rodríguez-Bailón is Professor of Social Psychology and Research Fellow at the Mind, Brain and Behaviours Research Center (CIMCYC) at the University of Granada. She is co-coordinator with Guillermo B. Willis of the Social Psychology of Inequality Lab. Her main research interests focus on the psychosocial antecedents and consequences of social and structural inequalities.

Luca Storti is Associate Professor of Economic Sociology at the University of Turin; a Research Fellow at the Ralph Bunche Institute at CUNY, The Graduate Center; and a Research Associate at the Institute for Social and Economic Research, University of Essex. He has held visiting appointments at several universities, including the University of Frankfurt and Free University of Berlin; the University of California, Los Angeles; and Pompeu Fabra University in Barcelona. His research examines wealth inequalities, as well as the infiltration of organized crime groups into the legal economy. His work has been published in various academic journals, including *Review of Social Economy*, *Modern Italy*, *Applied Geography*, *Sociologica*, and *Trends in Organized Crime*.

Megan Tobias Neely is Assistant Professor in the Department of Organization at the Copenhagen Business School and an affiliate of Stanford University's

Women's Leadership Innovation Lab. Her papers have appeared in journals such as the *Annual Review of Sociology*, *American Behavioral Scientist*, *Qualitative Sociology*, *Socio-Economic Review*, *Sociology Compass*, and *Social Currents*. She has authored two books: *Hedged Out: Inequality and Insecurity on Wall Street* (2022) and *Divested: Inequality in the Age of Finance*, with Ken-Hou Lin (2020).

Roland Verwiebe is Professor of Inequality Research and Social Stratification Research at the University of Potsdam. His research focuses on social inequality, digitalization, the labor market, migration, and quality of life as well as changing attitudes and values. His articles have appeared in journals such as *Social Justice Research*, *Journal of Ethnic and Migration Studies*, *International Migration*, *International Migration Review*, *European Societies*, and *European Sociological Review*.

Guillermo B. Willis is Associate Professor of Social Psychology and Research Fellow at the Mind, Brain and Behaviours Research Center (CIMCYC) at the University of Granada. His articles have appeared in journals such as the *Journal of Social Issues*, *Journal of Experimental Social Psychology*, *Journal of Experimental Social Psychology*, *Social Science Journal*, *International Review of Social Psychology*, and *Perspectives on Psychological Science*.

Cary Wu is York Research Chair and Associate Professor of Sociology at York University (Canada). His articles have appeared in journals such as *Dædalus—Journal of the American Academy of Arts and Sciences*, *Public Opinion Quarterly*, *Social Forces*, and *Social Science Research*.

List of Contributors

Lucy Barnes, Professor of Political Economy, Department of Political Science, University College London

Licia Bobzien, Postdoctoral Researcher with the Chair of Inequality Research and Social Stratification Research, University of Potsdam

Priya Chacko, Associate Professor of International Politics, University of Adelaide

Marc Dixon, Professor of Sociology, Dartmouth College

Francisco Duina, Charles A. Dana Professor of Sociology; Chair, Social Sciences Division, Bates College

Sam Friedman, Professor of Sociology, London School of Economics

Juan Diego García-Castro, Professor, University of Costa Rica; Adjunct Researcher, Centro de Estudios de Conflictos y Cohesión Social, Chile

Efraín García-Sánchez, Economic Research Fellow, SPARQ, Department of Psychology, Stanford University; Research Fellow, Mind, Brain and Behaviours Research Center (CIMCYC), University of Granada

Robert C. Hauhart, Professor of Sociology, Humanities, and Legal Studies, Saint Martin's University

Carola Hommerich, Professor of Sociology, Sophia University, Tokyo

Joanna Kitsnik, Researcher, Fondazione Eni Enrico Mattei

Hanna Kuusela, Associate Professor, Department of Social Sciences and Philosophy, University of Jyväskylä

Arvid Lindh, Associate Professor and Researcher, Swedish Institute for Social Research, Stockholm University

Liz Moor, Senior Lecturer in Media and Communications, Goldsmiths, University of London

Pía Riggirozzi, Professor of Global Politics, Department of Politics and International Relations, University of Southampton

Rosa Rodríguez-Bailón, Professor of Social Psychology; Co-Coordinator, Social Psychology of Inequality Lab, University of Granada

Luca Storti, Associate Professor of Economic Sociology, University of Turin; Research Fellow, Ralph Bunche Institute, City University of New York, The Graduate

Center; Research Associate, Institute for Social and Economic Research, University of Essex

Megan Tobias Neely, Assistant Professor, Department of Organization, Copenhagen Business School; Affiliate, Women's Leadership Innovation Lab, Stanford University

Roland Verwiebe, Professor of Inequality Research and Social Stratification Research, University of Potsdam

Guillermo B. Willis, Associate Professor of Social Psychology, University of Granada

Cary Wu, York Research Chair and Associate Professor of Sociology, York University (Canada)

Chapter 1
Introduction
The Logics of Acceptance

Francesco Duina and Luca Storti

How do people make sense of the existing economic inequalities in the world today? In this volume, we aim to identify and analyze the logics by which those economic inequalities are accepted, and even approved, by individuals and groups in society.

The question has gained momentum due to how significant those inequalities have become (Chancel and Piketty 2021; Huber and Stephens 2024; Milanovic 2023). Numerous studies have reported on the widening gaps between different social classes, increasing differentiation of economic resources within those classes, gargantuan levels of private wealth concentration, and rising poverty rates (Bourguignon 2015; Milanovic 2016a; Sayer 2015; Scheidel 2017). In a recent analysis, for instance, the Economic Policy Institute (2022) found that in the United States the total pay compensation for CEOs grew by 1,460% between 1989 and 2021. That of the typical worker grew by just 18%. Disparities in family wealth, in parallel, have steadily increased since 1989 (Congressional Budget Office 2022).

In China, India, Europe, and Russia, economic inequalities have increased in the last several decades (Inamdar 2024; Milanovic 2024). At the international level, the share of world income for the bottom 50% of the population has decreased since 1820, while that of the top 10% has gone up (Chancel et al. 2022, chapter 2). If we consider the very rich and what they have, a 2019 Oxfam report shows stunning and growing concentrations of wealth among the superrich, with the twenty-six richest billionaires owning, in 2018, as much wealth as the bottom half (around 3.8 billion people) of the world's population (Elliott 2019).

Such gaps have grown even as, according to some, inequalities on one front appear to have decreased: Those between countries (Milanovic 2024).

Francesco Duina and Luca Storti, *Introduction*. In: *The Social Acceptance of Inequality*. Edited by: Francesco Duina and Luca Storti, Oxford University Press. © Oxford University Press (2025).
DOI: 10.1093/oso/9780197814499.003.0001

That trend is, however, contested (Chancel et al. 2022), and, even if it is accurate, future developments may halt it depending on the growth rates of India, large African countries, and China (Guerriero 2024). In fact, some expect global income inequality between countries to start growing again (Kanbur et al. 2024). In any case, the situation remains quite clear: We have reached enormous gaps of inequalities between the rich, middle-class, and poor.

The general consensus is that the current levels of economic inequalities are problematic. This is the viewpoint of most of the media, politicians, international organizations such as the World Bank and the United Nations, and the public more generally.[1] Academics have also shared that position (Campbell 2018; Piketty 2014; Trigilia 2022). Some of the most pressing concerns focus on continued social cohesion, the erosion of social justice, the emergence of the so-called Great Gatsby Effect (i.e., the collapse of intergenerational mobility in the presence of high wealth concentration), and harmful exclusions (Atkinson 2015; Ayshford 2024; Krueger 2012). Attention has gone especially to certain constituents such as particular minorities, those suffering from the most pronounced types of insecurities, those living in developing countries, and migrants. Economic inequalities intricately intersect with variables such as age, gender, and ethnicity.

We too subscribe to this normative stance: We agree that current economic inequalities are highly problematic. However, the launching premise of this volume is that not everyone perceives them to be an issue. Instead, various actors actually see them as having little relevance. Some even welcome them. While the number of people who feel this way is not very large, it is not small either—as many of the chapters ahead show. As Lucy Barnes reports in Chapter 2, for instance, when examining data from twenty-nine countries across the globe, around 8% of the population (a segment that includes varying age, educational level, gender, and income groups) is accepting of income inequalities. In certain countries, the percentage of those accepting income or other types of economic inequalities is remarkably high. Cary Wu finds in Chapter 9 that, in 2019, the figure exceeded 60% when it related to income inequalities in China. In the case of Sweden, Arvid Lindh presents data in Chapter 12 on widespread support for welfare spending that discriminates against immigrants. In certain settings, such as in India, we also see that acceptance is growing even as inequalities are widening, as Priya Chacko shows in Chapter 13.

There is considerable acceptance of economic inequalities across countries and segments of societies. Such acceptance is not only counter to the more commonly held critical views of those inequalities but also, as all the chapters in this volume make clear, has profound implications for the sustenance and replication of those inequalities. The logics by which these inequalities are accepted are therefore the focus of this volume: We wish to identify and examine the multitudes of reasonings that actors adopt to reach their accepting attitudes toward economic inequalities in the world.

We proceed in this Introduction as follows. First, we introduce and elaborate on four major logics of acceptance: *market and economic*, *moral*, *cultural and institutional*, and *group and ethnic* logics. Second, we specify how our investigation not only builds on but also departs from existing research on economic inequality by adopting a wide-reaching comparative approach that moves across a rich variety of political, cultural, and economic contexts while also relying on different methodological approaches. Thus, third, we identify the main insights that emerge from the chapters: what they reveal about the four logics of acceptance. We close by outlining the organization of the volume and the Conclusion's discussion of how the logics, especially in combinations with each other, generate and replicate inequalities, possible initiatives for the reduction of those inequalities, and venues for future empirical research.

The Four Logics

Our specific focus is on four logics of acceptance of the existing economic inequalities in the world—primarily those in income, wealth, and the receipt of material benefits. Other types of inequalities, such as those in education or health, often intersect with economic ones. This means that the acceptance of economic inequalities also concerns other types of inequality. Several chapters of this volume point to this. For analytical purposes, however, the acceptance of economic inequalities—in whatever ways they may intersect with other types—remains our main object of interest. This allows for a clear guiding line of investigation across the chapters and the possibility of a sustained comparative assessment. We, of course, return to the concept of intersectionality throughout since it is relevant not only for what is in fact being accepted but also for who adopts these logics and how the logics are constructed.

We begin with some key specifications about the concept of "acceptance." By "acceptance" we mean the view, held by an actor or set of actors, that the economic inequalities in question—as perceived by the actor or actors—should not be contested or resisted but, rather, should be considered as something that is part of the order of things. We therefore distinguish acceptance from other orientations toward economic inequalities. These include various forms of rejection. They are different from acceptance, which, even when lukewarm, grants some degree of legitimacy to the inequality in question. Rejection of economic inequality questions whether it should exist: It fully or partially contests it. Acceptance, by contrast, does not.

We recognize that acceptance, regardless of the specific logic at work, may be held with varying degrees of enthusiasm. Indeed, at one extreme, actors may view inequality as a truly desirable outcome: something that is good and should happen. At the other extreme, they are far less happy with it and simply see it as an inevitable part of this world: They may be resigned, almost in fatalistic fashion, to its presence. Along the spectrum we can observe combinations of these two orientations.

In this volume, we include several contributions that examine instances of fairly enthusiastic acceptance: These are the more perplexing cases of acceptance given the magnitude of current economic inequalities. But they are not the only ones of relevance. Several other chapters therefore examine instances where inequalities are accepted with more moderation. Indeed, in some cases they even require the resolution of potentially contrasting views. They, too, contribute in their own manner to the overall societal acceptance of inequalities and must be understood.

We also recognize that any one logic of acceptance may come with varying degrees of prominence in actors' minds. By this we mean that individuals hold their views with more or less awareness, interest in the issue, and intensity of feelings (see, for instance, Savage et al. 2001). This should, of course, be expected: It is something that social theorists have posited occurs regularly in actors' lives when it comes to most issues or concerns. Max Weber, for instance, argued that actors engage in social life with varying degrees of consciousness, and that in most cases, they are only somewhat aware of how they perceive and make sense of their actions and the world around them (Weber 1978, 25). Pierre Bourdieu (1984) put forth a similar perspective when describing how broader economic and social landscapes shape how actors formulate viewpoints. More recently, pragmatists such as Gross (2018, 92) have emphasized the importance of habit as a driver of how actors generate their thoughts and then act. Much like other beliefs or dispositions, then, acceptance may be more or less at the forefront of people's minds. But this, of course, in no way detracts from the need to examine it. As Weber and many other theorists have reasoned, beliefs are highly consequential for what happens in society and the maintenance and evolution of the social order.

Importantly, we view the four logics of acceptance as essentially cultural material: They are collective representations used to make sense of the world. To use Émile Durkheim's (1982) terminology, the four logics represent "social facts": shared ways of seeing and feeling. This is more than a theoretical point. By highlighting that such logics are not a matter of individual dispositions but of wide-reaching attitudes, the observation highlights their stable and enduring qualities, and their hold over people's minds. As they subscribe to them, actors reflect and participate in broader collective interpretative frames or schemas. And these, as just noted, help shape the very worlds in which actors find themselves.

Above all, and as the coming empirical chapters show in revealing detail, we see these logics as serving to support and reinforce existing inequalities. They provide the conceptual underpinnings through which those inequalities become matter-of-fact aspects of everyday life. The logics lend legitimacy to the inequalities. As they do so, they also combine with other societal variables—such as the legal system, for instance, or the platforms of political parties and interest groups—to solidify or even further widen those inequalities.

Hence, our perspective is consistent with cultural approaches to inequalities that take seriously the role of shared ideas and values in shaping economic outcomes. Spillman (2023), for instance, has argued for the need to focus on cultural categorizations (rather than individual dispositions) for a more comprehensive understanding of inequalities. "Durable inequalities," she observed, rely on shared or collective ways of ascribing boundaries, stigma, and differences. Indeed, this is a view of culture and economy that dates as far back as Weber (1978, chapter 7) and continues with scholars such as Valentino and Vaisey (2022), Dorling (2015), Lamont and Small (2008), Tilly (1998), Bourdieu (1984), and Bourdieu and Passeron (1990). Their writings explore how multidimensional factors of a cultural and more broadly social nature shape economic inequalities, and how coexisting orders of justification of unequal economic arrangements become established (Boltanski and Thévenot 2006; Diaz-Bone 2015, 215). Several recent studies by economists and those adopting a materialistic approach have also emphasized how structured inequalities are intertwined with cultural processes. Piketty (2014, 2015) is especially pertinent here, as are works in the Marxist tradition on the naturalization of inequalities (Cook 2020).

With all this in mind, we propose here four types of logics of acceptance—each of which can be held with varying degrees of enthusiasm and prominence. They are market and economic logics, moral logics, cultural and institutional logics, and group and ethnic logics. Figure 1.1 captures their essential characteristics, with the understanding that we are concerned with those logics as they are presently at work and not, as might be interesting for other purposes, how they may have manifested in other historical periods across the globe. We describe the logics by considering their essence in its purest or ideal typical (to return to Weberian sociology) form, with the knowledge (as we discuss below and at length in the Conclusion) that in practice they often operate in combinations with each other.

Market and economic logics see people accept and even approve of economic inequalities because of the positive material outcomes for societies or significant segments of the population with which they are associated. Actors therefore do not accept inequalities as inherently desirable or good, but because they are externalities that result from dynamics that are deemed materially beneficial. For instance, people might view inequalities as deriving from efficient market-driven resource allocations that generate great wealth and lift everyone (or almost everyone) up. Resources go to the most productive elements of the economy. Everyone is accordingly better off, but those who created the relevant innovations or improvements will become much richer than before. The gap between themselves and others will therefore widen, but this should be of no concern. It should actually

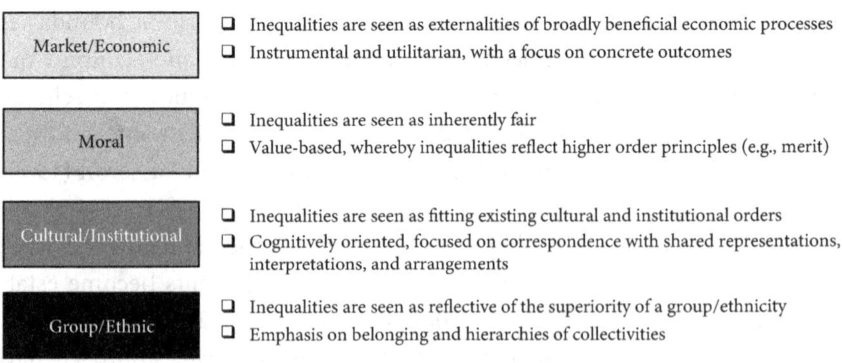

Figure 1.1 The four logics

be welcomed as indicative of positive developments for the whole. In fact, the absence of inequalities would signal a worrisome situation that would suggest the inefficient use of resources.

In another version of such market and economic logics, actors view inequalities as acceptable because they see them as resulting from the successes and failures of competition. And competition itself is deemed desirable because it encourages individuals and organizations to push themselves to outdo others. Such striving is the pathway to superior economic performance. It leads to new products and services, to the benefit, again, of society as a whole or at least a significant portion of the population. From this perspective, inequalities are therefore again the logical byproduct of a materially beneficial process. The opposite approach, after all, would entail either disincentivizing those who are willing to push themselves or somehow wasting previous resources on those who are not willing or capable to perform.

Moral logics, by contrast, see people positively inclined toward economic inequalities because they perceive them to be fair. Such fairness is rooted in "higher" or ethical principles. One such principle is meritocracy or one's willingness to apply oneself to certain ends. In this case, economic success is understood to be "deserved" or as the "proper" or "correct" reward for those who have "earned" it, while failures or lesser economic achievements are seen as resulting from incompetence, laziness, a disinterest in doing well, or other similar deficiencies or dispositions. Another such principle involves the view that the inequalities are reflections of, or belong to, broader arrangements or processes that are themselves seen as just or righteous—such as regulations that reward hard work or personal initiatives, or the belief that the government is looking out for the best interest of the people. As such, they are themselves accepted as fair.

Moral logics, thus, do not give weight to material calculations. Nor do they see inequalities as externalities to be accepted because of some benefit that is exogenous to them: Instead, they understand inequalities as containing elements of what is just and right, and this is what makes them acceptable and even desirable. Given this, as with market and economic logics but for different reasons, the absence of inequalities might actually raise questions. It could signal that differences that ought to manifest themselves are being somehow muted. Because of this, those who hold this view can be inclined to criticize policies, actors, or processes that interfere with the proper course of events.

Cultural and institutional logics present a third type of logic. Here, actors see economic inequalities as consistent with established or emerging outlooks, conventions, expectations, formal or informal policies, or organizational arrangements. Understanding those inequalities as fitting or resonating with that cultural and institutional material,[2] they base their acceptance on that perceived correspondence. Put differently, actors deem economic inequalities acceptable (and even desirable) because they see them as reaffirming shared ways of seeing and organizing the world. The inequalities "make sense" given those perspectives. Note that these are not moral considerations as such, which tend to be decontextualized. The emphasis is rather on the perceived complementarity between the inequalities and broader societal contexts.

A helpful illustration of this—one that Robert C. Hauhart examines with great sophistication in Chapter 11—is the acceptance of inequalities in the United States because they are seen as consistent with the American Dream. Another would be the view held by many in countries transitioning from socialist to market economies that, given the move to new approaches and policies, inequalities are logically going to manifest themselves.

Group and ethnic logics represent a fourth perspective. Here, people justify inequalities on the basis of hierarchical distinctions between collectivities that are seen as "superior" and others as "inferior." That distinction serves as the basis for acceptance: The superior groups, by virtue of who they are, are entitled to better economic conditions, while the inferior groups, by virtue of who they are, are not. In the most common and obvious cases this can be seen in the views that split society into two halves: "natives" or "true" citizens and "others" who are considered "foreign" (such as migrants). Inequalities in these cases are often not only deemed justified but even desirable, since they reflect how these groups should stand in relation to each other.

The logic can take on subtler versions. For instance, more inequality *within* a given collectivity may be deemed acceptable if it is seen as somehow related to the ability of that group or ethnicity to be more competitive or successful vis-à-vis others. This would be the logic we would expect to encounter, for instance, in at least some societies transitioning from situations of widespread poverty to affluence. Actors would see that there are differences among segments of their own population but find these acceptable because they are products of a transformation that improves the standing of the group or ethnicity in relation to others. In another version, inequality within a collectivity becomes acceptable when it is seen as reflective of inherent arrangements within that collectivity that are thought to be markers of its greatness as a whole. Here, the caste system in India would offer an example.

These four logics represent primary and conceptually distinct perspectives for how actors do or should make sense of economic outcomes. Although, as we note below, they may work together and combine with elements of each other (group and ethnic logics, for instance, may contain elements of moralistic notions), in their purest form they draw from different principles. In brief, as indicated in Figure 1.1, market and economic logics are in essence instrumental and utilitarian, with a focus on concrete outcomes. Moral logics are value-based, with an emphasis on coherence with abstract ethical notions. Cultural and institutional logics are cognitively oriented: continuity with transmitted shared representations, interpretations, and arrangements—which themselves guide people's minds—is prized. Group and ethnic logics emphasize belonging and adherence to one group and antagonisms toward other groups.

Yet, as just stated, these logics should not be seen as operating in isolation from each other. We can expect them to reinforce each other. In any case, the boundaries between them can be blurry. For instance, it is quite possible that group and ethnic logics invoke elements of moral ones: a collectivity may see itself as more "deserving" than others based on simply being a "better" or "worthier" people. Or cultural and institutional logics might contain elements that draw from market and economic logics, as might happen when an actor approves of inequalities because they see them as "fitting" the capitalist value system of their societies. Given this, we wish to investigate these logics as they actually manifest themselves. This is one of the advantages of a comparative volume such as this one—and something that we return to in the Conclusion.

We do not claim that the four logics are exhaustive: There may be others. So, why select these four? We do so for several reasons. First, as just noted, they represent primary and conceptually distinct perspectives. Second, the four logics are familiar in their various renditions to people across the world. As many of the chapters ahead show, they constitute widespread grounds for acceptance across many countries. Third, and relatedly, the logics have roots in different and long-standing intellectual traditions. Market and economic logics stem, for instance, from principles espoused by thinkers ranging from Adam Smith (1910) to the founders of the marginal revolution, such as William Stanley Jevons, Carl Menger, and Léon Walras, and thus the tradition of neoclassical economics (see Samuelson and Nordhaus 2009). These principles include the assessment of markets as capable of generating great wealth that, through trickle-down and other effects, can lead to a decrease in absolute poverty and ultimately benefit most, if not all, members of society (Campbell forthcoming).

Cultural and institutional logics are consistent with the works of scholars such as Thelen (2014) and Hall and Soskice (2001) but also more critical ones, such as Jessop (1990), who argue that societal actors' views on redistributional policies and class structures are heavily shaped by broader institutional and cultural contexts. There is a sense in these works of a certain degree of congruence or "fit" with social arrangements, which actors recognize and are generally inclined, for various reasons, to reaffirm (Bandelj and Sowers 2010).

As to moral arguments, Milton Friedman and Rose Friedman (1990) offered some of the most classic arguments in defense of unequal outcomes. People should be entitled to what they accrue due to their hard work, determination, and other personal traits. According to this perspective, the recognition of individual merit becomes an ultimate, nonnegotiable goal, regardless of any resulting effects in terms of the inequalities it may produce (Bruni and Santori 2022).

Group and ethnic logics draw, in turn, from those intellectual traditions emphasizing the primacy of collective identities in defining societies, social systems, and who is entitled to resources (Essed 1991, 2013; Ortiz 2021). The main references here are those works that investigate the processes of constructing antagonistic group identities based on opposition to other collectivities which are then identified as out-groups.

The four logics are thus rooted in well-established and fairly sophisticated perspectives on why actors should or in fact do accept and even approve of economic inequalities and are capacious in scope. Still, to reemphasize, we do not aim to be comprehensive in scope—that would be beyond the reach of any given volume. Rather, we wish to identify and analyze some of the most important and common logics of acceptance, and even approval, as they find specific articulations across different contexts, actors, and dimensions of inequality.

As we observed at the start, it is important to recognize that economic inequalities do not exist alone but intersect with other types of inequalities. These include those around gender, race, and ethnicity—all of which, it is worth pointing out, are also accepted by significant segments of societies (Patterson 1982; Smith 1990). Acceptance of economic inequalities, therefore, often means acceptance—with varying degrees of awareness—of more than a purely economic outcome. If so, we would expect the four logics to take the relevant intersectionalities into account, and, indeed, be built in their specific articulations around those intersectionalities.

In addition, the actors who hold these logics themselves operate at the intersections of factors such as race, ethnicity, religion, socioeconomic status, gender, and age, as well as broader value-systems. Because all these factors involve inequalities in their own right, we may say that subscribers to any given logic of acceptance find themselves in particular positions in social hierarchies. These positions may represent positions of advantage or disadvantage. This has implications for how they construct those logics: what they emphasize, exclude, and interrelate. Accordingly, it also means that the logics are often likely to benefit some actors and harm others.

In terms of geography and space, we see these logics of acceptance as present across the globe but as having particular articulations in national settings. The latter is where inequalities often manifest and are felt most clearly, relevant policies and debates on inequalities develop, and various institutional, political, and other factors interact with and drive those inequalities. At the same time, the logics certainly also interact with, and are influenced by and themselves shape, international and local factors. These include cross-border financial flows; networks of professionals; regional, metropolitan, and global economic developments; transnational cultural patterns; and political currents.

Hence, we recognize that many factors impact the overall nature of the four logics, their particular articulations, and why they are present and adopted in any given setting. These are not the main focus of our volume but are certainly part of the broader discussion. Many of the chapters ahead address them, and we will ourselves return to them in the Conclusion when thinking about how inequalities may be ameliorated. Throughout, it is therefore important to keep in mind for analytical purposes that these factors are distinct from the logics themselves or their articulations and adoption. This is so even when certain terms, such as "culture" or "the market," have relevance for both those factors and the logics themselves.

We can mention here a few of these causal factors. One concerns the accuracy of perceptions in the first place. Perceptions (of, for instance, others or of the extent of the inequalities themselves) affect how actors understand and judge inequalities. These themselves depend on variables such as operating biases, abilities to process information, and the availability of information, which might be scarce, for instance, when wealth is hidden (Trump 2023a; Zucman 2015). Here, the principle of "cognitive conformity," whereby individuals fail to engage critically with social reality and instead are subject to the hegemonic culture of the times (Gramsci 1992), might be relevant.

Periods of major economic, political, and demographic transitions may also explain the emergence and particular articulations of the observed logics. Increased levels of immigration, for instance, may lead to new interpretations of who is entitled to what. Broad institutional arrangements, such as, for instance, whether leading organizations or policies have favored and promoted certain perspectives in the first place, also matter. For example, established fiscal initiatives that favor entrepreneurship might promote certain market logics. Broader political economic contexts, such as whether neoliberal or coordinated market principles are dominant in a given national setting, surely influence dispositions toward particular logics and their elements.

Intersectionalities, in turn, play a role as well. Gender and race, for instance, intertwine to influence the particularities of the logics of acceptance we may observe in any one setting, just as they influence the content of any given element of culture. The same may be said when it comes to ethnicity, socioeconomic status, age, and political orientations. None of these factors operates in isolation. Instead, each can combine with others to define certain positionalities which, in turn, influence the articulation of any given logic. This means that the logics are not only held by actors in positions of intersectionalities but also stem from origins that are intersectional in nature. Figure 1.2 summarizes these analytical points.

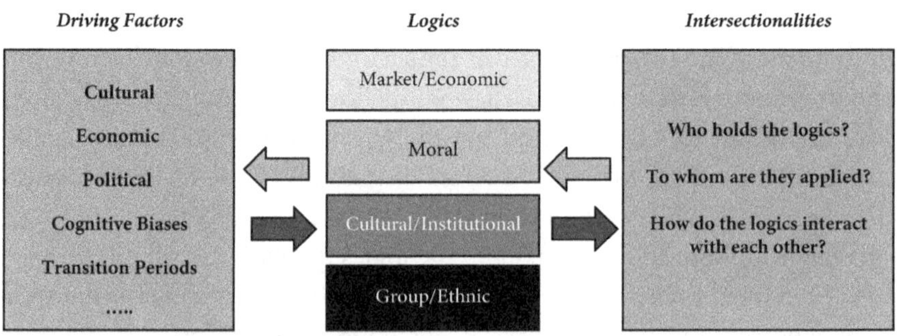

Figure 1.2 Driving factors and intersectionalities

The Literatures on Economic Inequality and Acceptance

Most of the existing research on economic inequalities does not concern itself with the logics of acceptance. Instead, it tackles three important but rather different themes. Our volume is in "conversation" with these research strands. We drew from some of these sources to set the context for our volume in the opening pages of this Introduction, and many of the chapters ahead do the same. We explain how this is so below before turning to the more limited literature on acceptance and the distinctive contribution of our volume to that research.

The Broader Literature: Trends, Drivers, and the Amelioration of Inequality

The first strand includes several important books, articles, and studies documenting the huge levels of economic inequalities across the globe and increasing inequalities within countries (Atkinson et al. 2011; Bourguignon 2015; Chanchel and Piketty 2021; Milanovic 2016a, 2016b; Saez and Zucman 2020; Sayer 2015; Scheidel 2017; Zucman 2019). We already pointed to some of the most important works in the opening pages of this Introduction. We add here that studies belonging to this strand address additional social and political cleavages that have emerged in connection to growing economic inequalities. Piketty and colleagues have, for instance, proposed that more economic inequality "has not led to wide-spread demands for redistribution or the revival of class conflicts" (Gethin et al. 2021, 7). Instead, there has been an increase in demands for identity politics, especially in marginal and peripheral areas (Rodríguez-Pose et al. 2023; Storti et al. 2023). Attention has thus gone to the intersections between economic inequalities and other kinds—based on race, for instance, or geographical location. Many of our chapters explore these intersectional dynamics and how the attitudes toward inequality are conditioned by belonging to certain social groups.

The second research strand examines the multitude of drivers that have consolidated and amplified inequalities over the last decades across the globe (Hurst et al. 2016; Krugman 2007; Markovits 2019; Piketty 2015). These works tend to be concerned with structural, economic, and political factors. These include major shifts in global production systems, international competition and the displacement of entire industries, networks of influence that promote the concentration of profits into the hands of a small percentage of the population, wars, and technological change. Particular emphasis is placed in these analyses on the role of financialization, which has led to capital returns being higher than economic growth itself. This process has purportedly amplified the accumulation of private wealth, thereby further increasing inequalities (Keister 2014; Piketty 2014). Policy choices have also played a major role: Since the 1980s, policymakers have reduced the progressivity of income taxes and introduced highly accommodative fiscal initiatives on intergenerational wealth transmission, capital income tax reductions, major corporate tax reductions, and the dismantling of the welfare state (Harrington 2012; Krugman 2007; Saez and Zucman 2019, 2021; Scheidel 2017).

Studies within this strand have also described the role of cultural factors. For instance, Piketty (2020) has argued that taking inequalities for granted—a shared mindset of sorts—is itself a driver of inequalities. Markovits (2019), in parallel, has suggested that the myth of meritocracy has narrowed the space for "social rights" and shifted the public and political debates toward individual variables (see also, Brint and Karabel 1989; Mijs 2021; Sandel 2020; Schimpfössl 2024). This has made it easier for inequalities to grow and be seen as part of the order of things, while in fact they are neither natural nor inevitable, but rather the outcome of more or less intentional processes of political economy rooted in values and ideology.

Our volume draws from these insights. The more culturally oriented causal explanations contain elements of precisely some of the logics we have articulated and that our chapters explore in great detail. The more policy and structural works speak to our consideration of what, in broader contextual terms, might be drivers of the four logics of interest.

The third strand includes mostly books on how those inequalities can be ameliorated (Atkinson 2015; Iceland et al. 2023; Reich 2020; Saez and Zucman 2019; Stiglitz 2015a, 2015b; Streeck 2016; Zucman 2015). Atkinson (2015), for instance, has put forth ideas for sustainable measures to reverse the effects of the wealth shift since the 1980s and the "Inequality Turn" from productive activities to rents and from new labor market flexibilities that have exacerbated asymmetries between workers and employers (see also, Krugman 2007). The proposed initiatives include more progressive taxation, consideration of "participation income," and the establishment of inclusive skill and educational programs. Zucman (2015) has, in turn, emphasized the need to prevent multinational corporations from evading taxes, implement effective wealth taxes on capital income, and make it more difficult for money to reach tax havens.

While a fair number of proposals are redistributive in nature, others seek to create opportunities for those with limited means (Huber and Stephens 2024). According to McCall (2013), for instance, the latter sort of policies are likely to garner consensus in the United States, where, given the historical tendency to view redistributive measures with some suspicion, measures that expand access to education, increase opportunities for labor market access, and provide adequate wage treatment are generally preferred. Stiglitz (2012) has similarly argued for the need to have evolving regulatory policies that promote widespread access to market opportunities. Not doing so means that a few entrenched actors turn into rent-seekers, with resulting drops in productivity. The same actors also tend to seek favorable measures (such as reducing the estate tax) that do not boost the economy and exacerbate inequalities and make them self-perpetuating.

Other recent studies consider the adoption of more radical measures, such as "universal basic income." For some, technological innovation—primarily artificial intelligence—tends to make many executive positions and many intermediate cognitive-level jobs redundant. This has the potential to displace a substantial number of workers who are not easily retrainable. Others see valuable opportunities: Never before has technological innovation promised to automate production and wealth creation, without the traditionally required labor costs. As a result, there are economic resources that can be redistributed through innovative measures, such as the reconceptualization of income as a citizenship right rather than the result of labor performance.

As with the two previous strands, this too is useful to us. While our main objective is to understand the logics of acceptance of economic inequalities, we are also interested in the implications of our analyses for the reduction of those inequalities. In other words, we wish to connect what we learn about those logics to possible initiatives for a less unequal world. Furthermore, the combination of logics and the intensity with which inequalities are accepted influences the type of policies that are most supported. Thus, we share the same impetus of this third strand of research and draw from its insights in the Conclusion as we advance several proposals.

Existing Research on the Acceptance of Economic Inequality

Research on the logics of acceptance is more limited but still substantively noteworthy. It is an emerging topic in some publications which cannot be easily placed in particular literature strands devoted to this question. To start, we can think of some classic precursors found in critical studies that delve into the concepts of ideology, hegemony, and discourse as tools through which powerful classes with economic resources render the established order acceptable—almost as if it were natural and inevitable—to subordinate classes (Gramsci 1992; Stoddart 2007). These include Marx on the ideology and hegemony through which capitalists obtain acquiescence from the working class (Briziarelli and Hoffmann 2017); Foucault on discourses through which power perpetuates the established order (Miller 1990); Moore (1978) on the social contracts that underlie and support asymmetrical class arrangements and that lead to the acceptance, tolerance, or simply "nonrecognition" of inequalities; and Patterson (1982) on the cultural conditions that made slavery acceptable in the United States. These may serve as reference points for articulating logics as they may apply to the current context.

When it comes to more contemporary works, it seems useful to distinguish between books and scientific articles. As to books, to our knowledge no single volume has sought to uncover the various logics of acceptance of inequalities—in their more abstract forms but also their actual manifestations as we move across contexts, actors, and dimensions of economic inequality. One important exception might be Dorling's (2015) *Injustice: Why Social Inequality Still Persists*. Dorling argues that five widely held "tenets" support and give legitimacy to growing economic inequalities. These include beliefs in the efficiency of elitism, the necessity of exclusion, prejudice as inevitable, the goodness of greed, and the impossibility of avoiding despair. The argument is made with the United Kingdom in mind above all, but at times extends beyond it. As such, several of its core ideas may be considered subsets of what we propose in our volume. For instance, the efficiency of elitism is closely associated with market and economic logics, while the necessity of exclusion may be considered a thread within group and ethnic logics.

A second book might be Piketty's (2020) *Capital and Ideology*. Its underlying thesis is that technological and economic drivers alone do not explain inequalities: Politics and ideological orientations must instead be part of the picture. Specifically, Piketty develops the idea of an "inequality regime." This is understood to comprise the justifications used to support a certain level of inequality at a given time and place. These justifications in turn correspond to institutional, fiscal, legal, and educational arrangements—as seen in his comparative and historical analyses. In relation to our proposed logics, we could think of an "inequality regime" as a social environment that prompts people to accept inequalities based on a combination of our four logics. As such, Piketty's work is broadly useful in terms of offering insights into certain elements of the logics of acceptance and the broader contexts that support them. It is, however, fairly generic when it comes to those logics and does not seek to analytically distinguish them for dissection.

A few other books offer relevant but tangential insights. Those written in the tradition of Bourdieu's work seem potentially relevant (see Schirato and Roberts 2020). They draw from his analysis of the relationship between social classes and symbolic capital. Symbolic capital can be designated as prestige or authority linked to the social position one occupies and which converts into recognized distinctions in social interaction practices (Bourdieu and Wacquant 2013, 297). This contributes to making both those who dominate and those who are dominated internalize power and social and cultural resource asymmetries. Ultimately, "status is thus naturalized, inferiority is internalized as self-deserved, and resistance is rendered futile" (Frank 2013, 22). The concept of *habitus* as a system of shared conceptions among members of the same social class or group also supports hierarchical relationships between different groups, which are taken for granted without questioning their utility or fairness (Bourdieu 1977, 86). This line of thinking resonates with our concept of group logic. On a more abstract level, we can recall here the work of Boltanski and Thévenot (2006) exploring how people justify their views of the world by appealing to certain logics, which may compete with each other and require, for social life to unfold normally, some degree of resolution.

The situation is different when it comes to scientific articles on the acceptance of inequalities. There are certainly a good number of articles aiming directly at the identification and analysis of distinct logics of acceptance. We see these, however, as limited in three important respects. First, most articles are devoted to single geographical cases and sets of actors or respondents. Thus, they do not offer a sustained analytical framework that moves across the four logics for assessment across different contexts. Second, those articles that are in fact comparative tend to focus on a single logic of acceptance.

As such, they too do not lead to synthetic conclusions that can only be reached when multiple logics are considered as we move across sets of actors or contexts. Third, the analyses tend to consider only certain aspects of the logics in question—their core elements, for instance, or the variables that explain their adoption, questions of intersectionality, and so on. While individually valuable, then, these articles offer rather selective insights. We can mention here some representative noteworthy examples.

When it comes to factors shaping the adoption of logics of acceptance, Mijs and Usmani (2024) demonstrate through a simulation model that highly unequal and segregated societies alter individuals' ability to infer the overall levels of social inequalities. In socially and spatially segregated societies disadvantaged individuals are not frequently in contact with those who have greater resources. As a result, they underestimate the level of their relative disadvantage and tend to be more accepting of the established order. This result is consistent with studies that have shown how the perception of inequality, in general, is not correlated to actual levels of inequalities (Trump 2023b) and can therefore be systematically biased. More broadly, McCall et al. (2017) and Lindh and McCall (2023) have examined how exposure to inequalities can generate concern, skepticism toward beliefs about opportunities, and support for targeted political initiatives.

Still in relation to the factors promoting the adoption of logics, scholars have described the phenomenon of "adaptive preferences." Individuals are so entrenched in the harshness of the socioeconomic contexts in which they find themselves that they conceive of the effort to escape them as enormous, and of the chances of success as very low. Therefore, they stop desiring what is almost impossible for them to achieve (Elster 1989; Sen 1997). This is so even if they are the ones to pay the highest prices from the existing arrangements (see, in the case of a book in this instance, Duina 2018).

Along the same vein, an elegant and classic article on the factors driving the logic of acceptance during the early stages of economic development is that of Albert Hirschman (1973). Hirschman compared the situation of growing inequalities in a developing country to being stuck in one of two lanes of a tunnel (hence the concept of the "tunnel effect") and seeing cars in the other lane moving. Initially, the movement in the other lane can generate hope and acceptance: Soon, one's own lane will also start moving. However, things can change in the long run. If the two lanes of traffic continue to move at unequal speeds, hope and acceptance can turn into resentment and lead to opportunistic behaviors, such as attempting to switch lanes even at the cost of violating traffic rules (Kohli 2013, 27). The tunnel effect is more pronounced when a society is culturally, demographically, and ethnically homogeneous. Then, one sees people with similar characteristics moving, and hopes of moving soon seem realistic. But, in the long run, homogeneity can exacerbate the counter-reaction, as it can lead to a sense of relative deprivation. The tunnel effect is relevant because it aligns well with analyses of countries like China (Durongkaveroj 2018; see also Chapter 9 in this volume).

When it comes to the core elements of the logics of acceptance, some of the most revealing works have examined how the wealthy and superwealthy strive to make their positions acceptable to themselves and others. One such strategy is their reliance on socially oriented philanthropy through which they support basic needs (McGoey 2012, 2021; McGoey and Thiel 2018; Storti and Dagnes 2021; see also, in the case of a volume, Sklair and Glucksberg 2021). This improves their standing in society and makes as a result the gap between them and others more agreeable. It generally relies on elements of market and economic logics as applied to specific settings and sets of actors: Mechanisms of great wealth generation are justified because of the material benefits they provide downstream.

Several similarly revealing works on the core elements of the logics of acceptance point to elements of moral and institutional-cultural thinking. Those on "system justification theory" offer excellent examples. The framework, itself rooted in social psychology, revolves around a cluster of empirically tested hypotheses. These include those on the rationalization of the status quo (Guinjoan and Rico 2018; Jost et al. 2004, 889; Laurin et al. 2013) and the tendency of people to judge more common events as more desirable than less common ones. They also include those on "favoritism towards out-groups," whereby those in less privileged positions tend to recognize superior qualities or capabilities in other groups compared to their own, thereby also accepting relationships of subordination or inferiority. Consistent with these hypotheses, "when income differences are perceived to be high, the public thinks of larger income inequality as legitimate" and thus "the public [often] reacts to inequality with adapted expectations, not increased demands for redistribution" (Trump 2018, 929).

To these we can add articles on how exposure to various political discourses molds redistributive preferences, thus indirectly impacting the level of acceptance of inequalities (Jedinger and Burger 2018) and on the inverse relationship between support for progressive taxation and belief in meritocracy (García-Sánchez et al. 2020, 2022). These underscore a correlation between specific fiscal arrangements (an institutional matter) and normative judgments about inequalities (per our moral logics above all).

With all the above said, we note that, while rare, some articles do offer valuable comparative analyses across contexts, sets of respondents, or logics. For instance, Weiss et al. (2022) compare different age cohorts in Germany and their acceptance of social inequalities. They find that "subjective social status significantly influences the acceptance of social inequalities among middle-aged and older adults, compared to young adults" (261). They then suggest that adherence to beliefs such as the possibility of upward mobility and merit—elements of what we call cultural and moral logics—is more pronounced in young individuals, likely due to factors associated with their stages of life. An example of how logics may, in turn, actually enter into tension with each other comes from Van den Haak and Wilterdink (2019). Employing a Bourdieusian perspective, they show how elements of cultural and group logics can prompt individuals to endorse a hierarchical stratification among social groups, despite the resistance on the part of the same individuals to moral justifications for unequal outcomes.

We see these various works as a valuable basis from which to launch our volume. We sought to contribute to it in a systematic, analytically sustained, and comparative manner. We discuss the chapters ahead in the next section.

The Chapters Ahead

We brought together scholars from across the world to investigate the four logics. The resulting thirteen chapters move across geographies, including the United States, Latin America, Europe (with special attention going to Scandinavia and the United Kingdom), India, China, Taiwan, Japan, and South Korea. Their primary aim is to illustrate how one or more of the logics in question are at work in those settings: the specific articulations and elements of those logics. How do those logics manifest in those contexts? What exactly is being invoked? What are the building blocks and claims? What aspects are emphasized?

In so doing, the chapters also show how actors adopt these logics with varying degrees of enthusiasm and with different levels of intensity, awareness, and interest. We also see how the logics can reinforce each other, while at the same translating into the acceptance of other kinds of inequalities that intersect with the economic ones. The chapters offer insights as well into the positionalities and vantage points of those employing the logics. In the process, they present valuable data on why those logics exist in the first place and the factors that promote their adoptions—from those at the macrolevel, such as reactions to international competition or threats, transitions to neoliberal or market economies, and the rise of populism, to those at the microlevel, such as perception biases. As they do all this, the chapters demonstrate how a range of qualitative and quantitative methods can be used for the empirical investigation of the logics.

In this section, we discuss the main highlights from the chapters, with the caveat that only a close reading of each chapter can provide an appreciation for its richness, nuances, and sophistication. Reflecting the organization of the volume itself, we proceed by type of logic and a consideration of the most relevant chapters on that logic.

Market and Economic Logics

As discussed earlier, when employing market and economic logics to accept economic inequalities, actors focus on broader principles of efficient capital allocation, greater wealth generation, and the benefits of competition in terms of motivating people to perform and succeed. They see inequalities as logical byproducts of these beneficial processes. Even if not desirable, inequalities should therefore be accepted and even welcome. Four chapters of the volume focus on these logics.

Lucy Barnes opens Chapter 2 by quantifying and describing, in the first place, the number of people who accept economic inequalities. This is useful overall information that lays the groundwork for the rest of the chapter and, indeed, other chapters as well. Barnes estimates the number by analyzing data from twenty-nine countries from the 2019 "Social Inequality" round of the International Social Survey Programme and by assessing the share of people who disagree with the notion that differences in income in their country are too large. The results vary noticeably across countries but average around 8% of respondents. In terms of demographics, the combination of male, high-income, younger, and postgraduate education seems to matter for acceptance. The association is, however, not particularly strong and many who accept inequalities do not have these particular traits. Briefly put, a small but not insignificant percentage of the population accepts inequalities, and that share is fairly diverse.

Barnes then turns to five countries (the United Kingdom, United States, France, Germany, and Denmark) to understand the logic driving this acceptance. There, she finds that over 80% of those unconcerned about inequality subscribe to what she terms "mainstream" or more "pro-market" views of how the economy works. With this in place, she observes that the majority holding these views have relatively "weak" pro-market stances. Specifically, they believe in the workings of supply and demand, and that exchanges make both parties better off. They are on the other hand hesitant to embrace what she calls more "radical" elements of pro-market thinking: the notions that lowering taxes will raise revenue, and that someone getting richer increases total wealth (as, for instance, trickle-down economics expects). In parallel, Barnes also finds that a different group altogether—those who hold more skeptical views of the market—are significantly less likely to accept inequalities.

Thus, the chapter offers three important takeaways when it comes to market and economic logics. First, the logics have several components, and these may actually be arranged along a continuum from mainstream to more radical. Second, most inequality-accepting actors appear to subscribe to the more moderate elements of these logics. Third, market and economic logics do seem, on the whole, to be drivers of acceptance.

Barnes presents further insights relevant for two other sections of this volume. It appears that elements of moral logics (specifically the belief in the fairness of inequalities) as well as group and ethnic logics (specifically the notion that certain groups of people as determined by gender, religion, ethnicity, nationality, or political orientation should be entitled to more or less) have considerable bearing on inequality acceptance. As to moral logics, however, the surprising finding is that of a negative correlation: Endorsing a moral view that fairness requires attention to deservingness reduces, rather than increases, acceptance.

Shifting methodological techniques, target population, and geographical setting, Megan Tobias Neely delves in Chapter 3 into the mindsets of hedge fund (HF), venture capital (VC), and technology startup (TS) workers in the United States. In particular, Tobias investigates through interviews how individuals in these industries articulate by way of sometimes considerable conceptual turns and efforts narratives that legitimize the wealth they accrue. Her overarching finding is that the interviewees from all three industries ultimately embrace narratives that cast economic inequalities as a justifiable externality of the consequences of work that they believe creates value that is widely beneficial in material terms to society. Here, trickle-down images are invoked either directly or indirectly. At the same time, Neely stresses that this overall perspective takes on important differences across the groups.

HF managers justify their work—and thus the resulting wealth—by reasoning that it creates more efficient markets, protects the savings of public institutions and pension workers through successful investments, and allows them to donate to the societal causes they care about. This last point comes with the conviction that philanthropy guided by personal preferences is likely to have superior impacts to other more traditional ways of redistributing income, such as through taxation and government spending: Wealthy people, after all, are obviously smart (otherwise they would not have gotten wealthy), and their judgment can accordingly be trusted. The concept of efficiency thus extends to impactful investments in parts of society that need it the most.

The story changes when it comes to TS founders and VC investors. These individuals say they want to create technologies that disrupt the status quo, revolutionize how business is done, and solve the major problems facing society. Some shared their ambivalence at the short-term outlooks common in those industries. But, on the whole, most thought that they function as facilitators of innovation by linking capital to ideas, and that this mechanism can generate great efficiencies, entirely new types of jobs, and new solutions to poverty, the underutilization of talent, and other challenges. This is a rather remarkable departure from the views of HF managers.

These differences in market and economic logics between industries suggest the presence of distinct institutional and cultural factors in those industries that shape values and perceptions. We can add here that Neely makes two additional and important observations. First, by and large, across all three industries white men are dominant. Women and people of color constitute minorities. At times, we read that they wish to challenge the dominant narratives to some degree. At the same time, one senses that they inevitably adopt many of its core tenets and contribute to the established narratives.

Second, at several turns, moral logics—particularly around meritocracy—are deployed along economic and market ones. This is consistent with Barnes's observations. In this case, inequalities are accepted not only as worthwhile externalities because of the greater economic goods being generated but also because, after all, they reflect the principle of earned and hence just compensation.

While Neely and Barnes are primarily concerned about the constitution of market and economic logics, Rosa Rodríguez-Bailón and colleagues shift the focus in Chapter 4 to the factors that shape, in the first place, how actors perceive economic inequalities. Among the most important is that people in general do not have accurate estimates of those inequalities. Various reasons account for such inaccuracies: These range from ignorance to cognitive biases and ideologies. A lack of clarity, among respondents, about what is meant by economic inequalities further clouds matters. In addition, it appears that researchers themselves may contribute to the confusion, since how they ask questions can influence the responses.

This contribution acquires particular relevance for our interest in market and economic logics as follows. Drawing from social psychology, Rodríguez-Bailón and colleagues propose that perceived economic inequalities have an effect on individuals' attitudes toward the need to redistribute resources or more generally address inequalities. Specifically, they propose that two factors—hitherto little understood—may impact how inequalities are perceived: the level of abstraction or specificity of the inequality individuals perceive and the extent to which it is meaningful and psychologically close to or distant from them. When economic inequality is presented in more general and abstract terms, people perceive it in such a way that they are less motivated to address it actively. Conversely, when economic inequality is brought closer to home and perceived within individuals' immediate social circles or communities, the motivation to address it may increase.

While not focused on the content of market and economic logics, the chapter thus does point to market and economic variables as key factors shaping acceptance: how individuals are exposed to those variables influences how they feel about them and what they wish to do about them. We will therefore return to these insights in the Conclusion when thinking about steps for the amelioration of inequalities.

Hanna Kuusela brings us back to Europe with Chapter 5—in this case Finland, a traditionally egalitarian country. She analyzes the parliamentary debates around the abolition of the wealth tax in Finland in 2006, exploring how a tax reform favoring the very wealthy was legitimized in times of deepening wealth inequalities. New moral and cultural attitudes toward inequality and wealth accumulation, she argues, have been articulated in the country in the last few decades. These parliamentary debates offer a great case study for the justificatory logics driving that shift. Those logics have been primarily market and economic ones with, however, concomitant elements of group logics as well.

Specifically, on the market and economic logic front, Kuusela shows that citizens have been called on to accept new levels of wealth—rather than inequality as such—based on the idea that, in a world of intense international economic competition where foreign capital can come into the country and take away local ownership and profits, domestic wealth can benefit the entire country. Finnish entrepreneurship, jobs, and the country's small and medium-sized family businesses will all do better if wealth is kept in Finland. In fact, perhaps paradoxically, some legislators reasoned that the move, while it would of course allow for inequalities to widen, would benefit the country's welfare state and its progressive programs. Thus, in line with trickle-down economic paradigms, abolishing the wealth tax was presented as an effective way to incentivize local wealthy Finns to continue owning and investing in Finland for the good of everyone in the country.

Crucially, such market and economic logic came with a not-too-subtle group and ethnic logic as well. Legislators presented their arguments by making broad distinctions between foreign capital owners and Finnish ones. The former represented a set of actors who are rapacious and uninterested in Finland's well-being. The latter were depicted as good actors naturally committed to that well-being. Kuusela therefore highlights a nationalistic, us-versus-them narrative underlying the arguments.

On the methodological front, the chapter's reliance on discursive analysis showcases an additional tool for empirical investigation of the logics of acceptance. The focus on legislators highlights how the logics can be spun in a top-down fashion by elites. The overall connections to broader cultural and moral shifts ties the logics to macrolevel contextual variables which they are both responding to and helping advance.

Moral Logics

When adopting moral logics to accept economic inequalities, actors rely on considerations of fairness. They view inequalities as containing elements of what is just and right, and this is what makes them acceptable and possibly even desirable. Calculations about material benefits do not matter. What is important are more abstract principles as reflected in those inequalities. Three chapters of the volume offer insights into these moral logics.

Joanna Kitsnik and Carola Hommerich undertake a comparative analysis in Chapter 6 of three East Asian countries: Japan, South Korea, and Taiwan. Utilizing data from the 2017–20 World Values Survey, they open by offering evidence of varying acceptance levels in those countries. Japanese respondents seem less accepting, while those from South Korea and Taiwan seem more so. At the same time, additional differences set them apart. For instance, when it comes to those with very high levels of tolerance of inequality, respondents from Taiwan figure prominently. To return to our earlier theoretical discussion of the logics, we see differences in the intensity of acceptance.

Kitsnik and Hommerich then assess which logics of acceptance seem most at play. They note that the World Value Survey includes variables consistent with our definition of moral logics. These are ones on individual responsibility, meritocracy, freedom over equality, and personal choice. In the three countries, the first three of these variables (along with an additional one that straddles both moral and market and economic logics: a preference for competition over the common good) seem especially predictive of acceptance of inequality. Two, in particular, are statistically significant across all three countries: individual responsibility and freedom over equality. Other factors, such as a respondent's structural determinants (class, education, mobility, and others) and various controls (such as gender and age) prove less relevant.

The main takeaway of this chapter, therefore, is that despite the macrolevel economic, cultural, and political differences that set these countries apart, respondents who accept inequalities have internalized a certain set of related moral ideas that seem constant across borders. Kitsnik and Hommerich close by generating ideas for possible ways of addressing income inequalities. In contrast to approaches that favor initiatives targeting structural factors or individual motivations, a more promising venue would be to tackle the deeply ingrained narratives that perpetuate and legitimize inequalities. Of course, this would have to be done with sensitivity to the very different specific contexts in which these narratives function. For instance, the concept of individual responsibility in Japan surely takes on connotations and associations that are distinct from those in, say, Taiwan.

Licia Bobzien and Roland Verwiebe effectively build on these insights in Chapter 7 by examining data from the International Social Survey Programme for European countries between 1992 and 2019. They show that the more people believe in meritocracy the less they are concerned about inequality. This is an important and straightforward application of the moral logics principle. But there is an important twist to this simple association: The more people believe in meritocracy (as a justification for inequality), the less likely they are to perceive inequality accurately. This, in turn, makes them less likely to be concerned about inequality. Hence, meritocratic beliefs have direct and indirect effects such that perceptions of inequality mediate the effects of meritocratic beliefs on inequality concerns.

Their analysis accordingly sheds valuable light both on the relevance of moral logics as something that people use to accept inequalities and, in tandem, how perceptions of inequality are in the first place formed inaccurately. On the latter point, Bobzien and Verwiebe suggest that selective processing of information drives inaccurate perceptions: Those who believe in meritocracy are prone to select data points that depict less inequality. They do so because the resulting picture confirms their beliefs and expectations about the world. As with the previous chapter, these findings have implications for initiatives aimed at changing those mindsets. Additionally, as to broader contextual factors, Bobzien and Verwiebe note that there are large differences between countries in the levels of beliefs in meritocracy, perceived inequality, and inequality concerns. They attribute this to cultural and institutional contexts—such as the characteristics of welfare programs and constellations of norms and values.

With Liz Moor and Sam Friedman, we move in Chapter 8 from national to individual cultural repertoires in the context of London. Inheritance is a mechanism for the preservation of inequalities. Justifying inheritance on moral grounds grants legitimacy to that mechanism. But the grounds for such justification are far from obvious: The inheritor typically cannot claim to have deserved the inheritance in any immediate sense. Meritocracy and "unearned" economic gifts are hard to reconcile. Through in-depth interviews of inheritors who used the received gifts to buy property in London, Moor and Friedman unveil how those individuals strive to infuse elements of deservingness in situations. Several observations emerge from the study.

First, the interviewees often felt the need to justify their situations and had to work to arrive at their conclusions. The process took effort, and thus—per our considerations of varying degrees of enthusiasm—the conclusion was reached with more or less confidence depending in part, and importantly, on one's positionality in various axes of privilege or discrimination. Second, the primary conceptual tool by which merit was inserted into the picture was by way of the "intergenerational self": The projection of themselves as somehow part of those from which the gift came. This meant reliance on a combination of three concepts: having "humble origins" at some point in one's extended family history, a familial narrative marked by hard work and meritocratic achievement, and an internalized familial ethos of frugality and caution. These concepts meant that the inheritors managed to make the gifted money "theirs" as well as "legitimate."

Third, a variety of other strategies helped introduce moral elements into the picture. For instance, references to other people who had far greater wealth or through illegitimate ways made their own inheritance seem fair. Another technique entailed downplaying housing wealth as contributing much to inequality. In the broader context of this volume, this chapter thus not only offers a compelling dissection of moral logics but also—in line with some of the chapters just discussed—provides insights into the shaping of perceptions of inequalities themselves as factors that promote the use of certain logics. In addition, the chapter has implications for potential solutions to inequalities, including on whether fiscal initiatives on inheritance tax, for instance, might prove realistic.

Cultural and Institutional Logics

Acceptance on the basis of cultural and institutional logics is primarily driven by the recognition that the observable inequalities somehow "fit" or resonate with established ways of perceiving and organizing the world. Actors see a complementarity or continuity between the inequalities and what they think are the perspectives and guidelines that shape and even define their societies. The inequalities thus "make sense" and are potentially even reassuring. Three chapters speak to these logics most clearly: one on China and two on the United States.

Cary Wu considers the case of China in Chapter 9, a country that has experienced immense changes in overall wealth generation, the rise of a large middle-class and a rich elite, and new levels of inequality. Methodologically, we move away from microanalyses and toward macrolevel investigations reliant on large-scale survey data. Wu opens by pointing out that, contrary to widely held claims, many Chinese accept economic inequalities. Indeed, they often approve of them. For instance, he reports the findings from an existing survey study indicating that nearly five times as many respondents agreed with the notion that "some people getting rich first will increase the opportunities for others to get rich" than with the proposition that "some people getting rich first will reduce the chances for others to get rich." How can such approval be explained?

His analysis of Asian Barometer Survey data indicates that beliefs in meritocracy play a significant role. However, he proposes a second, and in his view, more powerful, institutional (albeit with moral undertones) mechanism. Chinese citizens overwhelmingly trust the political system and think that those who run the government enact policies that benefit society, solve the problems society may face, and serve the best interest of the people. Such widespread support for the political system encourages and allows individuals to rationalize, rather than question, existing arrangements—not least income distributions. Chinese citizens thus view social arrangements as acceptable and fair because they see them as reflecting the intentions of a government that they believe in. As a result, they are inclined to support, reinforce, and justify various forms of social and economic inequality, even when the income distribution works to their disadvantage. Citizens see continuity, in other words, between their government, which they trust, and the economic arrangements around them, which they therefore accept.

To this overall argument, Wu returns to a theme that several other chapters consider as well: the accuracy of perceptions about inequalities. Individuals who tend to legitimize economic inequality, he writes, have weaker perceptions of that inequality. Their assessment is clouded by an a priori disposition to accept things as they are. Several important implications flow from this. Among the most pressing is that current claims made by observers of China about the instability of the system due to anger toward growing inequalities could very well be wrong. There is in fact little frustration. We return to this point in the Conclusion when thinking about possible steps to address those inequalities.

Moving the spotlight onto the United States, Marc Dixon draws in Chapter 10 from public opinion data and case studies of labor mobilization to examine the role of labor unions in promoting the societal acceptance of inequalities. The main claim is that, starting in the early 1980s, unions began a long period of decline during which they lost their "moral sway" and influence on society at large. Once seen as effective labor advocates working for a better world for all, they were increasingly perceived as greedy actors with special interests. This happened thanks to three particular union practices: two-tier bargaining, accepting deep concessions, and hunkering down.

Their resulting retreat from their historic role as defenders of working Americans became a major contributor to the acceptance, on the part of the American public, of neoliberal principles that showed very little concern for economic inequalities. Unions, themselves more tolerant of increasing inequalities, further facilitated a more general embrace of those inequalities. They made it easier for Americans to view those inequalities as a normal part of a new constellation of norms, expectations, and practices. The old vision of a more egalitarian society faded, and a new one—more inclined toward unequal outcomes—took hold.

As such, Dixon's chapter depicts a rich picture of unions as both actors accepting inequalities and as promoters—given the loss of their historical moral sway and now declining relevance—of the emerging neoliberal worldview. In a sense, they removed themselves as obstacles to the acceptance of inequalities—in what may be an example of a subtle, less than conscious mechanism by which then the American public felt "freer" to accept inequalities. On this, we can see parallels with Kuusela's analysis in Chapter 5 of Finnish legislators as both accepting and promoting emerging logics of inequalities. Dixon's chapter also relates the shift in unions' positions to the broader political and economic currents of the times. Here, too, we can appreciate that the observable dynamics around any given logic do not exist in isolation but unfold in wider contexts.

No discussion of the United States and inequality would be complete without attention going to the American Dream. In Chapter 11, Robert C. Hauhart points to widespread unhappiness and concern in the country regarding the increasing gap between those with more access, resources, and opportunities and those without. Yet, he observes, the situation is unlikely to change any time soon, and this is because something fundamental to American society sustains this seemingly fragile circumstance. Put in the analytical language of this volume, Americans are willing to accept these inequalities, even if in some cases with limited enthusiasm or awareness, because they see them as congruent with, and resulting from, the pursuit of the American Dream.

Hauhart accordingly engages in a deep and compelling analysis of that dream. The dream seems to exempt Americans from having to justify in any real sense their successes and, in turn, the failures of others. It serves as a convenient individualistically oriented cultural narrative that not only is part of the country's DNA but also is further promoted by the political and economic establishments—despite efforts at times by leaders such as Lyndon B. Johnson and John F. Kennedy to eradicate poverty. Americans see inequality as consistent with those cultural and institutional elements of their society. Importantly, in what is methodologically speaking a unique blend of cultural and historical analysis, Hauhart also stresses not only the durability but flexibility of the American Dream. It is continuously constructed and reconstructed over time and deployed by a variety of actors in their specific circumstances.

While the chapter is therefore pointing to a powerful cultural and historical logic, it also makes clear that parts of the American Dream itself contain moral elements. Hauhart describes it as a belief in the rewards of working hard and the results that come from one's dedication and pursuit of success, and a view that anyone can in fact achieve those results if they apply themselves. It is thus to some extent about fairness in success and, on the flip side, failure. Put differently, the cultural and institutional logic at work entails a recognition of continuity with cultural elements that are quite charged with moral content.

Group and Ethnic Logics

Group and ethnic logics see actors accepting inequalities on the basis of hierarchical distinctions between collectivities that are seen as "superior" and others as "inferior." The superior groups, by virtue of who they are, are entitled to better economic conditions, while the inferior groups, by virtue of who they are, are not. Perhaps the most familiar illustration of this are discourses about natives versus migrants. However, the logics can take on a variety of other manifestations. Recall our discussion of Kuusela's chapter on Finland and the elimination of the wealth tax advanced by legislators as a tool to retain domestic capital and save the country from the dangers of foreign investors. All of Finland became the "us" and foreign investors the "them," while a call was made to accept bigger domestic inequalities as a way to save the former from the latter.

Arvid Lindh continues the analysis of the Scandinavian context with a parallel argument in Chapter 12. Economic inequalities, along with their acceptance, have been on the rise in Scandinavia. This represents a departure from the traditional egalitarian picture of those countries. It merits close analysis. We wish to know more about what, exactly, is being accepted, by whom, and according to what logics. Contextual factors that might explain the trend itself are also of interest.

Lindh starts by considering the acceptance of two types of inequalities: income inequality and welfare chauvinism. The latter involves a distinction between those deemed deserving of welfare services and support, and those whose access should be limited or denied. Lindh's analysis—based on new data from the Swedish branch (to which Lindh belongs) of the International Social Survey Programme—indicates, first, that acceptance of welfare chauvinism may be more pronounced than of income inequality. Such acceptance is not universal of course: a significant cleavage exists that largely revolves around social class. Those in middle-class occupations, particularly sociocultural professionals (e.g., teachers, nurses, social workers), have more inclusivist attitudes than those located in the working classes. In terms of political orientation, those favoring welfare chauvinism tend to vote for far-right parties.

The results depict a more divided society than is traditionally imagined. And here, second, we see that group and ethnic logics often informed by populist conceptions are at play. Specifically, given the centrality of the welfare state to Swedish society, and given that historically contributions and benefits have involved native ethnic Swedes, those in favor of welfare chauvinism draw a line between ethnic Swedes and migrants: The latter are considered outsiders who simply cannot be entitled to the same resources as ethnic Swedes. An "us-versus-them" mentality is hence obviously at work here—one that also draws from elements of cultural-institutional logics (continuity with established institutional arrangements) and moral considerations of fairness and entitlement.

The case of India offers additional valuable material. Priya Chacko opens Chapter 13 by presenting data on inequality levels in the country. As India has experienced enormous growth overall, with millions being lifted out of poverty, inequalities have widened. Current figures are startling. The World Inequality Report 2022, for instance, indicates that the top 10% of income earners in India hold 57% of total national income, earning over twenty times more than the bottom 50%. Women, those from the lower castes, and migrant workers are among the groups experiencing the most unfavorable circumstances. The COVID-19 pandemic, coupled with government programs, further destabilized these and other groups, including Muslims.

Chacko examines how the four logics of this volume have been intertwined and used to promote acceptance of these inequalities. Her attention goes to the policies, pronouncements, and programs of the Bharatiya Janata Party (BJP) government since its re-election in 2014. The government has woven together those logics as part of its authoritarian populist project informed by neoliberal principles. What stands out as perhaps the most defining feature of its approach, however, is its glorification of its Hindu nationalist populism. At its core, this is a group and ethnic logic that effectively informs the other logics. Thus, for instance, when it comes to moral logics, calls to "duty" over "rights" help reaffirm the enduring caste order and its hierarchical organization of society, and thereby "naturalize" inequalities. When it comes to market logics, the emphasis on personal responsibility and more limited state intervention is connected to lessons from ancient Hindu texts. And when it comes to cultural logics, gender hierarchies are, for example, embedded in Hindu traditions of family organization and social order (which again, of course, includes considerations of castes).

While a variety of groups and collectivities are therefore affected by such an approach, Chacko notes that perhaps the most consistently disadvantaged segment of the population are India's Muslims—the poorest religious community in the country. The Hindu nationalist project implicitly and explicitly undercuts them, both in rhetoric and practice, when it comes to access to financial resources, education, infrastructure, and more. India is Hindu, and thus it follows, according to the BJP, that benefits go to those who belong to that group and not others (most notably Muslims).

With Pía Riggirozzi, the focus in Chapter 14 shifts to Latin America and the gendered dimension of poverty- and insecurity-induced migrations across the region. Vulnerable women and girls leave their countries in search of safer and more promising destinations. But, as they do so, they run into further gender-based discrimination—whether tacit or explicit—that affects them based on their gender identity. This need not be the result of openly discriminatory practices. Indeed, Riggirozzi's attention goes to governments and policies that are otherwise considered progressive, open, and human-rights-based. Those policies suffer, however, from gender-blindness: They ignore the realities of movement and the gendered risks that women and girls experience during migration. The result is the pursuit of migration management policies that in effect promote an acceptance of inequalities that further perpetuate the disadvantages afflicting women and girls. Furthermore, this confirms the double discrimination suffered by migrant women, both as women and as migrants. As a consequence, a system of stratification among migrants rigidly based on gender emerges, which in turn facilitates the acceptance of inequalities by creating a space of dominance for male migrants.

Governments thus contribute to the perpetuation of the acceptance of gender-based inequalities: Women and girls are seen as belonging to a group that is perceived to be, without contestation, disadvantaged. Little is done for them, and the cycle of inequality and its acceptance continues. Given this, Riggirozzi reasons that possible productive steps would entail initiatives designed to challenge those migration management practices and their underlying blindness to group differences. We note in this regard the regional dimension of her analysis—rather unique for this volume. These policy practices reflect regional cultural orientations toward gender and suggest, therefore, that the solutions must also be in a sense regional in scope.

The Organization of the Volume

As mentioned already, we have organized this volume into four main sections that correspond to the four logics of acceptance. Chapters were allocated to any given section based on the primary logic of acceptance on which they focus, with the understanding that several of the chapters consider more than one logic. We begin with chapters on market and economic logics and then proceed to ones on moral logics, cultural and institutional logics, and group and ethnic logics.

In the Conclusion, we leverage the takeaways from the chapters to reflect on three important matters. The first concerns how the logics function as mechanisms for the creation and replication of economic inequalities. We pay particular attention to what the chapters reveal in terms of combinations of logics. The second concerns possible initiatives for the reduction of those inequalities. The wealth of information emerging from the chapters allows us to gain new vantage points and articulate potentially compelling propositions particularly around how the logics themselves may be challenged: Perception biases, erroneous or untested assumptions about the world, and questionable expectations built into the logics themselves undermine their integrity or validity. Third, we consider promising venues for future empirical research by suggesting, for instance, units of analysis other than national contexts and by reflecting on qualitative versus quantitative approaches.

Notes

1. See, for instance, World Bank (2023) and Hasell et al. (2023).
2. We combine "cultural" and "institutional" here because, in line with current scholarship, there is a fluid continuity between the two variables, with "institutions" in effect representing subsets of cultural material that is more formally organized or crystallized (Duina 2011).

References

Atkinson, A.B. 2015. *Inequality: What Can Be Done?* Cambridge, MA: Harvard University Press.

Atkinson, A.B., T. Piketty, and E. Saez. 2011. "Top Incomes in the Long Run of History." *Journal of Economic Literature* 49 (1): pp. 3–71.

Ayshford, E. 2024. "How Inequality Around Us Shapes Our Perceptions of Morality." *Kellog Insight,* May 1. https://insight.kellogg.northwestern.edu/article/how-the-inequality-around-us-shapes-our-perceptions-of-morality.

Bandelj, N., and E. Sowers. 2010. *Economy and State: A Sociological Perspective.* Cambridge: Polity Press.

Boltanski, L., and L. Thévenot. 2006. *On Justification: Economies of Worth.* Princeton, NJ: Princeton University Press.

Bourdieu, P. 1984. *Distinction: A Social Critique of the Judgement of Taste.* Cambridge, MA: Harvard University Press.

Bourdieu, P. 1977. *Outline of a Theory of Practice.* Cambridge: Cambridge University Press.

Bourdieu, P., and J.C. Passeron. 1990. *Reproduction in Education, Society and Culture.* Vol. 4. London: Sage.

Bourdieu, P., and L. Wacquant. 2013. "Symbolic Capital and Social Classes." *Journal of Classical Sociology* 13 (2): pp. 292–302.

Bourguignon, F. 2015. *The Globalization of Inequality.* Princeton, NJ: Princeton University Press.

Brint, S., and J. Karabel. 1989. "American Education, Meritocratic Ideology, and the Legitimation of Inequality: The Community College and the Problem of American Exceptionalism." *Higher Education* 18 (6): pp. 725–735.

Briziarelli, M., and J. Hoffmann. 2017. "Hegemony in Marxist Traditions." *Oxford Research Encyclopedia of Communication.* https://doi.org/10.1093/acrefore/9780190228613.013.48.

Bruni, L., and P. Santori. 2022. "The Illusion of Merit and the Demons of Economic Meritocracy: Which Are the Legitimate Expectations of the Market?" *Journal of Business Ethics* 176 (3): pp. 1–13.

Campbell, J.L. 2018. *American Discontent: The Rise of Donald Trump and Decline of the Golden Age.* New York: Oxford University Press.

Campbell, J.L. Forthcoming. *Pay Up! Conservative Myths About Tax Cuts for the Rich . . . And Why They're Wrong.* New York: Cambridge University Press.

Chancel, L., and T. Piketty. 2021. "Global Income Inequality, 1820–2020: The Persistence and Mutation of Extreme Inequality." *Journal of the European Economic Association* 19 (6): pp. 3025–3062.

Chancel, L., T. Piketty, E. Saez, and G. Zucman. 2022. *World Inequality Report 2022.* World Inequality Lab. https://wir2022.wid.world/www-site/uploads/2021/12/WorldInequalityReport2022_Full_Report.pdf.

Cook, E. 2020. "Naturalizing Inequality: The Problem of Economic Fatalism in the Age of Piketty." *Capitalism: A Journal of History and Economics* 1 (2): pp. 338–378.

Congressional Budget Office. 2022. "Trends in the Distribution of Family Wealth, 1989 to 2019." https://www.cbo.gov/publication/58533.

Diaz-Bone, R. 2015. "Convention Theory and Neoliberalism." *Journal of Cultural Economy* 9 (2): pp. 214–220.
Dorling, D. 2015. *Injustice: Why Social Inequality Still Persists*. Bristol: Policy Press.
Duina, F. 2018. *Broke and Patriotic: Why Poor Americans Love Their Country*. Stanford, CA: Stanford University Press.
Duina, F. 2011. *Institutions and the Economy*. Cambridge: Polity Press.
Durkheim, É. 1982. *The Rules of Sociological Method*. New York: Free Press.
Durongkaveroj, W. 2018. "Tolerance for Inequality: Hirschman's Tunnel Effect Revisited." *Journal of International Development* 30 (7): pp. 1240–1247.
Economic Policy Institute. 2022. "CEO Pay Has Skyrocketed 1,460% Since 1978." https://www.epi.org/publication/ceo-pay-in-2021/.
Elliott, L. 2019. "World's 26 Richest People Own as Much as Poorest 50%, Says Oxfam." *The Guardian*, January 21. https://www.theguardian.com/business/2019/jan/21/world-26-richest-people-own-as-much-as-poorest-50-per-cent-oxfam-report.
Elster, J. 1989. *Nuts and Bolts for the Social Sciences*. Cambridge: Cambridge University Press.
Essed, P. 2013. "Entitlement Racism: License to Humiliate." In *Recycling Hatred: Racism(s) in Europe Today: A Dialogue Between Academics, Equality Experts and Civil Society Activists*, edited by European Network Against Racism, pp. 62–76. Brussels: European Network Against Racism.
Essed, P. 1991. *Understanding Everyday Racism: An Interdisciplinary Theory*. London: Sage.
Frank, A.W. 2013. "From Sick Role to Practices of Health and Illness." *Medical Education* 47 (1): pp. 18–25.
Friedman, M., and R. Friedman. 1990. *Free to Choose: A Personal Statement*. Boston: HarperCollins Publishers.
García-Sánchez, E., I. Correia, C.R. Pereira, G.B. Willis, R. Rodríguez-Bailón, and J. Vala. 2022. "How Fair Is Economic Inequality? Belief in a Just World and the Legitimation of Economic Disparities in 27 European Countries." *Personality and Social Psychology Bulletin* 48 (3): pp. 382–395.
García-Sánchez, E., D. Osborne, G.B. Willis, and R. Rodríguez-Bailón. 2020. "Attitudes Towards Redistribution and the Interplay Between Perceptions and Beliefs About Inequality." *British Journal of Social Psychology* 59 (1): pp. 111–136.
Gethin, A., C. Martínez-Toledano, and T. Piketty. Eds. 2021. *Political Cleavages and Social Inequalities in Fifty Democracies, 1948–2020*. Cambridge, MA: Harvard University Press.
Gramsci, A. 1992. *Prison Notebooks*. New York: Columbia University Press.
Gross, N. (2018. "Pragmatism and the Study of Large-Scale Social Phenomena." *Theory and Society* 47 (1): pp. 87–111.
Guerriero, A.Z. 2024. "A More Equal World? An Analysis of the Global Inequality Trends in the Period 2000–2020." IFSO Working Paper No. 29. University of Duisburg-Essen, Institute for Socio-Economics.
Guinjoan, M., and G. Rico. 2018. "How Perceptions of Inequality Between Countries Diminish Trust in the European Union: Experimental and Observational Evidence." *Political Psychology* 39 (6): pp. 1289–1303.
Hall, P.A., and D.W. Soskice. Eds. 2001. *Varieties of Capitalism: The Institutional Foundations of Comparative Advantage*. Oxford: Oxford University Press.
Harrington, B. 2012. "From Trustees to Wealth Managers." In *Inherited Wealth, Justice and Equality*, edited by G. Erreygers and J. Cunliffe, pp. 190–209. New York: Routledge.
Hasell, J., P. Arriagada, E. Ortiz-Ospina, and M. Roser. 2023. "Economic Inequality." *Our World in Data*. https://ourworldindata.org/global-economic-inequality.
Hirschman, A.O. 1973. "The Changing Tolerance for Income Inequality in the Course of Economic Development." *World Development* 1 (12): pp. 29–36.
Huber, E., and J.D. Stephens. 2024. *Challenging Inequality: Variation Across Postindustrial Societies*. Chicago: University of Chicago Press.

Hurst, C.E., H.M.F. Gibbon, and A.M. Nurse. Eds. 2016. *Social Inequality: Forms, Causes, and Consequences*. New York: Routledge.

Iceland, J., E. Silver, and I. Redstone. 2023. *Why We Disagree About Inequality: Social Justice vs. Social Order*. Hoboken, NJ: John Wiley & Sons.

Inamdar, N. 2024. "India's Economy: The Good, Bad and Ugly in Six Charts." *BBC News*, April 30. https://www.bbc.com/news/world-asia-india-68823827.

Jedinger, A., and A.M. Burger. 2018. "The Role of Right-Wing Authoritarianism and Political Sophistication in Shaping Attitudes Toward Redistribution." *European Journal of Social Psychology* 49 (3): pp. 560–573.

Jessop, B. 1990. *State Theory: Putting the Capitalist State in Its Place*. University Park, PA: Pennsylvania State University Press.

Jost, J.T., M.R. Banaji, and B.A. Nosek. 2004. "A Decade of System Justification Theory: Accumulated Evidence of Conscious and Unconscious Bolstering of the Status Quo." *Political Psychology* 25 (6): pp. 881–919.

Kanbur, R., E. Ortiz-Juarez, and A. Sumner. 2024. "Is the Era of Declining Global Income Inequality Over?" *Structural Change and Economic Dynamics* 70: pp. 45–55.

Keister, L.A. 2014. "The One Percent." *Annual Review of Sociology* 40 (1): pp. 347–367.

Kohli, A. 2013. "Albert Hirschman (1915–2012): An Intellectual for All Seasons." *Economic and Political Weekly* 48 (4): pp. 25–27.

Krueger, A.B. 2012. "The Rise and Consequences of Inequality in the United States." Speech at the Center for American Progress. January 12. https://obamawhitehouse.archives.gov/sites/default/files/krueger_cap_speech_final_remarks.pdf.

Krugman, P. 2007. *The Conscience of a Liberal*. New York: W.W. Norton.

Lamont M., and M.L. Small. 2008. "How Culture Matters: Enriching Our Understanding of Poverty." In *The Colors of Poverty: Why Racial and Ethnic Disparities Persist*, edited by A. Chih Lin and D.R. Harris, pp. 76–102. New York: Russell Sage Foundation.

Laurin, K., A.C. Kay, D. Proudfoot, and G.J. Fitzsimons. 2013. "Response to Restrictive Policies: Reconciling System Justification and Psychological Reactance." *Organizational Behavior and Human Decision Processes* 122 (2): pp. 152–162.

Lindh, A., and L. McCall. 2023. "Bringing the Market In: An Expanded Framework for Understanding Popular Responses to Economic Inequality." *Socio-Economic Review* 21 (2): pp. 1035–1055.

Markovits, D. 2019. *The Meritocracy Trap*. London: Penguin.

McCall, L. 2013. *The Undeserving Rich: American Beliefs About Inequality, Opportunity, and Redistribution*. Cambridge: Cambridge University Press.

McCall, L., D. Burk, M. Laperrière, and J.A. Richeson. 2017. "Exposure to Rising Inequality Shapes Americans' Opportunity Beliefs and Policy Support." *Proceedings of the National Academy of Sciences* 114 (36): pp. 9593–9598.

McGoey, L. 2021. "Hiding the Rentier Elephant in Plain Sight: The Epistemology of Vanishing Rent." *Sociologica* 15 (2): pp. 75–93. https://doi.org/10.6092/issn.1971-8853/12720.

McGoey, L. 2012. "Philanthrocapitalism and Its Critics." *Poetics* 40 (2): pp. 185–199. https://doi.org/10.1016/j.poetic.2012.02.006.

McGoey, L., and D. Thiel. 2018. "Charismatic Violence and the Sanctification of the Super-Rich." *Economy and Society* 47 (1): pp. 111–134. https://doi.org/10.1080/03085147.2018.1448543.

Mijs, J.J. 2021. "The Paradox of Inequality: Income Inequality and Belief in Meritocracy Go Hand in Hand." *Socio-Economic Review* 19 (1): pp. 7–35.

Mijs, J.J., and A. Usmani. 2024. "How Segregation Ruins Inference: A Sociological Simulation of the Inequality Equilibrium." *Social Forces*, soae033. https://doi.org/10.1093/sf/soae033.

Milanovic, B. 2016a. *Global Inequality: A New Approach for the Age of Globalization*. Cambridge, MA: Harvard University Press.

Milanovic, B. 2016b. "The Great Convergence Global Equality and Its Discontents." *Foreign Affairs*, July 14. https://www.foreignaffairs.com/world/great-convergence-equality-branko-milanovic.
Milanovic, B. 2024. "The Three Eras of Global Inequality, 1820–2020 with the Focus on the Past Thirty Years." *World Development* 177: p. 106516.
Milanovic, B. 2023. *Visions of Inequality: From the French Revolution to the End of the Cold War*. Cambridge, MA: Harvard University Press.
Miller, S. 1990. "Foucault on Discourse and Power." *Theoria: A Journal of Social and Political Theory* 76: pp. 115–125.
Moore, B., Jr. 1978. *Injustice: The Social Bases of Obedience and Revolt*. White Plains, NY: M.E. Sharpe.
Ortiz, S.M. 2021. "Racists Without Racism? From Colourblind to Entitlement Racism Online." *Ethnic and Racial Studies* 44 (14): pp. 2637–2657.
Patterson, O. 1982. *Slavery and Social Death: A Comparative Study*. Cambridge, MA: Harvard University Press.
Piketty, T. 2020. *Capital and Ideology*. Cambridge, MA: Harvard University Press.
Piketty, T. 2014. *Capital in the Twenty-First Century*. Cambridge, MA: Belknap Press.
Piketty, T. 2015. *The Economics of Inequality*. Cambridge, MA: Harvard University Press.
Reich, R.B. 2020. *The System: Who Rigged It, How We Fix It*. New York: Vintage.
Rodríguez-Pose, A., J. Terrero-Dávila, and N. Lee. 2023. "Left-Behind Versus Unequal Places: Interpersonal Inequality, Economic Decline and the Rise of Populism in the USA and Europe." *Journal of Economic Geography* 23 (5): pp. 951–977.
Saez, E., and G. Zucman. 2021. *How to Get $1 Trillion from 1000 Billionaires: Tax Their Gains Now*. Berkeley: University of California.
Saez, E., and G. Zucman. 2020. "The Rise of Income and Wealth Inequality in America: Evidence from Distributional Macroeconomic Accounts." *Journal of Economic Perspectives* 34 (4): pp. 3–26.
Saez, E., and G. Zucman. 2019. *The Triumph of Injustice: How the Rich Dodge Taxes and How to Make Them Pay*. New York: W. W. Norton & Company.
Samuelson, P.A., and W.D. Nordhaus. 2009. *Economics*. New York: McGraw-Hill.
Sandel, M.J. 2020. *The Tyranny of Merit: What's Become of the Common Good?* London: Penguin.
Savage, M., G. Bagnall, and B. Longhurst. 2001. "Ordinary, Ambivalent and Defensive: Class Identities in the Northwest of England." *Sociology* 35 (4): pp. 875–892.
Sayer, A. 2015. *Why We Can't Afford the Rich*. Bristol: Policy Press.
Scheidel, W. 2017. *The Great Leveler: Violence and the History of Inequality from the Stone Age to the Twenty-First Century*. Princeton, NJ: Princeton University Press.
Schimpfössl, E. 2024. "Rich Russians' Morality of Success." *East European Politics and Societies* 38 (1): pp. 283–302. https://doi.org/10.1177/08883254221139826.
Schirato, T., and M. Roberts. 2020. *Bourdieu: A Critical Introduction*. New York: Routledge.
Sen, A. 1997. *On Economic Inequality*. Oxford: Oxford University Press.
Sklair, J., and L. Glucksberg. 2021. "Philanthrocapitalism as Wealth Management Strategy: Philanthropy, Inheritance and Succession Planning Among the Global Elite." *Sociological Review* 69 (2): pp. 314–329.
Smith, A. 1910. *An Inquiry into the Nature and Causes of the Wealth of Nations*. London: J.M. Dent & Sons.
Smith. D. 1990. *Conceptual Practices of Power*. Boston: Northeastern University Press.
Spillman, L. 2023. "Morality, Inequality, and the Power of Categories." In *Handbook of the Sociology of Morality*, edited by S. Hitlin, S.M. Dromi, and A. Luft, vol. 2, pp. 373–385. Cham: Springer.
Stiglitz, J.E. 2015a. *The Great Divide: Unequal Societies and What We Can Do About Them*. New York: W. W. Norton & Company.

Stiglitz, J.E. 2015b. "Inequality and Economic Growth." *Political Quarterly* 86 (S1): pp. 134–155.
Stiglitz, J.E. 2012. *The Price of Inequality: How Today's Divided Society Endangers Our Future.* New York: W. W. Norton & Company.
Stoddart, M.C. 2007. "Ideology, Hegemony, Discourse: A Critical Review of Theories of Knowledge and Power." *Social Thought and Research* 28: pp. 191–225.
Storti, L., and J. Dagnes. 2021. "The Super-Rich: Origin, Reproduction, and Social Acceptance." *Sociologica* 15 (2): pp. 5–23.
Storti, L., G. Urso, and N. Reid. 2023. "Exiting the Periphery: Possible Pathways Towards a Socio-Economic and Institutional De-Marginalization of Places." *Regional Science Policy and Practice* 15 (7): pp. 1406–1424.
Streeck, W. 2016. *How Will Capitalism End? Essays on a Failing System.* London: Verso Books.
Thelen, K.A. 2014. *Varieties of Liberalization and the New Politics of Social Solidarity.* New York: Cambridge University Press.
Tilly, C. 1998. *Durable Inequality.* Berkeley: University of California Press.
Trigilia, C. Ed. 2022. *Capitalisms and Democracies: Can Growth and Equality Be Reconciled?* London and New York: Routledge.
Trump, K.S. 2018. "Income Inequality Influences Perceptions of Legitimate Income Differences." *British Journal of Political Science* 48 (4): pp. 929–952.
Trump, K.S. 2023a. "Income Inequality Is Unrelated to Perceived Inequality and Support for Redistribution." *Social Science Quarterly* 104 (2): pp. 180–188.
Trump, K.S. 2023b. "What Does It Take to Be Rich? Asking Reasonable Survey Questions About Income Inequality." *Research and Politics* 10 (3): pp. 1–7.
Valentino, L., and S. Vaisey. 2022. "Culture and Durable Inequality." *Annual Review of Sociology* 48: pp. 109–129.
Van den Haak, M., and N. Wilterdink. 2019. "Struggling with Distinction: How and Why People Switch Between Cultural Hierarchy and Equality." *European Journal of Cultural Studies* 22 (4): pp. 416–432.
Weber, M. 1978. *Selections in Translation.* Cambridge: Cambridge University Press.
Weiss, D., W. Greve, and U. Kunzmann. 2022. "Responses to Social Inequality Across the Life Span: The Role of Social Status and Upward Mobility Beliefs." *International Journal of Behavioral Development* 46 (4): pp. 261–277.
World Bank. 2023. "Inequality and Shared Prosperity." https://www.worldbank.org/en/topic/isp/overview.
Zucman, G. 2019. "Global Wealth Inequality." *Annual Review of Economics* 11 (1): pp. 109–138.
Zucman, G. 2015. *The Hidden Wealth of Nations: The Scourge of Tax Havens.* Chicago: University of Chicago Press.

PART I

MARKET AND ECONOMIC LOGICS

Chapter 2
Who Accepts Economic Inequality and Why?
Market Logics and the Acceptance of Inequality

Lucy Barnes

Introduction

In this chapter, I seek to provide a broad descriptive characterization of those who accept inequality and a more detailed account of the relationship between the way people understand how the economy works and their likelihood of accepting inequality.

I start with simple descriptions of those who accept inequality. The key takeaways here are that accepting inequality is a small minority position. Moreover, while younger, high-income men with postgraduate qualifications are more likely to accept inequality than those who are older, female, and have lower income and educational attainment levels (this leads to marginal overrepresentation within the group of accepters), we still find people from all groups who accept inequality.

Second, I consider the association between inequality acceptance and the specific content of market logics. That is, while the introduction to this volume highlights the kind of ("pro-market") reasoning with regard to material outcomes that may provide a logic for accepting inequality, I take a slightly broader view to examine how different kinds of orientations toward the market relate to acceptance of inequality. Endorsing a strongly pro-market view, while predictive of accepting inequality, is a relatively narrowly held kind of economic logic. Most people combine some elements of weaker pro-market thinking with (different patterns of) disagreement about some of

Lucy Barnes, *Who Accepts Economic Inequality and Why?*. In: *The Social Acceptance of Inequality*.
Edited by: Francesco Duina and Luca Storti, Oxford University Press. © Oxford University Press (2025).
DOI: 10.1093/oso/9780197814499.003.0002

its components. The small size of the pro-market group in the population means that it only provides about one-fifth of those unconcerned about inequality. More—indeed most—inequality accepters hold market views that are not particularly pro-market.

The chapter offers three important conclusions when it comes to market and economic logics. First, while some logics of acceptance of inequality can be characterized as market-oriented, not all logics of the market lead equally to the acceptance of inequality. Market logics have several components which may be arranged along a continuum from mainstream to more radical, but which also combine in interesting ways away from that unidimensional construct. Second, most inequality-accepting actors subscribe to relatively moderate elements of the kind of market logic that would underpin an acceptance of inequality. Nevertheless, variation in how people construct market and economic logics is associated with variation in levels of acceptance of inequality.

Who Accepts Inequality?

The first empirical task of this chapter is to put the subsequent findings (here and throughout the volume) into context by establishing the prevalence of the acceptance of inequality. That is, while the focus of the volume is largely to zoom in on those people who do not think economic inequalities should be contested or resisted, it is important to describe the size of this phenomenon. Data from the 2019 International Social Survey Programme (ISSP) on Social Inequality attests to the claim made in the Introduction to this volume that accepting inequality runs counter to a general consensus of concern. However, while accepting inequality is a minority position, it is one that draws support from across different types of people.

The 2019 ISSP survey asks respondents in twenty-nine countries[1] whether they agree or disagree with the statement that "[d]ifferences in income in [COUNTRY] are too large." Disagreement with this statement thus implies that existing levels of inequality are not a concern. The first descriptive parameter to calculate, then, is just how many people disagree that income differences are too large.[2] Overall, 8% of the populations surveyed accept inequality by this metric. Eighty-one percent explicitly agree that differences are too large—that inequality is a problem not to be accepted. The remainder neither agree nor disagree. An important implication of this is that while the social acceptance of inequality is important to understand, it is not the case that social attitudes, in broad terms, accept inequality explicitly. Broad popular acceptance of inequality in itself is unlikely to present a critical political barrier to egalitarian action.

However, if acceptance of inequality is concentrated in particular segments of the population, it might be the case that that 8% is a critical group. Including those who neither agree nor disagree that inequality is a problem increases the side of the group to 19%, a significant enough minority to be politically influential. Specifically, given known imbalances of influence in favor of those with higher incomes (Hacker and Pierson 2010), or higher education, and the overrepresentation of certain groups (older, men) in positions of power, it is important to consider whether acceptance of inequality gains amplified traction because of its concentration among those groups.

We can use the ISSP data to address this question also. Regression analyses allow us to consider the marginal associations of particular characteristics with the outcome of interest here: the acceptance of economic inequality. Specifically, I consider whether gender, age, income, and education groups differ systematically. For gender, I separate those who identify themselves as male from everyone else (those who are female and those who prefer not to use one of those two categories). I use four roughly equally sized groups to capture age, separating younger respondents (under 35), middle age (35–49), late middle age (49–64), and the oldest respondents (65 and over). For education, I use the six categories of qualification coded in the ISSP, which separate respondents according to level (no formal education, primary, secondary, tertiary, and postgraduate qualifications), with further distinctions between "lower" secondary qualifications, which do not allow entry to university; "upper" secondary qualifications, which do; and "postsecondary" qualifications which are non-tertiary qualifications oriented toward technical training or the labor market. Finally, for income I create five groups roughly equivalent to quintiles within each country.

Figure 2.1 shows the results of estimating binary logistic models on these lines. The figure shows the bivariate coefficients for each of the four characteristics discussed above, estimates from a multivariate model with all four variables entered simultaneously, and a final model that also adds the employment status of the respondent. The values plotted are on the scale of the underlying linear predictor, the log of the odds ratio between the different groups.

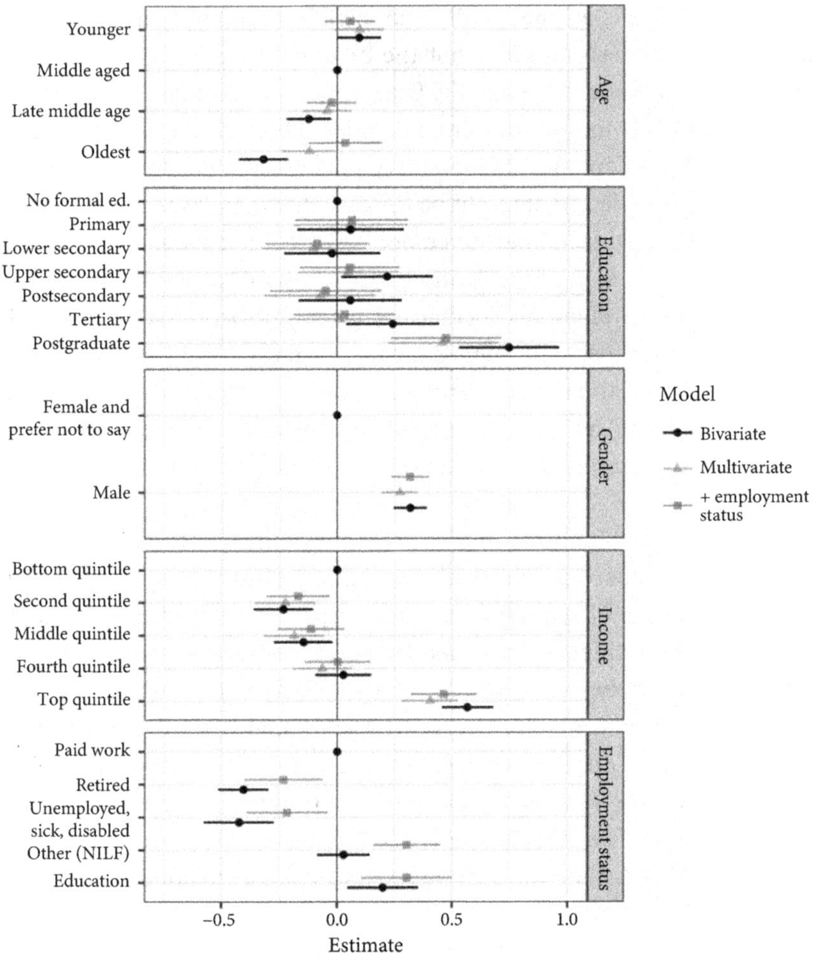

Figure 2.1 Logistic regression coefficient estimates of demographic characteristics' associations with accepting economic inequality

Data: ISSP Research Group (2022). Estimates from models with fixed effects for country.

Considering the bivariate associations (black circles), we see obvious gradients for age, and to some extent education: Younger people are more accepting of economic inequality, as are those with higher academic educational credentials. There are also big differences by gender, with men more likely to express acceptance of inequality. On income, we see increasing acceptance of inequality from the second quintile to the top, but the lowest income group is actually more likely to accept inequality than the second and middle groups.[3]

The multivariate treatment reveals that some of the descriptive differences describe overlapping populations. In particular, the strong age and education gradients in the bivariate data are attenuated when considered simultaneously. Interestingly, the positive association between tertiary education and accepting inequality disappears in the multivariate treatments (although a strong association with postgraduate qualifications remains). Similarly, the oldest group is less distinctively anti-inequality once education is taken into account. The bivariate relationships with income and gender, on the other hand, remain very similar in substantive terms regardless of the other variables included in the model. Men are significantly more accepting of inequality than women and those who prefer not to say (the latter two groups combined in Figure 2.1 for ease of presentation); and belonging to the highest income quintile too retains a strong association with accepting inequality across specifications.

These regression results make it clear that there are some systematic differences between types of people in terms of their tendencies to accept inequality. The differences are in the right direction for the argument that inequality-accepters might be exactly that group of people whose views might hold disproportionate influence: high-income men with postgraduate education. However, the regression results do not tell us directly what the overall composition of the inequality-accepting group looks like, and statistically significant differences at the margin do not automatically translate to large substantive differences. That is, it is premature to infer that a powerful, homogeneous group accepts inequality.

Table 2.1 shows the share of those who accept inequality that come from the group within each category where inequality acceptance is most and least likely, alongside those groups' shares of the overall population. The table indicates that the idea of a very particular "type" of person accepting inequality is, indeed, unwarranted. The group of people who accept inequality remains descriptively diverse, even as it deviates somewhat from the population averages as the regression results imply. Thus, it is simultaneously true that men are more likely to accept inequality and, at the same time, that over 45% of those who support inequality are not male. Similarly for the other characteristics, identifiable differences in the chance of accepting inequality do not cleanly separate homogeneous groups. Even for the biggest effects—those by income—the top quintile is hugely overrepresented among those accepting inequality, at 31%. Even so, half of those who

Table 2.1 Share of different groups among inequality-accepters and the general population

Category	Share of accepters	Share of pop.
Least likely groups		
Non-male	46	53
Oldest (65+)	18	23
Postsecondary ed.	10	13
Second income quintile	15	20
Most likely groups		
Male	54	47
Younger (<35)	28	24
Postgraduate ed.	16	12
Top income quintile	31	20

are unconcerned about inequality are drawn from the bottom three income quintiles within their countries.

The ISSP data thus show us two important things about who accepts inequality. First, it is a relatively small share of the population who is unconcerned about income differences between rich and poor. Second, while systematic patterns exist, those who accept inequality come from varied demographic groups within society. This broad descriptive mapping puts the findings of other contributions to this volume into perspective in important ways. Most basically, it points to the need for logics of justification where large economic inequalities are defended: Inequality does cut against the general predispositions in public opinion. But also, the most likely place to see these justifications in action is likely to be among those with high incomes, which the Neely and the Moor and Friedman chapters in this volume consider in detail. The levels of discomfort with large income differences even in these groups (even the share of young, top quintile, postgraduate-educated men who disagree that income differences are too high is 20%) underline the need for the kind of justificatory work undertaken to defend the deservingness or economic functionality of inequality.

Why Accept Inequality?

Having outlined the broad patterns of who accepts inequality, I now move to the more interesting considerations of why. Empirically, I link the endorsement of particular examples of each type of logic—market, moral, cultural-institutional, and group-based—to the acceptance of inequality, in broad-coverage survey data. I then move on to focus specifically on the market and economic logic in more detail. Thus, it is worth discussing this kind of logic in more depth. In particular, it is important to note that the argument is not that recourse to one type of reasoning rather than another—an appeal to the economic rather than the moral, for example—will be associated with a greater acceptance of inequality. Rather, there are particular types of logic within each category that provide a particular linkage between inequality and some value with market, moral, institutional, or group content or resonance.

Market Logics

The idea that appeals to the economic system provide an important justification of, and thereby logic of acceptance for, economic inequality is widespread. I pay particular attention to this logic here given the more detailed empirical investigation in the final part of the chapter.

Simply, and generally, the central reasoning in the market logic is that "inequality is necessary, even celebrated, because it is the natural outcome of an economic system that provides the greatest good to the greatest number" (Kwak 2018, 9). The inherent justice of a market process may be grounded in its contribution to other economic results (overall prosperity), or a more existential necessity of a broader capitalist system that derives its legitimacy elsewhere (Hochschild 1981, 67). An important component of this logic is a descriptive argument that inequality is necessary for good material outcomes.

There are different versions of this argument, articulated by different people, in different contexts. Neely (in this volume) outlines the particular narratives that highly remunerated finance and technology professionals use to understand the inegalitarian impacts of their work. Similar appeals to the necessity of unequal economic outcomes based on the natural, depoliticized workings of the economy feature in the economic reasoning of financial sector workers in London (Mosse 2021). Appeals to the incentives associated with high levels of inequality, and that broader benefits accrue from personal economic success, also represent a linkage between inequality and positive material outcomes. Sally, a lower-income participant in Hochschild's 1981 examination of Americans' views of distributive fairness, provides another such narrative: "by pushing yourself up, you're bringing other people with you" (cited by Hochschild 1981, 30).

In more technical treatments, market logic justifications for economic inequality are rooted in the idea of a trade-off between equality and (market) efficiency. A number of varieties of this general idea exist, from an aggregated analogy to specific equality-(Pareto) efficiency trade-offs in particular microeconomic interventions, on the one hand, to a broader question about the macroeconomic relationship between economic growth and equality (Jimènez-Buedo 2011). Under this view, growing inequalities are legitimized as the consequence of market mechanisms, or the conditions necessary for the effective functioning of those markets. These markets, in turn, are necessary for overall economic success—the growth of the pie for the common good.

This kind of market logic is often associated with neoliberal economic and political thought and is widely seen to have become more prevalent since the 1980s. By the 1980s, the group of intellectuals most closely associated with the development of that school of thought had coalesced on, among other things, the idea that pronounced economic inequalities were not only an unfortunate byproduct but also a functional characteristic of properly functioning market systems (Mirowski and Plehwe 2015).

Market logics, even in less overtly ideological forms, have also been argued to squeeze out the consideration of equality as a central criterion for the evaluation of policy. Popp Berman (2022) highlights how an emphasis on efficiency, even when not directly framed as in conflict with goals of equality (and indeed sometimes pursued in the service of egalitarian goals), reoriented American public policymaking in the decades after the 1960s. The use of this kind of "thinking like an economist" gave impetus to cost-containment and promoting competition within public policy, side-lining commitments to equality through the use of incentives and choice even as instrumental mechanisms rather than explicit goals in themselves (99).

The seeming naturalness of the equivalence between "pro-market" positions and those that are less concerned with inequalities points to the political success of this intellectual movement within economic policy and political expert discourse (Naidu et al. 2019). However, many economists (and others) reject the equation of "pro-market" with "anti-equality." They point instead to the existence of multiple different possible market logics. Empirical evidence on the compatibility of inequality and well-functioning markets is mixed at best (Jimènez-Buedo 2011; Ostry et al. 2014). It is clearly possible to make arguments against economic inequality from the basis of market-based logics (see Saez and Zucman 2020; Stockhammer and Onaran 2022). By the criterion of material success, if high inequality is associated with bad performance, a market logic could undermine the acceptance of inequality.

It also remains unclear whether the link between inequality and good market performance is widely held in public opinion, as opposed to elite discourse. On the one hand, mainstream formal accounts of economic performance in general are less common among the less well-off (Killick 2020). The efficiency-equality trade-off requires appeal to a number of "other-things-equal" assumptions, which expert positions tend to incorporate, while public understandings do not (Sapienza and Zingales 2013). Moreover, the efficiency-equality trade-off is not obvious in the empirical record (Kenworthy 1995). The idea that inequality is a corollary of good economic performance may not be obvious to the public.

Moreover, in other spheres of the macroeconomy, public economic psychology displays a "good-begets-good" heuristic where, even for variables that are commonly held by experts to be in trade-off with one another, performance on all outcomes is expected to move together (Leiser and Aroch 2009). Thus, the expected link could well be that more equal outcomes come with better overall material performance.

The Empirical Power of the Market Logic

It is thus the specific linkages within accounts of the market that determine their inequality-accepting or inequality-resisting direction. With large-scale survey data we can tap into endorsement of this kind of content and examine whether it does indeed correspond to the acceptance of inequality.

Data

Many existing datasets—like the ISSP—provide useful information on beliefs and attitudes about inequality. However, treatments of public conceptualizations and understandings of the economy are less common. Treatments of the rise of pro-market thinking have more typically been concerned with elite views (Mudge 2018; Popp Berman 2022) or high-level discourse (Schmidt 2016), than they have with public opinion, while treatments of public attitudes have tended to focus more directly on attitudes toward inequality and redistribution themselves rather than the content of the market linkages they draw (Hoy et al. 2024; Rueda and Stegmueller 2019; see also Barnes 2022).

To fill this gap, I fielded an original survey to nationally representative populations in the United Kingdom, Denmark, France, Germany, and the United States in 2020. The survey included questions on respondents' overall orientation to the economy and economic thinking, as well as a set of different questions about how respondents think the economy works. In particular, a number of questions track the underlying tenets of the idea that market allocation provides the positive social outcomes necessary for its invocation as a justification of inequality to be reasonable.

Market Linkages: Empirical Measurement

I use responses to six questions oriented toward the endorsement of a pro- or anti-market logic to describe different patterns of public thinking about markets and the economy.

First, I consider a simple microeconomic version of the idea of "anti-market bias," that economic transactions are zero-sum negotiations between unequal parties. I ask whether, in a sale of a bicycle for money, respondents consider the buyer, seller, both, or neither parties better off because of the deal. The "textbook" as well as the pro-market response is that both are better off; a strong anti-market view would be that neither is, while a more mercantilist view would imply that while the seller is better off, the buyer is not.

A second question asks directly how respondents think economic outcomes come about at the macro level:

> Here are some opinions about what affects the economy in [country]. Which of them comes closest to your view?
>
> - The economy in [country] depends on the operation of basic economic forces, like supply and demand.
> - The economy in [country] depends on the policy decisions of the government.

- The economy in [country] depends on the actions of a small group of influential rich people.
- Don't know.

While these are technically descriptive rather than evaluative statements, I order them from high to low in their "pro-market" nature with the supply and demand response being the most pro-market, and the "influential rich people" response the least. This last response allows for the idea of a "rigged" market logic, which rejects not only the idea that market outcomes are generally good but also the idea that current economic outcomes are driven by any kind of impersonal market forces at all.

These two survey questions, one at the micro- and one at the macro-level, do not necessarily capture a market linkage that we would expect to strongly drive support for inequality. However, they are central underlying premises for the notion that market organization underpins positive material outcomes.

I ask three questions with a similar format, with responses on a five-point scale from "strongly disagree" to "strongly agree," to gauge agreement with the following statements: additional workers increase demand for goods and services; economics and economic policy are about increasing the total level of resources available; a rich person getting richer increases total wealth. Each of these reflects the pro-market arguments in different ways. The first captures the macroeconomic efficiency of markets in the positive-sum rejection of the "lump of labor" fallacy. The second taps into the idea of generating wealth and making everyone better off through the pursuit of positive outcomes in the aggregate (without attention to the distribution of any benefits). The third poses this question in starker terms and comes the closest to a linkage that might directly underpin the acceptance of inequality, in stipulating that when the rich increase the gap between themselves and others, it is a sign of a benign aggregate expansion, rather than coming at the expense of others.

Finally, I ask about a shibboleth of the supply-side neoliberal approach, that reducing taxes will increase revenue due to its positive incentive effect. Respondents are asked whether a 10% tax cut will decrease taxes by more than 10%, exactly 10%, less than 10%, or not at all or even increase them. I denote this variable Laffer Curve. Expecting revenues to increase from a tax cut reflects a highly pro-market linkage within economic thinking. Not only is it closely conceptually tied to belief in efficient market-driven resource allocations that generate great wealth and raise all boats, but it is also politically and historically closely tied to these ideas.

Latent Class Analysis

I use latent class analysis to summarize the patterns of responses in the data. The key intuition behind latent class analysis is to assume an underlying categorical structure—there are different types of market logic represented in the population—and then to optimally separate these types based on maximizing between-group, and minimizing within-group, variation. The statistical analysis is unsupervised and "content free," optimizing the fit given the number of classes provided by the analyst. Substantive interpretation of the model output—the division of the population into these various classes—is thus an inductive interpretation.

I estimate and present the results of a six-class model, estimated using the poLCA package in R. A seven-class model provides marginal improvements to the Akaike Information Criterion and Bayesian Information Criterion, but at the cost of less readily interpretable patterns in conditional response patterns. Figure 2.2 shows the distributions of response probabilities across the market-logic questions within the latent classes generated by the model.

The figure shows the profile of response probabilities across the six items, within the six classes, with darker shading indicating a higher concentration of responses on the respective outcome category. Intuitively, the dark areas illustrate "where the people (in each group) are."

The most striking group pattern is the group at the bottom of the figure who tend to respond that they "don't know" across most or all these questions. This "don't know" group is not a huge share of people—around 5%—but it is a useful feature of the latent class analysis to separate out this kind of don't know response profile.

Second, we see a distinctive class in the third panel from the top whose responses are concentrated on the right-hand side of the substantive response categories. Given the construction of the figure, this reflects the consistent expression of a pro-market logic. This group comprises 12% of the sample. They are particularly distinctive in their endorsement of the positive effect of more workers on demand, and on the view that economics is about maximizing available resources. This group is also highly opinionated in the sense of giving very few "don't know" responses. In theoretical

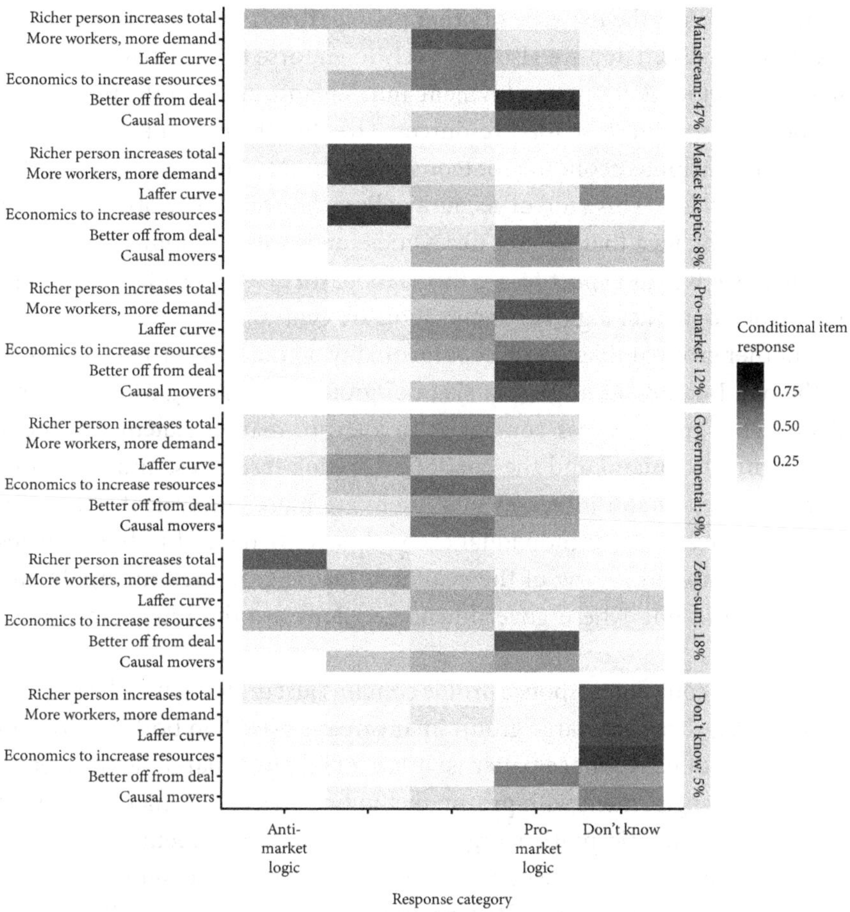

Figure 2.2 Conditional item responses for 6-class latent class analysis of market logics

Note: Darker cells indicate a higher probability of the relevant response category. Note that the causal movers variable has only four outcome levels (including "Don't know"); the least-market cell does not apply in those rows (see Appendix Table 2A for other outcome categories).

terms, this is the class whose particular version of an explanatory logic of the market is most likely to yield acceptance of economic inequality.

The second largest class in the analysis is a group (second panel from bottom) that is distinctive in having more responses concentrated on the left-hand side of the response categories, and in particular is characterized by disagreement with the idea that one person getting richer increases total wealth. This makes sense in a context where that person's increasing fortune comes at the expense of other people; thus I denote this group the "zero-sum" class. They are also less likely to endorse the positive-sum, pro-market statements about employment and demand, and that the purpose of economics is to increase total resources. They are the most likely of all the classes to attribute economic outcomes to a narrow, influential group (at 24% of the class). This kind of account of how the economy works is most at odds with the idea that market necessities can justify economic inequality. As such, we would expect to see this class particularly less likely to accept inequality, if market logics of justification are central.

Another group unlikely to accept inequality on the basis of a market logic is the one I denote as a "market skeptic" group, comprising 8% of respondents. This group is less convinced by the pro-market statements about employment demand and the goal of increasing resources, and responses to the "richer person increases total" item are more ambivalent. However, they still tend to think individual exchanges are beneficial to both parties and split between a view of the economy that is grounded in supply and demand, and one where government decisions are the important causal mover.

The most common response profile contains just under half of the respondents (47%). I call this large group "mainstream" based on both its size and the content of its response patterns. It has a fairly pro-market logic overall, anchored by agreement with pro-market interpretations of micro-exchange and macroeconomic market organization, including agreement with the idea that more workers create more demand. There is also agreement with the idea that the purpose of the economy is to increase overall resource availability. However, there is less enthusiasm for the idea that one person getting richer increases total wealth, and there is almost no endorsement of the "supply side" Laffer Curve dynamic.

The final group is one I label governmental. This group is distinctive in combining the attribution of economic outcomes to government (as the modal response within the class) with a more fiat-law expectation of the revenue consequences of a tax change in the Laffer Curve question (that the tax would raise the same amount as its rate increase). This group is also more evenly split between a view of individual exchange which sees both parties benefiting, and a "mercantilist" one in which only the seller is better off.

Overall, then, different groups of people combine different types of pro-market argument in different ways. The response profiles differ in their degree of general "pro-market" enthusiasm, but they are also different in the ways that they deviate from pro-market positions, for example, comparing the don't know, zero-sum, and governmental groups.

Market Logics and the Acceptance of Inequality

The final step is to consider the link between different market logics and the acceptance of inequality. We can see this in the patterns of association between each latent class and the same acceptance measure that we used in the ISSP analysis. I include latent class membership as a set of dummy variables in regressions including demographic characteristics (age, gender, income quintile, education level, employment status). I omit the large "mainstream" group as the reference group in the results presented in Table 2.2.

The expectations that we take from the content of the market logics are that the pro-market class would be more likely than the mainstream group to accept inequality, while both the zero-sum and market-skeptic logics should be less so. The governmental group may also be less likely to accept inequality, given their greater rejection of the benefits linkage of the "free market" arguments for unregulated economic transactions, and given their belief that government actions shape economic outcomes, their lower belief in existing inequalities as part of an inevitable order of things. Expectations about the "don't know" group are indeterminate.

Table 2.2 shows the results of a binary logistic random effects model (Model 1). Model 2 presents an alternative specification using fixed instead of random effects. Finally, Model 3 incorporates indicators of other, non-market, logics of acceptance.

The results broadly accord with theoretical expectations. The pro-market group is consistently estimated to be more accepting of inequality than the mainstream group, as well as (given their negative coefficients) all other groups. Similarly, the negative correlations for the market-skeptic and zero-sum groups, and for the governmental group, are recovered in the data. The group who responds disproportionately with "don't know" answers about the logic of the economy are also less accepting of inequality than the mainstream group. Note that while the coefficient for the don't know group becomes smaller and statistically insignificant with the inclusion of the variables tapping the other logics, this reflects respondents answering

Table 2.2 Multilevel logistic models of acceptance of economic inequality on markers of different logics

	Acceptance of inequality		
	Model 1	**Model 2**	**Model 3**
Don't know (?)	−0.88**	−0.87**	−0.59
	(0.43)	(0.43)	(0.62)
Zero sum (−)	−0.35**	−0.34**	−0.33*
	(0.16)	(0.16)	(0.18)
Market skeptic (−)	−0.62***	−0.62**	−0.93***
	(0.24)	(0.24)	(0.27)
Pro-market (+)	0.58***	0.58***	0.53***
	(0.13)	(0.13)	(0.15)
Governmental (−)	−0.77***	−0.77***	−1.17***
	(0.25)	(0.25)	(0.28)
Morality: deservingness (+)			−1.24***
			(0.20)
National redistribution (−)			−1.30***
			(0.42)
Group dominance (+)			3.95***
			(0.29)
Demographic controls	Yes	Yes	Yes
Country effects	Random	Fixed	Random
N	4722	4722	4159
Log Likelihood	−1459.02	−1448.41	−1186.30
AIC	2958.05	2942.82	2418.59
BIC	3087.25		2564.25

Note: Omitted market-logic category is the mainstream class. Signs in parentheses indicate direction of theoretical expectations. Demographic controls are age, gender, income quintile, education level, employment status.

"don't know" in the group dominance and morality questions being dropped from Model 3.

The estimated associations of the other groups with inequality acceptance also vary somewhat depending on the inclusion of the indicators of the other logics. On the one hand, compared to the mainstream group, the pro-market group is also more likely to endorse the morality of deservingness and group hierarchies, so accounting for this difference reduces the distinction on the basis of the market-logic grouping itself. On the other hand, the governmental and market-skeptic differences from the mainstream are exacerbated by the inclusion of the other logics in the model. These groups are also more oriented toward group dominance than the mainstream group, and in the case of the governmental group, also more deservingness-endorsing as a matter of morality, but because these tendencies weigh against the difference from the mainstream in terms of inequality acceptance, the distinctiveness attributable to the market logic is increased.

To provide an interpretable sense of the magnitude of these relationships, Figure 2.3 shows predicted probabilities estimated using Models 1 and 3 of Table 2.2. Focusing on the results for Model 3, among respondents who endorse "mainstream" market logics, the predicted probability of accepting economic inequality is just over 7.5%. Among the pro-market group, it is a little over 12.5%—a large difference. While they comprise 12% of the population, the pro-market group provides 20% of those who accept inequality.

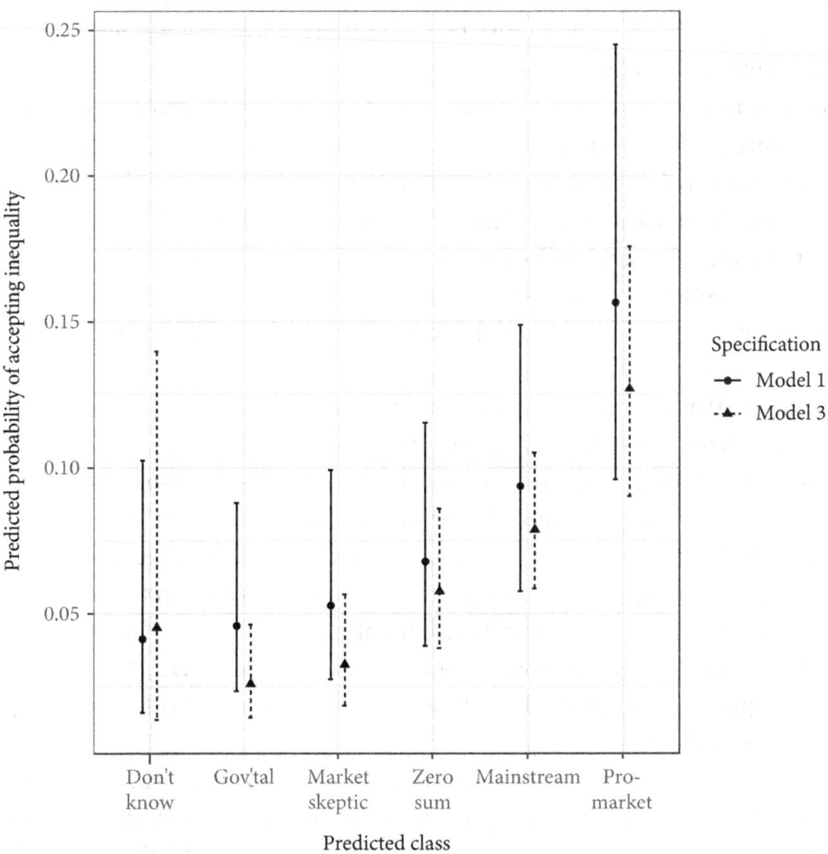

Figure 2.3 Predicted probabilities of accepting inequality, by market logic

Note: Other variables held constant at levels reflecting their share in the sample.

Similarly, the market-skeptic group is estimated to accept inequality only with a probability of 2.5%. These are very large differences in terms of the concentration of inequality acceptance across the different ways of thinking about the market.

Overall, then, there are clear connections between people's acceptance of inequality and the logics that they use to describe how markets work. These conform roughly to the expectations that we would have based on the way that the potential benefits of economic activities that might generate inequalities are understood. However, while people who ascribe to the most strongly pro-market logic are the most likely to accept inequality, two important caveats should be borne in mind. First, most people with strongly pro-market views nevertheless also think levels of inequality are too high. The predicted probability of accepting inequality in the pro-market group is still only 15%. Similarly, most people who accept inequality are not in fact strongly pro-market in their orientation. Only about a fifth of those who accept inequality are in the pro-market class. A majority (about 60%) of those who accept inequality come from the large "mainstream" category. As noted above, this group does exhibit recourse to market logics that are theoretically inequality-accepting—such as that the goal of economics and economic policy should be to increase resources overall—but as a group they also combine this view with a more skeptical view of the impact on total wealth when inequality increases.

The subtleties in the links between different types of idea within the economic sphere and economic inequality, in people's thinking, as well as the way that economic ideas themselves hang together—with some structure, but less than a unidimensional more-versus-less pro-market orientation—highlight the importance of looking at the details of the linkages in different kinds of reasoning about inequality, as well as the orientation toward different loci of evaluation. The results also highlight the diversity of logics within and between different groups: As with the demographic correlates of accepting inequality, acceptance does draw support from across different groups even in terms of market logics.

Meanwhile, systematic correlations between different market logics and the moral and group-based logics point to the overlapping and reinforcing interactions between these views: Greater adherence to the idea of the benefits of markets and economic transactions left alone tends to go along with a more positive assessment of the role of merit or deservingness in the moral sphere. This is consistent not only with the overlapping narratives highlighted elsewhere in this volume (e.g., Neely, Chapter 3, this volume) but also with other work highlighting the integration of the moral and the economic in popular (Prasad et al. 2016) and political thinking (Killick 2023, 16).

Conclusion

Considering variation across types of people in terms of their endorsement of different types of market-logic highlights that understanding the logics used to justify the acceptance of inequality remains complicated. Primarily, this is because the appeal of inequality-accepting logics is, in general, broader than the acceptance of inequality itself. That is, endorsing pro-market ideas about the benefits of market transactions is widespread in public opinion in the five countries studied here, while accepting inequality remains a minority position.

This feature of the shape of public opinion qualifies the discernible empirical differences between those with different visions of how the economy works, in terms of their acceptance of inequality. It is true that those with more pro-market visions of the economy are more likely to accept inequality, but the vast majority of even the most pro-market thinkers are concerned about economic differences between rich and poor, and most of those who accept inequality have quite mainstream economic views. Moreover, this mainstream economic thinking does not consist of widespread adherence to a strong set of neoliberal ideas, even in the background (Schmidt 2016): There is little support in this mainstream group for the idea of the Laffer Curve or for the idea that if the rich get richer, everyone benefits.

In zooming in on different kinds of arguments that might be made about the economy, this chapter has highlighted how there may be multiple, competing kinds of logic associated with justifications (or critiques) of inequality based in market reasoning. That is, the specific logic whereby inequality is justified comes not from evaluating inequality through a market lens in itself but from the specific ideas about how markets work. This will also be the same for the other types of logic: While justifications for inequality can be made with reference to certain types of moral logic, the fact of making the evaluation on moral grounds does not necessarily entail inequality acceptance, and so on.

Finally, it is important to conclude by reiterating the rarity and diversity of the acceptance of inequality. This is apparent in the analyses of the market logics but also in purely demographic terms. In the ISSP data, only 8% of respondents in the included sample disagree with the statement that income differences are too large. And while there are systematic differences across groups—especially regarding gender, education, and income—there are people from all demographic backgrounds among those who accept inequality. This recommends an essential caution around characterizing the social acceptance of inequality.

Appendix

Table 2A Market logic survey questions and response categories as used in analyses

Label	**Question text**	**Response categories** **Anti-market logic**			**Pro-market logic**
Better off from deal	Imagine that two people, Jack and Jill, both agree to a sale: Jill gladly sells Jack a bicycle at a price he is happy to pay. Without any further information being available, would you think that:	Both Jack and Jill are worse off because of the deal.	Jack, the buyer, is better off because of the deal, because he now has the bicycle.	Jill, the seller, is better off because of the deal, because she now has the money.	Both Jack and Jill are better off because of the deal.
Causal movers	Here are some opinions about what affects the economy in [country]. Which of them comes closest to your view?		The economy in [country] depends on the actions of a small group of influential people.	The economy in [country] depends on the policy decisions of the government.	The economy in [country] depends on the operation of basic economic forces, like supply, and demand.

Continued

Table 2A *Continued*

Label	Question text	Response categories Anti-market logic			Pro-market logic
Economics to increase resources	Economics and economic policy are about increasing the resources available.	Strongly disagree, disagree	Neither agree nor disagree	Agree	Strongly agree
More workers, more demand	New workers increase demand for goods and services and so create jobs for others.	Strongly disagree, disagree	Neither agree nor disagree	Agree	Strongly agree
Richer person increases total	If someone gets richer, it means that total wealth increases.	Strongly disagree, disagree	Neither agree nor disagree	Agree	Strongly agree
Laffer Curve	Imagine that the government cuts tax rates by 10%. What do you think will happen to the revenue that the government collects?	It will fall by more than 10% because the rate cut will also decrease economic activity.	It will fall by approximately 10% because that is the amount of the rate cut.	It will fall by less than 10% because the rate cut will increase economic activity. This will partly offset the lower rate.	It will remain the same or increase because the increase to economic activity will completely offset the lower rate or outweigh it.

Notes

1. Australia, Austria, Bulgaria, Switzerland, Chile, Czechia, Germany, Denmark, Finland, France, Great Britain, Croatia, Israel, Iceland, Italy, Japan, Lithuania, Norway, New Zealand, Philippines, Russia, Sweden, Slovenia, Serbia, Thailand, Taiwan, United States, Venezuela, South Africa.
2. This question refers explicitly to economic inequality within countries, which will continue to be our focus throughout the chapter. The ISSP also asks about differences in income levels between countries in a parallel question about whether "[p]resent economic differences between rich and poor countries are too large." The levels of acceptance of this kind of inequality are even lower (5% of the survey respondents disagree with the statement), and logics of acceptance of these international differences seem less closely tied to the logics of acceptance that are the focus of this volume, so I do not focus on this kind of inequality further.
3. These results remain similar if we code the "neither agree nor disagree" response as indicating acceptance of inequality.

References

Barnes, L. 2022. "Taxing the Rich: Public Preferences and Public Understanding." *Journal of European Public Policy* 29 (5): pp. 787–804.

Hacker, J.S., and P. Pierson. 2010. *Winner-Take-All Politics: How Washington Made the Rich Richer—and Turned Its Back on the Middle Class.* New York: Simon and Schuster.

Hochschild, J.L. 1981. *What's Fair? Americans' Beliefs About Distributive Justice.* Cambridge, MA: Harvard University Press.

Hoy, C., R. Toth, and N. Merdikawati. 2024. "A False Divide? Providing Information About Inequality Aligns Preferences for Redistribution Between Right- and Left-Wing Voters." *Journal of Economic Inequality.* https://doi.org/10.1007/s10888-023-09609-2.

ISSP Research Group. 2022. "International Social Survey Programme: Social Inequality V—ISSP 2019." GESIS, Cologne. ZA7600 Data file Version 3.0.0, https://doi.org/10.4232/1.14009.

Jimènez-Buedo, M. 2011. "The Political Uses of Some Economic Ideas: The Trade-Off Between Efficiency and Equality." *American Journal of Economics and Sociology* 70 (4): pp. 1029–1052. https://onlinelibrary.wiley.com/doi/abs/10.1111/j.1536-7150.2011.00801.x.

Kenworthy, L. 1995. "Equality and Efficiency: The Illusory Tradeoff." *European Journal of Political Research* 27: pp. 225–254. https://doi.org/10.1111/j.1475-6765.1995.tb00637.x.

Killick, A. 2023. *Politicians and Economic Experts: The Limits of Technocracy.* Newcastle-upon-Tyne: Agenda Publishing.

Killick, A. 2020. *Rigged: Understanding the Economy in Brexit Britain.* Manchester: Manchester University Press.

Kwak, J. 2018. *Economism: Bad Economics and the Rise of Inequality.* London: Vintage Books.

Leiser, D., and R. Aroch. 2009. "Lay Understanding of Macroeconomic Causation: The Good-Begets-Good Heuristic." *Applied Psychology* 58 (3): pp. 370–384.

Mirowski, P., and D. Plehwe. 2015. *The Road from Mont Pèlerin: The Making of the Neoliberal Thought Collective.* Cambridge, MA: Harvard University Press.

Mosse, J. 2021. *The Pound and the Fury: Why Anger and Confusion Reign in an Economy Paralysed by Myth.* Manchester: Manchester University Press.

Mudge, S.L. 2018. *Leftism Reinvented: Western Parties from Socialism to Neoliberalism.* Cambridge, MA: Harvard University Press.

Naidu, S., D. Rodrik, and G. Zucman. 2019. "Economics After Neoliberalism." *Boston Review,* February 27. https://www.bostonreview.net/forum/suresh-naidu-dani-rodrik-gabriel-zucman-economics-after-neoliberalism/.

Ostry, J.D., A. Berg, and C.G. Tsangarides. 2014. "Redistribution, Inequality, and Growth." IMF Staff Discussion Notes No. 2014/002. https://www.imf.org/en/Publications/Staff-Discussion-Notes/Issues/2016/12/31/Redistribution-Inequality-and-Growth-41291.

Popp Berman, E. 2022. *Thinking Like an Economist: How Efficiency Replaced Equality in US Public Policy.* Princeton: Princeton University Press.

Prasad, M., S.G. Hoffman, and K. Bezila. 2016. "Walking the Line: The White Working Class and the Economic Consequences of Morality." *Politics and Society* 44 (2): pp. 281–304. https://doi.org/10.1177/0032329216638062.

Rueda, D., and D. Stegmueller. 2019. *Who Wants What? Redistribution Preferences in Comparative Perspective.* Cambridge: Cambridge University Press.

Saez, E., and G. Zucman. 2020. *The Triumph of Injustice.* New York: WW Norton.

Sapienza, P., and L. Zingales. 2013. "Economic Experts Versus Average Americans." *American Economic Review* 103 (3): pp. 636–642.

Schmidt, V.A. 2016. "The Roots of Neo-Liberal Resilience: Explaining Continuity and Change in Background Ideas in Europe's Political Economy." *British Journal of Politics and International Relations* 18 (2): pp. 318–334. https://doi.org/10.1177/1369148115612792.

Stockhammer, E., and O. Onaran. 2022. "Growth Models and Post-Keynesian Macroeconomics." In *Diminishing Returns: The New Politics of Growth and Secular Stagnation*, edited by L. Baccaro, J. Pontusson, and M. Blyth, pp. 53–73. Oxford: Oxford University Press.

Chapter 3
Stewards of Capital
How Hedge Funds, Venture Capitalists, and Technology Startups Legitimize Inequality

*Megan Tobias Neely**

Introduction

Finance and technology have been major drivers of the top earnings that have widened income and wealth inequality over the past forty years (Galbraith 2000; Lin and Neely 2020; Piketty and Saez 2006; Roberts and Wolf 2018; Tomaskovic-Devey and Lin 2011). The financial sector's share of corporate profits in the United States, for one, has tripled over the last sixty years, yet fewer workers benefit than did in the manufacturing sector's heyday (Krippner 2005). Similarly, wages in high-tech industries are higher relative to their counterparts outside of tech and were projected to grow tremendously from 2016 to 2026, by 34.4% for high-tech goods and 14.4% for high-tech services (Roberts and Wolf 2018). That these high earners can influence politics to favor deregulation, leverage bargaining power within the sectors, and stimulate market demand for their products has transferred significant amounts of earnings to them (Hacker and Pierson 2010; Hart 2001; Lin and Neely 2020).

Previous research on finance and tech finds that the high earnings are legitimized by cultural beliefs about risk-taking, entrepreneurial innovation, technical expertise, and meritocracy (Balkin et al. 2000; Cooper 2014; Godechot 2016; Ho 2009; Neely 2022; Roth 2006; Souleles 2019). The dominant ideology within these industries holds that the merit, innovation, and risks legitimize the high rewards (Balkin et al. 2000; Ho 2009). According to this mindset, those who put their jobs and money on the line to take risks in the

Megan Tobias Neely, *Stewards of Capital*. In: *The Social Acceptance of Inequality*. Edited by: Francesco Duina and Luca Storti, Oxford University Press. © Oxford University Press (2025).
DOI: 10.1093/oso/9780197814499.003.0003

stock market or in entrepreneurship deserve higher incomes than people who play it safe in secure jobs.[1] This mindset reflects a market and economic logic of inequality.

The hedge fund (HF), venture capital (VC), and technology startup (TS) industries capture the core of finance capitalism in the United States. Each plays a central role in how capital is allocated in society and how these allocations influence economic and social inequality (Janeway et al. 2021; Nau 2013). Men, especially those who are white, monopolize all three fields (Alegria 2020; Catalyst 2018; Han and Tomaskovic-Devey 2024; Neely et al. 2023): managing 97% of HF assets (Barclays Global 2011; Kruppa 2018), holding 88% of the check-writing seats in VC (PitchBook and All Raise 2019), and receiving 85% of the venture-backed capital invested in TS (Clark 2018). White men's monopoly on capital in tech and finance not only exacerbates social inequality in society, it also enables these elites to amass the incomes and wealth driving economic inequality (Keister et al. 2021; Keister et al. 2022; Neely 2022; Yavorsky et al. 2019).

In this chapter, I ask: How do the drivers, mostly white men, of capital understand the impact of their work on society? And how does *who* composes these industries shape *how* they think about their work and its potential implications for inequality? To answer these questions, I interviewed and observed people working in the three industries.[**] While HF managers justify their work as creating more efficient markets, protecting the savings of public institutions and pension workers, and allowing them to donate to the societal causes they care about, TS founders and VC investors say they want to create technologies that disrupt the status quo, revolutionize how business is done, and solve the major problems facing society.

To gain insight into the social world and dominant ideology of these insular industries, I conducted in-depth interviews with forty-eight HF workers and seventy-four VC and TS workers. I supplemented interviews with field observations at twenty workplaces and fifty industry events, such as conferences, investor panels, and networking events, from 2013 to 2023 in New York, Texas, and California. Over one-third of all global HF industry assets are managed in New York, and California's Silicon Valley is the hub for VC and TS. For geographic variation, I selected Texas, a major industry hub with over 200 HFs and a growing TS scene. I recruited interviewees through mailing lists, events, and LinkedIn forums of professional associations. I used theoretical sampling by recruiting a sample more diverse than the industries to maximize variation (Small and Calarco 2022): women ($n = 71$) and people of color ($n = 53$, 33 of whom are Asian or Asian American).

My goal was to understand how people in these industries make sense of the societal implications of their work and industry, broadly defined, and then to understand how this shapes how they think about inequality—or perhaps whether they do not consider it at all. Thus, I asked them specifically, "What are the societal impacts of the work that you do?"; "Are there any moral values or goals that drive your work?"; "What benefits do you experience from the work that you do?"; and "What do you find most rewarding or satisfying about your work?"

The answers concerning how interviewees understood the impact of their work fell into three primary categories that correspond to logics of accepting inequality: earning high salaries to fund philanthropic causes they care about (moral logic); funding the building blocks of society (market and economic logic); and investing in ways that support entrepreneurs who create impactful ventures (market and economic logic). The interviewees did not necessarily speak directly to each logic; rather, how they understand the role of their work in society reflects the implicit, underlying assumptions that drive these logics of inequality (Spillman 2023)—what Abend (2014) calls "the moral background." By and large, the people I interviewed understood themselves as stewards of capital who take risks to invest in markets as a means to fuel economic growth, innovation, and charitable giving. According to this mindset, the winners in this market system get to become stewards of the capital they generate; thus, the steward reflects an ideology of meritocracy driven by the belief that amassing wealth is indicative of merit (Hecht 2022; Mijs 2021; Mijs and Savage 2020). Latent in these accounts is an implicit acceptance of the resulting social problems from this system, such as social and economic inequality, as the negative externalities of what are understood to be competitive and therefore meritocratic financial markets.

Philanthropy

"How do you like destroying the world?" The host of a Hamptons beach party teased Bradley, a white HF investor, to his chagrin. Bradley felt that HF managers had become scapegoats for American inequality:

> It's so easy for the media and for, you know, 99 percent of America to be like, "Look at this guy's house." It's like a $60 million apartment in New York City, or a $40 million house in the Hamptons, or x, y, and z. It's very easy for people to look at that and be like, "Look at that excess! It's not fair! Why aren't they more equitable in their distribution of wealth?"

Bradley understood that the opulence made people compare it to others' misfortune. But, he said, "I think that speaks to a much greater problem that we have in America rather than 'it's this person's fault.' I think people are looking for outlets to sort of place responsibility on certain people, and it's not fair." He said the real injustice is not the consumption practices of the exceedingly rich but the system that fails to provide basic support systems and distribute resources more evenly.

Next, Bradley echoed a common theme among my HF and VC interviews on philanthropic giving, reflecting moral logics that the winners of inequality are entitled to, and even have an obligation to, shape civil society by "giving back," a belief that is pervasive in the financial services industry and corporate sector in the United States (Daniels 1988; Giridharadas 2018; Sherman 2017; Spillman 2012). He touted how HF managers routinely redistribute their own wealth: "Most of these people are contributing a lot to charities . . . to further a lot of really good causes. Not to say that they are perfect, but, at the same time, I don't think the whole picture is being taken into account." Similarly, Lisa, an Asian-American HF investor, noted that her firm donates 10% of its profits to charity.

Several interviewees wanted to accrue personal wealth in order to enact their altruism. Cynthia, a white HF investor, said that the ability to give was her compensation's "true value" and "meaning of life." Cynthia, was unabashed in affirming: "So, I want to make a ton of money so that I can finance things, you better believe it." In particular, she cared deeply about funding research into childhood leukemia. She said, "If I could be there in that room when he [the doctor] can say to a mom, 'We've got the therapy. We're going to be able to.' I mean, what kind of greater victory can you have in the whole world?"

While Cynthia's hypothetical was touching, what she said next captured the moral and market and economic logics for accepting inequality. She argued for the option to pay no taxes and instead support charities:

> If I decide I made 20 percent in a year, and I want it to go to pay welfare, you can do it. If you want to pay for cancer research, fine. If you want it to go say build more Ronald McDonald houses, arthritis, whatever you want to do—"man on the moon," you know. So, I just think that's where the human spirit is. It's so exciting.

Cynthia evokes the neoliberal conception of redistribution (King 2006), assuming that rich people deserve to choose how best to distribute capital rather than paying taxes to fund social welfare.

Yet, citing the ability to engage in philanthropy as a reason for profit-seeking perpetuates the untenable but closely held idea that finance and other enormously compensated industries are, in fact, free-market meritocracies. I didn't doubt the sincerity of these scripts, as most of the HF and VC investors believed that a free-market system with limited interventions rewarded those who worked the hardest and, in turn, as hard workers, those who rose to the top were naturally best equipped to decide how to distribute their riches to the rest of society (picking charities like so many stocks and entrepreneurial ventures). Of course, the underlying implication is that this moral logic holds in both directions: that monetary success indicates personal merit and that having become multimillionaires and billionaires justifies stewardship over the distribution of capital to those presumably not smart enough or hard-working enough to have accumulated their own wealth.

That HF investors translated making money in financial markets into making a positive impact on society perpetuates neoliberal ideology: the best way to address society's needs is for financial markets to allow enterprising individuals, rather than government, to become stewards who accumulate and then redistribute resources, and so stripping away inefficiencies like bureaucracy and regulation is good for the people. Yet, they also consistently placed a premium on their ability to support social institutions and workers only with protective regulatory oversight. They saw little contradiction in favoring both unfettered markets and crucial government oversight.

Jennifer, a white woman in HF client services, critiqued the industry's dominant moral logic. She found it alarming that HF profits gave the industry a disproportionate ability to effect change. Beyond quibbles over fairness and the social good, Jennifer warned, the outsized remuneration may even undermine democracy. She said, "I think about these guys that are making money—a lot of money—on the backs of pensions, and they're starting to look bad." Their charitable giving wasn't enough—could never be enough—to justify the high earnings they accrued investing money for the working class.

During the Great Recession following the 2008 Financial Crisis, Jennifer reminded me, HF billionaire John Paulson had gifted $100 million to the Central Park Conservancy. When she read the news, she said, she exclaimed aloud,

> What an asshole?! He's lost so much fucking money [for his investors]. Right? And he [personally] has made all this money, and he's not making any money for his investors now, but he made boatloads of money . . . And

> he gives it to Central Park! Like, what the fuck? There are so many worse off people.

This is a key point: It's not hard to imagine that the priorities of HF managers may not align with the needs or wishes of most Americans.

Jennifer continued, "A lot these guys are making a lot of money with investments from endowments and pensions. These pensions are not making enough money, and they're not gonna make enough money from being in HFs" to support individual workers. Jennifer said,

> So, it's this vicious cycle. It's a little like liberal fantasy land. I wish these guys would think more about their impact and, you know, how what they do is perceived, and whether they could be more gracious about how they've achieved their wealth and more helpful in how they redistribute it.

Rather than focus on philanthropy, Jennifer thought, HF managers should lower their firms' profit margins to better support the students and workers affected by the endowment and pension money their firms manage, a concern shared by a subset of HF interviewees who countered the norm for embracing market logics.

Investing to Lift All Boats

Rather than "destroying the world," the people I interviewed often saw themselves as stewards posed to yield their capital to save at least some corner of it. At HF and VC firms, the investments were viewed as a vehicle for social change albeit in different ways. The HF investors I interviewed gained a sense of meaning from their work by building investment portfolios that could establish strong foundations for social institutions including governments, university endowments, pension funds, and arts foundations, which account for the majority of HF investments. VCs also invest for large institutions; however, they were less likely to identify that as the social value they generate. Instead, they pointed to the significance of their work in fostering entrepreneurship, creating jobs, and investing in transformative technologies.

The underlying assumptions driving these beliefs reflect an implicit market and economic logic of inequality that holds that if investors can drive economic growth, enable institutions and workers to amass wealth, and create entrepreneurial ventures and jobs, this will lift all boats and thus help to reduce inequality. The fact that inequality emerges in this system driven by market growth, then, is implicitly understood as an externality. Several people I interviewed, however, criticized these dominant views and pointed to the shortcomings of their industries. It is no coincidence that these concerns were expressed primarily by women and racial/ethnic minority men, who were more likely to reflect on their fields' broader impacts for society and inequality.

Funding Society's "Building Blocks"

When I asked about the social impact of their work, HF investors prided themselves on helping students, workers, and families by investing for the institutions that support their lives: pensions, 401(k)s, and endowments. Lisa told me, "Ultimately, if we make more money, the college endowments will be able to fund more scholarships and the pension funds can meet their funding requirements and the foundations can also make more grants for a certain project." "Most people kind of earn their salary and then spend it all on their life. That's it," said Scott, a white HF investor. He continued,

> But the way money and wealth are created, and true value gets added in this world is when you take whatever money you've earned and invest it in something and get a return on that. And those returns are what create wealth. Those returns are what get donated to charity. Those returns are what build infrastructure and what build societies. So, being a part of that is really exciting.

Reflecting market and economic logics, Scott understood his work as a financial investor as creating the building blocks of society, which is consistent with research on the US corporate sector more broadly (Spillman 2012).

HF manager Sharon, who is white, wanted a high income to be altruistic *and* to be a job creator via her investments: "I like money. I like things. I look at opportunities. I don't have a social consciousness to that. I want to do focused investing where I think I can have impact. I want to create markets. I want to create jobs." Sharon thought she could positively affect society through markets while also getting rich. She said, "I'm a capitalist. I believe in free economics. I have no problem with [free economics]." The assumption underlying Lisa, Scott, and Sharon's worldviews reflects market and economic logics for accepting inequality: The best way to distribute material resources is through markets and any inequalities that result from that market system is an undesirable externality. As capitalists, they serve an important role as stewards who put capital to productive use.

Much like Karen and other HF managers, the VCs I interviewed expressed pride in what they understand as venture's role in spurring innovation and job creation in the economy and their own role in supporting new founders grow their businesses. Angela, a white VC, stressed how she was "definitely trying to set all those founders on the best possible track and building things that can help them accelerate." Similarly, Mary emphasized a modest impact: "Obviously, you employ people who are going to work and produce products that make the world better, but a business isn't changing the world that much." Meanwhile, Jason, who is white, stressed the importance of funding entrepreneurs who could improve people's everyday lives, rather than the technology itself being the solution to societal problems. "I don't believe in technology being an unmitigated good . . . You could use it for good. You can use it for bad," he said. "So, the social impact I see in my work is I'm opening up possibilities by supporting entrepreneurs who are either saving people time, or helping them make more money, or giving people tools to do something that they couldn't do before."

Vihaan, an Asian-American man, defined VC in the broader sense of funding entrepreneurialism, and said,

> I think venture capital is an enormously influential industry . . . I would argue this is one of the most important things to get right for a country, for the world, to make it a better place. You know, as a capitalist, it is in my name: venture capitalist. I do believe in capitalism.

Acknowledging the problem of capitalism going to "extremes," he said, "But if you can solve for those, you can create enormous good." He then cited "venture capitalism," in the broader sense, as the reason why "China lifted a billion people out of poverty." To further explain, Vihaan gave examples of "the East India Company and Queen Isabella from Spain investing in Christopher Columbus." However, he did qualify this, saying, "I don't believe it [VC] can solve every problem or even a majority of the problems," and he stressed that the Silicon Valley had gotten too large and was prone to excess.

Echoing Vihaan's concerns, several of my HF interviewees went against the industry gain and thought HFs should be more mindful of the middle- and working-class workers whose pensions and retirement accounts pay their fees (Cassidy 2014). These concerns were expressed primarily by women and racial/ethnic minority men. When I asked Amanda, a white woman, how the HF she works for contributes to society, she looked out over the city and said, "I mean, we do manage money for, like, public clients and things like that. I do think we provide an important service. [The stock market] is extremely volatile and not very good at capital preservation, and those are the kind of services that we provide." Glancing toward the lobby to see if anyone was within earshot, Amanda lowered her voice, and quickly added, "I just think it's too expensive." "In terms of the fees?" I asked. Amanda nodded her head, smiled, and said with a laugh, "Just don't say that too loud here!"

Matthew, a Black man, imagined his end-client as the worker with a pension, which inspired caution in his stock market positions and a critique of the HFs' high fees:

> The costs to the institutional investors are very important to me because the individual investor has been sold a bill of goods . . . that by putting money into your 401(k), your pensions, 529s, all of this stuff, you will be able to at some point in time retire if you just do what you are supposed to do.

Of the current investment environment, Matthew concluded, "[It] creates a situation where essentially just the moving around of money makes a lot of people wealthy, but it doesn't serve the people who are actually committing the money to the market." Thus, it creates inequality between the financiers and the rest of society.

Espousing progressive views that contradicted the market and economic logics dominant in the industry, Matthew then said, "the price of real wages, the price of education, and the price of real wage inflation have gone in opposite directions." That divergence is what we call income inequality: "Now you have a situation where a lot of people who are saving all of this money are finding that they are unable to retire or the money that supposedly was going to cover them can't cover the current expenses that they have. And I just think it's a shame." Even if HFs lowered their fees, Matthew said, "People are still going to make money. Everybody is going to be fine. But you're not going to have guys who make $4 million a year [for] just picking up the phone," which he called "ridiculous." Becoming more animated, he continued:

> The service should be some reflection of the actual effort. How does that guy make $4 million a year? . . . He happens to be a salesperson that covers all of the big accounts for the big asset managers. Why does he cover all of those big asset managers? Because two of his frat brothers are portfolio managers at those asset managers. Kid you fucking not. That's the way it goes down.

Tax loopholes and lower capital gains taxes fuel these big payouts. Jennifer, for one, identified how HF philanthropy was only possible because HFs have "been able to make so much money by exploiting tax loopholes." Sharon, who earlier shared that she saw her work as creating jobs, returned to that logic: "I'm okay with tax breaks, if we're creating jobs. . . . I'm not okay with tax breaks just so that we give people tax breaks. I think that sucks. I think people have personal responsibility, and I think the government has responsibility." Sharon thought aloud through the competing ideologies surrounding the question of what makes a strong civic society, weighing individual responsibility vis-à-vis the stock market and social welfare that uses tax dollars to improve society as a whole.

Brian was the only white man I interviewed in HFs who criticized how the industry contributed to economic inequality. Of capital gains taxes, he said: "HFs are making 20% on profits, and if it's long-term gains, they only pay 15% in taxes. Is that fair? It's just not fair. It's scandalous and shameful." Brian cited these taxes as evidence of a "revolving table with Washington." He said, "People are just trying to make as much money as possible, but the whole system is flawed. [HF manager] Marc Lasry hired Chelsea Clinton. It's about access to politics." Meanwhile, he said, "people in politics want jobs and donations, so they don't charge the higher taxes." Brian further condemned the common practice of domiciling funds offshore to avoid paying domestic taxes. "[HF managers] rationalize it by giving money to charity," Brian said, "but they're stealing money from the government." While the dominant industry discourses in HF and VC were of the industries' role in creating value and jobs in society, those exceptions who pointed out the implications for inequality provide deviant cases that make apparent the market and economic logics pervasive in the industry that legitimize inequality.

Investing in the Future

The VC and TS industries embrace a dominant discourse of "disruption": The call to change how business is done. The biggest industry conference is called "Disrupt." On the whole, the "disrupt" discourse more often refers to creating market value than revolutionizing society. However, whether "disrupting" the status quo means working for the public good is a topic of debate. The VCs I interviewed often touted the good being done by the companies they invest in, yet described a dominant belief that social entrepreneurship is not profitable. Tom, who is a white man, gushed as he described at length a "favorite" startup working to improve global access to clean energy. Of the founders' pitch, he recalled:

> Rule one of the rules of venture investing, one of the rules of entrepreneurship, is don't try selling something to people who don't have any money right now. It's just one of those things, right? And we're thinking, "Guys, guys, we just love this idea, but it sounds like one of those social, do-good philanthropic kind of things that I don't know how this is going to work." And [name], the co-founder, comes over the table at us and he says, "You don't get it. If we're going to change the lives of 2 billion people on the planet. We got to build a big, scalable, sustainable, profitable, global multinational corporation!" I [was like] "Whoa, whoa, whoa." We love these guys. So, we were the first investors in this company.

The founder challenged Tom's assumption that social good can't be profitable, which Tom described as an industry tenet. Nonetheless, Tom's example reflected a deep-seated neoliberal belief among the VCs I interviewed that societal well-being can be achieved via capitalist for-profit means. This tension reflects market and economic logics that posit any harmful societal outcomes of the high competition in tech as merely negative externalities of the good created by capitalist innovation.

Mark, also a white man, espoused a common belief in technology's transformative potential. When asked how he would change venture or tech if he could, Mark replied, "I think the number one thing . . . is just getting more people involved, right?" He then continued:

> You can go back to the printing press with Gutenberg, people always complain about new technology. It doesn't matter what it is. New technology is always going to be the devil and destroy society. But if we're going to solve climate change, it's going to be through technology. It's not going to be through legislation because humans just can't agree on stuff. And so, the more people are involved in that, the better.

Mark captures a common libertarian ethos in the tech industry: Technology rather than government can fix societal problems by bringing people together. According to this mindset, VC investors and TS founders serve as stewards who put capital to productive use. Technology's shortcomings, according to this belief, lie in barriers to democratic involvement in the sense of getting more people involved in devising the solutions. Thus, social inequality is cast as a negative externality of the market, reflecting a market and economic logic for why inequality persists.

Annette, a white VC from Europe, provides a clue to the barriers to including more people in developing new technology: She recounted having to convince her partners, all men, to invest in a majority-woman-led startup developing air quality technology for "underserved communities." Annette said, "I fought for one year, and I fought with everything I had." Even though she signed the deal, she felt "defeated" and disappointed in her partners: "It leaves you with an aftertaste, just how you see people interact in those environments when those discussions." Annette was not alone in this fight: Other VC interviewees recounted pushback from colleagues when they wanted to invest in women-led and climate-focused startups. Several VCs who, like Annette, went against the industry norm of being upper-class white men described how this homogeneity influenced the extent to which VC and the tech it funds could transform society in meaningful ways. As such, they present cases that counter the dominant industry beliefs, making them more apparent.

My interviewees, both at VC and TS firms, who identified the barriers to using technology to solve societal problems often cited how the VC focus on shorter-term profits and big payouts prevented the industry from funding technology to solve social problems like climate change. For this reason, I often heard that VC is more likely to invest in software than hardware, which takes much longer to develop. I interviewed several founders of "clean tech" startups, including Mia, a white founder, who said,

> It's the desire to show returns in a short timeframe. You can't show that with hardware. At [my current firm], we're talking to VCs [and say], "How long did it take solar and wind to get to get to where we are today? Twenty years. I can do it [with this technology] in eight."

VCs, however, wanted shorter returns on their investments, which left Mia struggling to find funding. Mia said,

> My personal feeling about VC—it's a Ponzi scheme. You just have to stay away from that wave. You need someone to flip it to, whether it's the public or another investor. . . . Since it's all about flipping the deal, they have to network heavily to know where the Wall Street herd is going.

As Mia said, "It's because of the speed, the lightning speed" of finance, pushing for speedy returns on investments, that prevent them from investing in more impactful technologies.

Of the fundraising process, Mia recounted experiencing tokenism as a woman and said, "This is a demeaning process for everyone except for the select few, the select few is the MIT grad," referring to the premium placed on founders with elite credentials. Similarly, Travis, a white TS founder, identified how hardware technologies incurred a blue-collar stigma from VCs who are elites:

> No one knows about hardware in this world because if you're in the elite classes, that's how you get into VC, right? So you went to some fancy school, you're from some coastal city. . . . Those people don't build anything themselves. . . . So, it just seems like lame blue-collar shit. That's not cool.

This stigma, he thought, let a lot of important innovations go unfunded. In contrast, he said, "There's a lot of dumb people from Stanford who have no business getting funding, but somehow they got to the Stanford system or whatever," and so, he said, VCs would throw $2 or $8 million at Stanford B-school graduates just to give them a chance.

VCs who focused on impact investing described the need to play the game with the elite white men who run the industry and how this curtailed what could be accomplished with respect to social change. Andrés, a Latinx VC, stressed that the VC and TS opportunities go to elite graduates, and how, as a racial outsider, he needed to comply with the elite way of doing business in order to do work that reflects his values. "How do you actually make change in a country?" He said, "Unfortunately, it's by appealing to the elites, right? . . . It's a give-and-take negotiating with the people who have the power to let you, as the outsider, play with that." An Asian-American woman who had worked at an impact VC fund, Nari expressed concerns about its "impact" because all the partners were white men who, on principle, did not invest in first-time founders. This, she said, was "by nature excluding some founders who come from more less representative backgrounds, so like founders of color or women founders, right? Because usually these groups of people don't get second chances to try again if the first one didn't go as well."

Relatedly, Rose, an Asian-American VC, said the pursuit of the big "100x return" prevents "stakeholder capitalism" from being realized, whether it be in terms of the company "thinking about the environment, the community, the employees," referring to the need for a fairer distribution of earnings. Instead, she said, shareholder interests prevail, making it harder to do impact investing. A subset of my VC interviewees—more often women and men who are from racial/ethnic minority or working-class backgrounds—said that the cutthroat pursuit of profit prevents a more holistic approach to investing that could more meaningfully disrupt the status quo of finance capitalism by promoting more equitable and sustainable growth that invests in the public good. Following the market and economic logic of this mindset, inequality then is an externality of a competitive market system.

Conclusion

In contrast to the investment bankers, who believe that their vocation is to make companies and markets more efficient (Ho 2009), the people I interviewed at HF, VC, and TS firms believed their work helped to make technology, companies, and markets more efficient, *and* they embraced a broader vocation of allowing for investments in society's future well-being. These conceptions of the social value of their work informed how they either justified or critiqued the higher fees, lower taxes, fewer restrictions, workplace inequalities, and general excesses of their firms. Their accounts generally upheld free-market ideology, though the gaps and contradictions demonstrated a more complex understanding of financial markets, technological innovation, government interventions, and economic inequality.

HF and VC investments and philanthropy certainly can contribute to the social good; there is no doubt, for instance, that continued growth is the only way public pension funds will survive and continue to benefit workers. At the same time, the rhetoric of redistribution and giving back ultimately masks how this system transforms successful money managers and entrepreneurs into multimillionaires while indebting the middle class and risking the scant financial security available to students and the working class. Most Americans face stagnant wages, mounting debts, and insecure jobs—that rarely come with retirement benefits—and this is directly tied to the rise of the financial services and high-tech industries and the high earnings both demand (Lin and Neely 2020; Roberts and Wolf 2018).

Each industry embraced the stewards of capital mindset in a different way. While HF investors saw themselves as generating profits for large institutions who served average people and amassing fortunes as a means to create a better society, people at VC and TS understood themselves as building entrepreneurial ventures that devise better technologies, create new jobs, and, sometimes, make a social or environmental impact. All three reflect a market and economic logic of inequality embracing a legitimizing narrative that casts inequality as a justifiable externality of the consequences of their, according to them, exceptional work in competitive markets that spur innovation and extract value. This dominant cultural assumption, which has pervaded the mainstream, holds that amassing wealth is indicative of merit (Hecht 2022; Mijs 2021; Mijs and Savage 2020). Thus, the logic holds, these stewards of capital create market value that will eventually circulate in the economy in ways that benefit society more widely, so inequalities are an acceptable byproduct of that impact. These trickle-down market and economic logics legitimize the resulting inequality in society. The fact that the three fields feature durable social inequalities and financial capitalist ideology constrains their revolutionary potential, especially with respect to the pressing societal problems posed by climate change and widening inequality.

Notes

* I would like to thank Francesco Duina, Luca Storti, Lynette Spillman, and the other authors for their thoughtful comments on previous versions of this chapter. The findings on the hedge fund industry draw from my earlier work on this topic in *Hedged Out: Inequality and Insecurity on Wall Street* (2022).

** All interviewees' names were disguised to ensure anonymity.

1. Research finds that landlords similarly legitimize their profits based on how they perceive the risks they take in their investments (Desmond and Wilmers 2019).

References

Abend, G. 2014. *The Moral Background: An Inquiry into the History of Business Ethics.* Princeton, NJ: Princeton University Press.

Alegria, S. 2020. "What Do We Mean by Broadening Participation? Race, Inequality, and Diversity in Tech Work." *Sociology Compass* 14 (6): pp. 1–12.

Balkin, D.B., G.D. Markman, and L.R. Gomez-Mejia. 2000. "Is CEO Pay in High-Technology Firms Related to Innovation?" *Academy of Management Journal* 43 (6): pp. 1118–1129.

Barclays Global. 2011. *Affirmative Investing: Women and Minority Owned Hedge Funds.* Boston: Capital Solutions Group.

Cassidy, J. 2014. "The Great Hedge-Fund Mystery: Why Do They Make So Much?" *New Yorker*, May 12.

Catalyst. 2018. " Quick Take: Women in Financial Services." Catalyst.

Clark, K. 2018. "Female Founders Have Brought in Just 2.2% of US VC This Year (Yes, Again)." *TechCrunch*, November 4.

Cooper, M. 2014. *Cut Adrift: Families in Insecure Times.* Berkeley: University of California Press.

Daniels, A. 1988. *Invisible Careers: Women Civic Leaders from the Volunteer World.* Chicago: University Of Chicago Press.

Desmond, M., and N. Wilmers. 2019. "Do the Poor Pay More for Housing? Exploitation, Profit, and Risk in Rental Markets." *American Journal of Sociology* 124 (4): pp. 1090–1124.

Galbraith, J.K. 2000. *Created Unequal: The Crisis in American Pay.* Chicago: University of Chicago Press.

Giridharadas, A. 2018. *Winners Take All: The Elite Charade of Changing the World.* New York: Vintage.

Godechot, O. 2016. *The Working Rich: Wages, Bonuses and Appropriation of Profit in the Financial Industry.* London: Taylor & Francis Group.

Hacker, J.S., and P. Pierson. 2010. "Winner-Take-All Politics: Public Policy, Political Organization, and the Precipitous Rise of Top Incomes in the United States." *Politics and Society* 38 (2): pp. 152–204.

Han, J., and D. Tomaskovic-Devey. 2024. "Inertia, Progress, or Regress? Observing and Explaining Heterogenous Tech Firm Demographic Diversity Trajectories." *Work and Occupations* 52 (1): pp. 3–44.

Hart, D.M. 2001. "Why Do Some Firms Give? Why Do Some Give a Lot? High-Tech PACs, 1977–1996." *Journal of Politics* 63 (4): pp. 1230–1249.

Hecht, K. 2022. "'It's the Value That We Bring': Performance Pay and Top Income Earners' Perceptions of Inequality." *Socio-Economic Review* 20 (4): pp. 1741–1766.

Ho, K. 2009. *Liquidated: An Ethnography of Wall Street.* Durham, NC: Duke University Press.

Janeway, W.H., R. Nanda, and M. Rhodes-Kropf. 2021. "Venture Capital Booms and Start-Up Financing." *Annual Review of Financial Economics* 13: pp. 111–127.

Keister, L.A., H.Y. Lee, and J.E. Yavorsky. 2021. "Gender and Wealth in the Super Rich: Asset Differences in Top Wealth Households in the United States, 1989–2019." *Sociologica* 15 (2): pp. 25–55.

Keister, L.A., S. Thébaud, and J.E. Yavorsky. 2022. "Gender in the Elite." *Annual Review of Sociology* 48 (1): pp. 149–169.

King, S. 2006. *Pink Ribbons, Inc.* Minneapolis: University of Minnesota Press.

Krippner, G.R. 2005. "The Financialization of the American Economy." *Socio-Economic Review* 3 (2): pp. 173–208.

Kruppa, M. 2018. "The 'David' Problem." *Absolute Return*, September 7.

Lin, K.-H., and M. Tobias Neely. 2020. *Divested: Inequality in the Age of Finance.* Oxford: Oxford University Press.

Mijs, J.J.B. 2021. "The Paradox of Inequality: Income Inequality and Belief in Meritocracy Go Hand in Hand." *Socio-Economic Review* 19 (1): pp. 7–35.

Mijs, J.J.B., and M. Savage. 2020. "Meritocracy, Elitism and Inequality." *Political Quarterly* 91 (2): pp. 397–404.

Nau, M. 2013. "Economic Elites, Investments, and Income Inequality." *Social Forces* 92 (2): pp. 437–461.

Neely, M. Tobias. 2022. *Hedged Out: Inequality and Insecurity on Wall Street.* Berkeley: University of California Press.

Neely, M. Tobias, P. Sheehan, and C.L. Williams. 2023. "Social Inequality in High Tech: How Gender, Race, and Ethnicity Structure the World's Most Powerful Industry." *Annual Review of Sociology* 49 (1): pp. 319–338.

Piketty, T., and E. Saez. 2006. "The Evolution of Top Incomes: A Historical and International Perspective." *American Economic Review* 96 (2): pp. 200–205.

PitchBook and All Raise. 2019. *PitchBook-All Raise All In: Women in the VC Ecosystem.* November 11. San Francisco.

Roberts, B., and M. Wolf. 2018. "High-Tech Industries: An Analysis of Employment, Wages, and Output." *Beyond the Numbers: U.S. Bureau of Labor Statistics* 7 (7). Washington, DC: US Bureau of Labor Statistics. https://www.bls.gov/opub/btn/volume-7/high-tech-industries-an-analysis-of-employment-wages-and-output.htm.

Roth, L.M. 2006. *Selling Women Short: Gender and Money on Wall Street.* Princeton, NJ: Princeton University Press.

Sherman, R. 2017. *Uneasy Street: The Anxieties of Affluence.* Princeton, NJ: Princeton University Press.

Small, M.L., and J. Calarco. 2022. *Qualitative Literacy: A Guide to Evaluating Ethnographic and Interview Research.* Berkeley: University of California Press.

Souleles, D. S. 2019. *Songs of Profit, Songs of Loss: Private Equity, Wealth, and Inequality.* Lincoln: University of Nebraska Press.

Spillman, L. 2012. *Solidarity in Strategy: Making Business Meaningful in American Trade Associations.* Chicago: University of Chicago Press.

Spillman, L. 2023. "Morality, Inequality, and the Power of Categories." In *Handbook of the Sociology of Morality*, edited by S. Hitlin, S.M. Dromi, and A. Luft, vol. 2, pp. 373–385. Cham: Springer International Publishing.

Tomaskovic-Devey, D., and K.-H. Lin. 2011. "Income Dynamics, Economic Rents, and the Financialization of the U.S. Economy." *American Sociological Review* 76 (4): pp. 538–559.

Yavorsky, J., L. Keister, Y. Qian, and M. Nau. 2019. "Women in the One Percent: Gender Dynamics in Top Income Positions." *American Sociological Review* 84 (1): pp. 54–81.

Chapter 4
Effects of Meaningful Perceived Inequality on Well-Being and the Maintenance (or Challenge) of the Status Quo

Rosa Rodríguez-Bailón, Juan Diego García-Castro, Efraín García-Sánchez, and Guillermo B. Willis

Introduction

Economic inequality, often measured by the difference between the wealthiest and the least affluent members of society, is a multifaceted phenomenon. Beyond its economic implications, it permeates the social and psychological realms, leaving a mark on the well-being of individuals and shaping the dynamics of their relationships. This chapter seeks to illuminate the psychosocial consequences of economic inequality, shedding light on the interplay between economic disparities and the psychosocial dynamics of individuals that underlie them.

At the heart of our exploration lies the recognition that the tangible wealth gap does not solely define economic inequality but is equally influenced by the perception and the significant experiences of this divide within close social circles. The lens through which individuals perceive and interpret economic inequality (i.e., its meaning) plays a pivotal role in shaping their interactions with other individuals and groups. This intersection of objective economic realities and subjective perceptions lays the groundwork for understanding the psychosocial implications of economic inequality. Given our aims, we join Bobzien and Verwiebe (Chapter 7 in this volume) in examining how perceptions of inequalities are first formed and, once in place, how they shape the evolution of those inequalities.

To comprehend the full scope of the psychosocial consequences of economic inequality, we must first find a way to properly measure the appraisal

Rosa Rodríguez-Bailón et al., *Effects of Meaningful Perceived Inequality on Well-Being and the Maintenance (or Challenge) of the Status Quo*. In: *The Social Acceptance of Inequality*. Edited by: Francesco Duina and Luca Storti, Oxford University Press. © Oxford University Press (2025). DOI: 10.1093/oso/9780197814499.003.0004 of inequalities that may extend beyond material disparities and abstract ideas about them. It may encompass a spectrum of opportunities, access to education, healthcare, and even the ability to participate meaningfully in democratic societal processes. It would also be important to consider the most significant relationships individuals and groups have in everyday interactions that may impact these appraisals of inequality.

The chapter aligns with the market/economic logic regarding the acceptance of inequality from a psychosocial perspective because economic inequalities may be perceived as the natural byproduct of the normative competitive climate present in unequal social circles.

Perceived Economic Inequality

Perception is a cognitive process through which we recognize, organize, and make sense of environmental stimuli (Bruner and Goodman 1947). People are not passive or mechanical processors of information; they are active in configuring what they perceive and in giving meaning to it (Kunda 1990). Individuals build their comprehension of reality through their daily experiences and the narratives (i.e., ideologies and values) that give meaning to that reality. In the following sections, we will present empirical evidence and delineate several ideas examining why it is interesting to focus on how people perceive and give meaning to economic inequality, which, in turn, guides their responses to it.

Conceptual Bounds

Conceptualization and Measures of Perceived Economic Inequality

The perception of economic inequality is the individual perception of how financial resources are distributed among the people who make up a society (García-Sánchez, Matamoros-Lima et al. 2024).

Although there is no consensus among scholars on the criteria to assess actual economic inequality, people generally underestimate actual levels of inequality (Norton and Ariely 2011). Their perceptions of inequality correlate little, or not at all, with actual levels of inequality because of ignorance (e.g., lack of information about the income of elites; see Hing et al. 2019), cognitive biases (e.g., Eidelman and Crandall 2012; Jackson and

Payne 2021), or motivated reasoning, that is, ideologies (e.g., Franko 2017; Rodríguez-Bailón et al. 2017). Furthermore, evidence indicates that the way people are asked about the disparities they perceive affects their estimation of inequality (Bavetta et al. 2020; Hing et al. 2019). Scholars are still determining whether the representation of economic inequality that people use refers to inequalities in wages, income, wealth, economic opportunity, social mobility, or a combination of all five (Jachimowicz et al. 2022). Moreover, "objective" economic inequality could be measured by using different kinds of information (e.g., income, wealth, etc.), which makes it challenging to find clear correspondence between objective inequality and the subjective perception of it.

Given that economic inequality is not directly observable, individuals gather information to infer it from some indirect indicators (Bavetta et al. 2020). For example, it has been documented that people gather some information to estimate inequality through social sampling by using information about people close to them (such as family, friends, and workmates) and groups to infer inequality in society (Dawtry et al. 2015; García-Castro, González, et al. 2022) and to try to understand, explain, and justify it (see also, Moor and Friedman, Chapter 8 in this volume). Different measures of perceived economic inequality have been developed to date, but there is still no general consensus on the conceptualization, operationalization, and measures of the construct (Choi 2019). Thus, different methods may elicit different perceptions of inequality that capture unique ideas about what inequality is and how it can influence people's lives (Jachimowicz et al. 2022).

Furthermore, most measures used to assess the perception of economic inequality must be better conceptualized because they present serious construct validity problems and evaluate perceived economic inequality in abstract ways that are far from individuals' experiences (Knell and Stix 2020). Moreover, measures of perceived inequality relate very little to each other, capturing different dimensions of inequalities and a much lower relationship with objective inequality than expected (Castillo et al. 2022; Heiserman and Simpson 2021). The similarity between these measures is in their focus on quantifying economic gaps rather than in looking at individuals' psychological realities and the meaning they give to these inequalities in their daily lives. Despite their limitations, measures of perceived economic inequality provide an opportunity for scholars to study how people understand and engage in actions that counteract inequality.

Five data collection techniques are commonly used to capture perceived economic inequality (see Table 4.1 for examples). First, in one of the most influential research articles on this line, study participants estimate the economic resources of each quintile in US society (Norton and Ariely 2011). Yet, this technique is complex because it requires translating perceptions into numerical terms (Eriksson and Simpson 2013). Second, international surveys use Likert-type scales to gauge economic inequality (García-Castro, García-Sánchez, et al. 2022), but these indicators can be problematic as they often mix perceptions of inequality with attitudes toward it. Third, some measures ask about the wage gap between CEOs and unskilled workers, but respondents in these cases often rely on heuristics, which bias their responses (Castillo et al. 2022). Fourth, graphic evaluations present different resource distribution figures, asking participants to choose the one resembling their society (Castillo et al. 2022). Despite graphic evaluations being shown to have high predictive power, this technique is often criticized for its psychometric properties (Easterbrook 2021; García-Castro, García-Sánchez, et al. 2022).

Recently, different perceived inequality scales have been created to alleviate the above-mentioned weaknesses. These scales focus on general subjective perceptions instead of estimating numbers in people's heads about income or wealth gaps; for example, the Subjective Inequality Scale (Schmalor and Heine 2022) or the Perceived Economic Inequality Scale (Valtorta et al. 2024). However, both measures, apart from assessing perceived inequality, include an evaluation of respondents' attitudes toward inequality and the respondents' judgment of its perceived injustice. From these recently created scales, we will expand on the Perceived Economic Inequality in Everyday Life (PEIEL) scale in the following section (García-Castro et al. 2020). PEIEL fundamentally focuses on the perception of economic inequality as related to reference groups and individuals with whom respondents interact on an everyday basis and who give some proximity and meaning to economic inequality. Moreover, PEIEL has been used with good psychometric properties and predictive results in different cultural contexts (see Willis et al. 2024). This scale has the advantage of focusing on people's daily experiences, differentiating between perceptions and attitudes toward inequality.

Table 4.1 Measures of perceived economic inequality

Variable to be measured	Item's example asked to participants	Answer scale	Source
Perceived Distribution of Wealth	What percent of wealth do you think is owned by each of the five quintiles in [your country]?	Participants should estimate a percentage for each of the 5 quintiles of the population	Norton and Ariely (2011)
Perceived Economic Inequality	To what extend do you agree with the following statement: Differences in income in [your country] are too large.	5-point Likert-type response scale from "strongly disagree" to "strongly agree"	General Social Survey
Perceived Economic Inequality	What is your assessment about how income (the total sum of annual earnings) is distributed in [country]?	5-point response scale from "extremely unequally" to "rather equally"	Knell and Stix (2020)
Wage Gap	What is your estimation of the monthly salary of a CEO and unskilled worker in a typical company in [your country]?	Free answer. Logarithmic ratio between the two magnitudes is computed: ln (perceived earning highest paid worker/lowest paid worker)	International Social Survey Programme

Continued

Table 4.1 *Continued*

Variable to be measured	Item's example asked to participants	Answer scale	Source
Inequality the Graphic Notes Inequality Measure (GNIM)	Which graph most accurately represented the economic structure of [your country]? Choose the letter (from A to E) that corresponds to your answer.	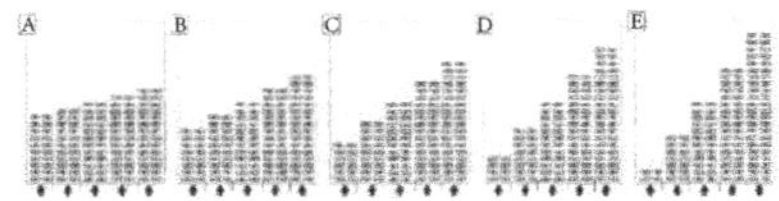	Rodríguez-Bailón et al. (2017)
Perceived Economic Inequality in Everyday Life	Includes twelve statements: e.g., "Among the people I surround myself with, there are some people who can afford access to a better health service than others."	7-point Likert-type response scale from "completely disagree" to "completely agree"	García-Castro et al. (2019)

Conceptualization and Measures of Meaningful Economic Inequality

Everyday life involves people's habitual experiences in their public and private lives, including their work or educational routines, day-to-day mobility, places they frequently visit, activities they do in their free time and home, etc. In this line of inquiry, the perception of economic inequality in everyday life is conceptualized as the habitual experiences in which the differences in people's economic resources occur (Willis et al. 2024). It is wrapped in individuals' significant experiences and related to contextual determinants, such as their place of residence, reference family or work groups, and their social comparison with other people and groups (García-Castro et al. 2023). Perceived economic inequality in everyday life allows people to better understand and make inferences about the reality of their environment (Sánchez-Rodríguez et al. 2023). These inferences, in turn, may help them better navigate these unequal contexts.

Some research supports the importance of measuring the perception of inequality in everyday life instead of the perception of inequality in general or abstract terms (Gimpelson and Treisman 2018; Mijs 2019) because it is better able to tap into people's psychological experiences and may be more closely related to some of its effects (García-Sánchez, Willis, Rodríguez-Bailón, García-Castro, et al. 2018; Newman 2014). People form their perception of meaningful inequalities through their everyday experiences not only by observing differences between groups of individuals but also through exposure to cultural narratives or artifacts, such as media, movies, books, stories, etc. As such, everyday experiences include both direct and indirect exposure to inequality situations between groups of people. Those who perceive disparities in the resources of people close to them—such as family, friends, and workmates—feel them more viscerally and immediately (Gugushvili 2020). In this way, perceiving inequality not just through economic resources but also through social classes (e.g., the elites vs. the poor), intergroup relations (e.g., discrimination, exclusion), public spaces (e.g., spatial segregation of housing, schools, hospitals), and work-related dynamics (e.g., income inequality, precarious jobs), that is, perceiving inequality in a more psychologically meaningful way, helps individuals to understand and better navigate through socially unequal contexts (García-Sánchez, Willis, Rodríguez-Bailón, Palacio Sañudo, et al. 2018).

The effects of perceived economic inequality in everyday life depend on how people understand and experience it (Willis et al. 2022). Individually, the proximity of inequality can provoke negative emotions (i.e., indignation, anger, sadness, etc.) that can lead individuals to change their attitudes toward economic redistribution. On the contrary, if inequality is seen as an abstract or psychologically distant issue from one's reality, it could make individuals not pay attention or not feel worried about it (García-Castro et al. 2023).

The Consequences of the Perception of Economic Inequality

Individual Consequences

The distribution of economic resources—such as wealth and income—shapes the dynamics of social interactions within a society, with important consequences at the individual level. According to Wilkinson and Pickett (2017), this happens for at least two reasons (see also Buttrick and Oishi 2017; Rodríguez-Bailón et al. 2020): On the one hand, it makes categories based on social class more salient, pushing people to compete for social status, supporting the economic logic by viewing the wealthy as the winners in the race for status while those with low socioeconomic status (SES) are seen as losers (Lakner and Milanovic 2016). On the other hand, the distribution of economic resources makes people believe that others are more different from themselves, increasing social distance, differences between groups, and reducing social trust.

First, economic inequality amplifies the importance of social rank. As such, in unequal societies, categories based on social class are relevant (see Tanjitpiyanond et al. 2022), and people value social status more, which in turn, could trigger an approach motivation for climbing the social ladder and an avoidance motivation for not wanting to lose their social position (Sommet and Elliot 2023). This is shown in some research where it is found that there is a positive association between economic inequality—measured at the country level—and comparisons with others (Delhey et al. 2017). Moreover, inequality increases status anxiety (Melita et al. 2021) and behaviors aimed at signaling social status, such as conspicuous consumption (Velandia-Morales et al. 2022) and the search for more luxury items (Walasek and Brown 2015). All this suggests that one of the main psychological effects of economic inequality is that it increases competition for status.

Second, economic inequality increases perceived social distance; that is, it makes people tend to perceive that others are more different from themselves (Sánchez-Rodríguez et al. 2019; Sánchez-Rodríguez et al. 2023). This could have relevant implications. For instance, inequality—at the country level—is related to decreased levels of social trust (Alesina and Ferrara 2002; Fairbrother and Martin 2013; García-Sánchez, García-Castro, et al. 2024). Additionally, there is a negative association between inequality and trust in institutions (García-Sánchez, Turner-Zwinkels, et al. 2024; Uslnaer and Brown 2005), which could be considered an extension of lowered social trust at the institutional level.

These two effects of economic inequality on status competition and perceived social distance could, in turn, influence individuals' well-being. All in all, when people tend to be worried and anxious about their societal position, and they constantly compare their social resources with others, they tend to report lower levels of happiness and well-being (Delhey and Dragolov 2014; Oishi et al. 2011). In addition, perceiving others as being more different from themselves may lower social trust, which could have some other negative effects. For instance, social distrust is also negatively related to well-being (Portela et al. 2013) and, more extremely, positively related to mortality indexes (Elgar 2010). These results suggest that economic inequality—through its effects on status competition and social distrust—has a negative influence on individuals' lives.

However, the empirical evidence on the relationship between inequality and well-being is mixed. Whereas some studies have shown that inequality is negatively related to happiness and well-being (Alesina et al. 2004; Oishi et al. 2011; Oishi and Kesebir 2015), other studies have failed to replicate these results (see Sommet and Elliot 2022; Kelley and Evans 2017). A meta-analysis of some of these studies also revealed that the association between inequality and well-being was close to zero (Ngamaba et al. 2018).

Trying to explain these inconsistent results, Willis et al. (2022) argued that the effects of economic inequality depend on its perception. They argued that objective economic inequality—measured at the county, state, or country level—may not be the best indicator for investigating the psychological effects of inequality, given that people tend to misperceive the levels of inequality around them (Gimpelson and Treisman 2018; Hauser and Norton 2017). This could happen because in more unequal societies, people, paradoxically, may have less contact with others from different social classes, which could impair their awareness of inequality. Moreover, people may also be motivated to perceive more or less inequality for ideological reasons. Summing up, Willis et al. (2022) posited that inequality is negatively associated with well-being, especially when people are aware of it and appraise it in a meaningful way that relates to their everyday life.

The association between perceived (but not objective) inequality and well-being has been corroborated in different studies. For instance, Oshio and Urakawa (2013) supported the association between them in Japan. Other studies have directly compared the effects of objective inequality and well-being in two European countries (measured at the province level). Vezzoli et al. (2023) and García-Sánchez, Turner-Zwinkels, et al. (2024) found that, in Italy and Spain respectively, perceived inequality, but not objective inequality, was negatively associated with well-being, and that concerns for status and social distrust partially explain these effects of economic inequality. These studies reveal the crucial role of the subjective component of economic inequality.

Social Consequences

One of the core assumptions regarding the social consequences of economic inequality is that it undermines social cohesion (Delhey and Steckermeier 2020). Although social cohesion can be an elusive concept, international research agrees that a cohesive society implies solid social ties, high levels of general and political trust, a sense of belonging and shared values, fairness perceptions, civic participation, solidarity, social order, and rule conformity, among others (Delhey et al. 2023). In this regard, empirical evidence supports the assumption that economic inequality erodes social cohesion, given that it reduces social and political trust (De Courson and Nettle 2021; García-Sánchez, Turner-Zwinkels et al. 2024), reduces civic participation and civic engagement (Du et al. 2021; Solt 2008), increase political polarization (Stewart et al. 2020; Winkler 2019), and undermines democracy (Andersen 2012; Scheve and Stasavage 2017). As such, economic inequality threatens social cohesion by hindering social interactions, impoverishing public life, and undermining the legitimacy of democratic governments.

But how does economic inequality divide us, weaken social and institutional ties, and foster social conflict? From a socioecological approach, economic inequality through the market and economic logics creates the conditions that foster people's thoughts, feelings, and behaviors, favoring conditions that may reinforce the status quo (Uskul and Oishi 2020). This perspective acknowledges that people shape their subjective reality and that psychological processes are fundamental to understanding the consequences, the maintenance, and/or the challenge of economic inequality on societal and individual outcomes (Gobel and Carvacho 2023).

Again, one of the psychological processes proposed to explain the consequences of objective economic inequality on societal outcomes is subjective views of inequality. The consequences of inequality will be shaped by how people perceive and understand such economic disparities (Willis et al. 2022). This idea has been supported by different psychosocial models that explain intergroup processes and political attitudes (Jetten et al. 2021; Osborne et al. 2022; Wienk et al. 2022). For instance, perceiving large and unfair inequalities leads people to support authoritarian leaders (Sprong et al. 2019) and populism (Jay et al. 2019) and to distrust political institutions (Du et al. 2023; García-Sánchez, García-Castro et al. 2024), which exacerbates affective polarization (García-Sánchez, Turner-Zwinkels et al. 2024) and social unrest (Jetten et al. 2020).

However, simply shaping people's subjective perceptions of inequality will not solve the problem of economic inequality harming social cohesion. On the contrary, misperceiving or justifying economic inequality augments and diversifies the pernicious effects of economic inequality. Impaired psychologically meaningful perceptions of inequality reinforce a vicious cycle of inequality by preventing people from taking action to redress inequality—it is difficult to address an issue that is not perceived, has no substantive meaning, or is misunderstood. Therefore, trying to make people perceive meaningful inequalities through their everyday experiences increases their support for redistribution and welfare programs aimed at reducing inequality, as shown in previous research (see Bussolo et al. 2021; García-Castro, González et al. 2022; García-Sánchez et al. 2020). Indeed, perceiving inequality in meaningful domains, such as income, health, and education, motivates people to engage in collective actions to redress such disparities (Soler-Martínez et al. 2023). Thus, subjective views on inequality that are significant for perceivers are pivotal to taking action to redress inequality.

In addition, being unaware of economic inequality, or perceiving it in very abstract terms and far from one's own reality, could intensify social and intergroup conflict by hindering people's reasoning about other social groups and the overall system. For instance, being unaware of economic inequality leads people to punish the disadvantaged for their situation (Hauser et al. 2021), exacerbates negative stereotypes of low socioeconomic groups (Tanjitpiyanond et al. 2022), and overlooks the role of structural factors attached to inequality (Davidai and Walker 2022). Thus, giving meaning to perceptions of inequality by making the indicators of structural inequality closer to perceivers' lives allows them to acknowledge the role of structural factors that cause them, avoiding victim-blaming narratives and informing people's attitudes that seek to reduce inequality (Amemiya et al. 2023).

Still, whether subjective views on inequality lead to social conflict and the maintenance of—or challenge to—inequality would depend on people's ideologies. In other words, the consequences of objective and perceived inequality will depend on the lenses through which people understand them. In the following section, we argue that the interplay between ideologies and perceptions of inequality shapes individuals and societal outcomes.

The Role of Ideologies in the Relationship Between Perceptions of Economic Inequality and Its Consequences

Social psychologists have shown that the perspective from which individuals view economic inequalities matters (Darby and Branscombe 2012). In addition to perceived inequality, assessments of inequalities as unfair or just play a crucial role in the individual and collective effects of economic inequality. As with other kinds of worldviews, ideologies about inequality are guiding forces that shape beliefs regarding the ideal structure of society. From this perspective, ideology offers both an interpretation and a prescription for how the environment should be organized (Zmigrod 2022). In the case of ideologies about inequality, they posit the question of how resources should be allocated within the collective context: Is it just or unjust for certain groups to possess more resources than others, and if so, under what circumstances and according to which principles (Sheehy-Skeffington and Thomsen 2020)?

Economic inequality and the ideologies that support it have been closely intertwined throughout history. Many ideologies have been used to legitimate economic inequality, ranging from the Protestant work ethic and meritocracy to social dominance orientation and the belief in a just world (Jost and Hunyady 2005). Interestingly, economic inequality and beliefs in meritocracy have increased hand-in-hand (see also, Bobzien and Verwiebe in this volume) over the last several decades (Mijs 2019), suggesting that changes in inequality elicit narratives to justify it.

Ideologies maintain economic inequality by impairing people's meaningful perceptions of inequality. People engage in motivated reasoning and moral logics, perceiving reality according to their ideological beliefs. As such, people who believe inequality is fair perceive less inequality (Du and King 2021). For instance, economic system justification systematically made people unaware of economic inequality (Waldfogel et al. 2021), and belief in a just world reduces the perceived unfairness in income distribution (García-Sánchez et al. 2022). Taken together, these findings suggest that inequality is in the eye of the beholder, as ideologies that legitimate inequality lead people to overlook the extent and meaningfulness of inequality (Kteily et al. 2017).

Ideologies also maintain economic inequality by impairing people's motivation to pursue social change. For instance, economic system justification beliefs mute people's biological and psychological responses toward inequality (Goudarzi et al. 2020), and meritocracy attenuates moral outrage that fosters responses against inequality (Wakslak et al. 2007). Indeed, system-justifying beliefs alleviate the discomfort of being oppressed or discriminated against (Sengupta et al. 2017). In sum, ideologies that legitimate the status quo weaken people's responses to address inequality.

Despite social sciences having focused on ideologies that seek to maintain the status quo, others promote social change. One of the ideologies most studied in social psychology about promoting social change and equality is egalitarianism. Egalitarianism refers to the belief in equality, especially in terms of political, social, or economic rights (Eldridge 2024). Egalitarianism and other ideologies that challenge inequality can be extended from the individual to the collective, representing a preference for the fundamental structure of equality, as opposed to hierarchy, to govern the distribution of resources within a society. The most used measure of anti-egalitarianism, known as social dominance orientation (SDO) (Pratto et al. 1994), operates under the group logic of acceptance/challenge of inequality and comprises two sub-dimensions that are contrary: SDO-E assesses preferences related to equality among social groups, while SDO-D gauges an inclination toward arranging groups in a dominance hierarchy (Ho et al. 2015).

While there is less research exploring these phenomena from the perspective of those advocating for equality, individuals high in SDO-E endorse legitimizing myths that work to diminish hierarchical structures, thereby advocating for the necessity of egalitarian policies. Specifically, they support ideologies that assert healthcare, education, or living wages as universal human rights, thereby challenging prevailing social inequalities

(Pratto et al. 2006). As these ideologies gain traction, even minimal group-based inequalities in these domains tend to be perceived as social issues warranting intervention (Kteily et al. 2017).

In this line of study, the general expectation for equal resource distribution correlates with a willingness to help and share resources, especially with groups possessing lower power. For instance, support for egalitarianism predicts a willingness to contribute through taxes to support universal health care, as evidenced across twenty-nine nations (Azar et al. 2018). These results suggest that such efforts are motivated by underlying concerns about equality rooted in resource distribution challenges.

As already posited, previous research has shown evidence of the interplay between egalitarianism and the perception of inequality on the motivation to challenge inequality. Importantly, some recent studies also revealed a reciprocal relationship between commitment to egalitarian principles and individuals' perceptions of societal-level inequality. For example, Kteily et al. (2017) found that individuals who reported higher levels of anti-egalitarianism exhibit reduced capacity to perceive inequality in society. Notably, this diminished sensitivity to inequality serves as a mediator for individuals' decreased endorsement of policies promoting egalitarianism.

Another important ideology related to the attenuation of inequality is feminism, conceived as a social and political ideology that emphasizes the recognition of patriarchy as a discriminatory system leading to various disparities, particularly against women. Feminism encourages collective efforts to transform this socially unequal reality (Sau 2000, 121). Feminism, as an inequality-attenuating ideology, seems important in the examination of gender inequalities (Zucker and Bay-Cheng 2010).

In the same line of inquiry as the results described above, feminist ideology positively predicts perceived inequalities and supports collective action to reduce inequality (Schwartz-Salazar et al. under review). Interestingly, the perception of inequality mediates the relationship between feminist ideology and support for collective action to confront not just gender inequalities but also economic-based inequalities.

In sum, the exploration of ideologies within this section illuminates their potential as catalysts for challenging entrenched inequalities, shaping perceptions of inequality, and fostering the groundwork for more equitable societies. By understanding how certain ideologies engage with and contest prevailing social disparities, we gain insights into their transformative power. The dynamic interplay between ideologies and perceived inequality underscores their profound impact on attitudes and actions toward the maintenance of or reduction in inequalities.

The Proposed Model of the Effects of Meaningful Perceived Inequality

As we have reviewed in this chapter, research in social psychology has provided insights about the importance of taking psychological factors into account, such as the perception of inequality, to predict the impact of economic inequality on individuals and groups.

Individuals perceive economic inequality from many different and varied cues that are not necessarily constrained to economic domains but are also related to their everyday lives, such as unemployment, poverty, and a lack of investment in education (Bussolo et al. 2021; García-Sánchez, Willis, Rodríguez-Bailón, García-Castro et al. 2018). Even when residing in the same location, individuals may be exposed to varying degrees of inequality and may be more attuned to certain aspects than others (Schmalor and Heine 2021). For example, consider the case of two families that live in the same middle-class neighborhood. The members of one family seldom leave the neighborhood, whereas the members of the other family work in the poorest neighborhood of their city. Certainly, they will perceive different levels of inequality around them. Likely, they will be touched in different ways by the levels of inequality they see in their close circles. It is very probable that if the second family has good relationships with people with low SES, their attitudes toward the reduction of inequality and toward improving low-SES people's lives are more positive than the ones from the first family.

Furthermore, we have also presented research that revealed the nuanced relationship between perceived economic inequality and some of its effects at the individual (e.g., on status anxiety) and societal levels (e.g., on attitudes toward redistribution or trust in democratic institutions).

In this regard, we propose that two of the factors that may impact these relationships are (a) the level of abstraction or specificity in the inequality individuals perceive and (b) the extent to which it is meaningful and psychologically close or distant from them (see Figure 4.1; García-Castro, Gonzalez et al. 2022; Knell and Stix 2020).

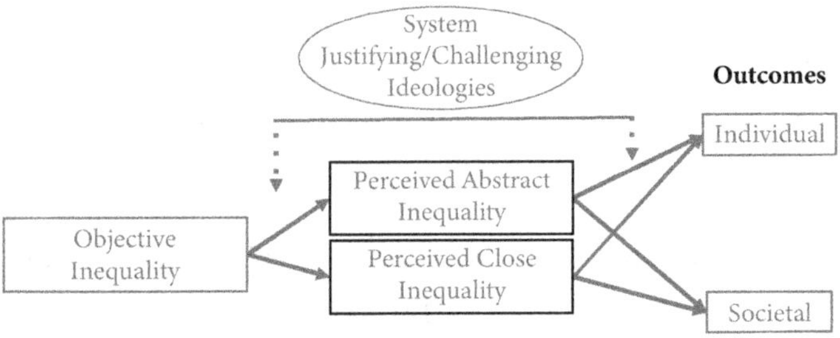

Figure 4.1 Proposed model of the influence of perceived inequality on individual and societal outcomes moderated by ideologies

Studies suggest that when economic inequality is presented in more general and abstract terms, people may not be as motivated to actively address it (e.g., García-Sánchez, Willis, Rodríguez-Bailón, Palacio Sañudo et al. 2018). For instance, people may know about inequality because they read a newspaper article discussing the Gini coefficient or by seeing data on social media about how economic inequality has changed in their country over the last few decades. From this perspective, this information alone may not be enough to mobilize them against inequality. This could be due to several reasons. First, abstract framing leads individuals to estimate levels of perceived inequality without a frame of reference, leading them to make estimations that are generally far from actual levels of national inequality on a national basis. Indeed, when asked to do this, individuals may use heuristics to respond. Therefore, measuring levels of perceived inequality using abstract frameworks will make the use of heuristics more likely, both for estimating actual inequality (e.g., anchor and adjustment) and for reporting attitudes toward it (i.e., ideal inequality or tolerance toward inequality) (Eidelman and Crandall 2012). Second, the abstract framing of inequality might lead individuals to view it as an inevitable or distant issue, reducing the perceived personal impact or responsibility as shown in contexts featured as high in power distance (Winterich and Zhang 2014).

On the contrary, when economic inequality is brought closer to home and perceived within individuals' immediate social circles or communities, the motivation to address it may increase. From this perspective, people may become aware of economic disparities because some family members are well-off, whereas others cannot make ends meet. Similarly, some of their friends or workmates may spend a lot of money on summer holidays, whereas others cannot afford to turn on the air conditioner during the hottest days. Research by García-Castro, Gonzalez et al. (2022) indicates that individuals are more likely to express less tolerance toward inequality and endorse more policies promoting equality when they perceive it as affecting people they know or when it directly impacts their immediate environment. This is what we conceive as meaningful inequality, that is, the level of inequality that is perceived at concrete levels (e.g., in relationships with others, at physical spaces, specific intergroup attitudes, etc.) and in close relationships with others.

In sum, evidence suggests that the level of specificity in perceiving economic inequality plays a role in motivating individuals to address it actively. We propose that more abstract and general perceptions of inequality may not elicit strong motivations to challenge it, but when inequality is perceived in close social circles, people may perceive higher levels of inequality, may judge them as more unfair or even trigger more anger, discomfort, and other negative emotions, which, in turn, could boost the motivation to take action to reduce it.

In this line of study, we can distinguish between individual and collective, positive and negative effects of perceived economic inequality (see Table 4.2). When economic inequality is perceived more abstractly, it may lead to fewer adverse effects on individuals, as it doesn't necessarily evoke discomfort or negative emotions. However, at the societal level, this abstract perception could be harmful, as it might not motivate individuals to actively oppose wealth disparities although these results are not clear in previous research. Conversely, when inequality is experienced more intimately and holds personal meaning, it could have negative implications for individuals. This would be particularly true when individuals perceive procedural injustice in the distribution of resources to the people they interact with on an everyday basis. Despite this, such meaningful experiences of inequality could serve as a catalyst for driving change, fostering a commitment with social groups to reduce inequalities and to promote social change.

Conclusion

All in all, the findings regarding the impact of perceived inequality on individual and collective selves highlight the intricate nature of the topic. While perceived inequalities provide insights into the circumstances and

Table 4.2 Proposed effects of perceived abstract vs. meaningful perceived inequality on individual and societal outcomes

Types of Inequality Perception	Individual	Societal
Abstract and General Perception of Inequality	Negative: increases status competition, status anxiety, and perceived social distance, reduces social trust and well-being	Not clear: it seems to increase ideal levels of inequality, tolerance toward inequality, and negative attitudes toward redistribution
Meaningful Perception of Inequality	Negative: increases indignation, anger, and status anxiety	Positive: increases identification with social classes, positive attitudes toward redistribution and other public policies to reduce inequality, motivation for collective action against inequality, and solidarity

reasons economic inequality can be detrimental to societies, they also appear essential in prompting individuals to actively address it.

Further research endeavors should delve into the exploration of the distinct antecedents and consequences associated with perceived meaningful inequality. By unraveling them, we can gain a more comprehensive understanding of their impacts on individuals and society, paving the way for more targeted and effective interventions to address the multifaceted challenges posed by economic inequality.

References

Alesina, A., R. Di Tella, and R. MacCulloch. 2004. "Inequality and Happiness: Are Europeans and Americans Different?" *Journal of Public Economics* 88 (9–10): pp. 2009–2042. https://doi.org/10.1016/j.jpubeco.2003.07.006.

Alesina, A., and E.L. Ferrara. 2002. "Who Trusts Others?" *Journal of Public Economics* 85: pp. 207–234.

Amemiya, J., E. Mortenson, G.D. Heyman, and C.M. Walker. 2023. "Thinking Structurally: A Cognitive Framework for Understanding How People Attribute Inequality to Structural Causes." *Perspectives on Psychological Science* 18 (2): pp. 259–274. https://doi.org/10.1177/17456916221093593.

Andersen, R. 2012. "Support for Democracy in Cross-National Perspective: The Detrimental Effect of Economic Inequality." *Research in Social Stratification and Mobility* 30 (4): pp. 389–402. https://doi.org/10.1016/j.rssm.2012.04.002.

Azar, A., L. Maldonado, J.C. Castillo, and J. Atria. 2018. "Income, Egalitarianism and Attitudes Towards Healthcare Policy: A Study on Public Attitudes in 29 Countries." *Public Health* 154: pp. 59–69. https://doi.org/10.1016/j.puhe.2017.09.007.

Bavetta, S., P. Li Donni, and M. Marino. 2020. "How Consistent Are Perceptions of Inequality?" *Journal of Economic Psychology* 78: p. 102267. https://doi.org/10.1016/j.joep.2020.102267.

Bruner, J.S., and C.C. Goodman. 1947. "Value and Need as Organizing Factors in Perception." *Journal of Abnormal and Social Psychology* 42 (1): pp. 33–44. https://doi.org/10.1037/h0058484.

Bussolo, M., A. Ferrer-i-carbonell, A. Giolbas, and I. Torre. 2021. "I Perceive Therefore I Demand: The Formation of Inequality Perceptions and Demand for Redistribution." *Review of Income and Wealth* 67 (4): pp. 835–871. https://doi.org/10.1111/roiw.12497.

Buttrick, N.R., and S. Oishi. 2017. "The Psychological Consequences of Income Inequality." *Social and Personality Psychology Compass* 11 (3): p. e12304. https://doi.org/10.1111/spc3.12304.

Castillo, J.-C., J.-D. García-Castro, and M. Venegas. 2022. "Perception of Economic Inequality: Concepts, Associated Factors and Prospects of a Burgeoning Research Agenda" [Percepción de desigualdad económica: conceptos, factores asociados y proyecciones de una agenda creciente de investigación]. *International Journal of Social Psychology* 37 (1): pp. 180–207. https://doi.org/10.1080/02134748.2021.2009275.

Choi, G. 2019. "Revisiting the Redistribution Hypothesis With Perceived Inequality and Redistributive Preferences." *European Journal of Political Economy* 58: pp. 220–244. https://doi.org/10.1016/j.ejpoleco.2018.12.004.

Darby, D., and N.R. Branscombe. 2012. "Egalitarianism and Perceptions of Inequality." *Philosophical Topics* 40 (1): pp. 7–25.

Davidai, S., and J. Walker. 2022. "Americans Misperceive Racial Disparities in Economic Mobility." *Personality and Social Psychology Bulletin* 48 (5): pp. 793–806. https://doi.org/10.1177/01461672211024115.

Dawtry, R.J., R.M. Sutton, and C.G. Sibley. 2015. "Why Wealthier People Think People Are Wealthier, and Why It Matters." *Psychological Science* 26 (9): pp. 1389–1400. https://doi.org/10.1177/0956797615586560.

De Courson, B., and D. Nettle. 2021. "Why Do Inequality and Deprivation Produce High Crime and Low Trust?" *Scientific Reports* 11 (1): p. 1937. https://doi.org/10.1038/s41598-020-80897-8

Delhey, J., and G. Dragolov. 2014. "Why Inequality Makes Europeans Less Happy: The Role of Distrust, Status Anxiety, and Perceived Conflict." *European Sociological Review* 30 (2): 151–165. https://doi.org/10.1093/esr/jct033.

Delhey, J., G. Dragolov, and K. Boehnke. 2023. "Social Cohesion in International Comparison: A Review of Key Measures and Findings." *KZfSS Kölner Zeitschrift Für Soziologie Und Sozialpsychologie* 75 (S1): pp. 95–120. https://doi.org/10.1007/s11577-023-00891-6.

Delhey, J., C. Schneickert, and L.C. Steckermeier. 2017. "Sociocultural Inequalities and Status Anxiety: Redirecting the Spirit Level Theory." *International Journal of Comparative Sociology* 58 (3): pp. 215–240. https://doi.org/10.1177/0020715217713799.

Delhey, J., and L.C. Steckermeier. 2020. "Social Ills in Rich Countries: New Evidence on Levels, Causes, and Mediators." *Social Indicators Research* 149: pp. 87–125. https://doi.org/10.1007/s11205-019-02244-3.

Du, H., A. Chen, P. Chi, and R.B. King. 2021. "Income Inequality Reduces Civic Honesty." *Social Psychological and Personality Science* 12 (4): pp. 537–543. https://doi.org/10.1177/1948550620929495.

Du, H., Y. Huang, L. Ma, X. Chen, P. Chi, and R.B. King. 2023. "Subjective Economic Inequality Is Associated with Lower Well-Being Through More Upward Comparison and Lower Trust." *Applied Psychology: Health and Well-Being* 16 (1): pp. 15–23. https://doi.org/10.1111/aphw.12467.

Du, H., and R.B. King. 2021. "What Predicts Perceived Economic Inequality? The Roles of Actual Inequality, System Justification, and Fairness Considerations." *British Journal of Social Psychology* 61: pp. 19–36. https://doi.org/10.1111/bjso.12468.

Easterbrook, M.J. 2021. "The Social Psychology of Economic Inequality." UNU WIDER Working Paper 43/2021. United Nations University World Instituto for Development Economics Research. https://doi.org/10.35188/UNU-WIDER/2021/981-5.

Eidelman, S., and C.S. Crandall. 2012. "Bias in Favor of the Status Quo." *Social and Personality Psychology Compass* 6 (3): pp. 270–281. https://doi.org/10.1111/j.1751-9004.2012.00427.x.

Eldridge, S. 2024. "Egalitarianism." *Britannica.* July 3. https://www.britannica.com/topic/egalitarianism.

Elgar, F.J. 2010. "Income Inequality, Trust, and Population Health in 33 Countries." *American Journal of Public Health 100* (11): pp. 2311–2315. https://doi.org/10.2105/AJPH.2009.189134.

Eriksson, K., and B. Simpson. 2013. "The Available Evidence Suggests the Percent Measure Should Not Be Used to Study Inequality: Reply to Norton and Ariely." *Judgment and Decision Making* 8 (3): pp. 395–396.

Fairbrother, M., and I.W. Martin. 2013. "Does Inequality Erode Social Trust? Results from Multilevel Models of US States and Counties." *Social Science Research* 42 (2): pp. 347–360. https://doi.org/10.1016/j.ssresearch.2012.09.008.

Franko, W.W. 2017. "Understanding Public Perceptions of Growing Economic Inequality." *State Politics and Policy Quarterly* 17 (3): pp. 319–348. https://doi.org/10.1177/1532440017707799.

García-Castro, J.D., E. García-Sánchez, G.B. Willis, J.C. Castillo, and R. Rodríguez-Bailón. 2022. "Perceived Economic Inequality Measures and Their Association with Objective Inequality and Redistributive Preferences." *Social Psychology* 53 (5): pp. 277–291. https://doi.org/10.1027/1864-9335/a000498.

García-Castro, J.D., R. González, C. Frigolett, G. Jiménez-Moya, R. Rodríguez-Bailón, G.B. Willis. 2022. "Changing Attitudes Toward Redistribution: The Role of Perceived Economic Inequality in Everyday Life and Intolerance of Inequality." *Journal of Social Psychology* 163 (4): pp. 566–581. https://doi.org/10.1080/00224545.2021.2006126.

García-Castro, J.D., R. Rodríguez-Bailón, and G.B. Willis. 2020. "Perceiving Economic Inequality in Everyday Life Decreases Tolerance to Inequality." *Journal of Experimental Social Psychology* 90: 104019. https://doi.org/10.1016/j.jesp.2020.104019/.

García-Castro, J.D., M. Venegas Márquez, L. Ramírez Cardoza, and F. Robles Rivera. 2023. "Evaluación de (in)justicia distributiva en jóvenes de Centroamérica." [Evaluation of Distributive (In)Justice Among Young People in Centroamérica]. *Andamios, Revista de Investigación Social* 20 (52): pp. 363–386. https://doi.org/10.29092/uacm.v20i52.1020.

García-Sánchez, E., I. Correia, C.R. Pereira, G.B. Willis, R. Rodríguez-Bailón, and J. Vala. 2022. "How Fair Is Economic Inequality? Belief in a Just World and the Legitimation of Economic Disparities in 27 European Countries." *Personality and Social Psychology Bulletin* 48 (3): pp. 382–395. https://doi.org/10.1177/01461672211002366.

García-Sánchez, E., J.D. García-Castro, G.B. Willis, and R. Rodríguez-Bailón. 2024. "Economic Inequality and Unfairness Evaluations of Income Distribution Negatively Predict Political and Social Trust: Evidence from Latin America over 23 Years." *Social Psychological and Personality Science* 0 (0). https://doi.org/10.1177/19485506231221310.

García-Sánchez, E., Matamoros-Lima, J., Moreno-Bella, E., Melita, D., Sánchez-Rodríguez, A., García-Castro, J.D., Rodríguez-Bailón, R., and G.B. Willis. 2024. "Perceived Economic Inequality Is Negatively Associated with Subjective Well-Being Through Status Anxiety and Social Trust." *Social Indicators Research* 172: pp. 239–260. https://doi.org/10.1007/s11205-024-03306-x

García-Sánchez, E., D. Osborne, G.B. Willis, and R. Rodríguez-Bailón. 2020. "Attitudes Towards Redistribution and the Interplay Between Perceptions and Beliefs About Inequality." *British Journal of Social Psychology* 59 (1): pp. 111–136.: https://doi.org/10.1111/bjso.12326.

García-Sánchez, E., F. Turner-Zwinkels, R. Kesberg, M. Marot, R. Rodríguez-Bailón, G.B. Willis, and T. Kuppens. 2024. "Economic Threats, Political and National Identification Predict Affective Polarization: Longitudinal Evidence from Spain." *International Review of Social Psychology* 37 (1): p. 5. https://doi.org/10.5334/irsp.838.

García-Sánchez, E., G.B. Willis, R. Rodríguez-Bailón, J.D. García-Castro, J. Palacio-Sañudo, J. Polo, and E. Rentería-Pérez. 2018. "Perceptions of Economic Inequality in Colombian Daily Life: More Than Unequal Distribution of Economic Resources." *Frontiers in Psychology* 9: pp. 1–11. https://doi.org/10.3389/fpsyg.2018.01660.

García-Sánchez, E., G.B. Willis, R. Rodríguez-Bailón, J. Palacio Sañudo, J. Polo, and E. Rentería Pérez. 2018. "Perceptions of Economic Inequality and Support for Redistribution: The Role of Existential and Utopian Standards." *Social Justice Research* 31 (4): pp. 335–354. https://doi.org/10.1007/s11211-018-0317-6.

Gimpelson, V., and D. Treisman. 2018. "Misperceiving Inequality." *Economics and Politics* 30 (1): pp. 27–54. https://doi.org/10.1111/ecpo.12103.

Gobel, M.S., and H. Carvacho. 2023. "The Dynamic Socioecological Model of Economic Inequality and Psychological Tendencies: A Cycle of Mutual Constitution." *Social and Personality Psychology Compass* 18 (1): p. e12875. https://doi.org/10.1111/spc3.12875.

Goudarzi, S., R. Pliskin, J.T. Jost, and E.D. Knowles. 2020. "Economic System Justification Predicts Muted Emotional Responses to Inequality." *Nature Communications* 11 (383). https://doi.org/10.1038/s41467-019-14193-z.

Gugushvili, A. 2020. "Which Socio-Economic Comparison Groups Do Individuals Choose and Why?" *European Societies* 23 (4): pp. 437–463. https://doi.org/10.1080/14616696.2020.1793214.

Hauser, O.P., G.T. Kraft-Todd, D.G. Rand, M.A. Nowak, and M.I. Norton. 2021. "Invisible Inequality Leads to Punishing the Poor and Rewarding the Rich." *Behavioural Public Policy* 5 (3): pp. 333–353. https://doi.org/10.1017/bpp.2019.4.

Hauser, O.P., and M.I. Norton. 2017. "(Mis)perceptions of Inequality." *Current Opinion in Psychology* 18: pp. 21–25. https://doi.org/10.1016/j.copsyc.2017.07.024.

Heiserman, N., and B. Simpson 2021. "Measuring Perceptions of Economic Inequality and Justice: An Empirical Assessment." *Social Justice Research* 34 (2): pp. 119–145. https://doi.org/10.1007/s11211-021-00368-x.

Hing, L.S.S., A.E. Wilson, P. Gourevitch, J. English, and P. Sin. 2019. "Failure to Respond to Rising Income Inequality: Processes That Legitimize Growing Disparities." *Daedalus* 148 (3): pp. 105–135. https://doi.org/10.1162/DAED_a_01752.

Ho, A.K., J. Sidanius, N. Kteily, J. Sheehy-Skeffington, F. Pratto, K.E. Henkel, R. Foels, and A.L. Stewart. 2015. "The Nature of Social Dominance Orientation: Theorizing and Measuring Preferences for Intergroup Inequality Using the New SDO_7 Scale." *Journal of Personality and Social Psychology* 109 (6): pp. 1003–1028. https://doi.org/10.1037/pspi0000033.

Jachimowicz, J.M., S. Davidai, D. Goya-Tocchetto, B. Szaszi, M.V. Day, S.J. Tepper, L.T. Phillips, M.U. Mirza, N. Ordabayeva, and O.P. Hauser. 2022. "Inequality in Researchers' Minds: Four Guiding Questions for Studying Subjective Perceptions of Economic Inequality." *Journal of Economic Surveys* 37 (5): pp. 1534–1561. https://doi.org/10.1111/joes.12507.

Jackson, J.C., and K. Payne. 2021. "Cognitive Barriers to Reducing Income Inequality." *Social Psychological and Personality Science* 12 (5): pp. 687–696. https://doi.org/10.1177/1948550620934597.

Jay, S., A. Batruch, J. Jetten, C. McGarty, and O. Muldoon. 2019. "Economic Inequality and the Rise of Far-Right Populism: A Social Psychological Analysis." *Journal of Community and Applied Social Psychology* 29 (5). doi: 0.1002/casp.2409.

Jetten, J., F. Mols, and H.P. Selvanathan. 2020. "How Economic Inequality Fuels the Rise and Persistence of the Yellow Vest Movement." *International Review of Social Psychology* 33 (1): p. 2. https://doi.org/10.5334/irsp.356.

Jetten, J., K. Peters, B. Álvarez, B.G.S. Casara, M. Dare, K. Kirkland, Á. Sánchez-Rodríguez, H.P. Selvanathan, S. Sprong, P. Tanjitpiyanond, Z. Wang, and F. Mols. 2021. "Consequences of Economic Inequality for the Social and Political Vitality of Society: A Social Identity Analysis." *Political Psychology* 42 (S1): pp. 241–266. https://doi.org/10.1111/pops.12800.

Jost, J.T., and O. Hunyady. 2005. "Antecedents and Consequences of System-Justifying Ideologies." *Current Directions in Psychological Science* 14 (5): pp. 260–265. https://doi.org/10.1111/j.0963-7214.2005.00377.x.

Kelley, J., and M.D.R. Evans. 2017. "Societal Inequality and Individual Subjective Well-Being: Results from 68 Societies and Over 200,000 Individuals, 1981–2008." *Social Science Research* 62: pp. 1–23. https://doi.org/10.1016/j.ssresearch.2016.04.020.

Knell, M., and H. Stix. 2020. "Perceptions of Inequality." *European Journal of Political Economy* 65: p. 101927. https://doi.org/10.1016/j.ejpoleco.2020.101927.

Kteily, N.S., J. Sheehy-Skeffington, and A.K. Ho. 2017. "Hierarchy in the Eye of the Beholder: (Anti-)egalitarianism Shapes Perceived Levels of Social Inequality." *Journal of Personality and Social Psychology* 112 (1): pp. 136–159. https://doi.org/10.1037/pspp0000097.

Kunda, Z. 1990. "The Case for Motivated Reasoning." *Psychological Bulletin* 108 (3): pp. 480–498.

Lakner, C., and B. Milanovic. 2016. "Global Distribution: From the Fall of the Berlin Wall to the Great Recession." *World Bank Economic Review* 30 (92): pp. 203–232.

Melita, D., G.B. Willis, and R. Rodríguez-Bailón. 2021. "Economic Inequality Increases Status Anxiety Through Perceived Contextual Competitiveness." *Frontiers in Psychology* 12: pp. 1–9. https://doi.org/10.3389/fpsyg.2021.637365.

Mijs, J.J.B. 2019. "The Paradox of Inequality: Income Inequality and Belief in Meritocracy Go Hand in Hand." *Socio-Economic Review* 19 (1): pp. 7–35. https://doi.org/10.1093/ser/mwy051.

Newman, B.J. 2014. "My Poor Friend: Financial Distress in One's Social Network, the Perceived Power of the Rich, and Support for Redistribution." *Journal of Politics* 76 (1): pp. 126–138. https://doi.org/10.1017/S0022381613001138.

Ngamaba, K.H., M. Panagioti, and C.J. Armitage. 2018. "Income Inequality and Subjective Well-Being: A Systematic Review and Meta-Analysis." *Quality of Life Research* 27 (3): pp. 577–596. https://doi.org/10.1007/s11136-017-1719-x.

Norton, M.I., and D. Ariely. 2011. "Building a Better America—One Wealth Quintile at a Time." *Perspectives on Psychological Science* 6 (1): pp. 9–12. https://doi.org/10.1177/1745691610393524.

Oishi, S., and S. Kesebir. 2015. "Income Inequality Explains Why Economic Growth Does Not Always Translate to an Increase in Happiness." *Psychological Science* 26 (10). https://doi.org/10.1177/0956797615596713.

Oishi, S., S. Kesebir, and E. Diener. 2011. "Income Inequality and Happiness." *Psychological Science* 22 (9): pp. 1095–1100. https://doi.org/10.1177/0956797611417262.

Osborne, D., J.C. Becker, J. Bahamondes, and E. García-Sánchez. 2022. "The Political Psychology of Inequality: Why Rising Rates of Economic Inequality Affect Our Health and Democracy." In *Cambridge Handbook of Political Psychology*, edited by D. Osborne and C.G. Sibley, pp. 363–381. Cambridge: Cambridge University Press.

Oshio, T., and K. Urakawa. 2013. "The Association Between Perceived Income Inequality and Subjective Well-Being: Evidence from a Social Survey in Japan." *Social Indicators Research* 116 (3): pp. 755–770. https://doi.org/10.1007/s11205-013-0323-x.

Portela, M., I. Neira, and M.D.M. Salinas-Jiménez. 2013. "Social Capital and Subjective Well-being in Europe: A New Approach on Social Capital." *Social Indicators Research* 114: pp. 493–511. https://doi.org/10.1007/s11205-012-0158-x.

Pratto, F., J. Sidanius, and S. Levin. 2006. "Social Dominance Theory and the Dynamics of Intergroup Relations: Taking Stock and Looking Forward." *European Review of Social Psychology* 17 (1): pp. 271–320. https://doi.org/10.1080/10463280601055772.

Pratto, F., J. Sidanius, L.M. Stallworth, and B.F. Malle. 1994. "Social Dominance Orientation: A Personality Variable Predicting Social and Political Attitudes." *Journal of Personality and Social Psychology* 67 (4): pp. 741–763.

Rodriguez-Bailon, R., B. Bratanova, G.B. Willis, L. Lopez-Rodriguez, A. Sturrock, and S. Loughnan. 2017. "Social Class and Ideologies of Inequality: How They Uphold Unequal Societies." *Journal of Social Issues* 73 (1): pp. 99–116. https://doi.org/10.1111/josi.12206.

Rodríguez-Bailón, R., Á. Sánchez-Rodríguez, E. García-Sánchez, K. Petkanopoulou, and G.B. Willis. 2020. "Inequality Is in the Air: Contextual Psychosocial Effects of Power and Social Class." *Current Opinion in Psychology* 33: pp. 120–125. https://doi.org/10.1016/j.copsyc.2019.07.004.

Sánchez-Rodríguez, Á., J. Jetten, G. Willis, and R. Rodríguez-Bailón. 2019. "High Economic Inequality Makes Us Feel Less Wealthy." *International Review of Social Psychology* 32 (1): p. 17. https://doi.org/10.5334/irsp.333.

Sánchez-Rodríguez, Á., R. Rodríguez-Bailón, and G.B. Willis. 2023. "The Economic Inequality as Normative Information Model (EINIM)." *European Review of Social Psychology* 34: pp. 1–41. https://doi.org/10.1080/10463283.2022.2160555.

Sau, V. 2000. *Diccionario ideológico feminista* [Feminist Ideological Dictionary]. Barcelona: Icaria.

Scheve, K., and D. Stasavage. 2017. "Wealth Inequality and Democracy." *Annual Review of Political Science* 20 (1): pp. 451–468. https://doi.org/10.1146/annurev-polisci-061014-101840.

Schmalor, A., and S.J. Heine. 2022. "The Construct of Subjective Economic Inequality." *Social Psychological and Personality Science* 13 (1): pp. 210–219. https://doi.org/10.1177/1948550621996867.

Schmalor, A., and S.J. Heine. 2021. "Subjective Economic Inequality Decreases Emotional Intelligence, Especially for People of High Social Class." *Social Psychological and Personality Science* 13 (2): pp. 608–617. https://doi.org/10.1177/19485506211024024.

Schwartz-Salazar, S., R. Martínez, and R. Rodríguez-Bailón. Under review. "Cultivating Change: The Role of Feminism in Perceiving and Addressing Inequalities."

Sengupta N.K., L.M. Greaves, D. Osborne, C.G. Sibley. 2017. "The Sigh of the Oppressed: The Palliative Effects of Ideology Are Stronger for People Living in Highly Unequal Neighbourhoods." *British Journal of Social Psychology* 56: pp. 437–454. https://doi.org/10.1111/bjso.12192.

Sheehy-Skeffington, J., and L. Thomsen. 2020. "Egalitarianism: Psychological and Socio-Ecological Foundations." *Current Opinion in Psychology* 32: pp. 146–152. https://doi.org/10.1016/j.copsyc.2019.08.014.

Soler-Martínez, F.M., E. García-Sánchez, and G.B. Willis. 2023. "Concerns About Inequality in Health, Education and Income Jointly Predict Collective Actions." *Revista Latinoamericana de Psicología* 55: p. 99. https://doi.org/10.14349/rlp.2023.v55.12.

Solt, F. 2008. "Economic Inequality and Democratic Political Engagement." *American Journal of Political Science* 52 (1): pp. 48–60. https://doi.org/10.1111/j.1540-5907.2007.00298.x.

Sommet, N., and A.J. Elliot. 2023. "A Competitiveness-Based Theoretical Framework on the Psychology of Income Inequality." *Current Directions in Psychological Science* 32 (4): pp. 318–327. https://doi.org/10.1177/09637214231159563.

Sommet, N., and A.J. Elliot. 2022. "The Effect of Local Income Inequality on Health Is Equivalent to Zero." *Quality of Life Research* 31: pp. 1999–2009.

Sprong, S., J. Jetten, Z. Wang, K. Peters, F. Mols, M. Verkuyten, B. Bastian, A. Ariyanto, F. Autin, N. Ayub, C. Badea, T. Besta, F. Butera, R. Costa-Lopes, L. Cui, C. Fantini, G. Finchilescu, L. Gaertner, M. Gollwitzer, . . . M.J.A. Wohl. 2019. "'Our Country Needs a Strong Leader Right Now': Economic Inequality Enhances the Wish for a Strong Leader." *Psychological Science* 30 (11): pp. 1625–1637. https://doi.org/10.1177/0956797619875472.

Stewart, A.J., N. McCarty, and J.J. Bryson. 2020. "Polarization Under Rising Inequality and Economic Decline." *Science Advances* 6 (50): pp. 21–23. https://doi.org/10.1126/sciadv.abd4201.

Tanjitpiyanond, P., J. Jetten, and K. Peters. 2022. "How Economic Inequality Shapes Social Class Stereotyping." *Journal of Experimental Social Psychology* 98: 104248. https://doi.org/10.1016/j.jesp.2021.104248.

Uskul, A.K., and S. Oishi. 2020. "Editorial Overview: What Is Socio-Ecological Psychology?" *Current Opinion in Psychology* 32: pp. 181–184. https://doi.org/10.1016/j.copsyc.2020.01.001.

Uslaner, E. M., and Brown, M. 2005. "Inequality, Trust, and Civic Engagement." *American Politics Research*, 33 (6): pp. 868–894. https://doi.org/10.1177/1532673X04271903.

Valtorta, R.R., M. Vezzoli, S. Mari, F. Durante, and C. Volpato. 2024. "Measuring Subjective Inequality: Development and Validation of the Perceived Economic Inequality Scale (PEIS)." *Spanish Journal of Psychology* 27: e2. https://doi.org/10.1017/SJP.2024.4.

Velandia-Morales, A., R. Rodríguez-Bailón, and R. Martínez. 2022. "Economic Inequality Increases the Preference for Status Consumption." *Frontiers in Psychology* 12: 809101. https://doi.org/10.3389/fpsyg.2021.809101.

Vezzoli, M., R.R. Valtorta, S. Mari, F. Durante, and C. Volpato. 2023. "Effects of Objective and Subjective Indicators of Economic Inequality on Subjective Well-Being: Underlying Mechanisms." *Journal of Applied Social Psychology* 53 (2): pp. 85–100. https://doi.org/10.1111/jasp.12928.

Wakslak, C.J., J.T. Jost, T.R. Tyler, and E.S. Chen. 2007. "Moral Outrage Mediates the Dampening Effect of System Justification on Support for Redistributive Social Policies." *Psychological Science* 18 (3): pp. 267–274. https://doi.org/10.1111/j.1467-9280.2007.01887.x.

Walasek, L., and G.D.A. Brown. 2015. "Income Inequality and Status Seeking: Searching for Positional Goods in Unequal US States." *Psychological Science* 26 (4): pp. 527–533. doi: https://doi.org/10.1177/0956797614567511.

Waldfogel, H.B., J. Sheehy-Skeffington, O.P. Hauser, A.K. Ho, and N.S. Kteily. 2021. "Ideology Selectively Shapes Attention to Inequality." *Proceedings of the National Academy of Sciences* 118 (14): e2023985118. https://doi.org/10.1073/pnas.2023985118.

Wienk, M.N.A., N.R. Buttrick, and S. Oishi. 2022. The Social Psychology of Economic Inequality, Redistribution, and Subjective Well-Being." *European Review of Social Psychology* 33 (1): pp. 45–80. https://doi.org/10.1080/10463283.2021.1955458.

Wilkinson, R.G., and K.E. Pickett. 2017. "The Enemy Between Us: The Psychological and Social Costs of Inequality." *European Journal of Social Psychology* 47 (1): pp. 11–24. https://doi.org/10.1002/ejsp.2275.

Willis, G.B., E. García-Sánchez, Á. Sánchez-Rodríguez, J.D. García-Castro, and R. Rodríguez-Bailón. 2022. "The Psychosocial Effects of Economic Inequality Depend on Its Perception." *Nature Reviews Psychology* 1: pp. 301–309. https://doi.org/10.1038/s44159-022-00044-0.

Willis, G.B., Y. Uchida, J.D. García-Castro, and K. Takemura. 2024. "High Relational Mobility Is Associated with Perceiving More Economic Inequality in Everyday Life." *Asian Journal of Social Psychology* 00 (1): pp. 1–12. https://doi.org/10.1111/ajsp.12597.

Winkler, H. 2019. "The Effect of Income Inequality on Political Polarization: Evidence from European Regions, 2002–2014." *Economics and Politics* 31 (2): pp. 137–162. https://doi.org/10.1111/ecpo.12129.

Winterich, K.P., and Y. Zhang. 2014. "Accepting Inequality Deters Responsibility: How Power Distance Decreases Charitable Behavior." *Journal of Consumer Research* 41: pp. 274–293. https://doi.org/10.1086/675927

Zmigrod, L. 2022. "A Psychology of Ideology: Unpacking the Psychological Structure of Ideological Thinking." *Perspectives on Psychological Science* 17 (4): pp. 1072–1092. https://doi.org/10.1177/17456916211044140.

Zucker, A.N., and L.Y. Bay-Cheng. 2010. "Minding the Gap Between Feminist Identity and Attitudes: The Behavioral and Ideological Divide Between Feminists and Non-Labelers." *Journal of personality* 78 (6): pp. 1895–1924. https://doi.org/10.1111/j.1467-6494.2010.00673.x.

Chapter 5
Accepting Great Wealth Inside the Nordic Model
The Case of Finnish Wealth Tax Reform

Hanna Kuusela

Introduction

The Nordic countries are well known for their welfare models, established in the aftermath of World War II. Characterized by high taxation, economic redistribution, universal public services, and corporatist bargaining, the model emerged as a blueprint for social stability, economic prosperity, and happiness. The model used to be articulated as a third way between socialism and capitalism, with an "idea that there is a Nordic recipe for how to alleviate the ills of capitalism while avoiding the pitfalls of socialism" (Koivunen et al. 2021, 6).

Yet, the past decades have in many ways challenged this recipe. As Lindh's chapter in this volume shows, the popular support for the Nordic model seems to be in flux, and different commentators have rejected the notion of the Nordic model as a third-way compromise, defining it instead as a combination of extreme individualism and a strong state that enables an efficient market economy (Koivunen et al. 2021, 2).

In concrete terms, the change in the recipe can, for example, be seen in how economic inequalities have developed in the Nordics. The deregulation of the financial markets, followed by structural changes in the 1980s and 1990s, transformed the situation in all Nordic countries. At the turn of the millennium, increases in economic inequalities in the Nordics were among the highest in the OECD. Particularly, new groups of wealthy elites emerged, as wealth and income increasingly accumulated at the top (Aaberge et al.

Hanna Kuusela, *Accepting Great Wealth Inside the Nordic Model*. In: *The Social Acceptance of Inequality*.
Edited by: Francesco Duina and Luca Storti, Oxford University Press.
DOI: 10.1093/oso/9780197814499.003.0005

2018; Atkinson and Piketty 2010; Kuusela and Kantola 2020; OECD 2015; Riihelä et al. 2010).

This chapter analyzes the cultural changes that have been needed to justify the new levels of inequalities in Nordic countries, particularly in Finland. Together with Lindh's chapter, this chapter explores the changing attitudes against the basic principles of the Nordic model, in this case with a focus on the top groups. This chapter depicts how the social acceptance of private accumulated wealth has been constituted anew in times of deepening economic inequalities and wealth accumulation at the top, exploring the changing *moral economies* around wealth accumulation in Finland.

Examining the different legitimization logics used to explain the inequalities driven by the top and the new policies that have followed, the chapter argues that the rising levels of private wealth accumulation have been accompanied by new moral economies or "cultures of private wealth" around the wealthy. Bringing forward current debates on economic inequalities in the intersection of political decision-making, political argumentation, and cultural processes, and following the core questions of this edited collection, the chapter unveils how new structured inequalities have intertwined with cultural processes in Finland. In their introduction to this volume, the editors present four key logics of how actors make sense of unequal economic outcomes. This chapter moves across the different—if not all the mentioned—logics, showing how the acceptance of great wealth in Finland has been driven not only by cultural and institutional logics but also by economic and moral logics, and finally by group and ethnic logics. Most clearly, the chapter examines how Members of Parliament (MPs) articulate an emergent market logic, and concomitant group logic, which together serve to justify inequalities. Finally, it shows how the *cultural* and *moral* norms in Finland get constructed anew by references to *market* and *group logics*.

The chapter gives an overall picture of the new situation based on different qualitative data, while also offering a new empirical case study on the abolition of the wealth tax in Finland in 2006. Given that redistribution—financed by high taxation—has been a core element of the Nordic model and understood as key to social trust and cohesion (Roikonen et al. 2021), this chapter looks at the cultural changes in the Nordic model from the perspective of how a new tax cut was discursively legitimized in the Finnish parliament.

In general, the chapter argues that the last several decades have witnessed significant changes in the ways in which the Finnish culture has approached private accumulated wealth. Rather than accepting new levels of *inequalities*, citizens have been called on to accept new levels of *wealth* with the idea that accumulated domestic wealth benefits the entire country.

Growing Economic Inequalities and the Nordic Model

The Nordic model can be seen both as an empirical, policy-based phenomenon and as a political idea (Koivunen et al. 2021). This chapter keeps both these dimensions in mind by using the concept of moral economy (Sachweh 2012; Sayer 2000, 2007; Svallfors 2006) to interpret how policy changes favoring the wealthy, like the abolition of the wealth tax, have become possible.

Together with other Nordic countries, Finland still tops global indexes for competitiveness, quality of life, prosperity, and equality. More recently, scholars have, however, started to ask "whether the 21st-century Scandinavian recipe for combining stable democracies, individual freedom, economic growth and comprehensive systems for social security is at a crossroad" (Koivunen et al. 2021, 2). Global digital economy, geopolitical tensions and changes in political culture are challenging the very basis of the Nordic model (Koivunen et al. 2021, 2), and the current crisis of the welfare state seems to reflect normative disorder as much as it does fiscal constraints (Sayer 2000).

In Finland, as in most countries, a period of financial deregulation increased wealth and income inequalities. While the income disparities in Finland diminished for decades after World War II (Atkinson et al. 1995), in the 1990s, economic inequalities grew rapidly. Along with other countries, Finland experienced a reversal of the equalization process, witnessing a significant increase in wealth inequality in the late 1990s (in parallel with an increase in income inequality), a leveling off in the early 2000s, and a new increase after the financial crisis (Törmälehto 2019). The abolition of the wealth tax, discussed in this chapter, happened amid these developments.

In addition to the wealth statistics—which are not particularly well suited for capturing the top groups—the changes in wealth inequality can be seen in the Finnish capital income statistics, as a significant part of income in the top groups consists of low-taxed capital income. The development has been fast: the 1% of the population with the highest capital income received about 14% of the total capital income in 1971, about 20% at the beginning of the 1990s, and 35% in 2004 (Riihelä et al. 2010). One reason is that share ownership is highly concentrated in Finland: in 2021, the top 1% owned 72% of all company shares in Finland (Heino 2024). In 2023, the Lorenz curve for financial assets placed Finland somewhere between the United States and Germany, thus, demonstrating that regarding ownership, Finland is not as equal as often thought (LIS 2023).

The shares of taxed wealth of the top groups (0.1% and 0.01%) more or less doubled in the two decades before the abolition of the wealth tax (Törmälehto 2019), and according to estimates, the share of net wealth of the top 1% of Finns grew from 8.1% in 1987 to 14.4% in 2019 (Riihelä and Tuomala 2022). Due to missing data at the top, this is likely to be a conservative estimate. These changes have made the taxation of wealth—in addition to income—a key question for the new conjuncture.

In the long run, such changes in the distribution also necessitate changes in their normative base. This is a topic that has traditionally been analyzed by scholars of "moral economy" (Sachweh 2012; Sayer 2007; Svallfors 2006), a term referring to social and economic exchanges grounded on a horizon of shared norms and values. According to such thinking, the economy is always embedded in social relations, and normative frameworks are seen as important motivations for individual actions, making the moral character of economic relationships an important object of investigation. A moral economy perspective focuses on norms and beliefs that structure economic practices by constituting what is considered acceptable and proper with respect to moral principles like justice, decency, or reciprocity.

In this chapter, I accompany recent research that has identified beliefs and justifications about the legitimacy of inequality (Sachweh 2012, 2014), particularly of unequal distributions, and how these have contributed to policy changes. When economies are understood as being embedded in social relations, moral norms are put into practice by political processes and legal structures, such as tax policies.

Changing Moral Economies in Finland

It is often argued that the Nordic success story was built on solidaristic and universalist ideals and a strong partnership ideology, involving compromises between classes (Kildal and Kuhnle 2005). Instead of celebrating wealth, success, and luxury, Nordic cultures have traditionally promoted a moral economy of equality and solidarity. The main argument of this chapter is that this situation is changing.

In my recent research, I have explored changes in the Nordic moral economy by focusing on different elite discourses concerning private wealth and economic inequalities in Finland since the 1980s. More specifically, I have explored how Finnish top earners (Kuusela 2022), business media (Kuusela 2024b), parliamentarians (Kuusela and Leinonen forthcoming), and mutual fund managers (Kuusela 2024a) have perceived economic inequalities and private wealth in recent times. While my research on mutual fund managers and top earners concerns only one point in history, the studies on parliamentary debates and Finnish business media have a historical time frame from the beginning of the 1980s until the early 2020s. All these data sets point to the same direction: private wealth accumulation has not only become more tolerable in Finland during these decades, but—more precisely—it has become celebrated.

The change is most notable in how Finnish business media has represented wealthy owners over the decades. I have argued elsewhere that the changes in the representations of richness and the rich between 1981 and 2021 demonstrate a rise of a new imaginary, in which private wealth accumulation is valued and perceived as a desirable goal both for individuals and society. The Finnish media bears witness to a new imaginary and new understanding of the social space, characterized by symbolic admiration for rich individuals. In this imaginary, private wealth accumulation—and wealth inequalities—are not only tolerated but also encouraged and idealized (Kuusela 2024b; for Sweden, see Vikström 2024).

Similar changes can be seen in how the Finnish parliament has debated private capital since the early 1980s. Based on our empirical research on the parliamentary discourse, my colleague Leinonen and I argue that there have been significant shifts in how the sociopolitical conflicts associated with, or seen as caused by, private capital have been articulated in the last decades (Kuusela and Leinonen forthcoming). The main shift has concerned the changing spatial dimensions of the conflict and capital's role in it. The conflict that in the 1980s was primarily understood in the parliamentary debates as one between the owners of capital and the workers—and as such as a conflict that gets structured and is felt inside the borders of the nation—has gradually been transformed into a conflict between the nation and different forces outside its borders. Domestic capitalists—who in the 1980s were regularly criticized for capturing too large a share of the national income—have gradually been rhetorically replaced by international capital markets, foreign capital, and venture capitalists, imagined as located outside the political community addressed in the parliamentary talks. Thus the conflict has been depersonalized and abstracted.

By showing how a national parliament of a Nordic welfare state loses sight of those internal dynamics that create inequalities, and the change of which would be in the parliament's power, we demonstrate how, in the era of globalization and financialization, along with jobs, conflict between the owners of capital and the rest has also been outsourced. In the parliamentary debates of the new conjuncture, capital is no longer treated as an entity, the owners of which produce and uphold social relations (which are relatable to the speaker and the audience), but it is, instead, treated as an increasingly uncontrollable force that operates outside national borders. A nationalistic (Fetzer 2022) rereading of good domestic vs. bad foreign wealth is at the core of this contemporary argumentation and can also be seen in the empirical case study discussed in this chapter.

Finally, the interviews among Finnish mutual fund managers, conducted in my research project, demonstrate how the professionals who provide services for the middle and upper-middle classes have also come to celebrate the rich. As I argued earlier, Finnish mutual fund managers primarily see the wealthy as a necessary and salutary part of the economy (Kuusela 2024a). Drawing on the logics of the market to explain inequalities, they perceive the rich as rectifying many of the drawbacks of the (financial) markets, so that the function of the rich individuals is to behave better than the markets. This type of common sense concerning the rich, I argue, helps to legitimize wealth accumulation at the top. In so doing, Finnish financial intermediaries occupied with wealth creation for the ordinary investors help to legitimate extreme wealth accumulation in a country with relatively modest, but rising, inequalities.

Together, these contemporary cultural currents demonstrate, I claim, a new culture of private capital in Finland, paving the way for a new economic regime that can be called neo-accumulationist, meaning a regime characterized by specific advantages for those with accumulated assets (Kuusela 2024b).

In this chapter, I elaborate further on this overall argument by analyzing the parliamentary debates concerning the abolition of the wealth tax in Finland. Many changes visible in other data can be seen in a concise form in these debates concerning the wealth tax in 2006.

Changing Moral Economies of Taxation

In the early twentieth century, modest annual taxes on wealth were introduced across the Western world. Since the 1990s, however, such taxes have been abandoned in many OECD countries (Lierse 2022; Perret 2021). These reforms illustrate an important break from policies that stressed redistribution, as wealth is spread far more unequally than income in most countries.

Scholars have offered different explanations for why the highly progressive tax systems have been deconstructed (Lierse 2022; Perret 2021), pointing to structural changes, such as capital mobility and trade (Lierse 2022; Perret 2021; Swank and Steinmo 2002), international tax competition (Genschel and Schwarz 2011), tax design issues (Perret 2021), and the rise of the knowledge economy (Hope and Limberg 2022.

This chapter (and this volume in general) tries to understand the role of culture and ideas in explaining such isomorphic changes. The cultural dimension is particularly salient for the analysis of the wealth tax. In addition to its economic dimensions, the wealth tax is of great symbolic relevance, as Hilmar and Sachweh (2022) have argued, because it reflects the commitment of the state to redress inequalities generated by the markets.

The cultural legitimization of tax reforms favoring the wealthy have just recently received growing attention. Understanding how such tax cuts have been legitimized in an era of rising inequality has been studied, for example, in Germany (Hilmar and Sachweh 2022; Lichtenstein et al. 2016) and the United States (Rademacher 2017, 2021), and discussed transnationally in review papers (Clark et al. 2020; Perret 2021). Most notably, Hilmar and Sachweh (2022) have investigated how the abolishment of the wealth tax in Germany, a country with high levels of wealth inequality, was debated in the parliament over a period of twenty years. One key finding of this previous research has been that arguments emphasizing potentially negative economic consequences of taxing wealth are prominent (Lichtenstein et al. 2016; Rieder and Theine 2019).

My study focuses on one moment, that of the abolition of the tax. The debates concerning the abolition can be understood as the intensification, or a moment of crystallization, of the new moral economy in Finland.

The Abolition of the Wealth Tax in Finland

The Finnish wealth tax was abolished by a coalition government formed by the Centre Party (KESK, a social liberal party), the Social Democratic Party (SDP), and The Swedish People's Party (RKP, a small centrist party). It is notable that the reform was introduced by a government in which The National Coalition Party (KOK, a center-right liberal conservative party), strongly in favor of the abolition, was not included, and in which the SDP held the position of minister of finance. This means that a significant part of the opposition was also in favor of the reform, whereas those forces, most notably the SDP, who could ideologically have been critical were in fact proposing it. So, in terms of changing political conjunctures toward the rich, the role of the Social Democrats seems to be key (Hilmar and Sachweh 2022). As Lierse (2022) has noted, the societal consensus for wealth tax cuts has been particularly pronounced under corporatism, where capital and labor have established an agreement not to tax wealth in return for (alleged) growth and employment.

The debate analyzed in this chapter includes altogether 174 individual parliamentary speeches during four plenaries. The most active debaters were the members of the two opposition parties: the KOK, with forty-six speeches; and the Left Alliance of Finland (VAS), with thirty-five speeches. The largest parties in the government, KESK and the SDP, were little less active, with twenty-nine and twenty-seven speeches. The Greens (VIHR), who were in opposition, followed with fifteen speeches, and the smaller parties, the Christian Democrats (KD), The Finns (PS), RKP, each held a few speeches (twelve by KD, nine by PS, and one by RKP).

The number of speeches more or less corresponds with the sizes of the parties, with the exception that the opposition parties were more active in the debate than government parties. The government's proposal was approved by clear majority. The SDP, KESK, KOK, and RKP were in favor of the abolition, with some social democrats voting against it and some being absent from the vote, whereas the VIHR, VAS, and PS were against the reform. The KD were split in the vote.

In the analysis, I focus on those speakers who were in favor of the reform, leaving criticism outside the scope, as the favorable opinions—which also turned out to be hegemonic—are the most significant for understanding the cultural acceptance of inequalities. It is noteworthy that those thirty-six SDP members who voted for the reform did not speak in the plenaries *at all.* Only those SDP members who voted against (seven) or those who were absent from the vote (nine) voiced their opinions publicly. (Exceptions were the minister of finance, who proposed the reform, and one MP, Arto Bryggare, who only noted that he agreed with the reform.) This implies that the SDP had challenges in legitimizing the reform discursively.

The most important arguments in favor of the reform can be grouped into three frames. The MPs supported the reform mainly by referring to (1) international competition, (2) the dynamic effects of the tax cut, and (3) the need to support domestic ownership. In many cases, these three frames overlap, but, for clarity, I discuss them separately. In addition to these frames, some MPs also argued that the tax should be abolished because it has been avoided regularly.

None of these arguments are new to the scholarship, which has been analyzing neoliberal rhetoric and trickle-down ideology since the 1990s. On the contrary, when compared with discussions in other countries, the Finnish case shows how homogeneous the argumentation has been across countries and regions (cf. Hilmar and Sachweh 2022; Lichtenstein et al. 2016; Perret 2021; Rademacher 2017, 2021). This isomorphism and its roots are certainly a feature that could be further investigated in future research.

An Answer to Global Competition

The first, and perhaps the strongest, argument in the plenary discussions on the wealth tax is international competition. MP Olavi Ala-Nissilä (Transcript 104/2005), a member of the KOK—an opposition party in favor of the reform—and a regular commentator in the debate, supported the reform by stating how "we are living in a competitive global economy, we are no longer living in a closed economy. . . . The idea that tax policy in Finland can be made without considering what is happening around us is wrong."[1]

Similarly, his party peer Ruut Sjöblom (Transcript 105/2005) referred to competition between countries: "International tax competition is directed at many factors of production, of which capital is the most mobile and sensitive to relocation. Therefore, the tax treatment of capital must be competitive, at least within the European Union. . . . In the OECD countries, wealth tax is levied in only seven countries apart from Finland. Some of them are still considering abolishing it."

These comments reflect the German debates of the 1990s, in which conservatives referred to the harsh realities of globalization, offering a narrative about how competitive markets and the mechanism of capital flight necessitate that national governments reduce taxes (Hilmar and Sachweh 2022). The tendencies toward globalization and capital deregulation in the 1980s rapidly reformed the economic policies and discourses in several countries toward what Jessop (2002) has labeled the Schumpeterian competition state. The main aim of the competition state is to secure economic growth within its borders by promoting conditions that are "deemed vital for success in competition with economic actors and spaces located in other states" (Jessop 2002, 96). The tendency toward isomorphism is noteworthy here, as different countries were set to compete with exactly the same means.

In the Finnish parliament, global tax competition is repeatedly associated with the attempt to keep capital inside the borders of the country or attract further capital. As KOK MP Reijo Paajanen (134/2005) stated, "it is extremely important for Finland to succeed internationally, and we must respond to this tax competition in various forms. I can see that the abolition of wealth tax will keep capital in Finland and thus also provide the dynamism we need."

Global competition has occupied the common sense of the parliamentarians to the extent that only mentioning that other countries have abolished the tax is often enough to support the reform in Finland. As KOK MP Kimmo Sasi (134/2005) noted, "The wealth tax is a very rare form of tax internationally. Until 50 years ago, 30 years ago, it was relatively common, but today more and more countries have abolished the wealth tax, and for that reason we too have had the reason to come to the same conclusion."

International comparison is also at the heart of the argumentation of SDP Minister of Finance Eero Heinäluoma (Transcript 104/2005), and of the government, "When you look at the justification for the government bill, it is clear that this is a very rare law in the world today and has been removed from many countries that are very close to our model of society."

Finally, competition also works as an argument to accept that the abolition of the tax favors those who are well-off. Letting inequalities grow is even considered ethical, as noted in this speech by Seppo Särkiniemi (Transcript 134/2005), a KESK MP:

> National economies are also competing with each other these days. It is true that the [abolition of the] wealth tax brings income to a section of the population that would not necessarily need it for consumption otherwise,

> but if this increases the propensity to invest and if it makes Finland better off as an economy than others, then I think this is an ethically sustainable solution.

Here moral, cultural, and economic logics intertwine. The reference to ethical behavior implies that the moral economy in Finland has already been shifting toward accepting that globalization produces inequalities, as if by necessity. Unavoidable competition becomes a moral reason to accept growing inequalities. Such comments uphold a cultural notion of (accumulated) private capital as something that needs to be served for it to benefit the society at large and that lowering taxes is an essential part of such service to the capital. As Bramall (2023, 101) writes, common sense about taxation is often strongly shaped by the idea to reduce taxes: "the orientation towards low taxation both in neo-liberal ideology and economic practice has been comparatively consistent, helping to secure its sedimentation in common sense." The common sense of the Finnish parliamentarians stresses competition instead of equality, and lower taxes instead of redistribution. These choices on what is being emphasized are significant from the perspective of the cultural acceptance of inequalities.

Belief in Dynamic Effects

In the parliamentarians' discourses, global competition is perhaps the most straightforward reason to remove the tax, while a more complex set of argumentation revolves around the mission to save jobs and the economy by not taxing wealth. This ideology—that links tax cuts to the boosting of the job market—informs the argumentation of all supporters, including the SDP Minister of Finance. He introduced his proposal by saying it is one in a series of reforms that "aim at strengthening employment performance and economic dynamism" (Heinäluoma, Transcript 104/2005). Similarly, Ala-Nissilä (Transcript 134/2005) proposed that the reform "is a very good package and will help create the dynamism that the Finnish economy needs, that domestic ownership needs, and that employment needs to improve." Just like the German conservatives who linked the competition trope to a much broader concern, claiming that German jobs depend on it (Hilmar and Sachweh 2022), Finnish parliamentarians link competition, employment, and economic dynamism together.

MPs regularly present the wealth tax as detrimental for economic growth. Referring to the (alleged) negative economic consequences of taxing wealth (Lichtenstein et al. 2016; Rieder and Theine 2019), Ala-Nissilä (Transcript 104/2015), for example, explained:

> The wealth tax has led to a sub-optimal channeling of investments in the economy, resulting in economic losses. The wealth tax has reduced government tax revenues through tax planning to avoid wealth taxation, for example by transferring funds to foreign deposits. Such practices are not conducive to jobs and entrepreneurship in Finland.

Previous research has shown how proponents of tax cuts for the rich often argue for their beneficial effects on economic performance (Hope and Limberg 2022; Lierse 2022; Rademacher 2017, 2021). As Bramall (2023, 99–100) writes, for decades, common-sense thinking about taxation has aligned the interests of the rich with the public interest, suggesting that taxation inhibits the entrepreneurial risk-taking of society's wealth creators. Bramall (2023) writes that such ideas legitimate wealth inequalities by implying that innovations derive (solely) from the risk-taking of entrepreneurs. Also, the German debates on wealth tax, studied by Hilmar and Sachweh (2022, 475), invoked "a language of fragility, protection, and safety, arguing that there is a need to protect the flow of capital in order to salvage jobs." In Germany, growth narratives highlighting tax cuts for the rich have appeared successful when they have been moralized by arguing that they generate a universal common good (Rademacher 2017, 2021). Arguing "that ending the wealth tax is in the interest of the economy as a whole, not of particular groups in society," was a strong trope in the German debates (Hilmar and Sachweh 2022, 476). This line of reasoning, focusing on efficiency gains and the removal of behavioral distortions, has also been behind several tax reforms in the United States (Gale and Samwick 2017). These arguments largely derive from the logics of the market and economy, discussed in this volume's introduction: Actors approve of growing inequalities because they view them as resulting from market-driven resource allocation that generates great wealth and lifts everyone up.

Slightly counterintuitively, in the Finnish debate, tax revenues are said to be saved by removing the tax, thanks to the assumed "dynamic effects." As MP Ala-Nissilä (Transcript 104/2005) stated, "I am quite sure that the dynamic effects of this tax proposal will have a greater impact on public finances than this loss of EUR 70 million in tax revenue."

His party peer, MP Sasi (Transcript 134/2005), described the dynamic effects as common sense:

> Then there has been discussion about whether the proposal has dynamic effects. I must say that common sense, if there is any, shows that the lower the tax on capital, the more likely it is that Finnish investments will remain in Finland and that we will also have the opportunity to attract foreign investments to Finland. At the moment, the biggest problem for Finns is that foreigners are not investing enough in Finland and that Finns are also moving their wealth out of Finland to other countries. In this respect, it is quite clear that Finland's competitiveness from these investments, will clearly be strengthened. And the more capital we have, the more opportunities we have to invest, and the more we invest, the more employment we have, and of course employment is the most important goal that every government must have in economic policy.

This comment deconstructs well the chain of argument, at the end of which is, "of course, employment" as the most important goal.

The MPs supporting the reform further hypothesized on the levels of the dynamic effects, concluding that the abolition of tax would not have negative fiscal effects. KESK MP Mauri Pekkarinen (Transcript 134/2005), said, "It is easy to believe the message that the respected chairman of the Finance Committee has cultivated here, when he testified how the dynamic effects of this reform are significant. I cannot say how significant. It may even be greater than the tax loss, but in any case, it will be very significant, up to tens, perhaps even hundreds of millions."

Such dynamic effects have recently been criticized by Hope and Limberg (2022) who studied the economic consequences of major tax reductions on the rich in eighteen OECD countries between 1965 and 2015. Estimating the effects of these reforms on key macroeconomic aggregates, they conclude that tax cuts for the rich lead to higher income inequality in the short- and medium term. Furthermore, according to them, reforms that rely on supply side theories do not have any significant effect on economic growth or unemployment, providing evidence against the idea—also prominent in the Finnish debates—that tax cuts for the rich trickle down.

Finally, according to Ala-Nissilä (Transcript 134/2005), "the dynamic effects are such that they safeguard the welfare society in Finland." This is an important aspect in terms of the cultural and moral legitimization of growing inequalities. Here, tax cuts are in fact deemed necessary to save the

Nordic model. As shown in my research with Kantola (2024) on Finnish top earners, members of the top groups often argue in favor of the welfare state by proposing cuts. According to this analysis, the top earners have created an establishment fantasy, being supportive of both the dismantling of the welfare state and its core principles by suggesting that it is possible to save the Nordic model by removing its central features like high taxation. Equally, in the parliamentarians' speeches, reforms that undermine the key principles of the welfare state, such as redistribution, are legitimized by referring to the moral need to save the welfare model. This "keeping the model while cutting it" (Kantola and Kuusela 2024) is an important trope to analyze when trying to understand the social acceptance of growing inequalities, as it promises to save what is still culturally and morally valued by many.

Support for Good Domestic Owners

Finally, the frameworks that emphasize global competition and dynamic effects give birth to a cultural and moral figure that, in many ways, explains why the growing inequalities driven by the top have been accepted with relatively little protest in Finland. In addition to a general discourse that presents the wealthy as important economic actors who generate growth and jobs, several commentators also engage in the construction of a more specific figure—that of the good domestic owner. This morally loaded figure is central for the legitimization of the new levels of inequalities and the new advantages for the top groups. Primarily, it grows out of group logics, discussed in this chapter's introduction: Actors see growing inequalities as acceptable or even desirable because they think that the world can be divided into "superior" collectivities that are more deserving than others. In my study, this group logics is attached to Finland as a nation, as opposed to other nations, and it quite peculiarly encourages acceptance of inequalities within a group (of Finns) to ensure that Finland succeeds vis-à-vis other nations.

In the parliament, the tax reform is repeatedly framed as supporting domestic ownership. KESK MP Pekka Nousiainen (105/2005) articulated this explicitly: "Above all, I think this is part of the Finnish corporate tax policy and the policy to support domestic ownership and entrepreneurship." Similarly, his party peer, Kimmo Tiilikainen (Transcript 134/2005), stated how the reform will "support the strengthening of entrepreneurship and Finnish ownership and thus employment." Finally, KESK MP Jukka Vihriälä

(Transcript 104/2005) saw the reform as part of a policy that advances "domestic ownership."

In other words, the abolition of the tax is presented as a means to guarantee that private capital stays in Finland. As KOK MP Pekka Kuosmanen (Transcript 134/2005) noted:

> [Y]ou don't have to be at all worried about the abolition of the wealth tax. For us, the most important thing is that capital remains in Finland. Capital has no home. Capital flows across national borders. In that sense, if we want to safeguard employment and investments, since investments are already escaping abroad . . . you will understand that the government has for once made the right decision when it abolishes the wealth tax.

Capital has no home, but if it has, it should be Finland. The domestic owner, as opposed to foreign owners, is repeatedly associated with enhanced employment. As KOK MP Arto Satonen (Transcript 104/2005) said:

> The government has taken the first step towards promoting domestic ownership and thus creating jobs here. Many of those who stand to benefit from this are family entrepreneurs, owner-managers, who employ over 100,000 people in this country. This will certainly have a very big impact. And the people who will benefit from this are those who work in these companies.

Here the workers are identified as the true beneficiaries of the tax reform. The general trickle-down ideology is given a more specific meaning: when the wealth of the *domestic owners* is not taxed, the *domestic workers* will automatically benefit. The same was said by KOK MP Jari Koskinen (Transcript 134/2005), according to whom, the reform "supports blue-white [the colors in the Finnish flag] ownership. I think that it is for the benefit of all of us Finns."

Just as in the argumentation concerning the dynamic effects, domestic rich individuals are represented here as forces that benefit the entire society. This notion is also found in other Finnish data from recent decades: Just like the fund managers (Kuusela 2024a) and the business journalists (Kuusela 2024b) who celebrate the rich, parliamentarians who subscribe to a new cultural understanding of accumulated domestic (and private) wealth see it as beneficial to everyone.

KESK MP Mikko Alatalo (Transcript 134/2005) also referred to jobs provided by domestic owners: "This wealth tax applies to around 3,000 family businesses in Finland. They are currently significant employers. They have paid a kind of employment tax for employing people in Finland and not exporting those jobs abroad." Alatalo portrayed family businesses as socially responsible companies, "not all of which may have huge incomes" and as the backbone of the national economy:

> These family businesses are still key to bringing Finland up to the level of the rest of Europe and the rest of the world in the service sector. The service sector provides employment even when big companies are squeezing out jobs. In fact, the future success of the internal market will very much depend on the service sector.

Just as in Germany, where the "Mittlestand" is often referenced in conjunction with the common good (Hilmar and Sachweh 2022, 475), in Finland, small and medium-sized family businesses are regularly used in the argumentation.

Such comments show the significance of nationalist discourse, everyday nationalism, and group ethics in framing narratives of economic and institutional change or economic policymaking (Fetzer 2022). Drawing on nationalist group ethics, such arguments draw a neat line between domestic and foreign owners.

I have argued elsewhere (Kuusela and Leinonen forthcoming), how, during the past few decades, the (good) domestic owner has become an important ideological figure, helping to obscure economic inequalities within countries. Instead of discussing how the share of national wealth, or income, gets distributed among different social groups, the new debate focuses on a nationalist demarcation between domestic and foreign (owners), helping to legitimize the rising levels of inequalities within a country. While in the Finnish debates of the 1980s capital accumulation was still associated with Finnish capitalists, whose privileged position was criticized, in the 1990s and the 2000s, unhealthy accumulation gets associated anew with foreign investors, venture capital, and Chinese or American pension funds, instead of with the domestic rich.

Quite curiously, however, in several parliamentary speeches these virtuous domestic owners are discussed side by side with the figure of the tax-avoider, as many MPs argue that the wealth tax was inefficient because it was easy to avoid. According to speakers, the wealth tax is "full of loopholes" (Pekkarinen, Transcript 134/2005), it has "provided exceptionally high opportunities for tax planning" (Heinäluoma, Transcript 104/2005), and it has been "a bad tax from a technical point of view" (Ala-Nissilä, Transcript 104/2005). Because the tax had been easy to circumvent, some speakers use these loopholes as a reason to eliminate it. Bramall (2023, 100, 104–5) has analyzed "the new visibility of tax-avoiding elites" in media and political discourse. This figure is used also in various speeches of Finnish parliamentarians, but this time as an unavoidable evil. Rather than trying to fix the loopholes, several parliamentarians use the figure of the tax-avoider as a reason to abolish the tax.

This figure is even used to argue that the true beneficiaries of the reform are ordinary citizens. Minister of Trade and Industry Pekkarinen (Transcript 134/2005), from the KESK, argued:

> The question was raised here, who will pay for this, this 60, 70, 80 million [of lost revenues]. Those who can play the games of the markets do not have to pay taxes. Many of them do not pay taxes. Those [who pay the wealth tax] are many times reasonably ordinary grandmothers and grandfathers who own some shares, some housing shares here and there, or a farm here and there, etc., just ordinary citizens.

Interestingly, both the figure of the tax-avoiding rich and the figure of the diligent business family are used to argue for the same tax cut, so that, in the end, the reform is said to benefit common citizens, grandmothers, and grandfathers, instead of the wealthy who work for the common good but are not being taxed anyway.

Conclusion

The moral economy enabling the tax cut for the rich owners in Finland largely builds on the transnational trickle-down ideology and a competition frame that emphasizes dynamic effects of tax cuts. Argumentation that draws on market logic and concomitant group logic serve to justify inequalities, as they are used to explain how reforms favoring the well-off benefit the economy and the society at large.

One key element in this argumentation has been the construction of the figure of the good domestic owner and a nationalistic demarcation between good (domestic) vs. bad (foreign) wealth. As after the deregulation of the financial market, no juridical boundaries between domestic and foreign capital exist anymore, these boundaries must be constructed culturally and morally to legitimate domestic policies that favor the (domestic) owners, still affected by national decision-making.

Together, the legitimizing logics discussed in this chapter point toward a larger cultural change in Finland that has made the pursuit of private wealth not only an acceptable but even more so, a desirable goal for all citizens. Rather than accepting new levels of inequalities, Finns have been called on to accept new levels of wealth with the idea that this benefits everyone and that this accumulation of wealth does not leave others with less.

While at first glance, changes in the perception of top groups might appear insignificant, from a moral economy point of view this is relevant: if norms of solidarity and equality are replaced with norms highlighting the importance of rich individuals, in the long run, this means a break from the basic principles of the Nordic model. Locally, this is a significant change. In future, understanding better both the local specificities and the transnational similarities of such transformations and their legitimization would benefit from comparatively oriented research.

Note

1. From here on, I refer to the transcripts of the plenary sessions of the parliament by using the number of the transcript.

References

Aaberge, R., C. André, A. Boschini, L. Calmfors, K. Gunnarsson, M. Hermansen, A. Langørgen, P. Lindgren, C. Orsetta, J. Pareliussen, P-O Robling, J. Roine, and J. Egholt Søg. 2018. "Increasing Income Inequality in the Nordics." Nordic Economic Policy Review 2018.

Atkinson, A.B., and T. Piketty. 2010. *Top Incomes: A Global Perspective*. Oxford: Oxford University Press.

Atkinson, A.B., L. Rainwater, and T. M. Smeeding. 1995. *Income Distribution in OECD Countries: Evidence from the Luxembourg Income Study*. OECD Social Policy Studies 18. Paris: OECD Publishing.

Bramall, R. 2023. "What Are We Going to Do About the Rich? Anti-Elitism, Neo-Liberal Common Sense and the Politics of Taxation." In *The Cultural Politics of Anti-Elitism*, edited by M. Ege and J. Springer, pp. 99–119. London: Routledge.

Clark, E., V. Gronwald, R.A. Guerrero Fernandez, and J.E. Ramírez Casillas. 2020. "Political Economy of a Net Wealth Tax." Wealth Tax Commission Background Paper No. 123.

Fetzer, T. 2022. "Beyond 'Economic Nationalism': Towards a New Research Agenda for the Study of Nationalism in Political Economy." *Journal of International Relations and Development* 25 (1): pp. 235–259.

Gale, W.G., and A.A. Samwick. 2017. "Effects of Income Tax Changes on Economic Growth." In *The Economics of Tax Policy*, edited by A.J. Auerbach and K. Smetters, pp. 13–39. New York: Oxford University Press.

Genschel, P., and P. Schwarz. 2011. "Tax Competition: A Literature Review." *Socio-Economic Review* 9: pp. 339–370.
Heino, S. 2024. *Rikkaiden vero*. Helsinki: Kalevi Sorsa säätiö.
Hilmar, T., and P. Sachweh. 2022. "'Poison to the Economy': (Un-)Taxing the Wealthy in the German Federal Parliament from 1996 to 2016." *Social Justice Research* 35 (4): pp. 462–489.
Hope, D., and J. Limberg. 2022. "The Economic Consequences of Major Tax Cuts for the Rich." *Socio-Economic Review* 20 (2): pp. 539–559.
Jessop, B. 2002. *The Future of the Capitalist State*. Cambridge: Polity Press.
Kantola, A., and H. Kuusela. 2024. "Vanguard Fantasies: The Wealthy Upper Classes as Politically Spirited Wealth Elite Establishment." *Sociological Review* 72 (2): pp. 359–377.
Kildal, N., and S. Kuhnle. 2005. *Normative Foundations of the Welfare State: The Nordic Experience*. London: Routledge.
Koivunen, A., J. Holmén, and J. Ojala. 2021. *Nordic Economic, Social and Political Model*. London: Routledge.
Kuusela, H. 2024a. "Better Than the Markets: Mutual Fund Managers' Perceptions of the Rich." *Sociology* 58 (1): pp. 213–230.
Kuusela, H. 2022. "The Hyperopia of Wealth: The Cultural Legitimation of Economic Inequalities by Top Earners." *Socio-Economic Review* 20 (2): pp. 515–538.
Kuusela, H. 2024b. "The Rise of the Owners and the Neo-Accumulationist Imaginary: Changing Perceptions of Private Wealth and Ownership in Finnish Business Media Between 1981–2021." *Economy and Society* 53 (4): pp. 651–674. doi:https://doi.org/10.1080/03085147.2024.2406088
Kuusela, H., and A. Kantola. 2020. "The Role of Ownership in Creating Top Incomes: Top 0.1% of Earners in Finland." In *Accumulating Capital Today: Contemporary Strategies of Profit and Dispossessive Policies*, edited by M. Benquet and T. Bourgeron, pp. 181–195. London: Routledge.
Kuusela, H., and P. Leinonen. Forthcoming. "Outsourcing Conflict: A Conjunctural Analysis of the Finnish Parliament's Discussions on Capital Between 1980–2020."
Lichtenstein, D., M. Rhomberg, and M. Böhme. 2016. "Konsonant oder interessengeleitet? Eine frameanalyse zur Berichterstattung über die Vermögensteuer im Wahljahr 2013" [Consonant or Interest-Led? A Frame Analysis of Reporting on the Wealth Tax in the 2013 Election Year]. In *Understanding Inequality: Social Costs and Benefits*, edited by A. Machin and N. Stehr, pp. 326–346. Wiesbaden: Springer VS.
Lierse, H. 2022. "Globalisation and the Societal Consensus of Wealth Tax Cuts." *Journal of European Public Policy* 29 (5): pp. 748–766.
LIS. 2023. Luxembourg Wealth Study Database. http://www.lisdatacenter.org/our-data/lws-database/. Luxembourg: LIS Cross-National Data Center.
OECD. 2015. *In It Together: Why Less Inequality Benefits All*. Paris: OECD Publishing.
Perret, S. 2021. "Why Were Most Wealth Taxes Abandoned and Is This Time Different?" *Fiscal Studies* 42 (3–4): pp. 539–563.
Rademacher, I. 2017. *Common Ground: Justifications of Neoliberal Tax Cuts in the US and Germany*. Osnabrück: University of Osnabrück.
Rademacher, I. 2021. "Winning the Votes for Institutional Change: How Discursive Acts of Compromise Shaped Radical Income Tax Reforms in the United States." *Policy Studies* 43 (6): pp. 1173–1194.
Rieder, M., and H. Theine. 2019. "'Piketty Is a Genius, But . . .': An Analysis of Journalistic Delegitimation of Thomas Piketty's Economic Policy Proposals." *Critical Discourse Studies* 16 (3): pp. 248–263.
Riihelä, M., R. Sullström, and M. Tuomala. 2010. "Trends in Top Income Shares in Finland 1966–2007." Tampere Economic Working Papers, University of Tampere.
Riihelä, M., and M. Tuomala. 2022. "Verotuksen rooli tulo- ja varallisuuserojen taustalla" [The Role of Taxation Behind Income and Wealth Differences]. In *Eriarvoisuuden tila Suomessa 2022*, edited by A. Rajavuori, pp. 19–50. Helsinki: Kalevi Sorsa säätiö.

Roikonen, P., J. Ojala, and J. Eloranta. 2021. "More or Less Equality? Facts, Debates, and Policies Related to the Nordic Model." In *The Nordic Economic, Social and Political Model*, edited by A. Koivunen, J. Ojala, and J. Holmén, pp. 62–91. London: Routledge.

Sachweh, P. 2012. "The Moral Economy of Inequality: Popular Views on Income Differentiation, Poverty and Wealth." *Socio-Economic Review* 10 (3): pp. 419–445.

Sachweh, P. 2014. "Unequal by Origin or by Necessity? Popular Explanations of Inequality and Their Legitimatory Implications." *European Journal of Cultural and Political Sociology* 1 (4): pp. 323–346.

Sayer, A. 2000. "Moral Economy and Political Economy." *Studies in Political Economy* 61: pp. 79–103.

Sayer, A. 2007. "Moral Economy as Critique." *New Political Economy* 12: pp. 261–270.

Svallfors, S. 2006. *The Moral Economy of Class: Class and Attitudes in Comparative Perspective*. Stanford: Stanford University Press.

Swank, D., and S. Steinmo. 2002. "The New Political Economy of Taxation in Advanced Capitalist Democracies." *American Journal of Political Science* 46 (3): pp. 642–655.

Törmälehto, V.-M. 2019. "Tulo-, kulutus- ja varallisuuseroista Suomessa" [About Income, Consumption and Wealth Differences in Finland]. *Kansantaloudellinen aikakauskirja*, 1/2019, pp. 41–65.

Transcript 104/2005. Plenary Session of the Finnish Parliament on October 12, 2005. https://www.eduskunta.fi/FI/taysistunto/Sivut/Taysistuntojen-poytakirjat.aspx.

Transcript 105/2005. Plenary Session of the Finnish Parliament on October 13, 2005. https://www.eduskunta.fi/FI/taysistunto/Sivut/Taysistuntojen-poytakirjat.aspx.

Transcript 134/2005. Plenary Session of the Finnish Parliament on December 8, 2005. https://www.eduskunta.fi/FI/taysistunto/Sivut/Taysistuntojen-poytakirjat.aspx.

Vikström, A. 2024. *The Mediated Representation of the Super-Rich: Secrecy, Wealth Taxation and the Tensions of Neoliberal Capitalism*. Örebro: Örebro University.

PART II
MORAL LOGICS

Chapter 6
What We Believe About Inequality Is Paramount
Shared Narratives Despite Diverging Paths in East Asia

Joanna Kitsnik and Carola Hommerich

Introduction

While global inequality has declined over the past several decades (Milanovic 2016), inequality within countries has increased, particularly in wealthier nations. This trend is driven by a complex interplay of factors, including globalization and the diffusion and impact of neoliberal ideas. By delving into specific ideologies and underlying narratives, we uncover how socioeconomic inequality becomes ingrained and accepted within societies. This chapter aligns with the overall goal of this volume: examining the various reasonings and logics that individuals adopt to justify their acceptance of economic inequalities. We argue that, by contributing to the moral logics behind accepting inequality, narratives that emphasize individual responsibility for economic success or failure, belief in meritocracy, hard work, or prioritizing individual freedom over equality play a significant role in discussions about economic inequality. These narratives, particularly those related to income inequality, are widespread and deeply entrenched in developed market economies, regardless of the specific type of capitalism in place (Kitsnik 2023). In this chapter, we investigate the extent to which these internalized inequality narratives explain individual acceptance of income disparities, especially compared to the impact of an individual's structural position.

While there has been a significant increase in cross-national comparisons on how individuals perceive and justify income inequality, these studies

Joanna Kitsnik and Carola Hommerich, *What We Believe About Inequality Is Paramount*. In: *The Social Acceptance of Inequality*. Edited by: Francesco Duina and Luca Storti, Oxford University Press. © Oxford University Press (2025). DOI: 10.1093/oso/9780197814499.003.0006 have primarily focused on Western countries (Blekesaune and Quadagno 2003; Finseraas 2009; Hadler 2005; Heuer et al. 2020; Linos and West 2003; McCall 2013; Roex et al. 2019). Despite a few exceptions (Kim et al. 2018; Tay 2015), comparative research on the economic powerhouses in East Asia has been so far notably scarce. For this reason, we focus on three economically developed East Asian countries—Japan, South Korea, and Taiwan—as representatives of an economically powerful, yet under-researched region. This allows us to illustrate the universal character of certain ideologies that contribute to similar patterns of inequality acceptance regardless of unsynchronized political and socioeconomic pathways. As such, our chapter complements Barnes's comparative analysis of twenty-nine countries (Chapter 2 in this volume) by placing a focus on East Asia.

Japan, South Korea, and Taiwan have all been labeled "developmental states" (Chi and Kwon 2012; Jones 1990), with their governments strongly pushing for fast economic growth to catch up with the already developed West. During this process of "compressed modernity" (Kyung-Sup 2010), social policies were subordinate to macroeconomic policies (Holliday 2000; Holliday and Wilding 2003; Kim et al. 2018), with little room for topics of social justice, social rights, and redistribution. While the rapid economic growth undergone by these countries may have increased the average standard of living, it has also been paired with more or less rapid increases in objective inequality. Still, as the seemingly successful West functions as a blueprint for the promise of economic prosperity, this development comes with an acceptance of inequality as a "necessary evil." To analyze the relationship between dominant narratives about economic inequality and the acceptance of such inequality across these three countries, we utilize a cross-sectional subset of the latest wave (2017–20) of the World Values Survey (WVS) for Japan ($N = 685$), South Korea ($N = 1202$), and Taiwan ($N = 1069$) (Haerpfer et al. 2020).

In the following sections, we first give a short overview of the different growth trajectories of our three countries and outline how individuals in Japan, South Korea, and Taiwan have responded to increasing inequalities over the past decades. Then, following an extended discussion of the most common inequality-legitimizing narratives, we introduce our empirical analysis of the effects of inequality-legitimizing narratives on inequality acceptance in our three East Asian countries.

Response to Rising Inequality in Japan, South Korea, and Taiwan

While similar in terms of recent trends of increasing economic inequality, Japan, South Korea, and Taiwan took different paths in their economic development.

The first East Asian country to successfully modernize, Japan experienced a period of fast economic growth during the 1970s and 1980s, which led to tangible improvements of living standards for large parts of the population. Since the burst of the so-called bubble economy in the early 1990s, however, the country has encountered big challenges to its economy, struggling with the effects of economic stagnation and a decreasing working-age population. Efforts to revitalize the economy have resulted in a stark segmentation of Japan's labor market, with more than a third of all workers being employed in part-time or temporary work by 2020 (Hommerich 2024). While this has led to levels of income inequality above the OECD average (OECD 2006), Japan is still often mistakenly looked on as a success story of equitable growth. Within Japan, the self-view has only slowly shifted from that of a "general middle-class society" (*sōchūryū shakai*) (Chiavacchi 2008; Chiavacchi and Hommerich 2017) to that of a "gap society" (*kakusa shakai*) marked by growing inequality (Tachibanaki 2005, 2006). While disposable household incomes increased in all other OECD countries over the past three decades, Japan has been an exception to this trend. Real incomes of those at the bottom of the income ladder have decreased compared to the mid-1980s (OECD 2011). Surprisingly, however, research on attitudes toward subjective income inequality indicates that the Japanese were relatively content with existing income inequalities throughout the 1990s and 2000s (Tay 2015). This acceptance of the unequal income distribution has been attributed to the mechanisms of the dual labor market, where non-regular workers and women are paid less and accept this pay disparity as just (Arita et al. 2019). More recent data, however, shows that the Japanese have become increasingly critical of growing inequalities and the increasing income gap (Pew Research Center 2019). This criticism, for example, is reflected in trends of subjective class identification, with fewer people identifying themselves as belonging to the middle class and more identifying themselves as belonging to the working class. The way people self-identify has also grown to be more closely connected to their actual objective social status over the past three decades, indicating a more realistic view of societal hierarchy compared to the economic boom years of the 1970s and 1980s (Hommerich and Kikkawa 2019; Hommerich et al. 2021). Over the same period, however, belief in the decisive role of education for economic success has weakened, and acknowledgment of non-meritocratic factors has increased (Kobayashi 2020). The shift in perspective is especially significant considering that Japan's economic and industrial growth in the 1970s and 1980s was largely attributed to the educational expansion among the population. Overall, rising awareness of growing income inequality comes with an increase in anxieties in the Japanese population and a weakening of social bonds (Hommerich 2024).

During the 1980s, rapid economic growth in South Korea—also known as the "Miracle on the Han River"—continued. This prioritized industrialization through a combination of state planning and private entrepreneurship, with family-owned conglomerates known as *chaebols* playing a central role. The influence of *chaebols* persisted even after the transition to democracy in the late 1980s and 1990s. The 1990s and 2000s saw a shift from labor-intensive to technology-driven industries, benefiting skilled labor but resulting in job insecurity and wage stagnation for others. While Japan's recognition of the disintegration of the social fabric and socioeconomic stability has been lagging behind the objective reality, the public opinion in South Korea has responded more promptly to increasingly unequal realities. Since the financial crisis in 2008, South Koreans have perceived their society as severely unequal with limited social mobility (Choi 2013; Kim et al. 2018). Yet, even earlier, the fruits of fast economic development were not evenly spread, with only 41% of South Koreans identifying as belonging to the middle class in 1999, and 19% saying that they had dropped from the middle class to the lower class (Koo 2007). More recent data indicates that 72% of South Koreans feel generally pessimistic about the possibility of reducing the gap between rich and poor (Pew Research Center 2019). Intergenerational mobility has also become increasingly challenging, a phenomenon described with the term "spoon class," which has emerged to express that individual life chances are highly dependent on parents' wealth and status. This illustrates awareness of structural inequality and increasingly challenging or nonexistent opportunities for intergenerational mobility (Kim 2023). Despite the critical self-view, it needs to be pointed out that in international comparison neither South Korea nor Japan has particularly high levels of income inequality (Pew Research Center

2019), with Gini coefficients hovering around the OECD average. Nonetheless, Choi (2013) found that South Koreans perceive income differences to be excessively inflated and comparatively unjust and have a low acceptance of unequal income distribution in comparison to nineteen OECD countries.

Similar to South Korea, Taiwan transitioned from labor-intensive sectors to technology-driven industries. The comparison by Weatherall et al. (2018) suggests that, although income distributions in Taiwan, Singapore, and South Korea were similar up until the early 2000s, an increase in income inequality has been especially pronounced in Taiwan following the 2008 financial crisis. Particularly affected by this shift are lower-income groups, who are experiencing a significant decrease in real wages. Taiwan's widening income gap is related to industry transformation with the latest economic growth being largely driven by capital paired with developments in the much-lauded automated high-tech industry. Particularly its semiconductor production, which has little demand for low-skilled workers and only seeks highly paid and highly educated professionals. However, the Taiwanese might not quite feel the pinch of the widening income gap yet, because, in contrast to other economies, Taiwan has a relatively higher purchasing power parity (PPP). This means that the Taiwanese people can enjoy better material conditions in Taiwan compared with their peers with the same level of income in places with lower PPP. When it comes to the perception of income inequality, Taiwanese people have exhibited relatively high awareness of the existing disparities, with over 90% recognizing income inequality to be a serious problem. Despite this concern, not much criticism regarding the fairness of the income distribution was expressed in the 2000s. Regarding opportunities, Kim et al. (2018) note that, when comparing China, Japan, South Korea, and Taiwan, Taiwanese people perceive their society to be comparatively fair. Hsiao and Wan (2014) find confidence about the future to be related to class status, with people belonging to the Taiwanese middle class being more pessimistic, and members of the higher and working class being more optimistic about their economic future.

Overall, the three East Asian countries under examination in this chapter have demonstrated divergent timelines in their reactions toward the steadily burgeoning socioeconomic inequality. In the case of Japan, previous studies indicate that the perception of income inequality as a problem came late. Meanwhile, public sentiment in South Korea has been critical of growing precariousness already since the Asian financial crisis in 1997–98. In Taiwan, people are also critical of wealth and income disparities, however, what sets them apart is the perception of opportunities for upward mobility and fairness in their society, which may be grounded in the more recent experience of economic upgrading compared to Japan and South Korea.

Inequality-Legitimizing Narratives as Predictors of Income Inequality Acceptance

These discrepancies in perception may be caused by different ways in which increasing economic inequality is discussed in these three societies. Public discourse often frames socioeconomic inequalities as outcome of individual success or failure rather than as created by structural or institutional issues (Piketty 2019). This has led to the internalization of narratives that legitimize inequality and encapsulate arguments used to defend the unequal distribution of wealth and income. Some of the most common narratives relate to economic growth, functional efficiency, meritocracy, individual responsibility, and fairness. They have continued to remain popular and are often utilized within the context of neoliberal political agendas.

Stubborn Orthodoxy of the "Trickle-Down Economics"

One of the central tenets of classical economics, going back to Adam Smith (1776/1976) and J.M. Keynes (1978), is the claim that inequalities are a "necessary evil" for the functioning of the free market and subsequently inevitable to maintain high economic growth rates. Trust in the "invisible hand" simultaneously functions as a widely accepted "moral justification for free market economics, namely that the pursuit of individual profit also provides the best mechanism for the pursuit of the common good" (Bauman 2013, 3). Another version of the same idea is the belief in the mechanisms of "trickle-down economics," which has been actively around since the Reagan administration and the tenure of Margaret Thatcher, and subsequently utilized within the neoliberal political and economic discourse throughout the world (Arndt 1983; Greenwood and Holt 2010; Morinobu 2021; Wisman and Smith 2011). "According to economic orthodoxy, a stiff dose of inequality brings more efficient and faster growing economies. This is because higher awards and lower taxes at the top—it is claimed—boost entrepreneurialism and deliver a larger economic pie" (Bauman 2013, 16), infamously encapsulated in the "Laffer Curve," which illustrates the idea that cutting taxes can result in increased total tax revenue (Laffer 2004; Mach 2019). Despite this theory having been repeatedly debunked, the idea itself has maintained its influence over the last forty years, and its underlying assumptions are by now deeply rooted within politicized capitalist discourse, especially in the right-wing political rhetoric and practice (Baker 2017). As such, it works as a great cautionary example of how poorly grounded theoretical conceptualizations can have a strong influential traction in the "real world" as they are kept alive to serve a specific political purpose.

Inequality as Functional Necessity for Economic Growth

The belief that reducing inequality will be detrimental for economic growth has been another line of discussion, particularly popular among economists who argue that inequality provides incentives for innovation and entrepreneurship, and subsequently contributes positively to economic growth (Lazear and Rosen 1981). This argument has had a notable appeal for governments, international institutions, policy and opinion makers, as it makes it easier to reduce social problems to extreme poverty. The implementation of social welfare programs that focus mainly on tackling poverty is a much more straightforward task than proposing fundamental reforms of the wider economic framework that is the source of the existing structural inequalities. Unsurprisingly, the assumed positive association between inequality and growth, however, has so far failed to find sufficient support in empirical analyses (Atkinson 2015).

Regardless of this, both national governments and intergovernmental organizations have had an important role in sustaining this narrative in policy development and implementation. Until very recently, policy recommendations from the international organizations overseeing economic development on the global scale (e.g., OECD and the International Monetary Fund (IMF)) has been narrowly focused on pro-growth policies (OECD 2014; Roaf et al. 2014). The IMF policy advice, for example, has long been that growth has to be sustained by lower taxes and minimal public expenditure (Alesina et al. 2018). Meanwhile, labor unions are seen as a major predicament for the efficiency of the markets (Betcherman 2012) Combined, these policies have contributed to an increase in wealth and income disparities, and it is only recently that the negative effects of a sole focus on growth have finally been acknowledged (OECD 2014).

Inequality as Unavoidable Side-Effect of a Meritocratic System

In a similar vein, proponents of inequality often refer to "inequality as incentive" to argue that social inequalities are functional for society because they motivate talented individuals to occupy essential positions (Veliz 2017). This hypothesis, based on Davis and Moore (1945) suggests that positions that are central to societal functioning should come with higher compensation, which in turn motivates people to work hard to fill these positions. We are trained to believe that the well-being of the many is best served by grooming and rewarding the abilities of the few, resulting in a pyramid-like hierarchy of social standings and privileges (Bauman 2013). This argument is often paired with the assumption of equality of opportunity and a selection of the best based on the principles of meritocracy, which renders resulting inequalities morally, ethically, and economically justifiable. The assumption that societal positions and the attached economic awards are allocated solely based on an individual's merit has maintained universal appeal due to its perceived ties to economic efficiency and fairness (Sandel 2020). Meritocracy assumes that an economic system that rewards effort, initiative, and talent is more productive and fairer than one that does not. As a result, meritocracy is seen as a universal social ideal, with proponents arguing that it does not discriminate on any basis other than achievement (Sandel 2020). However, the extent to which meritocratic principles have been applied in practice varies significantly (Larsen 2016; Neves 2000), and studies have highlighted its use for justifying inequality (Fong 2001; Kunovich and Slomczynski 2007; Locklear 1998; Mijs 2021; Roex et al. 2019; Sachweh 2017).

This narrative continues to have a powerful appeal at the individual level, as meritocracy's central promise emphasizes the importance of equal opportunities over equal outcomes (Reynolds and Xian 2014). This distinction is particularly significant because it enables us to differentiate between self- and exogenous determination of socioeconomic outcomes. Hence, meritocracy emphasizes individual responsibility for one's life outcomes, functioning as a powerful legitimator of inequality. However, this approach misrepresents how inequalities are created by disregarding structural processes framing inequality and privilege, thereby relating individual responsibility to individual failure (Bourdieu 1993). This misrepresentation works in both directions, as it gives the dominant groups an ideological justification for their position, while also providing non-dominant groups with an explanation for their position and the conditions for economic success (Bourdieu 1993). The belief in individual control of life outcomes through individual choice and the freedom to make these choices not only reflects individual-level values but also has broader societal implications, as it decreases support for policies that benefit society as a whole and increases support for measures that promote individual rights and freedoms (Savani et al. 2011).

Inequality Acceptance Based on Structural Position

A derivative from rational choice theory, the "structural position" hypothesis highlights the influence of an individual's social status position on their attitudes and beliefs. Its main assumption is that individuals are increasingly willing to accept income inequality, the higher their own socioeconomic status (education, income, occupation, subjective social class) is (Gijsberts 2002; Hadler 2005; Kelley and Evans 1993; Linos and West 2013; Wong et al. 2009). However, unequal structural conditions themselves are grounded in the ideas that have created them. This makes the narratives that the status quo is born out of particularly resistant to change. Significant change would necessitate not just a shift in ideas but also a transformation of the associated societal structures.

To better understand the interplay of ideas and societal realities in predicting acceptance of economic inequality, we include both in our analysis. We formulate three very general hypotheses to test the explanatory power of these two theoretical frameworks. First, we anticipate a positive association between higher socioeconomic status and acceptance of income inequality. Second, we assume that a stronger alignment with values inherent in the discourses of inequality-legitimizing narratives, presented above, will correlate positively with a stronger acceptance of income inequality. Last, we expect these relationships to exhibit moderate robustness across all three East Asian countries under comparison.

Data and Variables

For our analysis we utilize data from the WVS (Haerpfer et al. 2020), focusing on cross-sectional data from the most recent survey wave (2017–20) for Japan, South Korea, and Taiwan. This subset comprises 5,872 observations on 14 variables, with respondents for Japan, South Korea, and Taiwan, respectively (see Appendix Table 6A for descriptive statistics).

Dependent Variable

To effectively gauge the central topic of interest in this chapter—namely, the acceptance of socioeconomic inequality—we use a variable capturing respondents' normative attitudes toward income inequality. *Acceptance of income inequality* was measured by letting respondents indicate which of two opposing statements they agree with more on a 10-point scale, where 1 means "Incomes should be made more equal" and 10 represents the opposing "There should be greater incentives for individual effort." Higher values indicate higher acceptance of income inequality.

In Japan, *Acceptance of income inequality* is the lowest (mean = 5.36, SD = 2.04, Appendix Table 6A). In South Korea, the mean value leans more toward acceptance of income inequality as an incentivizing necessity (mean = 6.66, SD = 1.64); followed by Taiwan, which showed the highest acceptance of income inequality (mean = 7.22, SD = 2.23).

To offer a more detailed understanding of the distribution of the *Acceptance of income inequality* variable and its comparison among countries, it was collapsed into five levels: "Very High," "High," "Neutral," "Low," and "Very Low" for descriptive purposes (Figure 6.1). This reveals that, although South Korea and Taiwan exhibit the highest mean acceptance of income inequality, Taiwan has the greatest proportion of respondents with very high acceptance. In contrast, Japan has the highest proportion of respondents who are opposed to income inequality, as well as a large share of respondents (43%) who do not indicate a preference. Placing these results within the wider context of OECD countries (Figure 6.2), Taiwan has the second-highest acceptance of income inequality, immediately followed by South Korea. Japan, on the other hand, belongs to the group of countries with the smallest shares of respondents expressing high acceptance of income inequality.

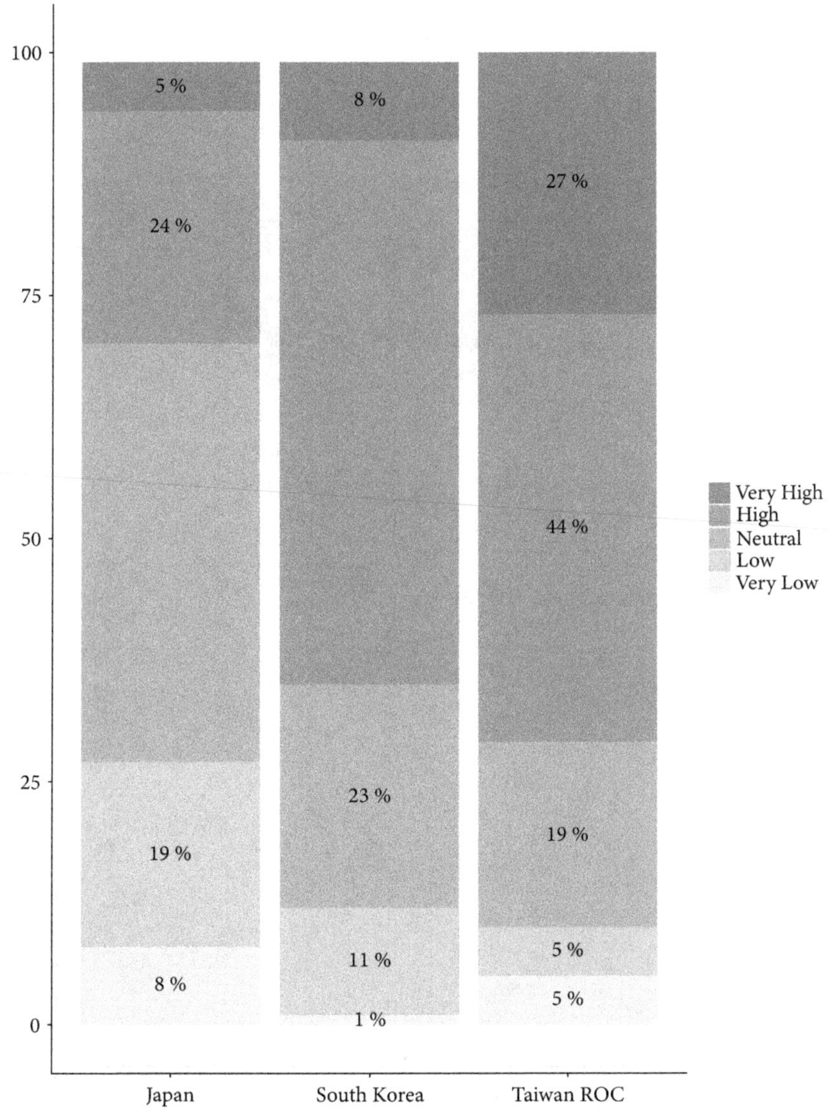

Figure 6.1 Proportion of acceptance of income inequality in Japan, South Korea, and Taiwan ROC

Source: Authors' calculations (World Values Survey 2017–20; Haepfer et al. 2020).

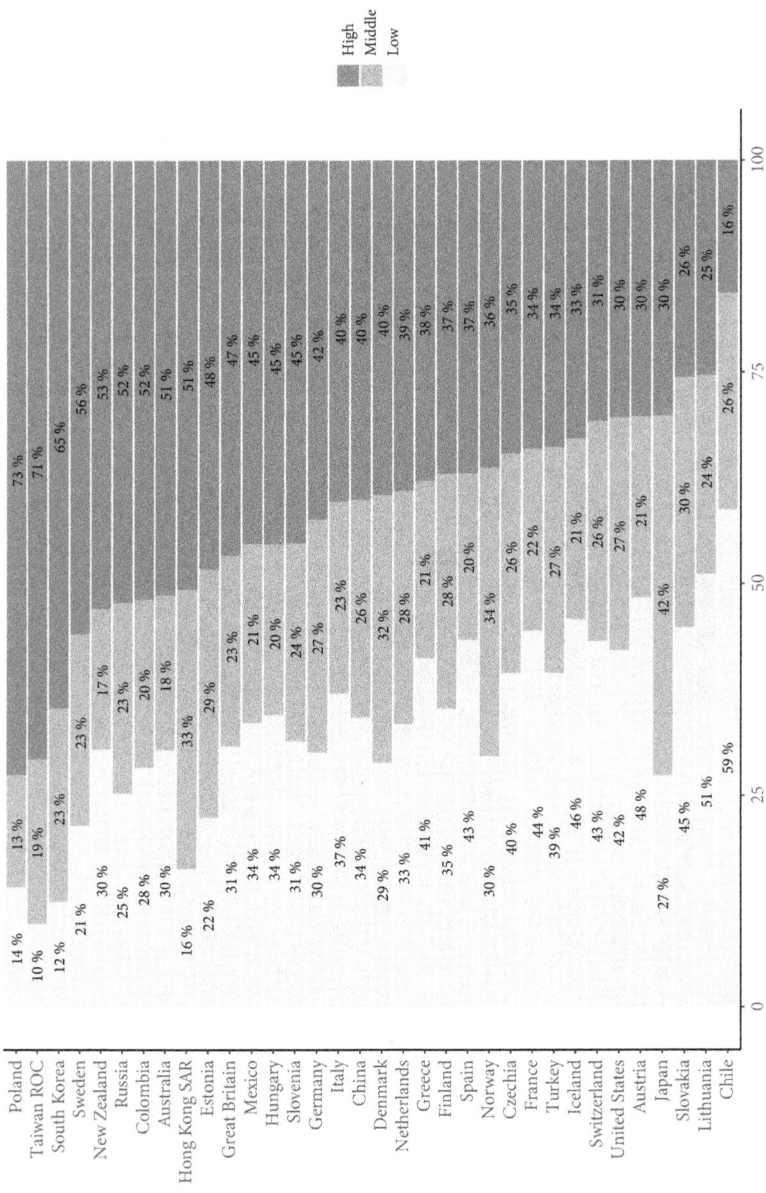

Figure 6.2 Proportion of acceptance of income inequality across thirty-four countries

Source: Authors' calculations (World Values Survey 2017–20; Haepfer et al. 2020).

Independent Variables

To examine the potential influence of inequality-legitimizing narratives on individuals' attitudes toward unequal income distribution, we developed an analytical framework centered around five key variables available in the WVS dataset: *Individual Responsibility*, *Competitiveness*, *Meritocracy*, *Choice*, and *Freedom vs. Equality*. These variables encapsulate some of the aspects of various arguments that, as previously discussed, have been employed to legitimize and normalize socioeconomic inequality in contemporary societies. The first variable, *Individual Responsibility*, was assessed using a 10-point scale. Respondents who chose a score of 1 indicated their agreement with the statement, "The government should take more responsibility to ensure that everyone is provided for," while those who selected a score of 10 expressed their agreement with the statement, "People should take more responsibility to provide for themselves." The *Competitiveness* variable is a continuous measure, gauging an individual's perspective regarding the value of competition as opposed to prioritizing the common good, where 1 indicated agreement with the statement "Competition is harmful," while 10 indicated agreement with the statement "Competition is good." *Meritocracy* captures an individual's adherence to meritocratic beliefs and was similarly measured on a 10-point scale. Selecting 1 indicated agreement with the statement "In the long run, hard work usually brings a better life," while 10 meant agreement with the statement "Hard work doesn't generally bring success—it is more a matter of luck and connections." This variable was reverse coded to match the direction of the other items. An individual's perceived control over their life, *Choice*, was also measured on a 10-point scale, with higher scores indicating a higher level of perceived control over the respondent's life. The last variable, *Freedom vs. Equality*, is a binary, categorical measure, capturing preference and prioritization of either individual freedom or equity.

To assess the structural position of individuals, we included four measures: *Educational Level*, *Subjective Household Income*, *Subjective Social Class*, *Experience of Social Mobility*. Socioeconomic status is, thus, captured as a mixture of objective and subjective measures. Descriptives of all variables are displayed in Appendix Table 6A.

Education was assessed asking respondents to state their highest level of education, based on the International Standard Classification of Education ISCED 2011 (UNESCO Institute for Statistics 2012), which comprises nine levels, from 0 = "early childhood education/no education," to 8 = "doctoral or equivalent." For descriptive purposes, we display the distribution of educational levels in our three countries recoded into three groups, as "Lower" (ISCED 0–2), "Middle" (ISCED 3–4), and "Higher" (ISCED 5–8) in Appendix Table 6A.

Subjective Household Income was measured by asking respondents to position the income of their household into one of ten income groups, with higher values indicating higher self-positioning on the income scale.[1] These groups were not connected to actual monetary figures, but positioning relied on respondents' subjective perception of the income hierarchy and their respective position within it. Unlike measures of objective income, this variable, thus, captures the comparative and subjective nature of respondents' socioeconomic position.

Subjective Social Class was measured on a categorical scale and captured subjective class placement, recoded from originally five classes into three different classes: lower class, middle class, and upper class. *Social Mobility* measured whether respondents' living standards had improved compared to their parents and was recorded on an ordinal scale with three levels: Downward Mobility, No Mobility, and Upward Mobility. As timelines for economic growth and recession differ between our three countries of interest, we included this item to control for and better understand the possible impact of personal experiences of profiting or suffering from economic changes.

While findings in prior research regarding the connections between age and acceptance of inequality are inconsistent (e.g., Dion and Birchfield 2010; Finseraas 2009; Roex et al. 2019), we here use *Age* as a control variable. *Gender* was also incorporated as a control variable, given that studies have found women to be more likely to support values related to greater equity (e.g., Iversen and Soskice 2001; Linos and West 2003). Additionally, binary variables encompassing whether respondents have children (*Children*) and whether they are married or cohabiting (*Married*) were also included as controls in the models.

Analytical Strategy

To examine the relationship between respondents' perception of inequality-legitimizing narratives, their position in the social hierarchy, and their acceptance of unequal income distribution across selected countries, we conducted linear regression analyses for each country (Tables 6.1, 6.2, 6.3). Assumptions for linear regression, including evaluations of standard residuals and absence of outliers, were satisfied. The variance inflation factor for control variables did not exceed 2. Assumptions of homogeneity of variance and linearity were met. The Breusch-Pagan test was employed to detect heteroskedasticity, and robust standard errors were applied for validity. Listwise deletion addressed missing cases. In our analytical models, we can include only some aspects of the inequality-legitimizing narratives we have discussed above, as we are constrained by the availability of appropriate operationalizations in the dataset.

Findings

The central research focus of the analysis was to examine the relationship between belief in inequality-legitimizing narratives (individual responsibility, belief in the merits of competition, meritocracy, belief in individual control of life outcomes, and prioritizing freedom over equality), social status, and acceptance of unequal income distribution in society. To test how these relationships play out in the three countries, separate models were constructed for each country. Before looking more closely at the importance and impact of specific determinants, we discuss the general explanatory power of structural position and inequality-legitimizing narratives on income inequality acceptance.

In Japan (Table 6.1, Model 1), a model with only control variables and variables capturing social status explained approximately 9% of the variance in *Acceptance of income inequality* (Adjusted $R^2 = 0.093$). The addition of variables capturing inequality-legitimizing narratives in Model 2 more than doubled the explanatory power to 22% (Adjusted $R^2 = 0.223$). In South Korea (Table 6.2, Models 1 and 2), a model with only control variables and social status did not achieve a good fit and explained *Acceptance of income inequality* only minimally (Adjusted $R^2 = 0.00005$). The inclusion of "inequality-legitimizing narratives" variables increased the explanatory power to around 5% (Adjusted $R^2 = 0.05$). In Taiwan (Table 6.3, Models 1 and 2), a model with control variables and social status explained approximately 7.5% of the variance (Adjusted $R^2 = 0.075$). The addition of inequality-legitimizing narrative variables nearly doubled the explanatory power to 10.5% (Adjusted $R^2 = 0.105$).

Table 6.1 Linear regression models—Japan

	Acceptance of inequality					
	Model 1			Model 2		
	B	SE B	β	B	SE B	β
Female (ref. male)	0.217	(0.139)	0.054	0.092	(0.138)	0.023
Not married (ref. married)	0.050	(0.213)	0.010	0.156	(0.206)	0.031
No children (ref. has children)	−0.047	(0.227)	−0.009	−0.107	(0.222)	−0.020
Age	−0.005	(0.006)	−0.034	−0.005	(0.006)	−0.036
Education	−0.005	(0.051)	−0.003	−0.091*	(0.051)	−0.063
Subjective social status						
Lower class (ref.)	–	–	–	–	–	–
Middle class	0.117	(0.170)	0.029	0.053	(0.168)	0.013
Upper class	0.890***	(0.233)	0.176	0.657***	(0.234)	0.128
Subjective income	0.118***	(0.031)	0.159	0.111***	(0.030)	0.149
Social mobility						
Downward mobility (ref.)	–	–	–	–	–	–
No mobility	0.533***	(0.193)	0.124	0.333*	(0.192)	0.077
Upward mobility	0.376*	(0.188)	0.093	0.322	(0.187)	0.080
Individual responsibility				0.231***	(0.031)	0.256
Competition is good				0.104***	(0.033)	0.112
Meritocracy				0.071*	(0.034)	0.077
Choice				0.065	(0.038)	0.062
Freedom (ref. equality)				0.526***	(0.143)	0.125
Constant	4.471***	(0.450)		2.464***	(0.521)	
Observations	797			702		
R^2	0.105			0.240		
Adjusted R^2	0.093			0.223		
Residual Std. Error	1.920 (df = 786)			1.774 (df = 686)		
F Statistic	9.202*** (df = 10; 786)			14.427*** (df = 15; 686)		

Note: *$p < 0.1$, **$p < 0.05$, ***$p < 0.01$.

Overall, in all three countries, a larger amount of variance in acceptance of income inequality was explained by beliefs in inequality-legitimizing narratives than by respondents' structural position. Among the three countries compared in the analysis, in Japan, social status and shared inequality-legitimizing narratives were the best predictors of acceptance of

Table 6.2 Linear regression models—South Korea

	Acceptance of inequality					
	Model 1			Model 2		
	B	SE B	β	B	SE B	β
Female (ref. male)	−0.016	(0.098)	−0.005	−0.037	(0.096)	−0.011
Not married (ref. married)	−0.191	(0.216)	−0.052	−0.276	(0.211)	−0.076
No children (ref. has children)	0.252	(0.223)	0.070	0.284	(0.218)	0.078
Age	0.007	(0.005)	0.062	0.003	(0.005)	0.029
Education	0.032	(0.036)	0.030	0.018	(0.035)	0.017
Subjective social status						
Lower class (ref.)	–	–	–	–	–	–
Middle class	−0.094**	(0.182)	−0.025	−0.037	(0.178)	−0.010
Upper class	−0.179	(0.235)	−0.040	−0.075	(0.230)	−0.017
Subjective income	0.094	(0.042)	0.078	0.048	(0.042)	0.040
Social mobility						
Downward mobility (ref.)	–	–	–	–	–	–
No mobility	0.083	(0.200)	0.022	0.112	(0.196)	0.030
Upward mobility	0.111	(0.185)	0.032	0.088	(0.184)	0.025
Individual responsibility				0.171***	(0.025)	0.202
Competition is good				0.055	(0.031)	0.056
Meritocracy				0.074**	(0.028)	0.085
Choice				0.044	(0.034)	0.037
Freedom (ref. equality)				0.275***	(0.098)	0.080
Constant	5.734***	(0.471)		4.042***	(0.540)	
Observations	1,202			1,202		
R^2	0.008			0.062		
Adjusted R^2	0.00005			0.05		
Residual Std. Error	1.635 (df = 1191)			1.594 (df = 1186)		
F Statistic	1.006 (df = 10; 1191)			5.245*** (df = 15; 1186)		

Note: $^{*}p < 0.1$, $^{**}p < 0.05$, $^{***}p < 0.01$.

income inequality. For South Korea, on the other hand, social status variables held only marginal predictive power and the explanatory power of inequality-legitimizing narratives for *Acceptance of income inequality* was also weakest among all three countries.

Table 6.3 Linear regression models—Taiwan ROC

	Acceptance of inequality					
	Model 1			Model 2		
	B	SE B	β	B	SE B	β
Female (ref. male)	0.165	(0.128)	0.038	0.085	(0.128)	0.020
Not married (ref. married)	−0.008	(0.177)	−0.002	−0.101	(0.176)	−0.023
No children (ref. has children)	−0.280	(0.216)	−0.062	−0.197	(0.215)	−0.043
Age	0.003	(0.006)	0.020	0.001	(0.006)	0.006
Education	0.249***	(0.041)	0.216	0.249***	(0.041)	0.216
Subjective social status						
Lower class (ref.)	–	–	–	–	–	–
Middle class	0.376**	(0.156)	0.081	0.285*	(0.156)	0.061
Upper class	0.354*	(0.191)	.072	0.249	(0.191)	0.050
Subjective income	0.058	(0.047)	0.046	0.037	(0.047)	0.029
Social mobility						
Downward mobility (ref.)	-	–	–	–	–	–
No mobility	−0.413*	(0.232)	−0.083	−0.431*	(0.229)	−0.086
Upward mobility	0.041	(0.211)	0.009	−0.006	(0.209)	−0.001
Individual responsibility				0.109***	(0.027)	0.120
Competition is good				0.111***	(0.036)	0.096
Meritocracy				0.002	(0.027)	0.003
Choice				0.028	(0.034)	0.025
Freedom (ref. equality)				0.390***	(0.131)	0.087
Constant	5.448***	(0.479)		3.860***	(0.592)	
Observations	1,085			1,078		
R^2	0.084			0.117		
Adjusted R^2	0.075			0.105		
Residual Std. Error	2.081 (df = 1074)			2.050 (df = 1062)		
F Statistic	9.785*** (df = 10; 1074)			9.392*** (df = 15; 1062)		

Note: *$p < 0.1$, **$p < 0.05$, ***$p < 0.01$.

While individual beliefs in narratives that legitimize inequality, such as emphasizing individual responsibility, competition, merit, freedom over equality, and personal choice, played a more significant role in explaining acceptance of income inequality compared to structural position across all three countries, the specific impact of these nuanced narratives varied to some extent. To determine the relative importance of the predictors within the respective country, we focus on a discussion of the standardized regression coefficients.

Comparing the three countries, social status variables had the strongest explanatory power in Japan (Table 6.1). A significant impact of subjective social status—identifying as "upper class" as opposed to "middle" or "lower class"—remained robust also when controlling for inequality-legitimizing beliefs. Subjective income had a similar impact (0.149, $p < 0.01$), with individuals with higher subjective incomes being more accepting of income inequality. An experience of downward mobility, as compared to one's parents, significantly reduced acceptance of income inequality. This effect remained significant also after controlling for inequality-legitimizing narratives in Model 2. Education showed to have a significant, albeit weak negative effect only after inequality-legitimizing narratives were controlled for (−0.063, $p < 0.001$), with individuals with higher educational levels being more critical of income inequality. In terms of inequality-legitimizing narratives, the belief in individual responsibility had the strongest impact on acceptance of income inequality in Japan (0.256, $p < 0.01$), followed by beliefs in individual freedom over equality (0.125, $p < 0.01$) and competition as positive incentive (0.112, $p < 0.01$). Acceptance of income inequality was also significantly impacted by the conviction that hard work, rather than luck, will lead to a better life (*Meritocracy*, 0.077, $p < 0.1$). Meanwhile, a belief in personal control over the course of one's life did not have a significant effect.

For South Korea, the structural position of an individual had no effect on acceptance of income inequality (Table 6.2). The inequality-legitimizing narratives, however, did explain some of the variance in inequality acceptance. Similar to Japan and Taiwan, the belief in individual responsibility to provide for oneself had the strongest effect (0.202, $p < 0.01$), followed by beliefs in meritocracy (0.085, $p < 0.05$), and individual freedom over equality (0.080, $p < 0.01$). Overall, the predictive power of the models is low for South Korea, pointing to additional decisive factors not controlled for in the models. Nonetheless, we find evidence that beliefs in narrative-legitimizing narratives are of significant importance for acceptance of income inequality also in South Korea, whereas the structural position of the respondents did not make a difference.

For Taiwan (Table 6.3), education had the overall strongest effect, which remained robust also when controlling for inequality-legitimizing beliefs (0.216, $p < 0.01$). Individuals with higher educational levels were more tolerant of income inequality. Despite the stable effect of education, neither belief in hard work (*Meritocracy*) nor the perception of life control (*Choice*) significantly predicted higher acceptance of income inequality. Among inequality-legitimizing beliefs, individual responsibility had the strongest effect (0.120, $p < 0.01$), followed by beliefs in competition as a positive incentive (0.096, $p < 0.01$), and personal freedom over equality (0.087, $p < 0.01$).

In summary, while nuanced differences emerged between countries, inequality-legitimizing narratives proved to be a more robust predictor of acceptance of income inequality than an individual's social status in all three countries. The belief that individuals are responsible to provide for themselves, rather than it being the government's duty to offer support, was the most powerful of the included narratives in all three countries. This belief was more pronounced in South Korea (mean = 5.27, SD = 1.93) and Taiwan (mean = 5.49, SD = 2.43) than in Japan (mean = 3.95, SD = 2.33), which may be related to experience with welfare provision in these societies. Japan, the most mature economy within our sample, also boasts the most developed welfare state among these three countries, although public social spending is just above OECD average and less generous than in Scandinavian countries, with the core of spending concentrating on health and pensions. That Japanese respondents were also more inclined to see the government as responsible for providing support goes hand in hand with the slightly lower levels of acceptance of income inequality in Japan (Appendix Table 6A).

Impact of Control Variables

While the focus of our analysis lies on the predictive power of structural position versus inequality-legitimizing beliefs, we also include a short discussion of the impact of our control variables.

The relationship between individuals' age and their values regarding acceptable levels of inequality in society has been a subject of much research (Ingelhart 2018; Inglehart and Appel 1989). However, the direction of this relationship remains inconclusive, as various studies have yielded contradictory findings. Some cross-national analyses of large-scale survey data have found a positive relationship between age and acceptance of inequality (e.g., Dion and Birchfield 2010), while others have found the opposite (e.g., Roex et al. 2019). Furthermore, some studies have found that the relationship between age and inequality values follows a U-shaped curve, with a positive relationship in young age and a negative relationship in old age (Finseraas 2009). Meanwhile, research on cross-sectional data from thirty countries has shown that individuals tend to become increasingly critical of unequal income distribution until the age of forty, beyond which the trend becomes less steep (Hadler 2005). The analysis at hand only adds to the uncertainty surrounding this relationship as age was not a statistically significant predictor of income inequality acceptance in Japan, South Korea, and Taiwan.

The effect of gender, parenthood, and marital status on acceptance of income inequality was also tested in this study, building on previous research by Cusack et al. (2006), Iverson and Soskice (2001), and Linos and West (2003). Prior studies have established that gender plays an important role in attitude formation, with women generally showing less acceptance of inequalities. However, in contrast to this, the role of gender was not statistically significant in any of the countries analyzed in this study. This finding suggests that at least in these East Asian countries gender is not a significant predictor of acceptance of income inequality. The continuous transformation and increasing flexibility of labor markets over the past few decades, along with the growing implications of increasingly segmented labor markets in Japan and South Korea, may have contributed to this shift. As income inequality has been on the rise since the 1980s, attitudes toward income distribution may have become more universally shared, transcending gender identity. These findings provide evidence of trends toward harmonization in attitudes toward income inequality, and further research may be necessary to explore the exact mechanisms driving this trend and the potential implications for policymaking.

As marriage represents an additional source of social and economic security, one may expect marital status to have a statistically significant impact on individual's attitudes towards unequal income distribution. However, being married or cohabiting did not have a statistically significant effect on income inequality acceptance in Japan, South Korea, and Taiwan. This finding may be attributed to the steadily increasing objective inequalities that might have surpassed the impact of cohabitation forms on attitudes toward unequal income distribution, similar to the effect observed for gender.

Despite inherent demographic similarities among the countries studied, the effect of the variable capturing respondents' parenthood was also not statistically significant.

Conclusion

This chapter presented results that highlight the scope and impact of moral logics legitimizing inequality. The arguments behind the steady increase in inequality have gained considerable public and political traction due to their promises of socioeconomic advancement. While it is evident that these promises have remained unfulfilled, globalization and the nearly universal shift toward a free-market economy have led to a gradual dissemination of emancipative and neoliberal values. This shift is noticeable from the West to the East, from established democracies to post-socialist nations, and from traditional markets to emerging global markets. While there has been a significant dispersion of values, norms, and policies across the globe that all play into the neoliberal call for continuous economic growth (Dobbin et al. 2007; Linos 2011, 2013; Simmons and Elkins 2004), the success of such cross-national influence of ideas of policy diffusion—also known as the diffusion pathway emulation—depends on the economic prosperity of the source country rather than the original success of the policy. This means that a policy is more likely imported from a country that is economically successful, as opposed to the geographical and cultural proximity. Moreover, as discussed by Bobzien and Verwiebe (Chapter 7 in this volume), the misinformed perception of inequality at the individual level is deeply rooted in the confirmation bias.

In this chapter we set out to investigate factors that contribute to people's acceptance of income inequality, focusing on three economically developed East Asian countries (Japan, South Korea, and Taiwan). Specifically, we tested to what extent social status and inequality-legitimizing narratives predicted acceptance toward income inequality. Our empirical findings provide evidence in support of the central argument of this chapter, stating that heightened acceptance of inequality-legitimizing narratives goes hand in hand with higher acceptance of income inequality in all three countries. What is more, beliefs in inequality-legitimizing narratives explained acceptance toward income inequality to a larger extent than people's social status.

While the general relationship was the same in all three countries, explanatory power varied significantly between the countries. Compared to South Korea and Taiwan, social status and beliefs in inequality-legitimizing narratives offered the strongest explanation for the acceptance of income inequality in Japan, the most mature economy of the three countries. The low explanatory power of our models, especially for South Korea, indicates that we fail to control for other factors that are decisive for income inequality acceptance. A possible supplementary explanation worth considering can be derived from the fact that individuals tend to significantly underestimate the existing levels of inequality (Osberg and Smeeding 2006). In South Korea, high societal pressure to succeed and conform socioeconomically while having limited possibilities for social mobility is well established. Therefore, one possible explanation for comparatively high acceptance of income inequality in South Korea could be derived from previous studies that have pointed out the role that narrow versus wide social comparisons play for perceiving existing inequality (Mijs 2021). This line of research argues that in societies where social comparisons are limited, aka "narrow," individuals tend to have a more restricted hence, invalid perception of income inequality, and claim that subsequently "people in more segregated societies are more likely to underestimate existing inequality" (Mijs 2021, 12). Similar to the conclusions made by Choi (2013), this research offers empirical support for the claim that the heightened acceptance of income inequality might be at least partly explained by the overflow of such overestimation. While there is a possibility that in the three countries compared in this chapter, the narratives might hold different meanings or interpretations, the results still show rather robust patterns.

While the statistical models presented here might suggest that the impact of some of the specified narratives for accepting income inequality are more powerful than others, it is crucial to revisit what these variables truly represent. We should refrain from making strong arguments that these models are sufficiently detailed or nuanced to support broad conceptual generalizations about the impact of specific ideas over others. The explanatory variables available in our dataset do not fully capture all aspects of the theoretical assumptions. Instead, they only address specific aspects relevant to these theoretical foundations. Therefore, caution is warranted when claiming that some ideas take precedence over others. Rather than drawing firm conclusions, we hope that these results serve to illustrate the collective impact of these narratives on the acceptance of inequality.

In summary, our research sheds light on the decisive nature of specific narratives that legitimize income inequality within developed market economies. It becomes evident that the degree of agreement with specific ideas surrounding the origins of socioeconomic inequalities and the attribution of individual responsibility for disparate outcomes significantly influences one's acceptance of inequality, as shown here for three East Asian countries. Throughout the course of this chapter, we delved into the economic trajectories of these East Asian nations, each navigating its unique set of challenges during periods of rapid economic growth paired with increasing inequalities. Despite the diverse historical and contextual variations, a common thread emerges—the impact of endorsing narratives that legitimize inequality remains a consistent predictor of attitudes toward economic disparities. In addition to conventional explanations rooted in objective circumstances, our findings underscore the importance of considering the influence of narrative agreement as a robust explanatory factor. This revelation offers an updated perspective to the persistence of inequality and suggests that the acceptance or rejection of certain ideas about inequality plays a pivotal role in shaping societal attitudes toward economic imbalances and is in line with previous research (Kitsnik 2022) underscoring that the impact of these narratives has been also strengthening over time.

As we contemplate the implications of our research, it becomes apparent that addressing income inequality requires a multifaceted approach. While conventional economic analyses often focus on structural factors and individual motivations, our study emphasizes the need to tackle the deeply ingrained narratives that perpetuate and legitimize inequality. By recognizing the role of these narratives in shaping perceptions, policymakers and advocates of social equity gain a more nuanced understanding of the mechanisms contributing to societal acceptance of economic disparities. In conclusion, our research hopes to contribute to the ongoing debate on how to tackle income inequality by highlighting the cross-cultural relevance of acknowledging the powerful impact of narratives that legitimize existing inequalities.

Appendix

Table 6A Summary descriptive statistics

	Japan (*N* = 1353)	South Korea (*N* = 1245)	Taiwan ROC (*N* = 1223)
Acceptance of Income Inequality			
Mean (SD)	5.36 (2.04)	6.66 (1.64)	7.22 (2.23)
Median [Min, Max]	5.00 [1.00, 10.0]	7.00 [1.00, 10.0]	8.00 [1.00, 10.0]
Missing	76 (5.6%)	0 (0%)	0 (0%)
Gender			
Female	763 (56.4%)	638 (51.2%)	629 (51.4%)
Male	590 (43.6%)	607 (48.8%)	594 (48.6%)
Married			
Married	994 (73.5%)	899 (72.2%)	680 (55.6%)
Not married	346 (25.6%)	346 (27.8%)	542 (44.3%)
Missing	13 (1.0%)	0 (0%)	1 (0.1%)
Children			
Children	1079 (79.7%)	902 (72.4%)	831 (67.9%)
No Children	255 (18.8%)	343 (27.6%)	392 (32.1%)
Missing	19 (1.4%)	0 (0%)	0 (0%)
Age (years)			
Mean (SD)	47.8 (14.3)	44.6 (14.1)	45.3 (14.7)
Median [Min, Max]	48.0 [18.0, 70.0]	46.0 [18.0, 70.0]	46.0 [18.0, 70.0]
Missing	319 (23.6%)	43 (3.5%)	118 (9.6%)
Education			
Lower	15 (1.1%)	50 (4.0%)	150 (12.3%)
Middle	584 (43.2%)	612 (49.2%)	442 (36.1%)
Higher	738 (54.5%)	583 (46.8%)	630 (51.5%)
Missing	16 (1.2%)	0 (0%)	1 (0.1%)
Subjective Social Class			
Lower class	487 (36.0%)	126 (10.1%)	506 (41.4%)
Middle class	571 (42.2%)	927 (74.5%)	391 (32.0%)
Upper class	223 (16.5%)	192 (15.4%)	312 (25.5%)
Missing	72 (5.3%)	0 (0%)	14 (1.1%)
Subjective Income Scale			
Mean (SD)	4.19 (2.67)	4.84 (1.38)	4.50 (1.75)
Median [Min, Max]	4.00 [1.00, 10.0]	5.00 [1.00, 8.00]	5.00 [1.00, 10.0]
Missing	148 (10.9%)	0 (0%)	0 (0%)

Continued

Table 6A *Continued*

	Japan (*N* = 1353)	South Korea (*N* = 1245)	Taiwan ROC (*N* = 1223)
Social Mobility			
Downward mobility	241 (17.8%)	93 (7.5%)	125 (10.2%)
No mobility	394 (29.1%)	310 (24.9%)	295 (24.1%)
Upward mobility	604 (44.6%)	842 (67.6%)	786 (64.3%)
Missing	114 (8.4%)	0 (0%)	17 (1.4%)
Individual Responsibility			
Mean (SD)	3.95 (2.33)	5.27 (1.93)	5.49 (2.43)
Median [Min, Max]	4.00 [1.00, 10.0]	5.00 [1.00, 10.0]	5.00 [1.00, 10.0]
Missing	37 (2.7%)	0 (0%)	0 (0%)
Competitiveness			
Mean (SD)	6.43 (2.28)	6.26 (1.67)	7.64 (1.93)
Median [Min, Max]	7.00 [1.00, 10.0]	6.00 [1.00, 10.0]	8.00 [1.00, 10.0]
Missing	83 (6.1%)	0 (0%)	0 (0%)
Meritocracy			
Mean (SD)	6.14 (2.19)	5.46 (1.87)	6.71 (2.45)
Median [Min, Max]	6.00 [1.00, 10.0]	5.00 [1.00, 10.0]	7.00 [1.00, 10.0]
Missing	80 (5.9%)	0 (0%)	0 (0%)
Choice			
Mean (SD)	6.05 (1.93)	6.98 (1.39)	7.34 (1.99)
Median [Min, Max]	6.00 [1.00, 10.0]	7.00 [1.00, 10.0]	8.00 [1.00, 10.0]
Missing	47 (3.5%)	0 (0%)	0 (0%)
Freedom vs. Equality			
Equality	462 (34.1%)	437 (35.1%)	462 (37.8%)
Freedom	772 (57.1%)	808 (64.9%)	752 (61.5%)
Missing	119 (8.8%)	0 (0%)	9 (0.7%)

Source: World Values Survey (2017–20); Haerpfer et al. 2020.

Note

1. While it would be preferable to also include an income measure that is attached to clearly specified monetary income groups, the WVS does not provide this kind of measurement.

References

Alesina, A., C.A Favero, and F. Giavazzi. 2018. "Climbing Out of Debt: A New Study Offers More Evidence That Cutting Spending Is Less Harmful to Growth Than Raising Taxes." *Finance and Development* 55 (1): pp. 6–11.

Arita, S., K. Nagayoshi, H. Taki, H. Kanbayashi, H. Takenoshita, and T. Yoshida. 2019. "Legitimation of Income Inequality in Japan: A Comparison with South Korea and the United States." Fondation France-Japon De l'EHESS (FFJ) Discussion Paper.

Arndt, H.W. 1983. "The 'Trickle-Down' Myth." *Economic Development and Cultural Change* 32 (1): pp. 1–10.

Atkinson, A.B. 2015. *Inequality: What Can Be Done?* Cambridge, MA: Harvard University Press.

Baker, P. 2017. "Arthur Laffer's Theory on Tax Cuts Comes to Life Once More." *New York Times*, April 25. https://www.nytimes.com/2017/04/25/us/politics/white-house-economic-policy-arthur-laffer.html.

Bauman, Z. 2013. *Does the Richness of the Few Benefit Us All?* Cambridge: Polity Press.

Betcherman, G. 2012. "Labor Market Institutions: A Review of the Literature." *World Bank Policy Research Paper*, 6276.

Blekesaune, M., and J. Quadagno. 2003. "Public Attitudes Toward Welfare State Policies: A Comparative Analysis of 24 Nations." *European Sociological Review* 19 (5): pp. 415–427.

Bourdieu, P. 1993. *Sociology in Question*. London: Sage.

Chi, E., and H.Y. Kwon. 2012. "Unequal New Democracies in East Asia: Rising Inequality and Government Responses in South Korea and Taiwan." *Asian Survey* 52 (5): pp. 900–923

Chiavacci, D. 2008. "From Class Struggle to General Middle-Class Society to Divided Society: Societal Models of Inequality in Postwar Japan." *Social Science Japan Journal* 11 (1): pp. 5–27.

Chiavacci, D., and C. Hommerich. Eds. 2017. *Social Inequality in Post-Growth Japan: Transformation During Economic and Demographic Stagnation*. London: Routledge.

Choi, J.W. 2013. "Crafting Public Perceptions of Inequality: Analysis of Korean Beliefs About Income Inequality." PhD dissertation. University of Illinois at Urbana-Champaign.

Cusack, T., T. Iversen, and P. Rehm. 2006. "Risk at Work: The Demand and Supply Sides of Government Redistribution." *Oxford Review of Economic Policy* 22: pp. 1–25.

Davis, K., and W.E. Moore. 1945. "Some Principles of Stratification." *American Sociological Review* 10 (2): pp. 242–249.

Dion, M.L., and V. Birchfield. 2010. "Economic Development, Income Inequality, and Preferences for Redistribution." *International Studies Quarterly* 54 (2): pp. 315–334.

Dobbin, F., B. Simmons, and G. Garrett. 2007. "The Global Diffusion of Public Policies: Social Construction, Coercion, Competition, or Learning?" *Annual Review of Sociology* 33: pp. 449–472.

Finseraas, H. 2009. "Income Inequality and Demand for Redistribution: A Multilevel Analysis of European Public Opinion." *Scandinavian Political Studies* 32 (1): pp. 94–119.

Fong, C. 2001. "Social Preferences, Self-Interest and the Demand for Redistribution." *Journal of Public Economics* 82 (2): pp. 225–246.

Gijsberts, M. 2002. "The Legitimation of Income Inequality in State-Socialist and Market Societies." *Acta Sociologica* 45 (4): pp. 269–285.

Greenwood, D.T., and R.P.F. Holt. 2010. "Growth, Inequality and Negative Trickle Down." *Journal of Economic Issues* 44 (2): pp. 403–410.

Hadler, M. 2005. "Why Do People Accept Different Income Ratios? A Multi-Level Comparison of Thirty Countries." *Acta Sociologica* 48 (2): pp. 131–154.

Haerpfer, C., R. Inglehart, A. Moreno, C. Welzel, K. Kizilova, J. Diez-Medrano, M. Lagos, P. Norris, E. Ponarin, and B. Puranen. Eds. 2020. *World Values Survey: Round Seven—Country-Pooled Datafile*. Madrid, Spain, and Vienna, Austria: JD Systems Institute & WVSA Secretariat.

Heuer, J.-O., T. Lux, S. Mau, and K. Zimmermann. 2020. "Legitimizing Inequality." *Comparative Sociology* 19: pp. 542–584.

Holliday, I. 2000. "Productivist Welfare Capitalism: Social Policy in East Asia." *Political Studies* 48 (4): pp. 706–723.

Holliday, I., and P. Wilding. Eds. 2003. *Welfare Capitalism in East Asia*. Basingstoke: Palgrave Macmillan.

Hommerich, C. 2024. "Social and Subjective Well-Being in Post-Growth Japan: Adapting to New Inequalities." In *Social Well-Being, Development, and Multiple Modernities in Asia*, edited by J. Yee, H. Harada, and M. Kanai, pp. 103–119. Singapore: Springer Nature. https://doi.org/10.1007/978-981-97-3866-3_7.

Hommerich, C., and T. Kikkawa. 2019. "Movement Behind the Scenes: The Quiet Transformation of Status Identification in Japan." *Social Science Japan Journal* 22 (1): pp. 11–24.

Hommerich, C., N. Sudo, and T. Kikkawa. Eds. 2021. *Social Change in Japan, 1989–2019: Social Status, Social Consciousness, Attitudes and Values*. London: Routledge.

Hsiao, H.-H.M., and P.-S. Wan. 2014. "Comparing Socio-Economic Attitudes of the Middle Classes." In *Chinese Middle Classes: Taiwan, Hong Kong, Macao, and China*, edited by H.-H.M. Hsiao, pp. 110–131. Milton Park: Routledge.

Inglehart, R. 2018. *Cultural Evolution: People's Motivations Are Changing, and Reshaping the World*. Cambridge: Cambridge University Press.

Inglehart R., and D. Appel. 1989. "The Rise of Postmaterialist Values and Changing Religious Orientations, Gender Roles and Sexual Norms." *International Journal of Public Opinion Research* 1 (1): pp. 45–75.

Iversen, T., and D. Soskice. 2001. "An Asset Theory of Social Policy Preferences." *American Political Science Review* 95 (4): pp. 875–893.

Jones, C. 1990. "Hong Kong, Singapore, South Korea and Taiwan: Oikonomic Welfare States." *Government and Opposition* 25 (4): pp. 446–462.

Kelley, J., and M.D.R. Evans. 1993. "The Legitimation of Inequality: Occupational Earnings in Nine Nations." *American Journal of Sociology* 99: pp. 75–125.

Keynes, J.M. 1978. *The General Theory and After: Part I. Preparation*. Vol. 13 of *The Collected Works of John Maynard Keynes*, edited by E. Johnson and D. Moggridge. Cambridge: Cambridge University Press.

Kim, C. 2023. "Stratification and Economic Inequality in South Korea." In *A Contemporary Portrait of Life in Korea*, edited by J. Kim, pp. 139–165. Singapore: Springer. https://doi.org/10.1007/978-981-99-5829-0_7.

Kim, H., S. Huh, S. Choi, and Y. Lee. 2018. "Perceptions of Inequality and Attitudes Towards Redistribution in Four East Asian Welfare States." *International Journal of Social Welfare* 27: pp. 28–39.

Kitsnik, J. 2022. "Untangling the Tolerance of Socioeconomic Inequality: Comparing Japan, the United States, South Korea, and the People's Republic of China." *Japanese Journal of Sociology* 31 (1): pp. 86–109.

Kitsnik, J. 2023. "Why We Don't Mind the Gap: The Robust Role of Individual Beliefs on Enduring Unequal Income Distribution—Evidence from 34 Countries." *Comparative Sociology* 22 (4): pp. 589–630.

Kobayashi, T. 2020. "Gensho suru chūryū shakaiishiki to kawaru nihonjin no shakaikan" [Waning Middle-Class Identification and Changing Japanese Attitudes Toward Society]. NHK Broadcasting Culture Research Institute. https://www.nhk.or.jp/bunken/english/research/yoron/20200501_7.html.

Koo, H. 2007. "The Changing Faces of Inequality in South Korea in the Age of Globalization." *Korean Studies* 31: pp. 1–18.

Kunovich, S., and K.M. Slomczynski. 2007. "Systems of Distribution and a Sense of Equity: A Multilevel Analysis of Meritocratic Attitudes in Post-Industrial Societies." *European Sociological Review* 23 (5): pp. 649–663.

Kyung-Sup, C. 2010. "The Second Modern Condition? Compressed Modernity as Internalized Reflexive Cosmopolitization." *British Journal of Sociology* 61: pp. 444–464.

Laffer, A.B. 2004. "The Laffer Curve: Past, Present, and Future." *Executive Summary Backgrounder* 1765 (1): pp. 1–16. https://iife.edu.vn/wp-content/uploads/2020/04/Laffer-Couver-Last-Present-and-Future-bg1765.pdf.

Larsen, C.A. 2016. "How Three Narratives of Modernity Justify Economic Inequality." *Acta Sociologica* 59 (2): pp. 93–111.
Lazear, E., and S. Rosen. 1981. "Rank-Order Tournaments as Optimum Labor Contracts." *Journal of Political Economy* 89 (5): pp. 841–864.
Linos, K. 2013. *The Democratic Foundations of Policy Diffusion: How Health, Family, and Employment Laws Spread Across Countries*. Oxford: Oxford University Press.
Linos, K. 2011. "Diffusion Through Democracy." *American Journal of Political Science* 55 (3): pp. 678–695.
Linos, K., and M. West. 2003. "Self-Interest, Social Beliefs, and Attitudes to Redistribution. Re-Addressing the Issue of Cross-National Variation." *European Sociological Review* 19 (4): pp. 393–409.
Locklear, S. 1998. "Meritocratic Image of Success and Its Determinants: A Comparison of Poland and Hungary, 1987–88 and 1992." *International Journal of Sociology* 28 (2): pp. 65–90.
Mach, P. 2019. "On the Origin of the Laffer Curve." *Economic Studies and Analyses/Acta VSFS* 13 (2): pp. 186–191.
McCall, L. 2013. *The Undeserving Rich: American Beliefs About Inequality Opportunity and Redistribution*. Cambridge: Cambridge University Press.
Mijs, J.J.B. 2021. "The Paradox of Inequality: Income Inequality and Belief in Meritocracy Go Hand in Hand." *Socio-Economic Review* 19 (1): pp. 7–35.
Milanovic, B. 2016. *Global Inequality: A New Approach for the Age of Globalization*. Cambridge, MA: Harvard University Press.
Morinobu, S. 2021. "Prime Minister Kishida's Growth and Redistribution Strategy: Will It Work?" Tokyo Foundation for Policy Research, November 21. https://www.tokyofoundation.org/research/detail.php?id=862.
Neves, L.M.P. 2000. "Putting Meritocracy in Its Place: The Logic of Performance in the United States, Brazil and Japan." *Critique of Anthropology* 20 (4): pp. 333–358.
OECD. 2014. *All on Board: Making Inclusive Growth Happen*. Luxembourg: OECD Economic Surveys.
OECD. 2011. *Divided We Stand. Why Inequality Keeps Rising. An Overview of Growing Income Inequalities in OECD Countries: Main Findings*. Paris: OECD Publishing. https://doi.org/10.1787/9789264119536-en.
OECD. 2006. *Labour Force Statistics 1985–2005*. Paris: OECD Publishing.
Osberg, L., and T. Smeeding. 2006. "'Fair' Inequality? Attitudes Toward Pay Differentials: The United States in Comparative Perspective." *American Sociological Review* 71 (3): pp. 450–473.
Pew Research Center. 2019. "Survey on Global Attitudes Spring 2019." Research Report.
Piketty, T. 2019. *Capital and Ideology*. Cambridge, MA: Harvard University Press.
Reynolds, J., and H. Xian. 2014. "Perceptions of Meritocracy in the Land of Opportunity." *Research in Social Stratification and Mobility* 36: pp. 121–137.
Roaf, M.J., M.R. Atoyan, M.B. Joshi, and M.K. Krogulski. 2014. *Regional Economic Issues—Special Report 25 Years of Transition: Post-Communist Europe and the IMF*. Regional Economic Issues Special Report. Washington, DC: International Monetary Fund. https://doi.org/10.5089/9781498305631.086.
Roex, K.L.A., T. Huijts, and I. Sieben. 2019. "Attitudes Towards Income Inequality: 'Winners' Versus 'Losers' of the Perceived Meritocracy." *Acta Sociologica* 62 (1): pp. 47–63.
Sachweh, P. 2017. "Criticizing Inequality? How Ideals of Equality Do and Do Not Contribute to the De-Legitimation of Inequality in Contemporary Germany." *Historical Social Research* 42 (3): pp. 62–78.
Sandel, M.J. 2020. *The Tyranny of Merit: What's Become of the Common Good?* New York: Farrar, Straus and Giroux.

Savani, K., N.M. Stephens, and H.R. Markus. 2011. "The Unanticipated Interpersonal Consequences of Choice: Victim Blaming and Reduced Support for the Public Good." *Psychological Science* 22: pp. 795–802.

Simmons, B.A., and Z. Elkins. 2004. "The Globalization of Liberalization: Policy Diffusion in the International Political Economy." *American Political Science Review* 98(1): pp. 171–189.

Smith, A. 1776. *An Inquiry into the Nature and Causes of the Wealth of Nations*, edited by R.H. Campbell, A.S. Skinner, and W.B. Todd, 1976. 2 vols. Oxford: Oxford University Press.

Tachibanaki, T. 2005. *Confronting Income Inequality in Japan*. Cambridge, MA: MIT Press.

Tachibanaki, T. 2006. "Inequality and Poverty in Japan." *Japanese Economic Review* 57 (1): pp. 1–27.

Tay, S. 2015. "Rethinking Income Inequality in Japan and China (1995–2007)." *China Report* 51 (3): pp. 230–257.

UNESCO Institute for Statistics. 2012. *International Standard Classification of Education ISCED 2011*. Montreal: UNESCO.

Veliz, P. 2017. "Functional Theory of Stratification." In *The Wiley-Blackwell Encyclopedia of Social Theory*, edited by B.S. Turner, K.-S. Chang, C. Epstein, P. Kivisto, W. Outhwaite, and J.M. Ryan, vol. 5, pp. 1–3. West Sussex: John Wiley & Sons.

Weatherall, M., M.H. Huang, and T. Whang. 2018. "The Malaise of Globalization in East Asia: Income Inequality, Perceived State Capacity, and Anti-Establishment Attitudes." *Korean Journal of International Studies* 16 (1): pp. 1–27.

Wisman, J.D., and J.F. Smith. 2011. "Legitimating Inequality: Fooling Most of the People All of the Time." *American Journal of Economics and Sociology* 70 (4): pp. 974–1013.

Wong, K.Y.T., P.S.S. Wan, and W.K.K. Law. 2009. "Public Perceptions of Income Inequality in Hong Kong: Trends, Causes and Implications." *Journal of Contemporary China* 18 (61): pp. 657–673.

Chapter 7
Linking Beliefs in Meritocracy and Concerns About Inequality
Perceived Inequality as Mediator

Licia Bobzien and Roland Verwiebe

Introduction

Inequality is on the rise in many countries. Across OECD countries, for instance, the average share of disposable income earned by the top 10% of earners has increased since 1990 and is now around five times higher than the income of the bottom 10% (OECD 2023). Empirically, concerns about inequality and demand for redistribution, however, remain relatively unrelated to actual levels of inequality (Trump 2023). Figure 7.1 shows a violin plot that illustrates inequality concerns by actual levels of inequality. Two observations stand out: First, individuals who live in more unequal countries are on average slightly more concerned about inequality than those living in more equal countries. Second, however, it shows that—independently from the actual level of inequality—individuals are very differently concerned about inequality. Some very concerned individuals live in low-inequality countries while others who are not concerned at all live in high-inequality countries.[1] This empirical observation of the unrelatedness between actual inequality and concerns about inequality has sparked the academic interest of social scientists as it is in conflict with standard theoretical expectations based on economic self-interest (Meltzer and Richard 1981) or based on values such as egalitarianism or fairness (Fong 2001; Rueda 2018).

There are two different explanations present in the literature to make sense of this empirical finding. First, following a moral logic, researchers argue that individuals justify inequalities and inequality dynamics using heuristics, such as the belief in meritocracy (Mijs 2021). Second, researchers

Licia Bobzien and Roland Verwiebe, *Linking Beliefs in Meritocracy and Concerns About Inequality*.
In: *The Social Acceptance of Inequality*. Edited by: Francesco Duina and Luca Storti, Oxford University Press.
 DOI: 10.1093/oso/9780197814499.003.0007

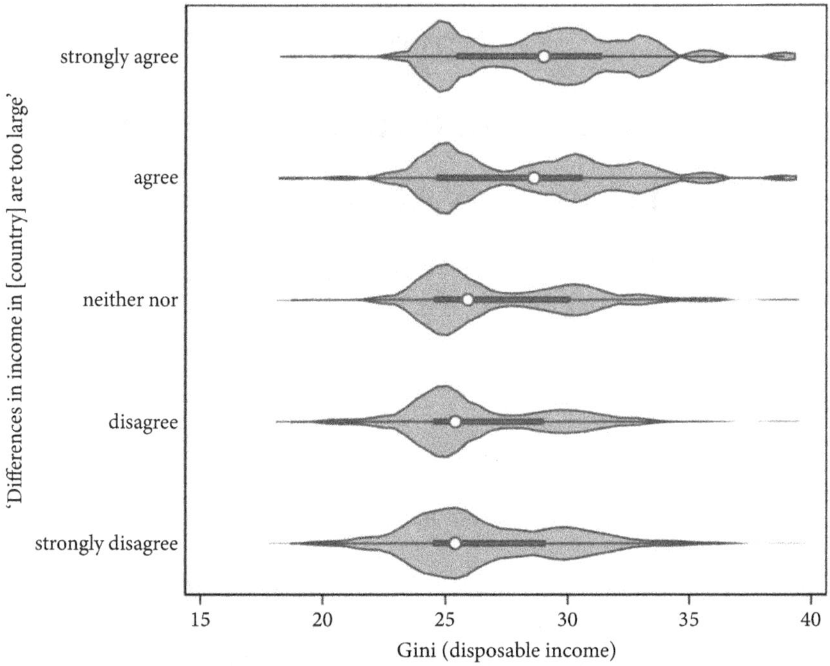

Figure 7.1 Violin plot: Inequality concerns by actual levels of inequality

Note: Violin plot with white dots reports the median Gini index for each answer category of inequality concerns; the box reports the first and third quartile; and the line, including the gray area, representing the density distribution.

Source: ISSP 1992–2019; N = 39,806, own calculation; actual inequality level based on Gini coefficient of disposable income.

argue that individuals are not accurately informed about inequalities; their perceptions are, however, relevant for the question whether they are concerned about inequality (Trump 2023). We know from past research that both explanations are empirically observable. Both inequality perceptions and beliefs in meritocracy are linked to inequality concerns and demand for redistribution. Yet, existing research also shows that inequality perceptions depend on an individuals' economic situation, such as income or education, as well as on individuals' attitudes and values, such as political beliefs (Roex et al. 2019; Trump 2018; Verwiebe and Wegener 2000; Wiesböck and Verwiebe 2023). Given these findings, we analyze how these two explanations are interwoven and investigate the ways in which perceived inequality mediates the link between beliefs in meritocracy and concerns about inequality. We argue that studying this mediation is crucial for a more comprehensive understanding of the dynamics at play.

Our results indicate, in line with past research, first, that beliefs in meritocracy are associated with inequality concerns and, second, that individuals' perceptions of inequality are associated with inequality concerns. Going beyond past research, we further find that individuals who believe in meritocracy perceive lower levels of inequality and show that this is an additional mechanism of how beliefs in meritocracy affect inequality concerns. We thus theoretically argue and empirically show that perceived inequality acts as a mediator that can help explain (parts of) the relationship between meritocracy beliefs and concerns about inequality. We explain this mediation by referring to selective attention as a mechanism that leads individuals to selectively process information about inequality, thereby focusing on information that serves their beliefs in meritocracy.

Theory

State of the Art: Making Sense of Inequality Concerns

Standard political economy explanations focusing on material self-interest as determinant for inequality concerns suggest that higher inequality should also lead to more concerns about inequality and more demand for redistribution (Meltzer and Richard 1981). However, empirical evidence is mixed (see Schmidt-Catran 2016) giving rise to a rich body of literature suggesting that determinants beyond material self-interest, such as other-regarding preferences and fairness concerns, matters to individuals (see Alesina and Glaeser 2006; Arts and Gelissen 2001). This literature has advanced our understanding yet still does not allow us to fully understand variation in inequality concerns and redistribution preferences across individuals. There are two explanations for this: Individuals often (1) legitimize inequalities by using justifications or (2) have biased perceptions about inequality. Such perceptions and justifications, in turn, matter for individuals' attitudes toward inequality.

Justifications

In the field of distributive justice and the study of how resources and opportunities should be allocated within a society, researchers argue that individuals' economic positions can be understood as an outcome of effort and circumstance/luck (Dworkin 2001; Roemer 1998). This implies that inequality is related to two dimensions of distributive justice: opportunities and outcomes. Following this line of argumentation, the structure of resources and opportunities matters for the evaluation of outcomes. In this context, *circumstances* are factors beyond people's control, such as the family one is born into. *Efforts*, in contrast, are actions, choices, and investments that individuals make, and it is considered within an individual's control, as it reflects personal choices and agency. There is evidence that individuals use this differentiation between circumstance and effort to (normatively) evaluate distributive outcomes in their everyday life. The general idea is that inequalities resulting from efforts are perceived as fair as they are a consequence of personal choices and agency while inequalities resulting from circumstances are perceived as unfair as they are a consequence of factors beyond people's control (Fong 2001; Heuer et al. 2020). Individuals then build their beliefs about whether outcome inequalities are meritocratic based on this differentiation between effort and circumstances. Beliefs in meritocracy thus represent the belief that societal success and the resulting inequalities are reflective of a meritocratic process,[2] with the American Dream standing as perhaps the most salient example of this legitimation process (see Hauhart, Chapter 11 in this volume). This mechanism is closely related to the concept of system justification, a concept that seeks to explain how individuals engage in cognitive and motivational processes to rationalize and justify existing social, economic, and political structures, even when they are characterized by inequality (Jost et al. 2004; van der Toorn et al. 2015). It is further closely related to the just world belief, a cognitive concept that reflects the tendency of individuals to believe that the world is fundamentally just, and that people generally get what they deserve. Such biases have been shown to be relevant for the study of fairness and inequality (Dallinger 2021; Trump 2018, 2020). There is also plenty of empirical evidence for the relevance of meritocracy beliefs: Fehr and Vollmann (2022), conducting an online survey experiment, show that economically successful participants overweigh the role of effort in their success and perceive high incomes as more deserved than unsuccessful participants. This, in turn, leads them to have lower demand for redistributive taxation. This finding is in line with several studies showing that individuals justify economic success (Heiserman et al. 2020; McCoy and Major 2007) and economic inequality by meritocracy (García-Sánchez et al. 2020; Mutz 2018).

Perceptions

The literature on justifications outlines that individuals tend to accept economic inequality if they believe that this is a consequence of a meritocratic process. There is, however, also an alternative explanation on why people accept inequalities: Literature focusing on biased perceptions argues that levels and changes of inequality are little related to concerns about inequality because people do not perceive such levels and changes (Trump 2023). The underlying assumption of this literature is that individuals would react in a self-interest manner if they were aware of the actual level of inequality. Because of often incomplete information, however, their preferences are not necessarily in line with self-interest mechanisms. There has been a growing interest in studying the relevance of inaccurate and biased perceptions of inequality to better understand whether there is empirical evidence for the theoretical mechanisms (see Rodríguez-Bailón et al., Chapter 4 in this volume). Evidence indicates that individuals indeed tend to misestimate the level of inequality (Bublitz 2022; Norton and Ariely 2011; Osberg and Smeeding 2006). If these perceptions (rather than justifications) matter, updating individuals' perceptions should also change the ways in which they think and feel about inequality. There is observational and experimental evidence that suggests that there is some evidence for this mechanism: Providing information on inequality, for instance in the form of providing information on the relative income position, influences individuals' inequality perceptions (Fernández-Albertos and Kuo 2018). The effect on preferences for redistribution is, however, context-dependent (Bublitz 2022), heterogeneous across individuals (Karadja et al. 2017), and effect sizes are rather small (Ciani et al. 2021; Weisstanner and Armingeon 2022).

Our Argument: Connecting Beliefs in Meritocracy to Perceived Inequality

Past literature shows that belief in meritocracy matters for concerns about inequality, indicating that individuals justify inequality using justifications such as the belief in meritocracy (Alesina and La Ferrara 2005; Mijs 2021). It further shows that inequality perceptions matter for individual political attitudes and preferences: Individuals who perceive less inequality also demand less redistribution (Bobzien 2020; Kuhn 2019; Willis et al. 2022). We argue that considering the interrelation between justifications (i.e., meritocracy beliefs) and perceptions (i.e., information about inequality) may help to better understand when and why individuals are concerned about inequality. Thereby, we follow Mijs (2021), who argues that "[r]ather than think[ing] of the role of cognition and morality [i.e., meritocracy] as competing explanations for the lack of popular concern about inequality, the two may in fact be connected" (11).

Justifications not only may influence individual attitudes toward inequality but also may influence individual perceptions thereof. A number of studies across different disciplines suggest that beliefs are crucial determinants of how individuals perceive the world. Such beliefs influence a variety of perceptions and views on the world such as climate change perceptions (Lacroix et al. 2020; Sambrook et al. 2021), social mobility perceptions (Dallinger 2010; Davidai and Gilovich 2015; Mijs and Savage 2020; Sandel 2020; Trevisan et al. 2022), or policy preferences and potentially political polarization (Di Tella and Rodrik 2020; Hochschild and Einstein 2015; Karadja et al. 2017; Ricci 2023). Following these findings, we argue that believing in meritocracy makes individuals less sensitive to perceiving inequalities, resulting in perceiving lower levels of inequalities relative to those who do not believe in meritocracy. Our argument builds on empirical findings by Du and King (2022), who find that individuals perceive different levels of inequality depending on normative responses: Individuals who consider inequality to be unfair perceive higher levels of inequality while individuals who consider inequality to be fair perceive lower levels of inequality. Similarly, Støstad (2024) shows in experimental settings that fairness beliefs causally affect perceived levels of inequality, suggesting that ideological beliefs alter how people perceive economic inequality. Such findings demonstrate the interrelation between beliefs and perceptions. We suggest that believing in meritocracy leads individuals to perceive less inequality as people selectively process information to maintain consistency in their existing beliefs. This cognitive mechanism is known as confirmation bias (Klayman 1995), "the seeking or interpreting of evidence in ways that are partial to existing beliefs, expectations, or a hypothesis in hand" (Nickerson 1998, 1089). This definition includes the tendency for individuals to favor information that confirms their preexisting beliefs while ignoring information that contradicts them. Applying that to the context of perceived inequality, this may mean that individuals tend to seek, interpret, and give more weight to information that aligns with their preexisting beliefs about inequality. For instance, if an individual believes that inequality is not a significant issue as well as that society is generally fair and social mobility high, they may tend to pay attention to information that supports this view while dismissing or downplaying information that suggests the contrary. Selective attention can facilitate such biases. Selective attention refers to the mechanism by which individuals focus their awareness on specific information while filtering out other information. For instance, if an individual holds specific beliefs, they may selectively consume information that support such existing beliefs reinforcing their confirmation bias. This is closely related to ideas around system justification theories suggesting that individuals try to justify existing social, economic, and political structures.

Against this background, we argue, first, that individuals justify inequalities by their beliefs in meritocracy (*justification* mechanism); and, second, have inaccurate perceptions of inequality (*perceptions* mechanism), which are, in turn, relevant for their inequality concerns. Our corresponding hypotheses are:

> H_1 (justification mechanism): *The higher the belief in meritocracy, the lower the inequality concerns.*
>
> H_2 (perceptions mechanism): *The higher the inequality perceptions, the higher the inequality concerns.*

We then argue that such two mechanisms, belief in meritocracy and perceived inequality, are interrelated: Individuals' perceived inequalities depend, among other factors, on the belief in meritocracy. This leads us to our third hypothesis:

> H_3 (interrelation): *The higher the belief in meritocracy, the lower the perceived inequality.*

From this it follows that we hypothesize a mediation effect between belief in meritocracy, perceived inequality, and inequality concerns. We suggest that this is due to consuming information selectively (see Figure 7.2):

> H_4 (mediation): *The effect of belief in meritocracy on inequality concerns is mediated by perceived inequality.*

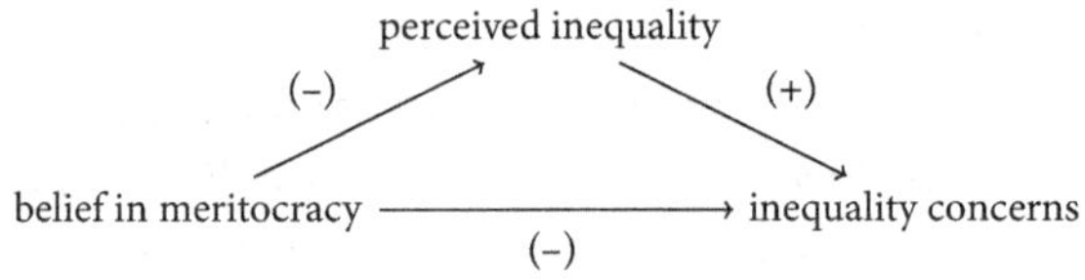

Figure 7.2 Illustration of the hypothesized mechanism
Source: Own illustration.

Method and Data

Data and Operationalization

To test the role of inequality perceptions in the relationship between beliefs in meritocracy and concerns about inequality, we analyze the Social Inequality modules I to V of the International Social Survey Programme (ISSP) (ISSP Research Group 2014, 2021). We use data from 1992, 2009, and 2019, excluding the year 1999 (module II) as it does not include a central item (belief in meritocracy) for our main independent variable. We focus on European countries included in at least one module: Austria, Belgium, the Czech Republic, Denmark, France, Germany, Hungary, Iceland, Italy, Latvia, Lithuania, Norway, Poland, Portugal, Slovakia, Slovenia, Spain, Sweden, Switzerland, and Great Britain (see Appendix Figure 7A for an overview of the included country-years). We include N = 39,806 observations across three time points ranging across more than twenty-five years after listwise deletion of cases containing missing values. We partly compensate for unit nonresponse error by weighting the data. All estimations discussed in the results section include these weights.

Dependent Variable: Inequality Concern

We measure individual inequality concerns using a question that asks respondents about their agreement to the following statement: "Differences in income in [country] are too large," with answer options *strongly agree*, *agree*, *neither agree nor disagree*, *disagree*, or *strongly disagree*. We recode the variable for easier interpretation; a higher value indicates that a respondent is more concerned about inequality. That is, someone who reports to strongly agree with the statement is assigned to a value of 5 while someone who strongly disagrees with the statement is assigned to a value of 1.[3]

Variables of Interest 1: Belief in Meritocracy

Following Roemer's (1998) differentiation between circumstances and effort, we build an index that considers the individually perceived importance of endogenous and exogenous factors for getting ahead in society. In doing so, we follow earlier work (Becker 2021; Fong 2001; Linos and West 2003). To measure the perceived importance of exogenous factors (*circumstance*), we use the following question: "[. . .] we have some questions about opportunities for getting ahead. How important is coming from a wealthy family?," with higher values indicating that it is less important. To measure the perceived importance of endogenous factors (*effort*), we use the following question: "How important is hard work?," with higher values indicating that it is more important. We then build an equally weighted index ranging from 1 to 5, with 1 indicating low belief in meritocracy and 5 indicating high belief in meritocracy.

Variables of Interest 2: Perceived Inequality

We operationalize perceived inequality using an item that ask individuals to reveal their perceived level of inequality using graphical visualizations. Respondents were asked to estimate how they think their society looks today: "These five diagrams show different types of society. Please [. . .] look at the diagrams and decide which you think best describes <country> [. . .]. What type of society is <country> today?" Following established standards of the research (Bobzien 2020; Gimpelson and Treisman 2018), we calculate Gini coefficients from these graphs (see Appendix Figure 7B for an overview of the visualizations).

Controls

Following past research on redistributive preferences and concerns about inequality, we add several control variables to minimize omitted variable biases. We add age (continuous, limited to sixteen to eighty), gender (female and male), three levels of education (<secondary, secondary, >secondary), employment status ((self-)employed, in education, retired, not in labor force, unemployed). We do not add income as an additional control variable as it is measured in the ISSP inconsistently across countries and across time making it difficult to harmonize the variables. We further use country- and year-fixed effects to sweep out the fact that our results are simply driven by structural differences between countries or general trends over time.

Results

We start our empirical analyses by specifying simple ordinary least squares (OLS) models including control variables as well as country- and time-fixed effects. In a next step, we use mediation techniques to disentangle the different effects on inequality concerns.

Figure 7.3 shows the linear predictions of inequality concerns (a) by belief in meritocracy and (b) by perceived inequality. It further shows (c) perceived inequality by inequality concerns. Corresponding with existing studies, we find that believing in meritocracy is associated with lower inequality concerns (Fehr and Vollmann 2022; McCoy and Major 2007; Mijs 2021). We further find, also in line with past research, perceiving higher levels inequality is associated with higher inequality concerns (Bobzien 2020; Du and King 2022; Willis et al. 2022). This indicates that beliefs in meritocracy as well as perceived inequality are relevant predictors for inequality concerns. These variables, however, are empirically not unrelated. Figure 7.3(c) shows that a higher belief in meritocracy is associated with lower inequality perceptions. We interpret that as a first indicator that believing in meritocracy may indeed make individuals less sensitive to perceiving inequality, through selective attention.

In a next step, we specify OLS models in which we add belief in meritocracy and inequality perceptions in a stepwise approach to gain knowledge of whether inequality perceptions mediate the relationship between belief in meritocracy and inequality concerns. Table 7.1 shows such models without controls (models 1 and 2) and with controls (models 3 and 4). Model 1 and model 3 include only belief in meritocracy as a variable of interest while model 2 and model 4 further include inequality perceptions.

Focusing on the full model 3, we see that believing in meritocracy is negatively associated with inequality concerns with a coefficient of −0.058 ($p < 0.01$) (H1). This reveals that individuals who believe in meritocracy tend to be less concerned about inequality. When adding inequality perceptions as additional variable in model 4, the effect of believing in meritocracy decreases to −.049 ($p < 0.01$); perceiving higher inequality, however, increases inequality concerns by 0.017 ($p < 0.001$) (H2). This indicates that belief in meritocracy as well as inequality perceptions are associated with inequality concerns and that the effect of belief in meritocracy may be partially mediated by inequality perceptions.

In a next step, we conduct a mediation analysis (MacKinnon et al. 2007) to test how much of the effect of belief in meritocracy on inequality concerns is

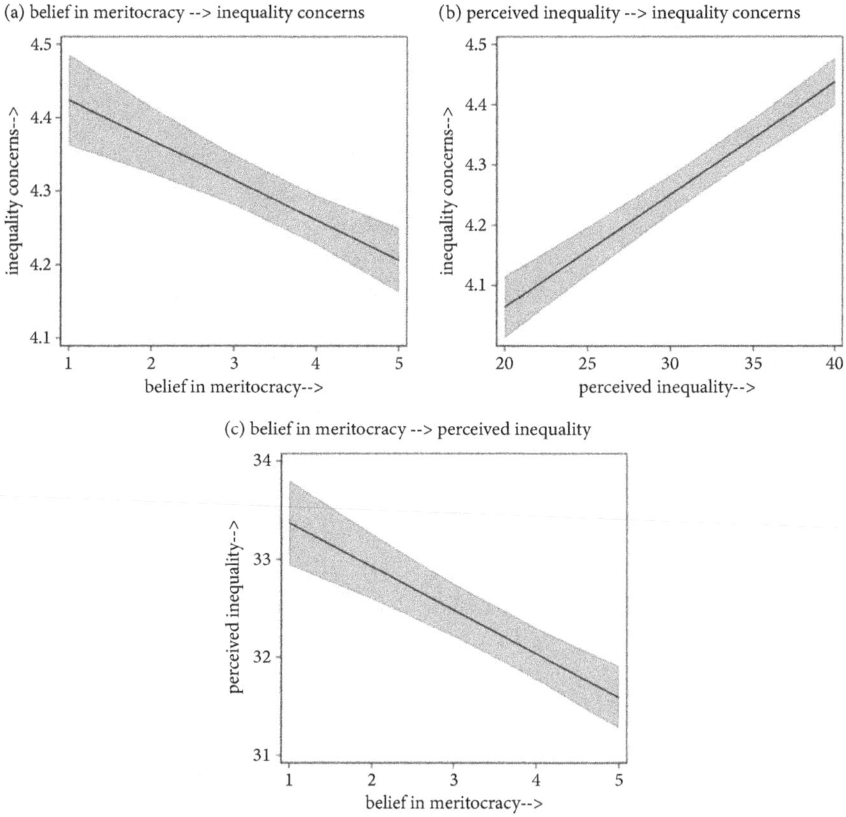

Figure 7.3 Linear predictions of (a) inequality concerns by belief in meritocracy, (b) inequality concerns by perceived inequality, and (c) perceived inequality by belief in meritocracy

Source: ISSP 1992–2019; N = 39,806, own calculation; controls country- and time-fixed effects not shown; 95% confidence interval.

mediated by perceived inequality. Thereby, we focus on the controlled direct effects. This is the effect of belief in meritocracy when taking the changes of the mediator into account (Acharya et al. 2016). This enables us to see how much of the main effect goes through perceived inequality. In the mediation analysis including controls (Figure 7.4 right), we include all control variables that have been included in the models (3) and (4) in Table 7.1, including country- and year-fixed effects. Figure 7.4 shows the indirect (mediation), direct (belief in meritocracy on inequality concerns), and total effect (the sum of these two effects) of belief in meritocracy on inequality concerns with perceived inequality as mediator without controls (left) and with controls (right). In the following, we focus our discussion on the model including controls as we consider that our final model specification.

Table 7.1 Regression analysis for inequality concerns

DV: inequality concerns	(1)	(2)	(3)	(4)
belief in meritocracy	−0.109***	−0.0752***	−0.0575**	−0.0488**
	(−4.80)	(−4.43)	(−3.39)	(−3.02)
perceived Gini		0.0283***		0.0183***
		(7.51)		(8.57)
constant	4.650***	3.619***	4.375***	3.804***
	(66.40)	(28.52)	(41.75)	(35.22)
country- and year FE	yes	yes	yes	yes
controls	no	no	yes	yes
N	39,806	39,806	39,806	39,806

Source: ISSP 1992–2019; $N = 39{,}806$, own calculation; controls not shown, t statistics in parentheses; $^{*}p < 0.05$, $^{**}p < 0.01$, $^{***}p < 0.001$ (see Appendix Table 7A for full regression table).

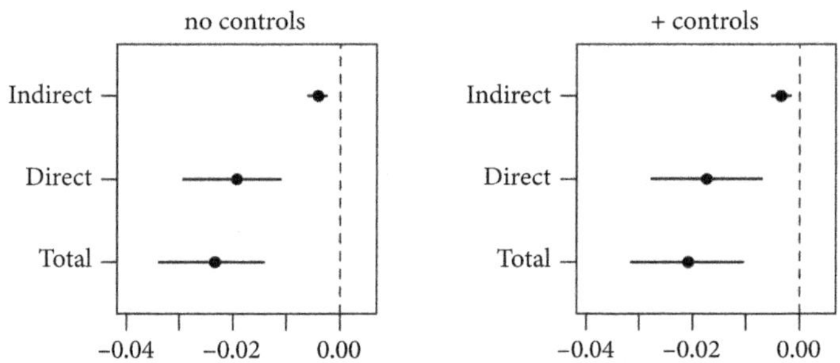

Figure 7.4 Mediation analysis of belief in meritocracy on inequality concerns mediated by perceived inequality

Source: ISSP 1992–2019; N = 39,806, own calculation; 95% confidence interval.

The mediation analysis shows an overall negative effect: Individuals who believe in meritocracy express lower levels of concern regarding inequality (total effect). The direct effect of belief in meritocracy on inequality concerns is substantial in effect size ($\beta = -.017$, $p < 0.001$). The indirect effect of perceived inequality on inequality concerns is relatively small in effect size (approximately a quarter of the total effect) but statistically significant ($\beta = -.003$, $p < 0.001$). This indicates that the perceived inequality as mediator may capture only a partial effect of belief in meritocracy on inequality concerns. We interpret these results as evidence that there are two mechanisms of how belief in meritocracy links to inequality concerns: There is a direct mechanism that leads individuals to be less concerned about inequality when believing in meritocracy. At the same time, there is a mediation through perceived inequalities: Believing in meritocracy is associated with lower inequality perceptions which, in turn, reduces inequality concerns.

Conclusion

In this chapter, we asked: Is the link between beliefs in meritocracy and inequality concerns mediated by perceived inequality? Existing research has shown that individuals use the concept of meritocracy to justify inequalities and that individuals often have biased perceptions of inequality that, in turn, influence the evaluation of such inequalities (H_1 and H_2). We suggested that beliefs in meritocracy and perceived inequality are interrelated determinants of inequality concerns (H_3): Those individuals who believe in meritocracy tend to perceive lower levels of inequality and, therefore, are less concerned about inequality due to selective attention and confirmation biases: Believing in meritocracy makes individuals selectively process information on inequality by focusing on observations that help them maintain their prior beliefs (H_4). Past research has argued that mechanisms such as selective attention leading to confirmation biases affect preferences and attitudes. We suggested that such mechanisms not only affect preferences but also perceptions of the status quo. From a theory-building perspective, acknowledging the interrelation of beliefs and perceptions may be a promising way for future research to better understand when and why individuals are concerned about inequality.

There are large differences between countries in the levels of belief in meritocracy, perceived inequality, and inequality concerns (see Appendix Figure 7C). This suggests that institutions such as the welfare state and culture are important determinants of such variables. That is, meritocracy beliefs, inequality perceptions, and inequality concerns do not exist in isolation but operate within the complex landscape of a variety of different societal and economic inequalities in many countries. Within the structure of this edited volume, we suggest that individuals apply moral logics, such as beliefs in meritocracy, to make sense of inequalities. The (non)existence of such a logic within societies is influenced by cultural and institutional contexts that shape social norms, expectations, and values (Almås et al. 2020; Thelen 2014). Moral logics are thus directly related to cultural and institutional logics.

Individuals can learn about the relevance of exogenous and endogenous factors by observing and experiencing their environment. For instance, beliefs in meritocracy are a function of one's own economic position and past experience (Mijs 2021). Empirically, higher inequality is associated with less economic mobility—usually considered a proxy for the existence of meritocracy (Corak 2013). At the same time, individuals living in high-inequality contexts often perceive lower levels of inequality than their counterparts in low-inequality contexts. This, partially counterintuitive finding, is explained by past research by segregation (Windsteiger 2022) and social comparison (Cansunar 2021). In this chapter, we suggested that selective attention and confirmation biases may be an additional mechanism explaining low-inequality perceptions in a high-inequality context.

We made the theoretical argument that perceived inequality may function as a mediator. However, there is evidence suggesting that the ways in which individuals react to perceived inequality may also depend on their beliefs. In this case, belief in meritocracy would moderate the relationship between perceived inequality and inequality concerns (García-Sánchez et al. 2020). Future research is needed to test the causal directions and interdependencies of these concepts empirically.

From a practical perspective, it is also important to ask: Does it really matter whether beliefs affect perceptions or preferences or both? Past research has shown that providing individuals with information about inequality, allowing them to update their perceptions, often has only small effects on preferences for redistribution and/or holds only for specific subgroups (Bublitz 2022; Cruces et al. 2013; Karadja et al. 2017). One explanation for that could be that individuals selectively process information applying heuristics such as confirmation biases. Thus, giving individuals information in an experimental context may only partially and selectively update their perceptions about inequality. This insight has been empirically shown in the literature aiming at understanding political polarization (Knobloch-Westerwick et al. 2020). Our results suggest that this also applies to the context of inequality concerns: It is not only important to ask how updating perceptions affects preferences and attitudes, as done by past research, but also to better understand the cognitive processes that lead to specific perceptions. This may enable researchers to understand which information in which context is used by individuals to update their perceptions and beliefs about inequality.

Our findings indicate that, beyond focusing on providing accurate perceptions to individuals, it may also be important to focus more strongly on perceptions of and beliefs about procedural inequalities and procedural fairness as well as cognitive biases individuals apply when building their perceptions and beliefs. Simply providing individuals with reliable information may not suffice to enable them to make realistic assessments because individuals may process information selectively. The objective should be to enable individuals to build accurate perceptions of the status quo. This is of practical importance because such perceptions matter for individuals' political preferences.

Appendix

Table 7A Full regression analysis including and excluding perceived Gini coefficient as independent variable

	(1)	(2)	(3)	(4)
DV: inequality concerns	b/se	b/se	b/se	b/se
belief in meritocracy	−0.109***	−0.0752***	−0.0575**	−0.0488**
	(−4.80)	(−4.43)	(−3.39)	(−3.02)
perceived inequality		0.0283***		0.0183***
		(7.51)		(8.57)
education (ref. < secondary)				
secondary			0.00467	0.00485
			(0.24)	(0.27)
>secondary			−0.208***	−0.188***
			(−5.33)	(−5.03)
employment status (ref. (self)employed)				
in education			−0.163***	−0.140***
			(−5.12)	(−4.57)
retired			0.0572**	0.0597**
			(3.13)	(3.39)
not in labor force			0.0259	0.0225
			(1.45)	(1.30)
unemployed			0.100***	0.0868***
			(4.56)	(4.22)
age in years			0.00197**	0.00165*
			(2.87)	(2.52)

Continued

Table 7A *Continued*

	(1)	(2)	(3)	(4)
male (ref. female)			−0.124***	−0.118***
			(−5.87)	(−5.80)
year (ref. 1992)				
2009			0.128	0.117
			(1.74)	(1.63)
2019			0.0648	0.0589
			(0.91)	(0.83)
constant	4.650***	3.619***	4.375***	3.804***
	(66.40)	(28.52)	(41.75)	(35.22)
Country FE	yes	yes	yes	yes
controls	no	no	yes	yes
N	39,806	39,806	39,806	39,806

Note: Country fixed effects not shown.
Source: ISSP 1992–2019; N = 39,806; t statistics in parentheses; $^{*}p < 0.05$, $^{**}p < 0.01$, $^{***}p < 0.001$.

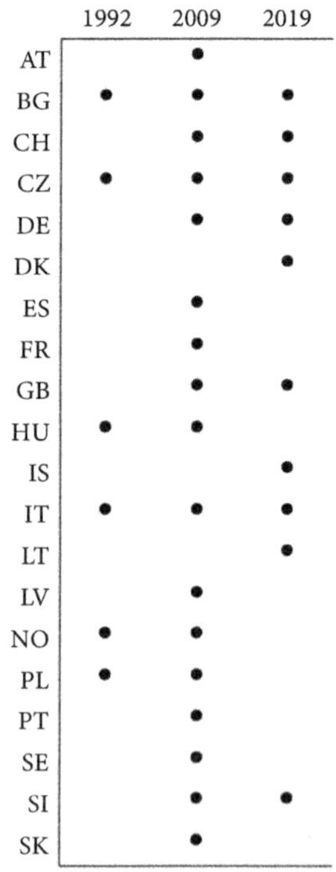

Figure 7A Overview of ISSP data (country-years) used for the analysis
Source: ISSP 1992–2019.

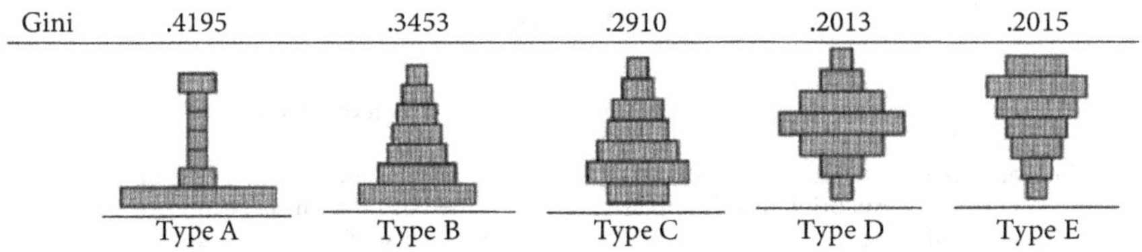

Figure 7B Operationalization of perceived inequality
Source: Master Questionnaire ISSP 2009.

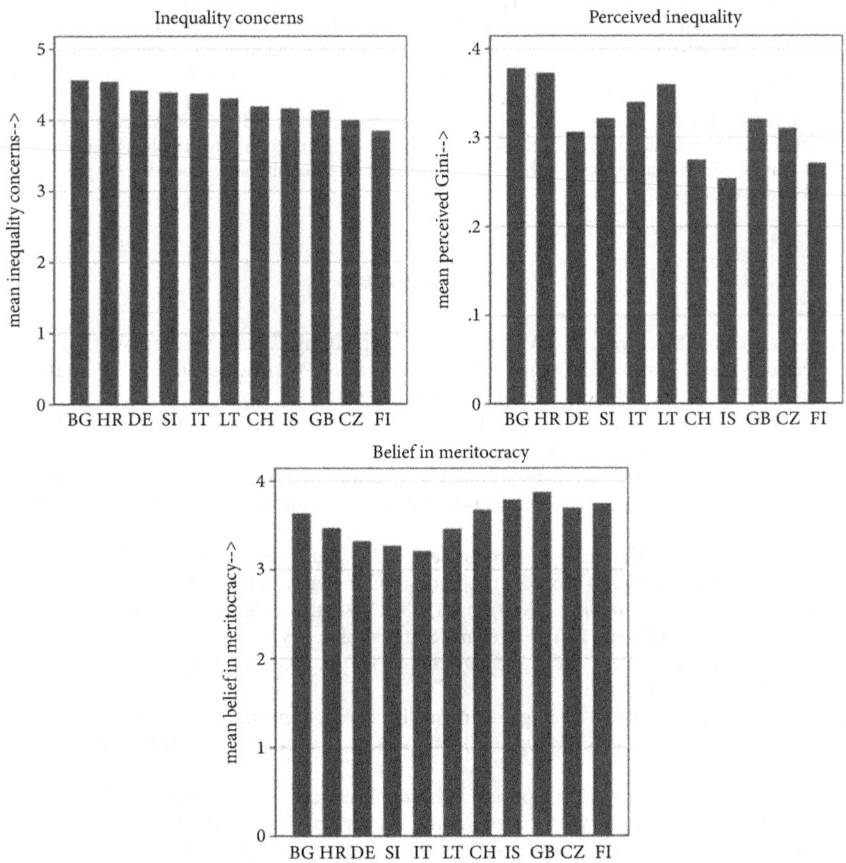

Figure 7C Country-means in inequality concerns, perceived inequality, and belief in meritocracy, 2019
Source: ISSP (2019) (own calculation).

Notes

1. Additionally, the predictive power of the actual inequality level on inequality concerns is rather low: $R^2 = 0.028$.
2. The concept of "meritocracy" has undergone an evolution since it was first introduced by Michael Young in an, originally dystopian, essay published in 1958. Initially conceived as a satirical critique of a society where social status was determined solely by one's talents and abilities, "meritocracy" has come to symbolize the ideal that individuals should be rewarded based on their hard work, skills, and efforts (for an overview, see Mijs and Savage 2020; Trevisan et al. 2022). While the meritocratic ideal is considered desirable by many, the term is being discussed more critically again; most prominently by Sandel (2020), who challenges the assumption that the distribution of wealth and status is solely a result of individual merit. Sandel suggests that this narrow focus on meritocracy has contributed to a sense of elitism and resentment among those who feel left behind in a system that celebrates winners and stigmatizes losers.
3. There is a large literature on preferences for public redistribution (see Dallinger 2010; Rueda 2018; Schmidt-Catran 2016). Here, we use concerns about inequality as a dependent variable rather than preferences for redistribution. Both concepts, however, are conceptually and empirically interwoven and highly correlated (corr(redpref, concerns) = 0.534, $p < 0.001$). We chose to focus on inequality concerns as this item focusses more on how individuals think about inequality rather than how individuals think about the government as an actor in changing inequality dynamics. At the same time, we benefit and build on the rich literature focusing on preferences for redistribution.

References

Acharya, A., M. Blackwell, and M. Sen. 2016. "Explaining Causal Findings Without Bias: Detecting and Assessing Direct Effects." *American Political Science Review* 110 (3): pp. 512–529. https://doi.org/10.1017/S0003055416000216.

Alesina, A., and E. Glaeser. 2006. *Fighting Poverty in the US and Europe: A World of Difference.* Oxford: Oxford University Press.

Alesina, A., and E. La Ferrara. 2005. "Preferences for Redistribution in the Land of Opportunities." *Journal of Public Economics* 89 (5): pp. 897–931. https://doi.org/10.1016/j.jpubeco.2004.05.009.

Almås, I., A.W. Cappelen, and B. Tungodden. 2020. "Cutthroat Capitalism Versus Cuddly Socialism: Are Americans More Meritocratic and Efficiency-Seeking Than Scandinavians?" *Journal of Political Economy* 128 (5): pp. 1753–1788. https://doi.org/10.1086/705551.

Arts, W., and J. Gelissen. 2001. "Welfare States, Solidarity and Justice Principles: Does the Type Really Matter?" *Acta Sociologica* 44 (4): pp. 283–299. https://doi.org/10.1177/000169930104400401.

Becker, B. 2021. "Temporal Change in Inequality Perceptions and Effects on Political Attitudes." *Political Research Exchange* 3 (1): pp. 1–21. https://doi.org/10.1080/2474736X.2020.1860652.

Bobzien, L. 2020. "Polarized Perceptions, Polarized Preferences? Understanding the Relationship Between Inequality and Preferences for Redistribution." *Journal of European Social Policy* 30 (2): pp. 206–224. https://doi.org/10.1177/0958928719879282.

Bublitz, E. 2022. "Misperceptions of Income Distributions: Cross-country Evidence from a Randomized Survey Experiment." *Socio-Economic Review* 20 (2): pp. 435–462. https://doi.org/10.1093/ser/mwaa025.

Cansunar, A. 2021. "Who Is High Income, Anyway? Social Comparison, Subjective Group Identification, and Preferences over Progressive Taxation." *Journal of Politics* 83 (4): pp. 1292–1306. https://doi.org/10.1086/711627.

Ciani, E., L. Fréget, and T. Manfredi. 2021. "Learning About Inequality and Demand for Redistribution: A Meta-Analysis of In-Survey Informational Experiments." OECD Papers on Well-Being and Inequalities, No. 2. Paris: OECD Publishing. https://doi.org/10.1787/8876ec48-en.

Corak, M. 2013. "Income Inequality, Equality of Opportunity, and Intergenerational Mobility." *Journal of Economic Perspectives* 27 (3): pp. 79–102. https://doi.org/10.1257/jep.27.3.79.

Cruces, G., R. Pérez Truglia, and M. Tetaz. 2013. "Biased Perceptions of Income Distribution and Preferences for Redistribution: Evidence from a Survey Experiment." *Journal of Public Economics* 98: pp. 100–112.

Dallinger, U. 2021. „Perzipierte Ungleichheit und politische Nachfrage" [Perceived Inequality and Political Demand]. *KZfSS Kölner Zeitschrift für Soziologie und Sozialpsychologie* 73 (4): pp. 473–500. https://doi.org/10.1007/s11577-022-00809-8.

Dallinger, U. 2010. "Public Support for Redistribution: What Explains Cross-National Differences?" *Journal of European Social Policy* 20 (4): pp. 333–349. https://doi.org/10.1177/0958928710374373.

Davidai, S., and T. Gilovich. 2015. "Building a More Mobile America—One Income Quintile at a Time." *Perspectives on Psychological Science* 10 (1): pp. 60–71. https://doi.org/10.1177/1745691614562005.

Di Tella, R., and D. Rodrik. 2020. "Labour Market Shocks and the Demand for Trade Protection: Evidence from Online Surveys." *Economic Journal* 130 (628): pp. 1008–1030. https://doi.org/10.1093/ej/ueaa006.

Du, H., and R.B. King. 2022. "What Predicts Perceived Economic Inequality? The Roles of Actual Inequality, System Justification, and Fairness Considerations." *British Journal of Social Psychology* 61 (1): pp. 19–36. https://doi.org/10.1111/bjso.12468.

Dworkin, R. 2001. "What Is Equality? Part 2: Equality of Resources." In *The Notion of Equality*, edited by M. Hajdin, pp. 283–345. London: Routledge. https://doi.org/10.2307/2265047.

Fehr, D., and M. Vollmann. 2022. "Misperceiving Economic Success: Experimental Evidence on Meritocratic Beliefs and Inequality Acceptance." CESifo Working Paper No. 9983. München: Ifo. https://doi.org/10.2139/ssrn.4241623.

Fernández-Albertos, J., and Kuo, A. 2018. "Income Perception, Information, and Progressive Taxation: Evidence from a Survey Experiment." *Political Science Research and Methods* 6 (1): pp. 83–110. https://doi.org/10.1017/psrm.2015.73.

Fong, C. 2001. "Social Preferences, Self-Interest, and the Demand for Redistribution." *Journal of Public Economics* 82 (2): pp. 225–246. https://doi.org/10.1016/S0047-2727(00)00141-9.

García-Sánchez, E., D. Osborne, G.B. Willis, and R. Rodríguez-Bailón. 2020. "Attitudes Towards Redistribution and the Interplay Between Perceptions and Beliefs About Inequality." *British Journal of Social Psychology* 59 (1): pp. 111–136. https://doi.org/10.1111/bjso.12326.

Gimpelson V., and D. Treisman. 2018. "Misperceiving Inequality." *Economics and Politics* 30 (1): pp. 27–54. https://doi.org/10.1111/ecpo.12103.

Heiserman, N., B. Simpson, and R. Willer. 2020. "Judgments of Economic Fairness Are Based More on Perceived Economic Mobility Than Perceived Inequality." *Socius* 6: pp. 1–12. https://doi.org/10.1177/2378023120959547.

Heuer, J.-O., T. Lux, S. Mau, and K. Zimmermann. 2020. "Legitimizing Inequality: The Moral Repertoires of Meritocracy in Four Countries." *Comparative Sociology* 19 (4–5): pp. 542–584. https://doi.org/10.1163/15691330-BJA10017.

Hochschild, J.L., and K.L. Einstein. 2015. "Do Facts Matter? Information and Misinformation in American Politics." *Political Science Quarterly* 130 (4): pp. 585–624. https://doi.org/10.1002/polq.12398.

ISSP Research Group. 2014. "International Social Survey Programme: Social Inequality I–IV—ISSP 1987–1992–1999–2009." GESIS Data Archive, Cologne. ZA5890 Data file Version 1.0.0'. https://doi.org/10.4232/1.11911.

ISSP Research Group. 2019. "Study: ZA7600 - International Social Survey Programme: Social Inequality V - ISSP 2019." GESIS Datenarchiv, Köln. http://dx.doi.org/10.4232/1.14009.

ISSP Research Group. 2021. "International Social Survey Programme: Social Inequality V—ISSP 2019." GESIS Datenarchiv, Köln. ZA7600 Datenfile Version 2.0.0, https://doi.org/10.4232/1.13829.

Jost, J.T., M.R. Banaji, and B.A. Nosek. 2004. "A Decade of System Justification Theory: Accumulated Evidence of Conscious and Unconscious Bolstering of the Status Quo." *Political Psychology* 25 (6): pp. 881–919. https://doi.org/10.1111/j.1467-9221.2004.00402.x.

Karadja, M., J. Mollerstrom, and D. Seim. 2017. "Richer (and Holier) Than Thou? The Effect of Relative Income Improvements on Demand for Redistribution." *Review of Economics and Statistics* 99 (2): pp. 201–212. https://doi.org/10.1162/REST_a_00623.

Klayman, J. 1995. "Varieties of Confirmation Bias." In *Psychology of Learning and Motivation*, edited by J. Busemeyer, R. Hastie, and D.L. Medin, pp. 385–418. San Diego: Academic Press. https://doi.org/10.1016/S0079-7421(08)60315-1.

Knobloch-Westerwick, S., C. Mothes, and N. Polavin. 2020. "Confirmation Bias, Ingroup Bias, and Negativity Bias in Selective Exposure to Political Information." *Communication Research* 47 (1): pp. 104–124.

Kuhn, A. 2019. "The Subversive Nature of Inequality: Subjective Inequality Perceptions and Attitudes to Social Inequality." *European Journal of Political Economy* 59: pp. 331–344. https://doi.org/10.1016/j.ejpoleco.2019.04.004.

Lacroix, K., R. Gifford, and J. Rush. 2020. "Climate Change Beliefs Shape the Interpretation of Forest Fire Events." *Climatic Change* 159 (1): pp. 103–120. https://doi.org/10.1007/s10584-019-02584-6.

Linos, K., and M. West. 2003. "Self-Interest, Social Beliefs, and Attitudes to Redistribution: Re-Addressing the Issue of Cross-National Variation." *European Sociological Review* 19 (4): pp. 393–409. https://doi.org/10.1093/esr/19.4.393.

MacKinnon, D.P., A.J. Fairchild, and M.S. Fritz. 2007. "Mediation Analysis." *Annual Review of Psychology* 58 (1): pp. 593–614. https://doi.org/10.1146/annurev.psych.58.110405.085542.

McCoy, S.K., and B. Major. 2007. "Priming Meritocracy and the Psychological Justification of Inequality." *Journal of Experimental Social Psychology* 43 (3): pp. 341–351. https://doi.org/10.1016/j.jesp.2006.04.009.

Meltzer, A.H., and S.F. Richard. 1981. "A Rational Theory of the Size of Government." *Journal of Political Economy* 89 (5): pp. 914–927. https://doi.org/10.1086/261013.

Mijs, J.J.B. 2021. "The Paradox of Inequality: Income Inequality and Belief in Meritocracy Go Hand in Hand." *Socio-Economic Review* 19 (1): pp. 7–35. https://doi.org/10.1093/ser/mwy051.

Mijs, J.J.B., and M. Savage. 2020. "Meritocracy, Elitism and Inequality." *Political Quarterly* 91 (2): pp. 397–404. https://doi.org/10.1111/1467-923X.12828.

Mutz, D.C. 2018. "Status Threat, Not Economic Hardship, Explains the 2016 Presidential Vote." *PNAS* 115 (19): pp. E4330–E4339. https://doi.org/10.1073/pnas.1718155115.

Nickerson, R.S. 1998. "Confirmation Bias: A Ubiquitous Phenomenon in Many Guises." *Review of General Psychology* 2 (2): pp. 175–220. https://doi.org/10.1037/1089-2680.2.2.175.

Norton, M.I., and D. Ariely. 2011. "Building a Better America—One Wealth Quintile at a Time." *Perspectives on Psychological Science* 6 (1): pp. 9–12. https://doi.org/10.1177/1745691610393524.

OECD. 2023. "Income Distribution." OECD Social and Welfare Statistics (database). *OECD iLibrary*. 10.1787/data-00654-en.

Osberg, L., and T. Smeeding. 2006. "'Fair' Inequality?: Attitudes Toward Pay Differentials: The United States in Comparative Perspective." *American Sociological Review* 71 (3): pp. 450–473. https://doi.org/10.1177/000312240607100305.

Ricci, D. 2023. *Post-Truth American Politics: False Stories and Current Crises*. New York: Cambridge University Press.

Roemer, J.E. 1998. *Theories of Distributive Justice*. Cambridge, MA: Harvard University Press.

Roex, K.L.A., T. Huijts, and I. Sieben. 2019. "Attitudes Towards Income Inequality: 'Winners' Versus 'Losers' of the Perceived Meritocracy." *Acta Sociologica* 62 (1): pp. 47–63. https://doi.org/10.1177/0001699317748340.

Rueda, D. 2018. "Food Comes First, Then Morals: Redistribution Preferences, Parochial Altruism, and Immigration in Western Europe." *Journal of Politics* 80 (1): pp. 225–239. https://doi.org/10.1086/694201.

Sambrook, K., E. Konstandinidis, S. Russell, and Y. Okan. 2021. "The Role of Personal Experience and Prior Beliefs in Shaping Climate Change Perceptions: A Narrative Review." *Frontiers in Psychology* 12: pp. 1–7. https://doi.org/10.3389/fpsyg.2021.669911.

Sandel, M.J. 2020. *The Tyranny of Merit: What's Become of the Common Good?* New York: Farrar, Straus and Giroux.

Schmidt-Catran, A.W. 2016. "Economic Inequality and Public Demand for Redistribution: Combining Cross-Sectional and Longitudinal Evidence." *Socio-Economic Review* 14 (1): pp. 119–140. https://doi.org/10.1093/ser/mwu030.

Støstad, M.N. 2024. "Fairness Beliefs Affect Perceived Economic Inequality." Working Paper [Preprint].

Thelen, K.A. 2014. *Varieties of Liberalization and the New Politics of Social Solidarity.* New York: Cambridge University Press.

Trevisan, F., P. Rusconi, P. Hanna, and P. Hegarty. 2022. "Psychologising Meritocracy: A Historical Account of Its Many Guises." *Theory and Psychology* 32 (2): pp. 221–242. https://doi.org/10.1177/09593543211057098.

Trump, K.-S. 2018. "Income Inequality Influences Perceptions of Legitimate Income Differences." *British Journal of Political Science* 48 (4): pp. 929–952. https://doi.org/10.1017/S0007123416000326.

Trump, K.-S. 2023. "Income Inequality Is Unrelated to Perceived Inequality and Support for Redistribution." *Social Science Quarterly* 104 (2): pp. 180–188. https://doi.org/10.1111/ssqu.13269.

Trump, K.-S. 2020. "When and Why Is Economic Inequality Seen as Fair." *Current Opinion in Behavioral Sciences* 34: pp. 46–51. https://doi.org/10.1016/j.cobeha.2019.12.001.

van der Toorn, J., M. Feinberg, J.T. Jost, A.C. Kay, T.R. Tyler, R. Willer, and C. Wilmuth. 2015. "A Sense of Powerlessness Fosters System Justification: Implications for the Legitimation of Authority, Hierarchy, and Government." *Political Psychology* 36 (1): pp. 93–110. 10.1111/pops.12183.

Verwiebe, R., and B. Wegener. 2000. "Social Inequality and the Perceived Income Justice Gap." *Social Justice Research* 13 (2): pp. 123–149. https://doi.org/10.1023/A:1007545823040.

Weisstanner, D., and K. Armingeon. 2022. "Redistributive Preferences: Why Actual Income Is Ultimately More Important Than Perceived Income." *Journal of European Social Policy* 32 (2): pp. 135–147. https://doi.org/10.1177/09589287211037912.

Wiesböck, L., and R. Verwiebe. 2023. „Sind Einkommensunterschiede zu groß? Eine Analyse von Einstellungen in der österreichischen Bevölkerung"[Is Income Inequality Too High? An Analysis of Attitudes in the Austrian Population]. *Österreichische Zeitschrift für Soziologie* 48 (1): pp. 53–66. https://doi.org/10.1007/s11614-023-00514-6.

Willis, G.B., E. García-Sánchez, A. Sánchez-Rodríguez, J.D. García-Castro, and Rosa Rodríguez-Bailón. 2022. "The Psychosocial Effects of Economic Inequality Depend on Its Perception." *Nature Reviews Psychology* 1 (5): pp. 301–309. https://doi.org/10.1038/s44159-022-00044-0.

Windsteiger, L. 2022. "The Redistributive Consequences of Segregation and Misperceptions." *European Economic Review* 144: p. 104073. https://doi.org/10.1016/j.euroecorev.2022.104073.

Chapter 8
Justifying Inherited Wealth
A UK Case Study on Conflicting Orders of Worth

Liz Moor and Sam Friedman

Introduction

The extent of contemporary wealth inequality is epitomized by one startling statistic: Eight billionaires now own as much wealth as the bottom 50% of the world's population (Lawson et al. 2020). In the United Kingdom, this inequity is particularly acute: The distribution of wealth is significantly more unequal than income and is growing at a faster rate (World Inequality Database 2020). Key to understanding this inequality, and particularly its reproduction across generations, is intergenerational gifting or the inheritance of wealth, particularly via housing (Christophers 2018). Such transfers have been steadily growing in recent years, yet the paradox is that reliance on such intergenerational support has grown at precisely the same time as ideals of meritocracy have become more and more entrenched (Mijs 2019; Savage 2015). One question, then, is whether and how people can reconcile beliefs in meritocratic achievement with accepting large and unearned economic gifts?

In this chapter, we address this question by drawing on research with twenty-seven homeowners in London who had recently bought property with financial help from their parents or wider family. We wanted to understand whether they experienced any tension in receiving financial gifts, and if so, how they justified it to themselves. In framing this research, we draw on the sociology of critical capacities (see, for example, Boltanski and Thévenot 2006) to foreground the explanations people offer for their actions and their attempts to find legitimate ways of justifying inherited wealth.

Liz Moor and Sam Friedman, *Justifying Inherited Wealth*. In: *The Social Acceptance of Inequality*.
Edited by: Francesco Duina and Luca Storti, Oxford University Press. © Oxford University Press (2025).
DOI: 10.1093/oso/9780197814499.003.0008

We find that there is widespread—though not universal—discomfort at receiving unearned gifts, and that interviewees employ distinctive strategies both to justify their receipt and to offset the feelings of discomfort about inequality. In particular, interviewees deploy "origin stories" that tend to downplay aspects of their own, often privileged, upbringings and instead situate their subjectivity as rooted in working-class or upwardly mobile extended family histories. This expression of an "intergenerational self" (Fivush et al. 2008) thus attempts to reconcile the apparent tension between meritocracy and the receipt of unearned gifts, deflecting suspicions of "unfair" privilege and instead positioning gifted money as interviewees' "own" through a multigenerational conception of subjectivity. We also observe a tendency to draw boundaries between one's own story of relatively "deserving" housing wealth and the less deserving wealth of others. Finally, we find some efforts to downplay housing wealth as a site of wealth inequality, or of intergenerational gifts as a cause of housing inequality, and instead to shift the narrative to other forms of inequality that are presented as more egregious and in need of reform. We understand these strategies for defusing the tension that arises with awareness of inequality as forms of justification, in Boltanski and Thévenot's (2006) sense, because they emerge in response to a perceived conflict between different kinds of moral logic: The "domestic" and family-oriented on the one hand, and the civic "general will" on the other.

Our findings provide insight into *how* people reason about inequality, particularly housing inequality, and show how even relatively privileged people labor discursively to incorporate a narrative of meritocratic achievement (a moral logic based on civic norms) into their accounts of their own economic experience, even while they also justify receipt of gifts through the "naturalness" of giving to kin (a moral logic based on the "domestic" ideal). This bears comparison with Neely's findings in this volume (Chapter 3). In our case, we find evidence of people trying to engage with conflicting normative claims about intergenerational gifting, and sometimes to resolve them. This has important implications for existing work on intergenerational transfers. Work in this area has tended to foreground the *intrafamilial* relational issues raised by gifting, but we show that there are wider *social* tensions that interviewees seek to resolve. These are most notable when interviewees talk about friends who do not have the same resources or when they reflect on the fairness of intergenerational transfers more broadly. In this way, our findings speak directly to the question of how inequality comes to be justified through particular forms of reasoning, and the appeal to different kinds of moral logic.

Our work also contributes to contemporary policy debates about intergenerational wealth transfers and taxation. We suggest that there is a conflict at the heart of these debates, between what Boltanski and Thévenot (2006) term different orders of worth (or what this volume calls different logics): The value of family ties and loyalty, on the one hand, and social values of meritocracy on the other. Yet, our findings suggest that one reason why this tension has not generated political appetite for policy changes such as increased inheritance tax is that many people feel that they can successfully reconcile these competing logics. By recasting familial gifts as evidence of one's place within an extended family project of multigenerational upward mobility, or by positioning gifting as a mechanism for supporting "ordinary" working- or lower middle-class families, our interviewees make these seemingly conflicting principles compatible.

Inheritance and the Reproduction of Wealth Inequality

In recent years, there has been a renewal of social scientific interest in the topic of wealth inequality (see Karagiannaki 2015; Piketty 2014; Savage 2015). In the United Kingdom, wealth has long been more unequally distributed than income, and such inequities continue to grow. A key dimension of wealth inequality, particularly relevant for its reproduction across generations, is the intergenerational transfer of economic capital. Here, parents (or other family members) gift, loan, or bequest wealth to their children either in vivo or when they die. Homeownership is, increasingly, the main reason for such transfers and a growing prerequisite for getting on the housing ladder is parental economic support. This "bank of mum and dad" is often decisive in Britons' pathways to homeownership, providing access to the kind of lump-sum capital necessary to reach deposit thresholds (Heath and Calvert 2011). For example, the proportion of UK first-time buyers dependent on financial support from family members rose from 10% in the mid-1990s, to around 45% in 2017, and it is now estimated to have risen to up to 60% (Udagawa and Sanderson 2017).

The growing association between homeownership and the "bank of mum and dad" has significant implications for the reproduction of inequality. Most obviously, it ensures that access to most people's key wealth-generating asset—housing—increasingly depends on class (and often also racial) privilege (Shapiro 2004). Indeed, as Adkins et al. (2020) have recently argued, the increase in inter vivo wealth transfers may be playing a major part in a reordering of the class structure whereby access to asset ownership—particularly housing—is becoming the key determinant of life chances.

Yet, there is an intriguing paradox here: Reliance on intergenerational support has grown at precisely the same time as norms of meritocracy have become more entrenched (Mijs 2019; Savage 2015). The idea here is that the most meritorious accumulate the most economic capital based on their own talent and hard work. Recently, a burgeoning literature has critiqued many of the assumptions underlying this "meritocratic ideal," variously questioning the arbitrary ways that merit is (mis)recognized as such (Khan 2011), the hubris meritocracy generates among its winners (Sandel 2020), how it contributes to the stigmatization of working-class destinations (Littler 2018), and a misplaced belief among all that the inequalities it produces are fair (Mijs 2019). However, one relatively unexplored theme in this recent work is how people reconcile benefiting from "unearned" inherited wealth and claiming a belief in or adherence to dominant principles of meritocracy. Only Shapiro (2004) has examined this in real depth, finding a widespread trepidation, discomfort and even denial in interviews about inheritance with white middle-class interviewees in the United States (see also, Sherman 2017). These inheritors, he argues, experience the tension between inheritance and meritocracy as a troubling "collision" and respond by laboring discursively to position their inherited assets as both deserved (i.e., by downplaying their significance vis-à-vis the greater assets they had accumulated through merit and hard work) and non-transformational (i.e., in terms of impacting their relative life chances).

Inheritance vs. Meritocracy: Reconciling Competing Orders of Worth

One way to think about this collision that Shapiro (2004) identifies is that it reflects socioeconomic arrangements that are governed by *competing* principles or moral logics. In the case of parental financial transfers to children, there is a "domestic" logic at play—one in which personal ties and attachments dominate, and giving economic aid to one's children reflects the natural order of things (see Boltanski and Thévenot 2006, 8).[1] However, this domestic logic sits rather awkwardly with a competing moral logic, based in societal beliefs about meritocracy and "fairness." After all, the meritocratic ideal—which pivots on the idea that rewards should be based on the abilities, skills, and achievements of the *individual*—is clearly undermined where people's ability to realize, or "cash in," their respective talents is contingent on the help of others. Following Boltanski and Thévenot (2006), disputes around the appropriate governing principles for a given situation—in this case, the allocation of housing—typically provoke forms of *justification*, which, in turn, reveal more starkly the underlying "forms of generality" or "forms of worth" governing areas of conflict and the extent to which they can be made compatible with one another.

In approaching our interviews, we draw on this framework to highlight intergenerational gifting as an exemplar of the type of everyday conflict or dispute that Boltanski and Thévenot (2006) suggest characterizes social life. It is a topic that is in principle open to a variety of possible normative claims and forms of justification and has questions of or "fairness" at its heart. The accounts that people produce of having received familial financial gifts reveal some of the tensions between different understandings of "fairness" and the different forms of justification they mobilize to support their views. We also follow Boltanski's (2011) claim that one of the purposes of sociology is to draw attention to these tensions or unresolved conflicts (Telling 2016).

In doing this, we also seek to exploit some of the differences between their sociology of critical capacities and the work of Pierre Bourdieu (see, for example, Celikates 2012; Guggenheim and Potthast 2012). On the one hand, the discourse of meritocracy has become so powerful that it might be described as a key component of contemporary *doxa*, i.e., an arbitrary but unquestioned and taken-for-granted "truth" existing in "the universe of the undisputed" (Bourdieu 1972). As such, we might expect our interviewees to both acknowledge norms of meritocracy in their accounts and instinctively position their receipt of gifts as adhering to such a doxic norm. On the other hand, meritocracy is not the only thing that interviewees talk about, and the palpable tensions we observe in people's accounts of inherited wealth, particularly when they talk about relations with less advantaged friends, suggest that there may be more going on than simple strategic positioning in relation to current norms. The conflict between a public discourse of meritocracy and people's own experiences of relative advantage through inherited or gifted wealth (itself socially validated through tax law) generates a discomfort that many interviewees seem compelled to try to resolve, often through rehearsing and testing out competing moral logics. Here Boltanski and Thévenot's (2006) approach has the advantage over Bourdieu of bringing out the *multiple* logics that may govern a particular situation, as well as "socially rooted, contextual forms of criticism" (Boltanski 2011, 5) in which people often engage and which may in turn form the basis for broader social theories of domination.

As we show below, most (although not all) of our respondents saw a tension between their receipt of an unearned monetary gift and the ideals of meritocracy, and they raised the associated question of "fairness" on their own initiative early in the interview. However, different kinds of "justificatory work" then followed as part of the substance of each interview, which either appealed to different overarching principles, or set them out in such a way as to attempt to resolve them. This justificatory work—ultimately oriented to finding ways of being comfortable with housing inequality—took three main forms that we outline briefly below, before moving to our empirical findings.

The main way that respondents justified their own experience of inheritance/gifting was by drawing attention to a particular construct, which, following Fivush (Fivush et al. 2008; Merrill and Fivush 2016), we call the *intergenerational self*. This intergenerational self—in which people understand their social identity not only in terms of their own life experience but also in terms of their parents' and grandparents' lives—provided a key means through which many respondents justified or attempted to resolve the tension between receiving unearned capital and adhering to the ideal of meritocracy. As we show, the advantages associated with parental gifts or inheritances were strongly offset, obscured, or deflected by a self-understanding that reached back beyond the influence of one's own, often privileged background, to a more humble and often working-class, multigenerational family history.

A second way in which people justified their own receipt of an unearned financial gift was by contrasting their own economic experience with that of real or imagined others. Here, we draw on Lamont's (1992) notion of "boundary work" and the various repertoires of evaluation people draw on to symbolically demarcate themselves from others. Specifically, we show how interviewees mobilized a complex combination of political and moral grounds to draw symbolic boundaries between their own inherited wealth and that of others. Crucial here were the narration of particular, meritocratically legitimate, wealth "origin stories" that were then positioned against friends or peers (and sometimes public figures) who had benefited from wealth that was greater, had been acquired through illegitimate family ties, or through other means that were less clearly tied to hard work.

Finally, some respondents mitigated the tension associated with the receipt of unearned income by resituating questions of wealth inequality and fairness away from housing. Here, we found efforts—often quite subtle—to underplay housing wealth as a site of inequality, or of intergenerational gifts as a problem, and instead to shift the narrative to other forms of inequality or unfairness that were claimed to be more problematic. Here, some forms of inequality become socially accepted, while others are positioned as more worthy of challenge.

Design and Methodology

Our fieldwork consisted of twenty-seven semistructured interviews (lasting between one and one-and-a-half hours) with twenty-one individuals and three couples who had bought their first property in London with financial support from a family member, usually a parent or grandparent. Appendix Table 8A provides demographic information about the gender, ethnicity, age, occupation, and class origin (in terms of parental occupation) of each interviewee.[2] Appendix Table 8A also details the value of the financial gift or inheritance received by most interviewees (seven declined to provide details). Notably, the sums received were greater than in other studies (see, for example, Druta and Ronald 2017; Heath and Calvert 2013), reflecting the later time of our study, the buoyant housing market at the time, and the fact that interviews were conducted in London. At the bottom end of the range, some participants received approximately £5,000, but at the upper end, the gifts extended above £500,000. The mean amount received was £76,000, and the median was £50,000.

Interviews were conducted in interviewees' homes and structured across four sections. First, interviewees were initially asked about their family background, education, occupation, and housing history. Second, we asked about the process of buying their current property and particularly the process of negotiating financial transfers with parents. Third, we asked about how they felt about having received financial help, and how their housing situation compared with that of peers and siblings. Finally, we asked their opinion on policies concerning inheritance tax and inter-vivo gifting.

The sociological interview is clearly a co-production (Rapley 2001), and we cannot guarantee that our findings would be replicated. Nonetheless, one of the affordances of the interview is that it provides interviewees with an opportunity to "reason out loud" about an area where they may have thoughts or feelings that have not previously been fully explored (Pugh 2013). This may be heightened in this case by the fact that both the event and topic of our research, as well as our positionality as critical academics, have the potential to elicit feelings of defensiveness. For example, justifications and explanations concerning inherited wealth may have emerged precisely because interviewees wanted to resist sociological stereotypes about middle-class entitlement that they felt may be being imposed on them by two critical sociologists (Savage and Flemmen 2019; see also Boltanski 2011, 3).

The interview context also helps us to think through one of the limits of Boltanski and Thévenot's (2006) initial formulation of regimes of justification and "orders of worth." As Wagner (1999) points out, these were originally seen as "constitutively public," but it is not clear that the same regimes apply in other "less public, more individual or localized ways in which a human agent engages with his or her environment" (347). Here, it may also be useful to consider Butler's (2005) suggestion that, while the terms through which we give an account of ourselves are unavoidably social in character, we nonetheless "come into contact with these norms through proximate and living exchanges, in the modes by which we are addressed and asked to take up the question of who we are and what our relation to the other ought to be" (30). Sociological interviews pose such questions in ways that invite abstract reflection and reasoning but also offer a certain intimacy. Tellingly, one interviewee described the interview discussion as "like therapy," while another said they would continue the discussion of inheritance tax in the pub with friends later. Both suggest something other than a purely public account of oneself, but they also suggest that, despite its artificiality, the prearranged interview had some continuity and resonance with conversations that might take place elsewhere in interviewees' lives.

Making Sense of Unearned Wealth: The Intergenerational Self

The tension between using family money to buy property and beliefs in meritocracy was evident in almost all interviews. In some cases, it was a source of guilt and political uneasiness, while in others it was simply something in need of explanation. The "need to explain" comes, we suggest, from a widespread awareness that although receiving money from parents is common, it is also at odds with dominant values of meritocracy:

> *I feel strange* in a position whereby my art is all about feeling sort of not looked after or in a difficult place in the city . . . and yet we're in a position now where we are in the top bracket [emphasis added]. (Georgia)[3]
>
> I've got loads of friends who would never be able to afford [it], um, and it does make you *feel a bit weird* . . . [emphasis added]. (Simon)
>
> I sort of feel, *I definitely feel kind of guilty* [emphasis added]. (Harriet)

This tension was often also articulated in political terms, as a kind of betrayal of strongly held commitments to equality and meritocracy. It represented, as Carol explained, a "personal conflict between what is best for your family and what is best on a national level" or, as Miles put it, a "lefty cognitive dissonance to live with constantly."

Significantly, most interviewees negotiated this tension by deploying various kinds of explanation or *justification*. The overarching theme flanking such justifications was, following Fivush et al. (2008), the idea of an intergenerational self. This had three distinct but interlinked elements: having "humble origins" at some point in one's extended family history, a familial narrative marked by hard work and meritocratic achievement, and an internalized familial ethos of frugality and caution.

Almost every respondent foregrounded their humble origins in some form. While this was sometimes expressed in conventional terms of parental occupation or income during the interviewee's own childhood, in most cases it was achieved by placing one's own background within the context of a much longer family history. Initially, this often involved deflecting presumptions of privilege. Nina, for example, was keen to emphasize that despite "this very posh voice . . . I've had, with money, definitely a really strange upbringing." From here, many chose to place emphasis on their *parents*' early-life struggles and class background, rather than their own. Hannah emphasized her father's experience of working in factories and garages (he now runs a successful business), while Harriet explained how her mother had squatted in London before buying her now quite valuable home.

Many went further, narrating their humble origins through the experiences of their grandparents and sometimes even great-grandparents. Alicia provided a notable example. When we asked about her background, she chose to narrate her origins not in relation to her wealthy entrepreneur father but instead through the story of her grandfather, who grew up impoverished and "basically dying of hunger" before becoming a businessman. Here, as with other interviewees, stories of intergenerational hardship and the modest beginnings of parents and grandparents were foregrounded and perhaps even inflated, as if to imply that the interviewee's current security was earned or deserved.

A second element of the intergenerational self was an emphasis on parental or grandparental hard work, meritocratic achievement, and upward social mobility. This was closely linked to the notion of "humble origins" but distinct from it, because it attempted to illustrate how humble origins had been transformed into economic prosperity, and, ultimately, the parental economic support interviewees had benefited from. It was also a way of explaining *why* such financial gifts are legitimate.

For example, Philippa, who had bought property in London with a partner in her late twenties, described her parents as having "come from relatively poor backgrounds and *worked hard and built up* [emphasis added]." Les similarly described his father having to "work hard . . . and *go without* [emphasis added]" to buy a house—something, he implied, that other people were not always willing to do. Indeed, almost all respondents whose parents had middle-class occupations emphasized that their parents had more working-class *origins* and had once been "just starting out" at the bottom rung of the ladder. Their current situation, therefore, was to be understood as the outcome of hard work during a lifetime, rather than early advantage. These parents were now business owners, managers, marketing consultants, and doctors (among other roles), but their lives were narrated as a success against the odds.

The narratives deployed here serve to justify current good positioning in the housing market by emphasizing that any money received has come as the legitimate result of meritocratic achievement, rather than as a form of unearned wealth. Thus, through the logic of an *intergenerational* self, the hard work of previous generations means that a financial windfall in the present does not need to be understood as "unearned."

The final element of the "intergenerational self" involved folding narratives of parental or grandparental hard work into one's own subjectivity in the present. This was achieved via their continuation of an enduring family "ethos" of hard work and frugality, especially in terms of homeownership:

> [My parents] never really earned a lot of money but they were always careful with money *and that's rubbed off on me.* . . . [I was] living on sofas and that sort of thing and putting a bit of money aside and living within your means and not running up credit card debts and all that kind of stuff. We were brought up with that sense of needing to be sensible about money. (Lucy)

> I could have spent all that money on iPads and phones and everything else. I didn't because I know that my dad didn't do that. He was training at uni [university] for, like, nine years . . . he was like, we had a black and white telly [television] in the eighties . . . there was no fancy stuff. (Les)

What is significant here is how both Lucy and Les attribute their parents' wealth to being "careful" and "sensible" with money, and they argue that adopting such an ethos has been formational in their pathway to homeownership, unlike imaginary others who "fritter away" money on consumer goods. There is a clear moral logic here, and a sense that certain groups may be entitled to better outcomes, due to imagined sacrifice. Homeownership here is constructed as a responsible form of consumption (Druta and Ronald 2017, 2–3) but also presented as contingent on the possession of a particular financial ethos that can then be used to deflect any implied criticism of family wealth.

What all three elements of the intergenerational self—that is, "humble origins," hard work/meritocracy, and an internalized familial ethos of frugality and caution—had in common was that each served to justify or contextualize the money interviewees had received. On the one hand, the gifted money could be construed as in some way "their" money (rather than their parents' or grandparents') through the extended sense of intergenerational subjectivity. On the other hand, the money itself could be seen as legitimate because its origins and means of accrual could be demonstrated to lie in (often intergenerational) hard work over time—a clear moral virtue.

The Limits of the Intergenerational Self

While elements of the intergenerational self were deployed as a form of justification in every interview, their ability to resolve respondents' subjectively felt tensions (the "weird" or "guilty" feelings noted at the beginning) differed in important ways. For a small number of respondents, the narration of an intergenerational self appeared effective at eliminating tensions between receiving gifts and a belief in meritocracy. In these cases, the intergenerational self enabled interviewees to fold parental gifts into a story of upward mobility. These cases fell along a spectrum of more or less tension, but there appeared to be a series of "mitigating circumstances" that were felt by interviewees (and often by us as interviewers) to be credible ways of evidencing a story of humble origins, parental hard work, or meritocratic achievement.

The first was, unsurprisingly, parental occupation. In cases where parents were more objectively working-class, i.e., employed in routine/manual jobs such as taxi driver, car mechanic, cleaner, cook or care worker, interviewees showed markedly less tension or anxiety at having received financial gifts. Thus, having at least one parent in a working-class occupation—even if the other parent had a more middle-class job or the interviewee had received a large sum of money from a *partner's* family—tended to be associated with stories of advancement that felt less ambivalent.

A second familial circumstance contributing to less ambivalent narratives was family migration, which precipitated the need to "start again," sometimes in the face of racism and hostility. Such stories fell along a spectrum. For example, stories in which a white parent or grandparent had migrated to a majority (or dominant minority) white country did not necessarily resolve tensions as credibly as those cases where nonwhite parents had migrated to the United Kingdom. Among interviewees with parents from Black African, Middle Eastern, or South Asian backgrounds, parents had come from differing class backgrounds and entered different occupations and achieved varying levels of wealth since arriving in the United Kingdom. Yet, what these families had in common was an experience of restricted social mobility, exclusion from certain kinds of opportunities, and a sense of having to work harder than white and/or "native" peers with equivalent qualifications.

A third type of mitigating circumstance was seen in cases where the interviewee's parents had divorced, leading to a childhood characterized by downward social mobility for the mother and a single, often very low, family income. For example, Nina described a "solidly middle class" father living in another country but a childhood on a restricted income with a mother in domestic service. Another interviewee had been raised by a single mother whose home was repossessed. Even when these interviewees had, later in life, been given fairly substantial gifts to buy property, or had entered middle-class professions, their narrative of "humble origins" felt more secure than those raised in a double-income home. What we take from these "mitigating circumstances" is that—as the editors of this volume note—people find themselves in particular positions in a social hierarchy—at the intersection of various axes of privilege or discrimination—and these positionalities influence how, and with what kind of authority, they are able to construct and deploy particular moral logics.

In contrast to these relatively smooth accounts of an intergenerational self, it is important to note that in most interviews there remained a clear residue of discomfort or conflict concerning parental gifts. In particular, these interviewees struggled to bridge the gap between the objective privileges they had enjoyed and the intergenerational story of humble origins they sought to tell. This tension typically came out when respondents described talking to friends about money and property. For example, Alicia, born outside the United Kingdom, described her family's substantial wealth in terms that emphasized generations of hard work and meritocratic achievement but observed that she still felt that she was made to feel uncomfortable about her wealth by British friends:

> I only feel uncomfortable about my parents' money when I speak to people in Britain about it . . . Sometimes when you talk about that kind of thing here I get some looks that make me feel like people assume that because of all these things I should be rolling in it.

This sense of persisting tensions was evident in many other interviews too. As above, it often came to the fore when people compared their situation with that of their friends, especially friends who were unable to buy property, despite having similar occupations and incomes:

> Sometimes when people ask me how the flat's going, and I sort of complain about how we haven't got anything sorted . . . and then, they're just like [.] "I'm never going to be able to buy somewhere." (Simon)

> I felt really guilty when I got given the money. . . . I was just really aware that other people couldn't afford to do this and everyone else was working as hard as I was. (Amanda)

Respondents often also described awkwardness when talking about financial gifts with friends and a reluctance to publicize details of the money they had received. Philippa acknowledged, for example, there were "not many people I would have told [about] how much help we had," and Jim explained that there were some friends who "I am definitely a bit more reluctant to talk about the details of buying a house with" because he didn't want to "rub their face [in it]." Sara similarly said she wouldn't "flaunt it" and "would probably be quite vague with people who aren't in my close circle."

Thus, despite proffering a humble intergenerational self in some parts of the interview, elsewhere it was clear that such justificatory narratives had not entirely resolved the tension these interviewees felt in relation to gifting, and their sense that there was indeed a conflict between their belief in meritocracy and their receipt of an unearned gift. In particular, as discussions turned toward proximate others, and interviewees reflected relationally on their economic privilege, their sense of discomfort was often very clear.

Boundaries Between Self and Others

Given these conflicts and tensions, it is unsurprising that interviewees often justified the receipt of financial assistance in other ways too. One common strategy, often deployed alongside acknowledging awkwardness with some friends, was to draw boundaries with *other* friends (or peer group members). The point of contrast here was often those who had benefited from greater wealth, capital that had been acquired through illegitimate family ties, or other means that were less clearly tied to "hard work." Nadia, for example, contrasted her own situation with that of friends whose parents "own three or four properties, and that is insane." In fact, while a few respondents had parents who made money from rental income on second properties, others used rental income as a key example of "illegitimate" wealth against which their own meritocratic story could be contrasted. Here, the social or political conflict between meritocratic achievement and familial gifting is kept alive, but the interviewee insists on their own position on the "correct" side of that split.

The drawing of boundaries between one's own property story and that of wealthier others also came up when interviewees were asked to talk about the "bigger picture" of the politics of housing inequality. We will discuss this further in the next section, but here it is worth noting that some respondents' political awareness meant that even when they had recounted stories of humble origins and intergenerational hard work, they still recognized the role that parental gifting played in perpetuating inequality. This usually emerged—sometimes prompted by the interviewer—as a kind of "reasoning out loud" about the pros and cons of taxing parental gifts or raising inheritance tax. The following example is typical:

> I: Some people would say you shouldn't be able to give huge amounts of money to your children because it's not fair on people who don't have that advantage. . . .
>
> R: I see both side of the coin. I see both perspectives. I say well, potentially yeah, that's true, but also you can't tell someone not to give the money to their kids. The kids haven't earned the money, fine, they haven't. But at the same time you know that's their parents' choice. . . . You can't tell someone what they can and can't do. (Neil)

It is in such comments that we see most clearly the attempt to engage with competing moral logics and "orders of worth," and the acknowledgment—here mostly implicit—that resolution of the tension may not be possible. Elsewhere, when respondents were critical of inheritance tax (which many, although not all, were), we observed frequent efforts to make the logic of family ties and family loyalty fit within a more recent social norm of meritocracy. Here, interviewees often grounded their criticism in the idea that wealthier others would be able to pay such taxes, whereas "ordinary" families (including themselves) would not, leading to perverse and unfair outcomes. For Arthur:

> Yes, inheritance probably should be taxed on balance but I think if you look at someone who has a private wealth of hundreds of millions the fact that they can then hand on that money to their child doesn't change the fact that they have this huge private wealth in the first place. So that is in itself unbalanced.

A number of interviewees contrasted the situation of these "ordinary" (but usually middle class) families with that of celebrities or the aristocracy. For Tom, "if you are Gary Lineker earning £1.8 million a year, or you're Hugh Grant or whoever . . . maybe it [paying inheritance tax] doesn't make much difference to you." Others, like Neil, thought that inheritance tax was unfair because it didn't distinguish between the level of wealth of different recipients: "if you think about someone like Prince William, he doesn't need his grandma's inheritance as much as say somebody else, you know." For Elliott:

> If it [the inheritance] is enough to buy a nice house and be able to support your family in a nice area that's fine. But if it's enough to buy ten mansions, maybe there is a case for taxing them a little more.

Georgia distinguished between the "upper class" who have "got millions anyway" and wouldn't suffer from inheritance tax, and the middle class, "where someone has maybe given their son or daughter some money to start a business" but who wouldn't be able to afford inheritance tax. There is some truth in the argument that inheritance tax falls more heavily on some people than others. In the United Kingdom, unlike in some other OECD countries, inheritance tax is not progressive or "tiered" into different brackets, and those with lower incomes and/or standing to inherit smaller estates pay tax at the same rate (if they actually met the threshold for doing so, which very estates few do) as those standing to inherit a lot more (Goss 2024). Nonetheless, the language in which some of these claims were cast ("ten mansions," millionaires, references to the aristocracy, etc.) also suggested an attempt by interviewees of quite varied wealth backgrounds to discursively position themselves as relatively humble, even poorly off.

In these instances, we see how interviewees often very effectively reconciled competing orders of worth. Here, they positioned their "modest" gifts not only as reflecting "natural" expressions of familial loyalty, love, support, and interdependence but also as having unique meritocratic legitimacy; meritocratic in terms of how the capital was accumulated in the first place, and meritocratic also in the forms of ordinary striving it helped facilitate. Moreover, this reconciliation was aided by boundary-drawing with the aristocracy and super-wealthy, whose gratuitous and conspicuous transmissions of wealth were cast as neither deserving nor necessary to fostering familial interdependence. Some forms of inequality remained unacceptable, while others were felt to be manageable.

Downplaying the Significance of Gifting to Inequality

The final way that interviewees justified financial gifts was to dispute housing wealth as a significant source of inequality. This was done in various ways. Almost all respondents started by acknowledging that inequality was a problem, but then went on to either deny that housing wealth was a central aspect of inequality, assert more powerful sources of inequality, or discuss wider issues of housing inequality but downplay the role of intergenerational transfers.

First, people were keen to diminish the significance of intergenerational gifting by contrasting it with a bigger picture of inequality. A number of respondents began by agreeing that inheritance tax (or other taxes on monetary gifts) might be a way of addressing wealth inequality but then qualified their support by rehearsing a series of objections or proposing other policy levers instead. Miles explained that he would vote in favor of inheritance tax but added that "I don't know if that would be the best way to stem structural inequality." While it would be the most "obvious" way to do it, he personally would "take away private schools" charitable status' because "that's just as important as inherited wealth." Here, there is some acknowledgment of the principle of meritocracy (or at least of fairness and equality), but a denial that the transmission of wealth between generations—and the logic of loyalty to kin that it implies—is a significant obstacle to this, and thus a truly *competing* "order of worth." For Arthur, similarly:

> I would personally suggest that it is more important to try and create a sort of fairer society where you don't have footballers earning hundreds of millions of pounds and then having to tax it.

Lucy conceded that inheritance tax might be legitimate but thought that "[the government] are better off utilising other revenues . . . they've got to sort out these huge corporations who are paying minimal tax." For Les, the problem of wealth inequality was reframed as one of unequal access to getting on the housing ladder in the first place. As he explained: "The real cause[s] of *high house prices* are things like land banking, [buy-to-let] investors [and] green belt rules [emphasis added]." In different ways, then, respondents deployed their "inequality knowledge" in a way that worked to simultaneously blur the significance of gifting and foreground other "inequality culprits," such as buy-to-let landlords, tax-avoiding global corporations or companies engaged in "land banking." What we find, in other words, is not so much that people downplay levels of inequality, but rather that they deflect the problem of inequality toward locations in which they themselves are less directly (and uncomfortably) implicated.

While respondents receiving the largest sums of money from family often went to some lengths to downplay the significance of these transfers relative to a bigger picture of social inequality, those receiving relatively smaller amounts from their parents were often quite unabashed in their defense of such gifts. Indeed, it was striking that opposition to inheritance tax was typically strongest among respondents whose own story of meritocratic advancement was objectively the most credible, and whose gifts were often relatively small.[4] They defended the right to give and receive financial gifts far more vigorously, and in a less coded way, than those who had received larger (often considerably larger) amounts:

> Well I think they've already paid taxes on whatever their income was. So I would say I see inheritance tax as double tax. . . . I think it's quite bad that it gets taxed again. (Georgia)

> I would be very angry if someone told me that I couldn't give my children money. I'd be very angry. (Alison)

For these respondents, far from being a source of inequality that needed to be addressed or excused, financial gifts, and inheritances from parents—and the housing wealth that followed—were seen as a form of "leveling up" for the less well off. As Alison put it:

> Especially with the more working class families, some of those parents have absolutely killed themselves with those houses. They've done everything for them, and . . . all that hard work's going to be stripped away from the children because they're can't afford the tax on it. It breaks my heart.

Among these interviewees there was a genuine sense of unfairness at the idea that either financial gifts or inherited property might be taxed—"I just don't understand what that would do" (Georgia, 17)—or that the fruits of their parents' work might be taken away.

Discussion and Conclusion

In this chapter, we have examined the competing moral logics deployed to justify inequality, by focusing on the way people justify inherited wealth or inter-vivo gifts from family members. We show that people benefiting from inter-vivo gifting experience discomfort not only at the level of family relations, as some previous authors have shown, but also socially as a tension between benefiting from unearned gifts and living up to a wider "meritocratic ideal" (Littler 2018). As our results show, this tension between competing moral logics—in Boltanski and Thévenot's (2006) terms between the familial "domestic principle" and the meritocratic "general will"—generated various forms of justification and attempts to resolve these conflicts.

Most significantly, in our study respondents attempted to downplay the ascribed privilege (and implications of unfair inequality) associated with gifting by deploying particular "origin stories." Here, they reached back into extended family histories to tell stories of the past—of working-class struggle, of upward social mobility, of meritocratic striving—that sought to cast their receipt of unearned capital in a deserving (and therefore moral) light. In some cases, where this aligned with more "objective" experiences of upward mobility, these origin stories acted to fairly effectively resolve tensions. However, in the majority of cases, a residue of discomfort remained, particularly among those from the most privileged backgrounds and those receiving the largest amounts. Notably, discomfort here was experienced most acutely when these individuals talked and thought *relationally*—either in terms of friends who did not have access to such gifts or when reflecting on the wider societal fairness of intergenerational transfers. In addition, interviewees deployed further justificatory strategies—drawing boundaries between their own wealth and the greater or less legitimate (i.e., less morally acceptable) wealth of others or disputing and downplaying the significance of gifting in relation to other forms of inequality. Here, we see how justifying one form of inequality (in this case housing inequality) is sometimes made possible by drawing attention to apparently starker or more egregious forms of inequality elsewhere.

Our chapter also claims that these social discomforts and tensions can often be understood through Boltanski and Thévenot's (2006) notion of competing "orders of worth" (or in the language of this volume, competing moral logics). In many of our interviews, people's justifications of their own views or experiences could be read not only as self-interested social positioning (although this was clearly part of it) but also as evidence of people identifying conflicting principles at work in their own lives, and trying to either justify adhering to one principle or the other, or—more commonly—to make the competing principles compatible. There may be a broader value to this approach for studies of inequality because it may enable us to identify those areas of public or private discourse where social conflicts and tensions remain open and unresolved (and therefore, in Bolatnski's (2011) sense, a possible basis for broader social critique), and those, by contrast, where conflict and critique has been effectively shut down.

Finally, our research may shed some light on recent political debates about inheritance tax in the United Kingdom and elsewhere. Despite the clear role that intergenerational transfers play in reproducing wealth inequality (Christophers 2018) and the tensions between meritocracy and gifting, public and political support for taxing such practices remains low in the United Kingdom (Rowlingson et al. 2017), with inheritance tax widely viewed as the "most unfair" tax (Shakespeare 2015). Our analysis suggests that one previously underexplored reason for this may be that recipients simply do not see their *own* gifts as significantly contributing to inequality, and indeed—by reaching back two or more generations—may actually see their family story as one of meritocratic struggle. Here, unequal outcomes can be more easily accepted if they are seen as linked to meritocracy rather than inherited advantage. While our respondents acknowledged that peers with less family wealth struggled more, they also identified *other* friends (or celebrities) who had benefited from more excessive or less "legitimate" parental wealth and saw their own gifts as small or normal in comparison. Thus, even though they understood the relationship between transfers and inequality, and were sometimes politically sympathetic to addressing it, their support was often somewhat qualified. Seeing their own family story as a meritocratic one, a tax on the "fruits" of that story could be construed, in effect, as a punishment of meritocratic hard work. In this way, a belief in meritocracy could be made compatible with a rejection of inheritance tax.

This line of reasoning suggests that one of the difficulties for inheritance tax (and other attempts to tackle inequality) as a *political* project is that it is a site where two competing moral logics or orders of worth (Boltanski and Thévenot 2006) meet and interact. While these logics—of family loyalty and personal ties, on the one hand, and a "civic will" of meritocracy on the other—may seem to be objectively in conflict, we have shown that people are often able to discursively bring these competing principles into a kind of alignment, and that in many cases, people deploy an "intergenerational self," characterized by humble origins, hard work, and upward mobility, to recast familial gifts, and the unequal housing outcomes they generate, as evidence of multigenerational meritocratic success.

Appendix

Table 8A Table of interviewees

Pseudonym	Age	Gender	Occupation	Ethnicity	Recruiter	Amount	Mother's occupation	Father's occupation
Nadia	20s	F	Teacher	Black/African/Caribbean/Black British	Y	Missing	Nursing home	General practitioner
Aaron	30s	M	Doctor	Other ethnic group	N	£30,000	SAHM	Doctor
Louise	30s	F	Doctor	White British	N	£30,000 (Partner's family)	SAHM	Ecologist
Harriet	20s	F	Political fundraiser	White British	N	£50,000	Medium-size business owner	Medium-size business owner
Jim	20s	M	Teacher	White British	N	£7,000	Professor	Engineer
Carol	20s	F	Primary teacher	White British	N	£10,000	Primary teacher	Chief executive
Alison	30s	F	Craft worker	White British	Y	5,000	Teaching assistant	Further education lecturer
Nina	30s	F	Publishing Assistant	Asian/Asian British	N	£51,500	Cleaner/Domestic Work	Business Owner

Continued

Table 8A *Continued*

Pseudonym	Age	Gender	Occupation	Ethnicity	Recruiter	Amount	Mother's occupation	Father's occupation
Georgia	30s	F	Musician	White British	Y	Missing	Musician	Music teacher
Tom	40s	M	Recruitment consultant	White British	Y	Missing	Missing	Missing
Paul	30s	M	Accountant	White British	Y	£10,000	Secretary	Taxi driver
Phillippa	20s	F	Corporate fundraiser	White British	N	£50,000	Teacher	Public Relations consultant
Les	30s	M	Technical writer	White British	Y	25,000	Typist	Doctor
Nigel	30s	M	Housing policy officer	White British	N	35,000	Missing	Missing
Neil	30s	M	Educational administration officer	White British	Y	Apprx. £73–146,000 (exact figure undisclosed)	Fashion designer	Graphic designer
Simon	30s	M	PhD Student	White British	N	343,000	Missing	Missing
Alicia	20s	F	Theater public relations	White other	N	£550,000	SAHM	Large business owner
Miles	40s	M	Postdoctoral researcher	White British	N	Apprx. £40–80,000 (exact figure undisclosed)	Educational admin	Musician

Hannah	30s	F	Publishing manager	Asian/Asian British	N	£70,000	Administrative assistant	Small business Owner
Arthur	30s	M	E-Learning manager	White British	N	£15,000	Journalist	Advertising creative director
Rania	30s	F	Personal assistant	Black/African/ Caribbean/Black British	Y	£20,000 (Partner's family)	Cleaner/Domestic work	Psychiatric nurse
Michael	30s	M	Project Manager	White British	Y	5,000	Dinner Lady	Construction Manager
Lucy	40s	F	Business owner	White British	Y	Apprx. £80–100,000 (exact figure undisclosed)	Business owner	Social worker
Gregor	20s	M	Insurance Broker	White British	Y	Apprx. £100–150,000 (exact figure undisclosed)	SAHM	Stockbroker
Elliott	30s	M	Photographer	White British	Y	35,000	SAHM	Business owner
Amanda	30s	F	Musician	White British	Y	50,000	Nurse	Civil servant
Sara	30s	F	Solicitor	Asian/Asian British	Y	£55,000	Craft worker	Factory worker
Nadia	20s	F	Teacher	Black/African/ Caribbean/Black British	Y	Missing	Nursing home	General practitioner

Note: Stay-at-Home Mother (SAHM).

Notes

1. As former UK Prime Minister David Cameron asserted in 2011: "[The desire to 'pass something on' to younger generations] is about the most basic, human and natural instinct there is . . . that home that you have worked and saved for belongs to you and your family—you should be able to pass it on to your children" (Customs Today 2015).
2. In assigning interviewees to these categories, we draw on the three-class schema National Statistics Socio-Economic Classification (NS-SEC).
3. Pseudonyms are used throughout.
4. These interviewees were also among the least likely to ever be affected by inheritance tax.

References

Adkins, L., M. Cooper, and M. Konings. 2020. *The Asset Economy*. Oxford: Polity.

Boltanski, L. 2011. *On Critique: A Sociology of Emancipation*. Cambridge: Polity.

Boltanski, L., and L. Thévenot. 2006. *On Justification: Economies of Worth*. Translated by C. Porter. Princeton, NJ: Princeton University Press.

Bourdieu, P. 1972. *Outline of a Theory of Practice*. Cambridge: Cambridge University Press.

Butler, J. 2005. *Giving an Account of Oneself*. New York: Fordham University Press.

Celikates, R. 2012. "Systematic Misrecognition and the Practice of Critique: Bourdieu, Boltanski and the Role of Critical Theory." In *Recognition Theory and Contemporary French Moral and Political Philosophy*, edited by M. Bankowsky and A. Le Goff, pp. 160–172. Manchester: Manchester University Press.

Christophers, B. 2018. "Intergenerational Inequality? Labour, Capital, and Housing Through the Ages." *Antipode* 50 (1): pp. 101–121.

Customs Today. 2015. "Cameron Announces Plan to Cut Inheritance Tax to Protect Millions from 'Death Duty.'" *Customs Today*, April 14. https://customstoday.media/cameron-announces-plan-to-cut-inheritance-tax-to-protect-millions-from-death-duty/.

Druta, O., and R. Ronald. 2017. "Young Adults' Pathways into Homeownership and the Negotiation of Intra-Family Support: A Home, the Ideal Gift." *Sociology* 51 (4): pp. 783–799.

Fivush, R., J. Bohanek, and M. Duke. 2008. "The Intergenerational Self: Subjective Perspective and Family History." In *Self Continuity: Individual and Collective Perspectives*, edited by F. Sani, pp. 131–143. London: Psychology Press.

Goss, D. 2024. *The Future of Inheritance Tax*. London: Demos.

Guggenheim, M., and J. Potthast. 2012. "Symmetrical Twins: On the Relationship Between Actor-Network Theory and the Sociology of Critical Capacities." *European Journal of Social Theory* 15 (2): pp. 157–178.

Heath, S. and E. Calvert. 2013. "Gifts, Loans and Intergenerational Support for Young Adults." *Sociology* 47 (6): pp. 1120–1135.

Heath, S., and E. Calvert. 2011. "The Role of Family and Friends in the Housing Pathways of Single Young Adults." ESRC Centre for Population Change Briefing 6. November.

Karagiannaki. E. 2015. "The Impact of Inheritance on the Distribution of Wealth: Evidence from Great Britain." *Review of Income and Wealth* 63 (2): pp. 394–408.

Khan, S. 2011. *Privilege: The Making of an Adolescent Elite at St. Paul's School*. Princeton: Princeton University Press.

Lamont, M. 1992. *Money, Morals and Manners: The Culture of the French and American Upper-Middle Class*. Chicago: University of Chicago Press.

Lawson, M., A. Parvez Butt, R. Harvey, D. Sarosi, C. Coffey, K. Piaget, and J. Thekkudan. 2020. *Time to Care: Unpaid and Underpaid Care Work and the Global Inequality Crisis*. Geneva: Oxfam International.

Littler, J. 2018. *Against Meritocracy: Culture, Power and Myths of Mobility*. London: Routledge.

Merrill, N., and R. Fivush. 2016. "Intergenerational Narratives and Identity Across Development." *Developmental Review* 40: pp. 72–92.
Mijs, J. 2019. "The Paradox of Inequality: Income Inequality and Belief in Meritocracy Go Hand in Hand." *Socio-Economic Review* 19 (1): pp. 7–35. https://doi.org/10.1093/ser/mwy051.
Moor, L., and S. Friedman. 2021. "Justifying Inherited Wealth: Between 'the Bank of Mum and Dad' and the Meritocratic Ideal." *Economy and Society* 50 (4): pp. 618–642.
Piketty, T. 2014. *Capital in the 21st Century*. Cambridge, MA: Harvard University Press.
Pugh, A. 2013. "What Good Are Interviews for Thinking About Culture? Demystifying Interpretative Analysis." *American Journal of Cultural Sociology* 1 (1): pp. 42–68.
Rapley, T. 2001. "The Art(fulness) of Open-Ended Interviewing: Some Considerations on Analysing Interviews." *Qualitative Research* 1 (3): pp. 303–323.
Rowlingson, K., R. Joseph, and L. Overton. 2017. *Inter-generational Financial Gifts and Inequality: Give and Take in 21st Century British Families*. Basingstoke: Palgrave Macmillan.
Sandel, M. 2020. *The Tyranny of Merit: What's Become of the Common Good?* London: Allen Lane.
Savage, M. 2015. "Introduction to Elites from the 'Problematic of the Proletariat' to a Class Analysis of 'Wealth Elites.'" *Sociological Review* 62 (2): pp. 223–239.
Savage, M., and M. Flemmen. 2019. "Life Narratives and Personal Identity: The End of Linear Social Mobility?" *Cultural and Social History* 16 (1): pp. 85–101.
Shakespeare, S. 2015. "Voters in All Parties Think Inheritance Tax Unfair." *YouGov*, March 19. https://yougov.co.uk/topics/politics/articles-reports/2015/03/19/inheritance-tax-most-unfair.
Shapiro, T. 2004. *The Hidden Cost of Being African American: How Wealth Perpetuates Inequality*. Oxford: Oxford University Press.
Sherman, R. 2017. *Uneasy Street: The Anxieties of Affluence*. Princeton, NJ: Princeton University Press.
Telling, K. 2016. "Pierre Bourdieu and the Problem of Reflexivity: Recent Answers to Some Old Questions." *European Journal of Social Theory* 19 (1): pp. 146–156.
Udagawa, C., and P. Sanderson. 2017. *The Impacts of Family Support on Access to Homeownership for Young People in the UK*. London: Social Mobility Commission.
Wagner, P. 1999. "After Justification: Repertoires of Evaluation and the Sociology of Modernity." *European Journal of Social Theory* 2 (3): pp. 341–357.
World Inequality Database. 2020. "Income and Wealth Inequality, United Kingdom, 1895–2017." https://wid.world/country/united-kingdom/.

PART III

CULTURAL AND INSTITUTIONAL LOGICS

Chapter 9
Why Do Chinese People Accept Income Inequality?
A Political System Justification Theory

Cary Wu

Introduction

This chapter focuses on China, where rapid economic growth and modernization over the last several decades have led to substantial increases in income inequality. Statistical estimations suggest that China has become one of the most unequal countries in the world. China's Gini coefficient, which was around 0.30 in 1980, nearly doubled to 0.55 by 2012 (Xie and Zhou 2014). In a different measure, the portion of national income for the top 10% of income earners in China increased from 27% to 41% between 1978 and 2015, whereas the bottom 50% saw a decrease from 27% to 15% (Piketty et al. 2019). Despite a recent trend of slowing growth in inequality (Kanbur et al. 2021), China today continues to grapple with persistently high levels of income inequality (see Walder 2023; Wan and Knight 2023).

As in many other countries, popular acceptance of current inequalities is widespread in China. Surveys and qualitative evidence suggest that most Chinese citizens do not seem to be angry about the income gap and largely perceive the income distribution as fair (see Østerby-Jørgensen 2023; Whyte 2010; Wu 2009; Xie et al. 2012). More surprisingly, Chinese from lower socioeconomic status and from rural areas are most likely to find income inequality acceptable (Whyte 2010). Thus far, three major theories have been proposed to explain the widespread acceptance of inequality among Chinese citizens. An economic modernization theory suggests that the high tolerance of income inequality among Chinese citizens comes from their understanding of income inequality as a welcome byproduct of

Cary Wu, *Why Do Chinese People Accept Income Inequality?*. In: *The Social Acceptance of Inequality*.
Edited by: Francesco Duina and Luca Storti, Oxford University Press. © Oxford University Press (2025).
DOI: 10.1093/oso/9780197814499.003.0009

economic modernization as well as their perception of improved life conditions (Whyte and Im 2014; Wu 2009). A cultural theory suggests that high tolerance is rooted in Chinese people's meritocratic beliefs (Østerby-Jørgensen 2023; Xie 2016). A political control theory attributes the acceptance of income inequality among Chinese citizens to political control and propaganda (Song 2023; Whyte 2010).

In this chapter, I introduce a political system justification perspective highlighting Chinese people's high trust in the government in shaping their views of income distribution. Survey studies have shown that Chinese citizens hold very high levels of trust in their government (Wang 2005; Wu and Wilkes 2018b). Building on this fact and prior work on system justification (Haack and Sieweke 2018; Jost et al. 2004), I argue those who trust the people who run the government to do what is right are more likely to believe that existing social and political arrangements are fair, legitimate, and necessary, and as a result, are inclined to support, reinforce, and justify various forms of social and economic inequality, even when the income distribution works to their disadvantage. Empirically, bringing together existing theories of Chinese acceptance of high inequality, I seek to test whether economic modernization, meritocratic beliefs, and political propaganda as well as political trust all play a role in shaping how people perceive income fairness among Chinese citizens. My analysis of data from two recent China samples of the Asian Barometer Survey (ABS) not only confirms that most Chinese citizens perceive income distribution as fair but also reveals that there is an observable upward trend in this perception from the 2015 to 2019 period. Regression analysis finds strong empirical support for the moral logic: High political trust but also economic modernization, meritocratic beliefs, and political propaganda all contribute to Chinese people's perception of income fairness and therefore their acceptance of the significant inequality in China.

Explaining Chinese Acceptance of Inequality

Current literature offers three distinct explanations for the high acceptance of income inequality among Chinese citizens. An economic modernization theory associates the Chinese acceptance of inequality with economic growth and improved life opportunities. A cultural perspective underscores the influence of meritocratic beliefs. A political control theory posits that political propaganda and censorship are fundamental mechanisms. Let's take each in turn.

Economic Modernization

The most dominant, and perhaps the most conceivable, driver of why people perceive income distribution as acceptable in China is the economic gains and improved life opportunities from China's rapid modernization. In this view, economic growth, even though unequal, is real and encouraging. Two described pathways underlie how economic growth may have made people believe income inequality is fair. One is that Chinese citizens seem to understand and accept the "no pain, no gains" logic that inequality is a byproduct of development and growth (Xie 2016). Supporting this perspective are findings by Piketty et al. (2019) about the economic gains and their coexistence with inequality in China. They suggest that the key difference between China and the United States since the 1970s is that, in China, the bottom 50% has benefited enormously from growth. Its average income grew by five times in real terms, which is less than macro growth and top income growth but still substantial. This increase presumably made rising inequality more acceptable, especially since living standards were very low in 1978. By contrast, income growth for the bottom 50% in the United States has been negative (–1%). Another is that Chinese citizens largely perceive that their living conditions have improved significantly compared to the past, and therefore, they generally do not view variations in overall enhanced income and life opportunities as unfair (Whyte and Im 2014; Wu 2009). This is described as the "tunnel effect" (Hirschman and Rothschild 1973; Larsen 2016). For example, Wu (2009) examined people's tolerance of inequality and their perceptions of legitimate earnings inequality and opportunities in two Chinese societies through individual population surveys in China and Hong Kong. His analysis revealed that both Mainland and Hong Kong respondents were optimistic about opportunities for social mobility, which is positively associated with their sense of the fairness of income distribution. Taken together, the economic development theory suggests that China's rapid economic modernization and improved living conditions have led to the high acceptance of inequality among ordinary citizens.

Meritocratic Beliefs

Many suggest that Chinese tolerance of inequality is cultural. More specifically, it is the meritocratic belief that leads to Chinese acceptance of high inequality. This corresponds to Østerby-Jørgensen's (2023) meritocratic framing. Meritocracy is optimistic about the prospects of upward mobility and opportunities to get ahead through talent, education, and hard work, and such values help legitimize patterns of inequality, as the public still believes in the equality of opportunity (Wu 2009; Xian and Reynolds 2017). For example, Whyte (2010) conducted his first systematic, nationwide survey of ordinary Chinese citizens on inequality and distributive justice in 2004. He showed that the prevailing view was that the overall patterns of inequality in China allow ordinary citizens to succeed through hard work, talent, and training. Xie (2016) also points out that many Chinese today find inequality acceptable because of the cultural beliefs held widely by the Chinese that everyone has the opportunity to achieve higher socioeconomic status through individual effort.

Political Propaganda

China's high tolerance of inequality can also be political. In the contemporary world, political actors wield considerable power to reconstruct social reality in a way that hides real disparities in society. This is particularly pronounced in non-democratic settings, like China's, where the State possesses almost unlimited powers to shape narratives, emphasizing certain facets of inequality while downplaying others. Growing studies have highlighted the potential role political control may have on people's beliefs surrounding inequality in China. For example, Whyte (2010) showed that most Chinese seemed to accept Deng Xiaoping's view that "it is good for some people to get rich first." In his 2004 survey of income inequality and social justice, respondents were asked which of two statements they agreed with more: "Some people getting rich first will reduce the chances for others to get rich" and "Some people getting rich first will increase the opportunities for others to get rich." Many more respondents favored the second option (by 48.6% to 11.1%), shining light on the important link between political propaganda and perceptions about inequality. More recently, Song (2023) constructed a database that includes articles with the keyword "inequality" published in major newspapers, magazines, and online digital news media between 2003 and 2018, to evaluate the effectiveness of media control on both the production of news, in terms of the volume and variety of inequality news across media outlets, and the consumption of news, in terms of media users' behaviors and beliefs about the level of inequality. Her analysis demonstrated that Chinese citizens who consume state-owned media are more likely to underestimate the level of inequality compared with those who follow the internet or marketized media (Song 2023). Hence, Chinese citizens may be misinformed about inequality because of the government's control over media via propaganda and censorship.

Most recently, to understand how the Chinese make sense of the high inequality in everyday life, Østerby-Jørgensen (2023) identified three framings of inequality based on his interviews with seventy-five Chinese people. Specifically, a developmental framing underscores that despite increased economic inequality, everyone is materially better off than before. A meritocratic framing attributes inequality to variations in effort, ability, or contribution. Last, a difference-order framing highlights the notion that individuals are born into diverse families with varying resource levels, and hence income difference is not inherently unfair. These popular framings underscore why regular Chinese citizens tend to justify rather than question the significant levels of inequality. These framings are also closely related to the three distinct explanations for the widespread acceptance of high inequality in China we discussed above.

A Political System Justification Theory: The Role of Political Trust

In this study, I outline a moral logic that highlights the role of Chinese people's high trust in their government in shaping how they perceive income distribution. Chinese citizens are very trusting in their government. National and international surveys have consistently shown that the majority of Chinese citizens believe that they can trust their government, especially their central government (Wang 2005; Wu and Wilkes 2018a). The high political trust among Chinese citizens is found to be genuine, not out of political fear (Stockmann et al. 2018). While democracies around the world experienced declining levels of political trust, the authoritarian Chinese government maintained unexpectedly high and stable levels of trust (Fairbrother et al. 2022; Wu and Wilkes 2018a).

Prior literature has shown a close relationship between political trust and income inequality. In this line of literature, scholars have focused on how both actual inequality and perceived inequality can negatively affect people's trust in their government (Barreiro et al. 2019; Lee et al. 2020). In the case of China, for example, Hutchison and Xu (2017) show that individuals living in provinces with higher levels of inequality and openness tend to be less trusting of the government. Lei (2020) found a statistically significant correlation between discontent with income inequality and distrust of the provincial and county governments. However, the high levels of political trust in China even in the face of growing inequalities challenge the seemingly straightforward negative relationship between political trust and inequality.

Does high political trust help explain Chinese citizens' tolerance of inequality? Thus far, limited research has considered how political trust may influence people's views of inequality. One line of political trust literature suggests that people's trust in government does not always reflect government performance or citizens' evaluation of it, but instead it is rooted in political cultures and individuals' early life socialization (Dalton and Welzel 2014). In the case of China, traditional Chinese values, with their emphasis on hierarchy, group orientation, and paternalism, may be the key drivers for China's high political trust (Shi 2008; Wu and Wilkes 2018b). In this view, political trust is learned early in life, and learned trust tends to be stable and does not change easily (Fairbrother et al. 2022). Accordingly, it seems more logical to suspect that Chinese citizens' political trust may come before their views of income inequality.

Here, I argue that high political trust in China could be one reason why Chinese citizens are not angry about the widespread income disparities. Specifically, politically trusting individuals are more likely to hold a political system justification belief. A political system justification belief builds on the system justification theory but focuses more on the political aspect. The system justification theory provides a widely accepted explanation of why people believe the world is just despite growing economic disparities. The theory suggests that people, fueled by a common desire to uphold favorable opinions of themselves and their social connections, tend to also cultivate positive views regarding the social, economic, and political structures that they live in (Jost 2019; Jost and Banaji 1994). In this view, the legitimacy of inequality—where certain individuals possess more money, power, opportunities, or resources than others—can be attributed, in part, to the human tendency to seek justification and support for the systems within which they operate. This inclination endures even when such systems prove detrimental to individuals or their respective groups (Haack and Sieweke 2018; Samson 2018). In fact, strong evidence has shown that system-justifying beliefs diminish inequality aversion (Goudarzi et al. 2020). High and growing income inequality can even further strengthen people's belief in a just world (Malahy et al. 2009).

In the context of China, several studies have already shown that system justification belief leads to lower perceived economic inequality. For example, in a three-wave longitudinal study among 1,525 Chinese adolescents, Li et al. (2023) show that system justification belief leads to lower perceived economic inequality longitudinally. Specifically, I argue that widespread support for the political system allows individuals to rationalize, rather than question, the unfair income distribution. In other words, politically trusting individuals are more likely to believe that existing social and institutional arrangements are fair, legitimate, and necessary, and therefore, are more inclined to support, reinforce, and justify various forms of social and economic inequality, even when the income distribution works to their disadvantage. Individuals who tend to legitimize inequality have weaker perceptions of income inequality (Du and King 2022), leading to their high acceptance of unfair income distribution.

Data and Measures

Data

Data for empirical demonstrations come from the ABS conducted by the Hu Fu Center for East Asia Democratic Studies in Taiwan. The ABS is a cross-national survey project that provides high-quality data to comprehensively explore public opinion and political behavior across diverse Asian countries. The samples selected for the ABS represent the totality of the adult, voting-age population in each country surveyed. China has been part of the survey program since it was first launched in 2001. Thus far, five waves have been conducted in Mainland China. In this study, I use data from the two most recent waves of China surveys, conducted in 2015 (N = 4,043) and 2019 (N = 4,941).

Focal Measures

People's acceptance of income inequality can be reflected in whether they perceive differences in income as fair (Almås et al. 2010). I use two different questions. One question asks, "How fair do you think income distribution is in the country?" Another asks, "Considering all the effort that you and your family members have made in the past, do you think the income that your family currently receives is fair or not fair?" Responses for both items were coded on an ordinal scale including four categories: 1 = very unfair, 2 = unfair, 3 = fair, and 4 = very fair. My calculation of the polychoric correlation, a statistical measure used to assess the strength and direction of the relationship between two ordinal variables, indicates a strong positive association ($r = 0.58$) between these two measures. Individuals perceiving income distribution or family income as more fair indicate their higher acceptance of income inequality.

Economic Modernization

Economic development is measured using two items: (1) "How would you describe the change in the economic condition of our country over the last few years?," and (2) "How would you compare the current economic condition of your family with what it was a few years ago?" Responses were coded on a 1–5 scale from 1 = much worse now, 2 = a little worse now, 3 = about the same, 4 = a little better now, and 5 = much better now. A principal components analysis (PCA) is used to create an economic development index that represents the overall level of perceived change in the economic condition held by each respondent. The results of the PCA supported a reduction into one overall measure, as one component with an eigenvalue above 1 was produced that accounts for more than half of the variance (68. 2%), with loadings at 0.83 for both items. Enhanced life opportunities variable is measured using the item that asks "As compared to my parent's generation, my generation has more or fewer opportunities to improve one's standard of living or social status?" Responses included 1 = substantially fewer opportunities, 2 = fewer opportunities, 3 = about the same, 4 = more opportunities, and 5 = substantially more opportunities.

Meritocratic Belief

Meritocratic belief is measured by the question: "Please tell me how you feel about the following statement: Wealth and poverty, success and failure are all determined by fate. Would you say you strongly agree, somewhat agree, somewhat disagree, or strongly disagree?" The item is reversely coded to indicate people's beliefs that wealth and success can be achieved by hard work.

Political Propaganda

It is difficult to find a direct measure of political propaganda. The effect of political propaganda is often captured by exposure to different media outlets (see Song 2023). We follow this common way of capturing the effect of political propaganda using media exposure to different news channels. In ABS, the item asks: "Which one is the most important channel for you to find information about politics and government?" Answers include television, newspaper (print and online), internet and social media, radio, other channel (please specify). The variable is recoded into three categories: 1 = traditional media including television, newspaper, radio; 2 = internet and social media; and 3 = other media.

Political Trust

Political trust is measured by the question, "Generally you can trust the people who run our government to do what is right. Would you say you strongly agree, somewhat agree, somewhat disagree, or strongly disagree?" This is a long-standing measure of political trust that has been used to study the topic for decades (Wu et al. 2022).

Political System Justification

Political system justification is measured by the question: "Over the long run, our system of government is capable of solving the problems our country faces. Agree or disagree." I should note here that political system justification is slightly different from the well-established system justification belief. The focus is on the political aspect. We largely follow the conceptualization from Li et al.'s (2023) study, where they measure political system justification using several items including "In general, I find Chinese society to be fair," "In general, Chinese political system operates as it should," and "Chinese society is getting worse every year" (reverse-scored).

Control Variables

The analysis also includes a wide range of demographics including gender or sex (0 = male, 1 = female), age (in years), marital status, education (years in school), level of household income (quintile steps), and geographic region.

Plan of Analysis

The analysis takes two general steps. First, I describe the overall patterns of perceived fairness among Chinese citizens. I separate between the 2015 sample and the 2019 sample to show whether there is any change in the survey period in perceived fairness. I also describe variations in perceived fairness based on the key indicators of economic modernization, meritocratic belief, political propaganda, and political trust. Second, I estimate two ordinal logistic regression models given the outcome variables (perceiving income distribution as fair and perceiving family income as fair) are coded on a 4-point Likert scale from 1 = strongly disagree to 4 = strongly agree. The first model includes all major predictors of economic modernization, meritocratic belief, political propaganda, and political trust as well as a wide range of controls. The second model adds a political system justification measure of "Over the long run, our system of government is capable of solving the problems our country faces. Agree or disagree." This is to suggest whether political system justification belief may partially explain the connection between political trust and perceived fairness.

Results

Table 9.1 illustrates the distribution and over-time trend of how people perceive income inequality in China. In 2015, approximately 45% of Chinese citizens expressed the view that income distribution in China is fair. This rose to 60% by 2019. Likewise, nearly 70% of respondents felt that their family's current income was fair, with this percentage climbing to 79% in 2019. These numbers suggest that a substantial majority of Chinese citizens hold the belief that income distribution in the country is fair, and there is an observable upward trend in this perception over the survey period.

Table 9.1 Perception of fairness in China, ABS 2015–19

	Q1: How fair do you think income distribution is?		**Q2: Considering all the effort that you and your family members have made in the past, do you think the income that your family currently receives is fair or not fair?**	
Distribution	2015	2019	2015	2019
Very unfair	10.1	4.5	3.6	1.3
Unfair	44.4	35.3	26.5	19.6
Fair	42.4	58.7	65.5	76.0
Very fair	3.0	1.5	4.4	3.1
Trend	2015	2019	2015	2019
Overall (Fair or very fair)	45.4	60.2	69.9	79.1

To provide a further understanding of the upward trend, I consider how this perception varies by age. If younger generations tend to show higher perceptions of fairness, the overall perception of fairness will increase over time. Figure 9.1 shows this is indeed the case. Panel A focuses on the perception of fair income distribution by year. The data indicates that individuals born in the 1970s, the Cultural Revolution period, tend to have a notably lower perception of fair income distribution. Conversely, both older and younger generations exhibit a higher perception of fairness in income distribution. Focusing on the perception of fair family income, Panel B shows a similar pattern. The higher perception of fairness among younger generations suggests that shifts in generations could have contributed, at least in part, to the increase in fairness perception from 2015 to 2019.

Table 9.2 provides descriptive variations in the perception of income inequality according to four sets of factors. Set A concentrates on variables related to economic development. The findings reveal a strong correlation between individuals who perceive an improvement in economic conditions and increased life opportunities and their higher perception of fairness.

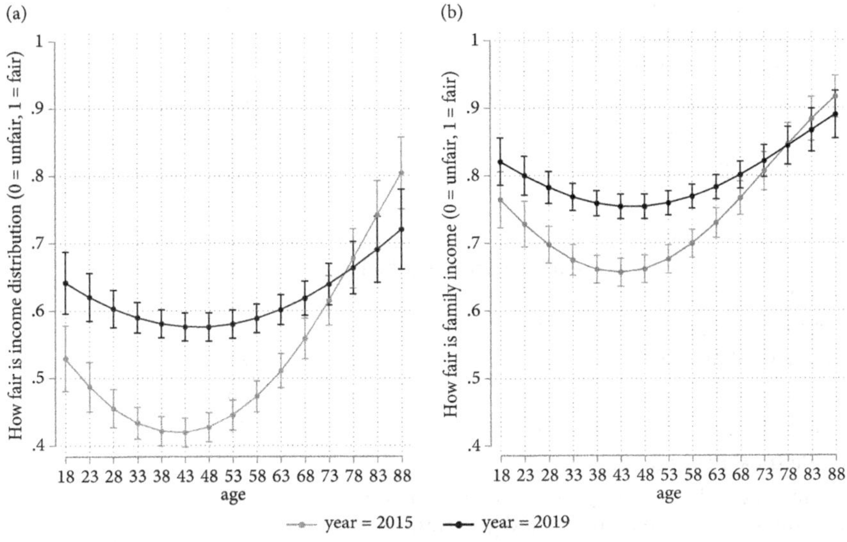

Figure 9.1 Perception of fairness by age, ABS 2015–19

Note: The nonlinear relationships were captured using logistic regressions involving age and its interaction term as well as a list of controls including gender, education, marital status, household income, and urban and geographic region. Panels A and B display the predictive margins with 95% confidence intervals.

Table 9.2 Variations in the perception of fairness by economic, cultural, and political factors, ABS 2015–19

	Income distribution is fair	Family income is fair
A. Economic development		
How would you describe the change in the economic condition of our country over the last few years?		
Much worse	18	45
A little worse	36	65
About the same	39	63
A little better	54	75
Much better	63	81
How would you compare the current economic condition of your family with what it was a few years ago?		
Much worse	31	45
A little worse	42	59
About the same	42	65
A little better	57	77
Much better	63	87
As compared to my parent's generation, my generation has more or fewer opportunities to improve one's standard of living or social status?		
Substantially fewer opportunities	15	40
Fewer opportunities	38	61
About the same	42	62
More opportunities	54	72
Substantially more opportunities	59	82
B. Cultural framing		
Wealth and poverty, success and failure are not all determined by fate.		
Strongly disagree	53	71
Somewhat disagree	53	71
Somewhat agree	54	76
Strongly agree	56	79
C. Political propaganda		
Which one is the most important channel for you to find information about politics and government?		
Traditional (TV, newspaper, radio)	61	79
Internet	60	80
Other	66	77

	Income distribution is fair	Family income is fair
D. System support		
You can generally trust the people who run our government to do what is right.		
Strongly disagree	32	60
Somewhat disagree	49	72
Somewhat agree	61	79
Strongly agree	66	81
Over the long run, our system of government is capable of solving the problems our country faces.		
Strongly disagree	21	58
Somewhat disagree	34	62
Somewhat agree	57	77
Strongly agree	62	81

For instance, 63% of those expressing that the country's economic conditions have significantly improved consider the income distribution to be fair, whereas only 18% of those reporting a much worse economic condition perceive the income distribution as fair. Similarly, among respondents who believe their generation has more opportunities for improving living standards and social status, 59% view the income distribution as fair, in contrast to the 15% who think it's fair among those who perceive fewer opportunities for such improvements.

Set B focuses on the cultural framing perspective. The results indicate that individuals who hold the belief that individual actions can influence outcomes are more inclined to perceive both the income distribution and family income as fair, in contrast to those who believe that wealth, poverty, success, and failure are predetermined by fate.

Set C considers the effect of political propaganda. The findings suggest that individuals who identified the internet as their primary source for information and news are less prone to perceive the income distribution as fair compared to those who rely more on traditional media. However, the distinction in media preferences is less evident when considering the perception of fair family income.

Finally, Set D considers political trust and system support variables. Results reveal a strong correlation between individuals who express trust in the government and believe in the government's capability to address the country's challenges, and their likelihood to perceive both the income distribution and family income as fair. To illustrate, 66% of those who strongly agree that government officials can be trusted consider the income distribution as fair, whereas only around 32% share the same perception among those who strongly disagree with the trustworthiness of government officials.

Table 9.3 provides ordinal logistic regressions predicting the effects of economic modernization, meritocratic belief, political propaganda, and political trust on the perception of fairness (see Appendix Table 9A for full results). Results show that all these factors play a significant role in shaping how people perceive the fairness of income distribution and family income. Specifically, Model (1) shows that individuals experiencing improved economic conditions and expanded life opportunities are markedly more likely to perceive the income distribution as fair. Similarly, respondents endorsing the belief that individual effort can alter destiny exhibit significantly higher odds of considering the income distribution as fair. This pattern is also observed among those who primarily rely on the internet for news and information. In particular, we also see that individuals who express higher levels of trust in the government show significantly higher odds of perceiving income distribution as fair, with a unit increase in political trust measures leading to about a 41% increase in the odds of saying the income distribution as fair in relative to unfair. Model (2) adds a system justification variable to the base model. It shows that individuals who hold the belief that over the long run, their system of government is capable of solving the social problems of their country faces are significantly more likely to perceive the income distribution as fair. While the effect of political trust in Model (2) remains significant, the decrease in odds ratio from Model (1) to Model (2) suggests that system justification belief may partially explain the effect of political trust on perceived income fairness. Model (3) and Model (4) repeat the analysis using the perceived family income fairness as outcome variables. The overall patterns are very similar. Figure 9.2 provides a visualization of the main findings. Taken together, the overall findings show evidence to support the significant role of political trust in shaping perception of income fairness, even with controlling the established theories and a wide range of demographics.

Discussion

This study makes several major contributions to the study of subjective inequality in China. First, it shows that Chinese acceptance of inequality remains widespread. Recent research suggests that Chinese people may have

Table 9.3 Ordinal logistic regressions predicting perception of fairness, ABS 2019

	Model (1)	Model (2)	Model (3)	Model (4)
	How fair is income distribution		How fair is family income	
Economic development				
Improved economic condition	1.374***	1.373***	1.457***	1.455***
	(6.71)	(6.72)	(7.30)	(7.23)
Enhanced life opportunities	1.382***	1.365***	1.512***	1.483***
	(4.82)	(4.63)	(6.47)	(6.09)
Meritocratic belief				
Self-effort belief	1.313***	1.307***	1.328***	1.319***
	(3.98)	(3.90)	(3.46)	(3.37)
Political propaganda				
Traditional media (TV,	ref	ref	ref	ref
newspaper, and radio)	0.804*	0.806*	0.829	0.834
Internet	(−2.11)	(−2.08)	(−1.55)	(−1.49)
Other channels	1.439*	1.808**	0.980	1.196
	(2.10)	(3.17)	(−0.11)	(0.86)
Political trust				
Trust the people who run our government to do what is right	1.410***	1.379***	1.481***	1.420***
	(4.81)	(4.47)	(4.34)	(3.83)
System justification				
Over the long run, our system of government is capable of solving the problems our country faces		1.261*		1.461**
		(2.00)		(2.61)
Controls	yes	yes	yes	yes
Cut points				
cut1	0.309*	0.533	0.147**	0.356
	(−2.01)	(−0.97)	(−2.83)	(−1.33)
cut2	5.398**	9.332***	3.267	7.967**
	(2.92)	(3.45)	(1.78)	(2.74)
cut3	701.9***	1222.0***	612.2***	1520.6***
	(10.94)	(10.65)	(9.39)	(9.43)
N	2833	2833	2917	2917
pseudo R^2	0.051	0.052	0.065	0.067

Note: Exponentiated coefficients; t statistics in parentheses. $^{*}p < 0.05$, $^{**}p < 0.01$, $^{***}p < 0.001$

become more critical about rising income inequality. For example, analyzing data from two waves of the China National Survey on Inequality and Distributive Justice collected by Whyte (2016), Lei (2020) shows that Chinese people's attitudes toward inequality changed little between 2004 and 2009, but they have become increasingly critical of both inequality and its seeming disjuncture with China's socialist principles between 2009 and

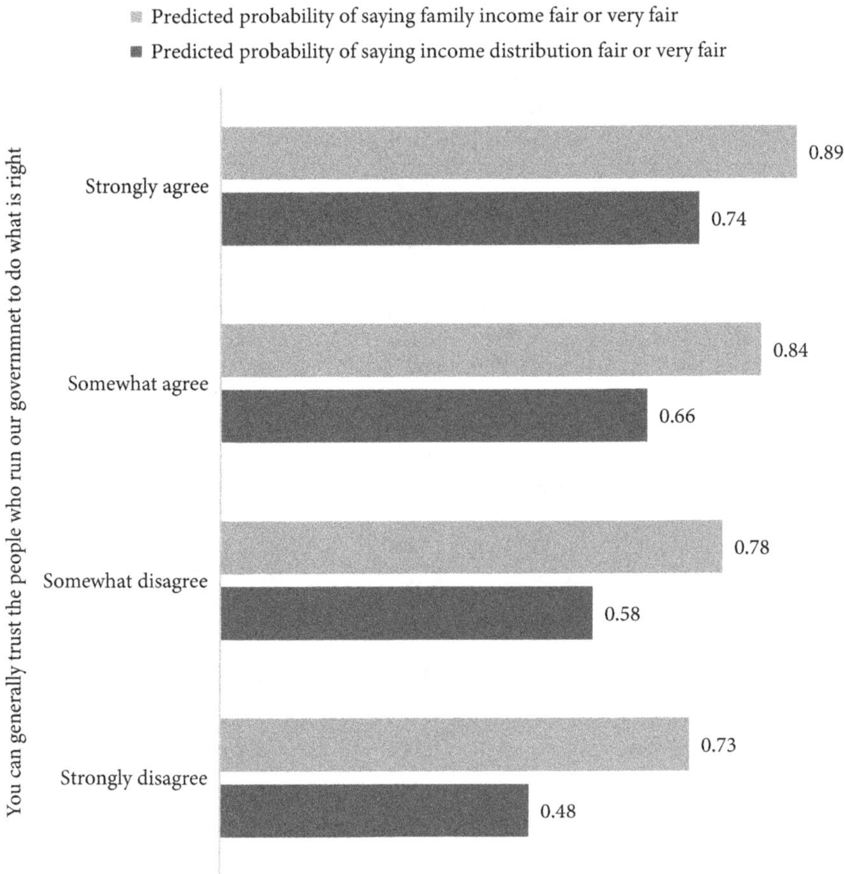

Figure 9.2 Predicted perceived fairness of income inequality and family income, ABS 2015–19

2014. There is also research indicating specific segments of the Chinese population—such as the middle class or educated youth—have begun to show signs of anger and resentment against growing inequality (Jin 2022). Nonetheless, my analysis shows that the broader pattern persists—Chinese society as a whole continues to accept and accommodate inequality. There is even an observable upward trend in this perception from 2015 to 2019.

Second, this study not only brings together major established theories of Chinese acceptance of inequality and subjects to empirical scrutiny, but it also highlights the role of political trust in shaping how people perceive income inequality. Survey studies have shown that Chinese citizens hold very high levels of trust in their government (Shi 2001; Wang 2005; Wu and Wilkes 2018b). Despite prior literature suggesting that high levels of income inequality, both actual and perceived, undermine people's trust in their government (Barreiro et al. 2019), including in the context of China (Hutchison and Xu 2017; Lei 2020; Yu and Yang 2021), the high levels of political trust in China, even in the face of growing inequalities, challenge the seemingly straightforward negative relationship between political trust and inequality. Here I suggest that Chinese citizens' trust in the political system may come before their views of income inequality. This is because the high political trust among Chinese citizens could be rooted in political culture, and people learn to trust their government largely from early life socialization (Fairbrother et al. 2022; Shi 2001). Because Chinese citizens trust and support their government, they hold a system justification belief that legitimatizes income inequality. My empirical analysis shows the significant positive effect of political trust on perceived fairness while controlling economic modernization, cultural belief, and political control factors. Chinese citizens who believe over the long run their government is capable of solving the social problems the country faces show significantly higher odds of perceiving both the income distribution and family income fair.

Finally, the study also contributes to the "social volcano" debate. Over the last several decades, the widening gap between the rich and the poor in China has led to widespread concerns about its political ramifications. Harvard sociologist Martin Whyte characterized the potential threat of high inequality to political stability in China as a "social volcano" (Whyte 2010). However, the question of whether this "social volcano" will continue to lie dormant or could erupt at any moment has been a subject of considerable debate (see, Wei 2022). Some suggest the probability of this "social volcano" erupting is low, as Chinese citizens do not show anger but instead exhibit a high level of acceptance and tolerance toward the prevailing income disparities in the country (Song 2023; Wei 2022; Wu 2009; Xie 2016). Whyte himself presented three pieces of evidence against his "social volcano" thesis. First, average citizens in China show lower levels of discontent with income inequality compared to citizens in many other societies. Second, despite a continuous rise in income inequality, there is no widespread surge in popular anger on the issue. Third, there is a relatively lower degree of criticism among economically disadvantaged rural Chinese populations, who have gained less from the nation's economic growth compared to their urban counterparts (Whyte 2016; Whyte and Im 2014).

Others, however, suggest that the "social volcano" exists, and the high inequality could have political consequences. Zhou and Jin (2018) point out that there is a social volcano because provincial inequality has negative effects on individuals' trust in the local government and distrust in the local government implies distrust in the central government. Lei (2020) also suggests that Chinese individuals who think that the level of inequality has violated socialist principles are more likely than others to distrust the central, provincial-level, and county-level governments. She underscores the potential political repercussions associated with elevated levels of inequality.

Here I show that because Chinese citizens continue to perceive income distribution as largely fair, and they still show high trust in both local and national government (Fairbrother et al. 2022), there may not be a "social volcano" effect of the high income gap in China. Indeed, Lei (2020) found no statistically significant correlation between discontent with income inequality and distrust of the central government in China. Hutchison and Xu (2017) also show that the negative effects of inequality and openness are largely offset by the strong positive effect of economic growth, leading to Chinese citizens maintaining a high level of political trust.

Conclusion

Misperception of actual inequality is widespread globally. Individuals' social and economic status, their ideological beliefs, and the broad social, economic, and political contexts they are in can all shape how people perceive inequality (Gimpelson and Treisman 2018; Wu et al. 2024). Chinese citizens also widely consider income distribution fair even though China is among the most unequal countries in the world (Whyte 2010; Wu 2009; Xie 2016). In this study, I have provided an overview of current theories that seek to explain the widespread acceptance of income inequality in China. I have also introduced a new perspective that highlights the role of political trust in shaping perceived income fairness in China. My empirical analysis using data from the ABS shows that Chinese society as a whole continues to accept and accommodate inequality, and a combination of economic, cultural, and political factors together explains why this is the case. In particular, I have shown that politically trusting individuals are more likely to perceive income distribution as fair, and this is partially because they tend to hold a system justification belief that helps legitimize income inequality and are confident that their government can solve the inequality issue over the long run. The consistently high levels of political trust and fairness perception maintained by Chinese citizens challenge the notion that high inequality inevitably leads to political instability.

Appendix

Table 9A Ordinal logistic regressions predicting perception of fairness, ABS 2019

	Model (1)	Model (2)	Model (3)	Model (4)
	How fair is income distribution		**How fair is family income**	
Economic development				
Improved economic condition	1.374***	1.373***	1.457***	1.455***
	(6.71)	(6.72)	(7.30)	(7.23)
Enhanced life opportunities	1.382***	1.365***	1.512***	1.483***
	(4.82)	(4.63)	(6.47)	(6.09)
Meritocratic belief				
Self-effort belief	1.313***	1.307***	1.328***	1.319***
	(3.98)	(3.90)	(3.46)	(3.37)
Political propaganda				
Traditional media (TV, newspaper, and radio)	ref	ref	ref	ref
Internet	0.804*	0.806*	0.829	0.834
	(−2.11)	(−2.08)	(−1.55)	(−1.49)
Other channels	1.439*	1.808**	0.980	1.196
	(2.10)	(3.17)	(−0.11)	(0.86)
Political trust				
Trust the people who run our government to do what is right	1.410***	1.379***	1.481***	1.420***
	(4.81)	(4.47)	(4.34)	(3.83)
System justification				
Over the long run, our system of government is capable of solving the problems our country faces		1.261*		1.461**
		(2.00)		(2.61)
Controls				
Female	1.130	1.137	1.010	1.018
	(1.48)	(1.55)	(0.10)	(0.19)
Age	0.956**	0.955**	0.941**	0.940**
	(−2.67)	(−2.70)	(−2.86)	(−2.90)
Age-sq	1.000*	1.000*	1.001**	1.001**
	(2.53)	(2.53)	(2.93)	(2.93)

Continued

Table 9A *Continued*

	Model (1)	Model (2)	Model (3)	Model (4)
	How fair is income distribution		How fair is family income	
Education in years	1.017	1.016	1.038**	1.037**
	(1.48)	(1.37)	(2.93)	(2.76)
Marital status_single	ref	ref	ref	ref
Married	0.885	0.896	0.971	0.992
	(−0.76)	(−0.68)	(−0.15)	(−0.04)
Widowed/separated	0.694	0.708	0.953	0.976
/divorced	(−1.61)	(−1.52)	(−0.18)	(−0.09)
Household income_Step1	ref	ref	ref	ref
Household income_Step2	0.861	0.866	1.146	1.142
	(−0.92)	(−0.88)	(0.73)	(0.71)
Household income_Step3	0.839	0.837	1.138	1.128
	(−1.11)	(−1.12)	(0.69)	(0.64)
Household income_Step4	0.816	0.817	1.368	1.351
	(−1.08)	(−1.08)	(1.43)	(1.37)
Household income_Step5	0.753	0.749	2.304**	2.278**
	0.883	0.884	1.093	1.085
Did not answer	(−0.88)	(−0.87)	(0.53)	(0.49)
	(−1.08)	(−0.87)	(0.84)	(0.49)
Urban	0.817*	0.814*	1.032	1.033
	(−2.08)	(−2.11)	(0.28)	(0.28)
Geographic region_North	ref	ref	ref	ref
Northeast	2.940***	2.888***	1.634*	1.474
	(5.56)	(5.14)	(2.17)	(1.59)
East	1.684***	1.727***	1.221	1.177
	(3.53)	(3.39)	(1.12)	(0.83)
South Central	1.210	1.319	0.951	0.885
	(1.31)	(1.75)	(−0.29)	(−0.63)
Southwest	1.450*	1.458*	1.302	1.216
	(2.40)	(2.25)	(1.35)	(0.92)
Northwest	0.675	0.698	0.776	0.726
	(−1.51)	(−1.28)	(−0.93)	(−1.08)
Cut points				
cut1	0.309*	0.533	0.147**	0.356
	(−2.01)	(−0.97)	(−2.83)	(−1.33)
cut2	5.398**	9.332***	3.267	7.967**
	(2.92)	(3.45)	(1.78)	(2.74)
cut3	701.9***	1222.0***	612.2***	1520.6***
	(10.94)	(10.65)	(9.39)	(9.43)
N	2833	2833	2917	2917
pseudo R^2	0.051	0.052	0.065	0.067

Note: Exponentiated coefficients; t statistics in parentheses. $^{*}p < 0.05$, $^{**}p < 0.01$, $^{***}p < 0.001$

References

Almås, I., A.W. Cappelen, E.Ø. Sørensen, and B. Tungodden. 2010. "Fairness and the Development of Inequality Acceptance." *Science* 328 (5982): pp. 1176–1178.

Barreiro, A., W.F. Arsenio, and C. Wainryb. 2019. "Adolescents' Conceptions of Wealth and Societal Fairness amid Extreme Inequality: An Argentine Sample." *Developmental Psychology* 55 (3): p. 498.

Dalton, R.J., and C. Welzel. Eds. 2014. *The Civic Culture Transformed: From Allegiant to Assertive Citizens.* Cambridge: Cambridge University Press.

Du, H., and R.B. King. 2022. "What Predicts Perceived Economic Inequality? The Roles of Actual Inequality, System Justification, and Fairness Considerations." *British Journal of Social Psychology* 61 (1): pp. 19–36.

Fairbrother, M., J. Mewes, R. Wilkes, C. Wu, and G.N. Giordano. 2022. "Can Bureaucrats Break Trust? Testing Cultural and Institutional Theories of Trust with Chinese Panel Data." *Socius* 8: p. 23780231221126879.

Gimpelson, V., and D. Treisman. 2018. "Misperceiving Inequality." *Economics and Politics* 30 (1): pp. 27–54.

Goudarzi, S., R. Pliskin, J.T. Jost, and E.D. Knowles. 2020. "Economic System Justification Predicts Muted Emotional Responses to Inequality." *Nature Communications* 11 (1): p. 383.

Haack, P., and J. Sieweke. 2018. "The Legitimacy of Inequality: Integrating the Perspectives of System Justification and Social Judgment." *Journal of Management Studies* 55 (3): pp. 486–516.

Hirschman, A.O., and M. Rothschild. 1973. "The Changing Tolerance for Income Inequality in the Course of Economic Development: With a Mathematical Appendix." *Quarterly Journal of Economics* 87 (4): pp. 544–566.

Hutchison, M.L., and P. Xu. 2017. "Trust in China? The Impact of Development, Inequality, and Openness on Political Trust Across China's Provinces, 2001–2012." *Asian Journal of Comparative Politics* 2 (2): pp. 176–195.

Jin, S. 2022. "Does Soft Propaganda Work? The Impact of Inequality Rhetoric on Opinions Toward Economic Inequality in China." *China Review* 22 (3): pp. 211–241.

Jost, J.T. 2019. "A Quarter Century of System Justification Theory: Questions, Answers, Criticisms, and Societal Applications." *British Journal of Social Psychology* 58 (2): pp. 263–314.

Jost, J.T., and M.R. Banaji. 1994. "The Role of Stereotyping in System-justification and the Production of False Consciousness." *British Journal of Social Psychology* 33 (1): pp. 1–27.

Jost, J.T., M.R. Banaji, and B.A. Nosek. 2004. "A Decade of System Justification Theory: Accumulated Evidence of Conscious and Unconscious Bolstering of the Status Quo." *Political Psychology* 25 (6): pp. 881–919.

Kanbur, R., Y. Wang, and X. Zhang. 2021. "The Great Chinese Inequality Turnaround." *Journal of Comparative Economics* 49 (2): pp. 467–482.

Larsen, C.A. 2016. "How Three Narratives of Modernity Justify Economic Inequality." *Acta Sociologica* 59 (2): pp. 93–111.

Lee, D., C.Y. Chang, and H. Hur. 2020. "Economic Performance, Income Inequality and Political Trust: New Evidence From a Cross-National Study of 14 Asian Countries." *Asia Pacific Journal of Public Administration* 42 (2): pp. 66–88.

Lei, Y.W. 2020. "Revisiting China's Social Volcano: Attitudes Toward Inequality and Political Trust in China." *Socius* 6: 2378023120915382.

Li, W., J. Wu, Y. Yang, M. Yuan, J. Lin, and Y. Kou. 2023. "Longitudinal Relations Between Perceived Economic Inequality and Prosocial Behavior Among Chinese Adolescents: The Mediating Role of System Justification." *Children and Youth Services Review* 155: p. 107316.

Malahy, L.W., M.A. Rubinlicht, and C.R. Kaiser. 2009. "Justifying Inequality: A Cross-Temporal Investigation of US Income Disparities and Just-World Beliefs from 1973 to 2006." *Social Justice Research* 22: pp. 369–383.

Østerby-Jørgensen, A.M. 2023. "There Is High, and There Is Low: A Qualitative Examination of Framings of Inequality That Chinese People Apply." *Socio-Economic Review* 21 (2): pp. 1083–1101.

Piketty, T., L. Yang, and G. Zucman. 2019. "Capital Accumulation, Private Property, and Rising Inequality in China, 1978–2015." *American Economic Review* 109 (7): pp. 2469–2496.

Samson, K. 2018. "Trust as a Mechanism of System Justification." *PLoS One* 13 (10): p. e0205566.

Shi, T. 2008. "China: Democratic Values Supporting an Authoritarian System." In *How East Asians View Democracy*, edited by Y. Chu, L. Diamond, A.J. Nathan, and D.C. Shin, pp. 209–237. New York: Columbia University Press.

Shi, T. 2001. "Cultural Values and Political Trust: A Comparison of the People's Republic of China and Taiwan." *Comparative Politics* 33 (4): pp. 401–419.

Song, X. 2023. "Understanding Subjective Inequality in China." *European Sociological Review 39* (4): pp. 545–568.

Stockmann, D., A. Esarey, and J. Zhang. 2018. "Who Is Afraid of the Chinese State? Evidence Calling into Question Political Fear as an Explanation for Overreporting of Political Trust." *Political Psychology 39* (5): pp. 1105–1121.

Walder, A.G. 2023. "China's Extreme Inequality: The Structural Legacies of State Socialism." *China Journal* 90 (1): pp. 1–26.

Wan, H., and J. Knight. 2023. "China's Growing But Slowing Inequality of Household Wealth, 2013–2018: A Challenge to 'Common Prosperity'?" *China Economic Review* 79: p. 101947.

Wang, Z. 2005. "Before the Emergence of Critical Citizens: Economic Development and Political Trust in China." *International Review of Sociology* 15 (1): pp. 155–171.

Wei, L. 2022. "When the Wall Is Broken: Rural-to-Urban Migration, Perceived Inequality, and Subjective Social Status in China." *Research in Social Stratification and Mobility* 82: p. 100731.

Whyte, M.K. 2016. "China's Dormant and Active Social Volcanoes." *China Journal* 75 (1): pp. 9–37.

Whyte, M.K. Ed. 2010. *One Country, Two Societies: Rural-Urban Inequality in Contemporary China*. Vol. 16. Cambridge, MA: Harvard University Press.

Whyte, M.K., and D.K. Im. 2014. "Is the Social Volcano Still Dormant? Trends in Chinese Attitudes Toward Inequality." *Social Science Research* 48: pp. 62–76.

Wu, C., K. Sharma, E. Haddon, and F. Duina. 2024. "Political Polarization and the Dynamics Between Actual Income and Perceived Income Inequality in the United States, 1987 to 2021." *Socius* 10: p. 23780231231225580.

Wu, C., and R. Wilkes. 2018a. "Finding Critical Trusters: A Response Pattern Model of Political Trust." *International Journal of Comparative Sociology* 59 (2): pp. 110–138.

Wu, C., and R. Wilkes. 2018b. "Local–National Political Trust Patterns: Why China Is an Exception." *International Political Science Review* 39 (4): pp. 436–454.

Wu, C., R. Wilkes, and D.C. Wilson. 2022. "Race & Political Trust: Justice as a Unifying Influence on Political Trust." *Daedalus* 151 (4): pp. 177–199.

Wu, X. 2009. "Income Inequality and Distributive Justice: A Comparative Analysis of Mainland China and Hong Kong." *China Quarterly* 200: pp. 1033–1052.

Xian, H., and J. Reynolds. 2017. "Bootstraps, Buddies, and Bribes: Perceived Meritocracy in the United States and China." *Sociological Quarterly* 58 (4): pp. 622–647.

Xie, Y. 2016. "Understanding Inequality in China." *Chinese Journal of Sociology* 2 (3): pp. 327–347.

Xie, Y., A. Thornton, G. Wang, and Q. Lai. 2012. "Societal Projection: Beliefs Concerning the Relationship Between Development and Inequality in China." *Social Science Research* 41 (5): pp. 1069–1084.
Xie, Y., and X. Zhou. 2014. "Income Inequality in Today's China." *Proceedings of the National Academy of Sciences* 111 (19): pp. 6928–6933.
Yu, Y., and Z. Yang. 2021. "Unevenness vs. Unfairness: Perceptions of Economic Inequality and Political Support in China." *China: An International Journal* 19 (2): pp. 1–24.
Zhou, Y.J., and S. Jin. 2018. "Inequality and Political Trust in China: The Social Volcano Thesis Re-examined." *China Quarterly* 236: pp. 1033–1062.

Chapter 10
Labor's Moral Sway in the Era of Union Decline
The Case of the United States

Marc Dixon

Introduction

The United States stands out relative to many rich capitalist democracies both for its high level of economic inequality and its comparatively weak labor movement. A vibrant research literature demonstrates the surge in income inequality in the United States over the last four decades and the critical role of union decline in this process (Jacobs and Dirlam 2016; Rosenfeld 2014; VanHeuvelen 2018, 2023). The steep decline of unions, which accelerated in the 1980s, is shown to account for a fifth to up to a third of the growth in earnings inequality. The effects of unions are especially marked for blue-collar workers, and the share of income going to the working class declined considerably during this period. Yet, unions are also found to provide a check on executive pay and to impact a host of stratification outcomes beyond earnings. For all these reasons, labor advocates and many academics point to union revitalization as key to reducing inequality and its deleterious effects (Isaac 2023).

The relationship between union decline and popular responses to inequality is less clear. The basic headline is that increases in inequality to levels outpacing the 1920s have not increased Americans' support for redistribution, and unions, in their shrunken state, appear unable to inspire much public outrage to change this (McCall 2013; Saez and Zucman 2020). In this chapter, I fill in the story by considering how unions shaped public understanding of inequality during their heyday and the ways in which this influence, or unions' moral sway, was undermined during labor's steep

Marc Dixon, *Labor's Moral Sway in the Era of Union Decline*. In: *The Social Acceptance of Inequality*.
Edited by: Francesco Duina and Luca Storti, Oxford University Press. © Oxford University Press (2025).
DOI: 10.1093/oso/9780197814499.003.0010

decline. I suggest that union decline, a process marked not only by steep membership losses but also a growing acceptance by unions of the new normal of high inequality, helped facilitate a broader cultural logic of acceptance of inequality marked in part by diminished expectations of fairness in the labor market.

The labor movement, of course, is not the only actor whose notable shifts have likely contributed to the acceptance of inequality. The Democratic Party in the United States and left parties elsewhere have increasingly embraced markets and market solutions over redistribution (Berman 2022; Mudge 2018), often sidelining labor in the process. My focus here, however, is on changing union practices and unions' relationship to civil society and to average workers. As the most forceful advocate for economic equality in the twentieth century, it is instructive to clarify what unions once did, their potential role in the seeming indifference to inequality today and what, if anything, might change the course.

Stratification research on unions provides a useful jumping off point by identifying direct and indirect pathways through which unions impact inequality. This research shows that unions impact inequality directly by raising the wages of their members and through threat effects whereby nonunion employers raise wages to head off the threat of unionization (Rosenfeld 2014). Yet, there are also a host of indirect pathways through which unions matter for inequality, from calling out exorbitant executive pay to promoting norms of fairness and imbuing workers with more egalitarian views. For Western and Rosenfeld (2011), these political and cultural practices were central to unions' twentieth-century role as a pillar of the moral economy, or "norms prescribing fair distribution that are institutionalized in the market's rules and customs" (517). Whereas unions were an important anchor of the moral economy in the three decades following World War II, union decline has weakened generalized norms of fairness and contributed to earnings inequality beyond their direct effects on the wages of union members (VanHeuvelen 2018).

Why did unions' egalitarian claims resonate in the first place? Unions were able to promote norms of fairness in part because of their size and effectiveness at the bargaining table, as I describe later. Yet, unions' moral sway rested on more than numbers. It depended on unions being seen as legitimate representatives of workers' interests. Chaison and Bigelow (2002) distinguish between unions' pragmatic and moral legitimacy. Unions hold pragmatic legitimacy to the extent members and potential members see unions as effective bargaining agents that deliver meaningful material gains. Unions hold moral legitimacy to the extent that key constituents—especially workers and the public—see unions as producing something of greater value to the community (i.e., beyond union members). Unions arguably need both to inspire the public on issues of inequality.

Understanding how unions matter (or not) means thinking about ways in which this legitimacy is upheld or undermined. Here I turn to the crisis period of union decline in the 1980s. I suggest how certain union practices, mostly survival strategies, signaled their acceptance to growing inequality and undermined unions' image as an egalitarian force. Whereas acts and effects of solidarity were visible and on display during the peak of union strength, the decline period was instead highlighted by concessions and a growing disconnect between unions and average workers. This coupled with the shrunken state of the labor movement and its retreat from mainstream civic life made it difficult for unions to shed the greedy special interest label applied by their opponents. In this context, most union appeals fell flat.

I begin by describing union strength and influence in the post–World War II era and their steep decline at the end of the twentieth century. I then turn to the relationship between unions and inequality attitudes today before considering how union practices during the decline period and the changing relationships between unions, civil society, and average workers may have facilitated a broader cultural acceptance of inequality. I conclude by examining the recent uptick in worker activism on the heels of the COVID-19 pandemic. I ask what it would take for unions to promote and enforce economic fairness today and whether union revitalization could be part of the solution to inequality growth.

Union Influence Then and Now

Labor unions were the key equalizing force of the mid-twentieth-century boom years—a period marked by strong economic growth and relatively low inequality. A third of the workforce belonged to unions. Unions boosted the wages and benefits of average workers through collective bargaining agreements, and these gains often spilled over to nonunionized workers as well, boosting millions into the middle class and effectively compressing the income distribution (Farber et al. 2018). The median earner saw their wages double in the two decades following World War II and collective bargaining agreements helped keep wages in tandem with productivity growth into the 1970s (Morris and Western 1999).

The success of unions in facilitating such widely shared prosperity during this period is sometimes described as a part of a "social contract" on work or a "capital–labor accord" (Dixon 2020; Kochan 2000). Here, large firms and the public mostly accepted unions as legitimate representatives of worker interests, unions did not challenge managerial prerogatives over the organization of work, and workers were rewarded with rising incomes. There were limits, of course. Many small firms still fiercely resisted labor. Union strength was highly uneven across regions and mostly absent in the growing Sunbelt states. Manufacturing work, the bulwark of the labor movement, was still dangerous and often dull. Racial, ethnic, and gender hierarchies in the workplace persisted despite, and sometimes due to, union policies. Still, unions, for all their limitations, helped promote a more equitable wage distribution through the economic gains and rights secured in private sector collective bargaining contracts and through electoral mobilization and lobbying in Congress for liberal economic and social welfare policies (Jacobs and Dirlam 2016; Western and Rosenfeld 2011).

It is the combination of worker mobilization and electoral support for left parties, as power resources theory suggests, that facilitates redistributive policies and why union strength is typically associated with lower inequality across capitalist democracies (Pontusson 2013). In the United States, however, fights over redistribution were often carried out in the private sector, arguably heightening the role of unions (Galbraith 1958). Unions helped to make health insurance, pensions, and generous unemployment insurance a reality for average workers. In addition to collective bargaining and political mobilization, unions mattered by shaping workplace culture and solidarity, by promoting "norms of equity" and shaping public perception of what counts as a fair return from work (Western and Rosenfeld 2011). This indirect influence of unions on economic inequality rested on union legitimacy, that is, that unions were seen as effective and capable actors that produced something of greater value to the community (Chaison and Bigelow 2002). Consistently high public approval for unions and strong union election win rates in the early postwar decades are indicative of such legitimacy and arguably gave weight to union claims on inequality.

The boom years proved exceptional. Labor's influence unraveled quickly as economic crises and increased global competition roiled the economy in the 1970s. While unions declined across most Western countries in the late twentieth century, union decline in the United States began earlier and was especially steep. The United Auto Workers and the United Steelworkers, the biggest industrial unions, each lost more than 400,000 members between 1979 and 1984 alone (Windham 2017). Decline was not limited to the manufacturing core or those sectors most impacted by global competition. Union strongholds in construction and transportation also saw huge declines. Union density, the percentage of workers belonging to unions, declined from a mid-century peak of 35% in the mid-1950s to 23% in 1980 and 13% in 2000. The severity of the decline is masked in part by the gains of public sector unions in the 1970s. Private sector union density fell from just over 24% in the 1970s to below 10% by the late 1990s.

Following President Ronald Reagan's firing of more than 10,000 striking air traffic controllers in 1981, new union organizing attempts fell by half. Union organizing has not sniffed pre-Reagan levels since (Tope and Jacobs 2009). Whereas striking in highly unionized industries was associated with wage gains in the early postwar decades (Rubin 1986), strikes also declined in the 1970s and 1980s and became decoupled from wage gains (Rosenfeld 2006). By the end of the twentieth century, the American labor movement had a far lower union coverage rate (the share of all workers covered by collective bargaining contracts whether members or not) than other Western countries (Godard 2009).

Though surveys routinely show a latent demand for unions, this has not translated into a reversal or even a halting of union decline (Kochan et al. 2023). Several factors contribute to the exceptional decline and its persistence. These include economic and technological change and the growth of the nonunion sector relative to traditionally union jobs (Farber and Western 2001; Kimeldorf 2013), business resistance to unions (Clawson and Clawson 1999), political opposition and legal restrictions (Tope and Jacobs 2009), and union stagnation and organizing failures (Voss and Sherman 2000). This is not all for a lack of trying on unions part. A host of new union organizing strategies and insurgent movements within and outside of the main US labor federation, the AFL-CIO, have shown promise, but have failed to reverse the downward trend (Martin 2008).

The relationship between the steep decline in unions and the rise in economic inequality is well documented. As unions fell, wages in the middle of the income distribution stagnated and inequality accelerated. This was punctuated by the extraordinary income growth of top earners (Saez and Zucman 2020). Union wage effects are strongest for blue-collar workers and for men, but unions are also found to keep runaway executive pay in check (Shin 2014; Western and Rosenfeld 2011). Two of the big changes are depicted in Figure 10.1 with union decline and the ratio of CEO-to-worker pay moving in opposition directions. The CEO-to-worker pay ratio first rises in the 1980s and then accelerates in the 1990s. It has been at or above 300-to-1 for much of this century. As Galbraith (1958) described, unions were once a countervailing power to corporations. Their decline left a void that has been filled by a patchwork of social movements and corporate social responsibility initiatives with far less power and/or will to change pay-setting practices.

Researchers find union decline to account for a fifth to up to a third of the total growth in earnings inequality over the last four decades (VanHeuvelen 2018). Beyond income inequality, union decline has led to increased working poverty (Brady et al. 2013; VanHeuvelen and Brady 2021), and there is suggestive evidence that it has contributed to growing political inequalities of access and influence (Feigenbaum et al. 2018; Page et al. 2013).

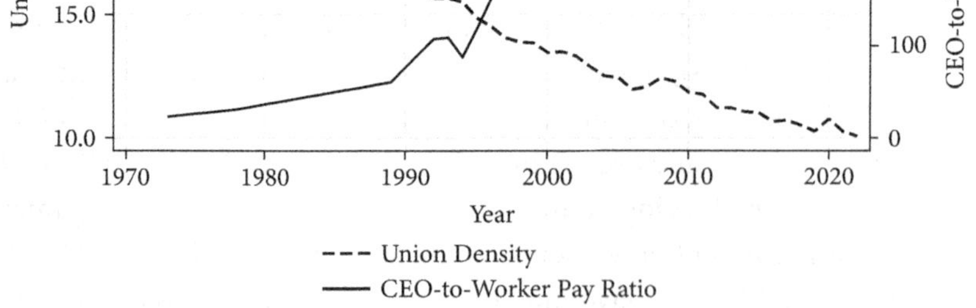

Figure 10.1 Union density and CEO-to-worker pay, 1973–2022

Note: Union density from Hirsch et al. (2024). CEO-to-Worker Pay Ratio from the Economic Policy Institute (Bivens and Kandra 2023). The ratio represents the average annual executive compensation for the 350 largest publicly traded firms owned in the United States over the annual average compensation for private sector nonsupervisory workers.

Union Decline and the Acceptance of Inequality

It is safe to say that American unions have been unable to muster significant public resistance to rising economic inequality or support for redistributive policies to combat it. The largest public outcry against inequality in the last several decades, *Occupy Wall Street*, occurred mostly *in the absence* of unions. One notable exception has been the success of minimum wage ballot initiatives at the state level where unusually large shares of voters (sometimes exceeding 70%) have supported increases to the minimum wage (Congressional Research Service 2021).

Scholars agree that public desire for reduced inequality is modest in the United States relative to other countries (Lindh and McCall 2022). Steep increases in inequality highlighted by the runaway growth of top earners have not changed this. McCall (2013) finds that public objection to income inequality peaked in the United States in the mid-1990s and then dropped as inequality continued to rise. As inequality rose, public recognition of inequality *decreased* (Waight and Goldstein 2019).[1] Americans tend to be more accepting of income inequality when they believe there is equality of opportunity and belief in the latter appears to be growing. As inequality has grown across OECD countries, so have meritocratic beliefs justifying it such that residents who came of age under rising inequality believe more strongly in meritocracy. Not surprisingly, this pattern is especially marked in the United States (Mijs 2021).

The limited ability of unions to muster resistance to rising inequality is due in part to the shrunken state of the labor movement, as fewer members of the public have direct exposure to unions and collective bargaining. Others, like Pontusson (2013), suggest that the changing composition of national labor movements, whereby more union members are now higher earners, may weaken union support for redistribution. Still, union influence, like that of other voluntary organizations, cannot be reduced solely to membership rates. Moreover, throughout the decline period, union members, higher earners or not, were still more likely to recognize inequality than nonmembers, and they were more likely to engage in protest and to vote as well (Caren et al. 2011; Kerrissey and Shofer 2013; Waight and Goldstein 2019).

Here I suggest an additional and related route through which union decline may contribute to the acceptance of inequality by considering the actions of unions themselves. This coupled with their growing isolation in social and political life undermined labor's moral sway and gave fuel to critical portrayals of unions as out of touch and greedy special interests.

Acceptance in Action

Union Practices

The last decades of the twentieth century were troubling times for the labor movement. Collective bargaining contracts in the two decades following World War II almost always included gains for workers, often substantial gains. Beginning in the 1970s and 1980s, contracts were more often marked by deep concessions in wages and benefits. Some of these undermined the union ethos by abandoning principles of wage uniformity. Historian Nelson Lichtenstein (2002, 238) describes the crisis facing American unions during these years as "an ideological challenge, from within and without, that questioned the very meaning of trade unionism."

What did this look like in practice? In the face of steep membership losses, heightened business resistance and an often-hostile state, union leaders actively pushed for concessions to save jobs. Big visible events like the Chrysler bailout in 1979 set the tone as the Democratic administration and union leadership collectively pushed for and sold significant pay cuts for workers. This agreement broke up wage uniformity among the big Detroit automakers. Ford and General Motors followed by slashing jobs while other employers soon pushed for similar givebacks (Lichtenstein 2002).

When unions did push back, they often lost. President Reagan's firing of more than 10,000 striking air traffic controllers, a move he made with considerable public backing, was followed by high-profile failed strikes in mining, meatpacking, and heavy manufacturing. Despite employing innovative tactics including the use of "corporate campaigns" to target the financial institutions supporting struck companies, many strikes in the 1980s ended with the elimination of the existing union. Some firms even began "baiting" unions into strikes with the aim of replacing their workforce with strikebreakers (Martin and Dixon 2010). Losses were not limited to strikes. Employer opposition to union organizing became more sophisticated and effective. Union representation elections, which fell by half during these years, also reached historically low success rates. Every year between 1980 and 1998, unions lost a majority of representation elections held by the National Labor Relations Board (NLRB). Many unions simply "hunkered down" and abandoned new organizing entirely (Clawson and Clawson 1999; Stepan-Norris and Kerrissey 2023).

In this context, it is not surprising that many unions viewed concessions as more palatable than fighting back. While concessions during troubled economic times may signal that labor is a reasonable actor with the public good in mind, they also erode the view of unions as capable and effective bargaining agents, among union members and nonmembers alike. The latter became more likely as what was first a desperate attempt to save jobs during the depths of the recession of 1981–82 persisted as the economy improved and spread beyond troubled industries. After years of economic expansion, the majority of collective bargaining contracts in the late 1980s either "lowered wages, weakened benefits, or altered standard methods of pay to workers in cost-reducing ways" (Bell 1989, 44). Heavy manufacturing led the way, but, by the mid-1980s, concessions had spread to relatively healthy industries including aerospace, hotels and restaurants, and publishing. Companies not in any immediate distress saw the success of their peers in getting concessions from unions and soon demanded the same (Bluestone and Harrison 1988). By the end of the decade, eight of the ten largest unions made concessionary settlements in a majority of their contract negotiations.

Hard concessions were followed by something arguably more damaging to the union idea in two-tiered bargaining. Two-tiered bargaining is marked by clauses in union contracts whereby new workers are hired at significantly lower rates than existing workers to lower the wage bill and save current jobs. Two-tiered bargaining was sold by union leadership (and many union members) as the only way out of massive job loss and plant closures. Given that the cuts come at the expense of new and yet to be hired employees, two-tiered bargaining necessarily erodes solidarity and exacerbates inequality within unions. It pits the interests of younger (lower tier) workers against older workers. Journalist Steven Greenhouse (2008) puts a face on this by describing a scene where a father and son worked in the same agricultural equipment factory in the Midwest. The son lamented his new work reality in that he will never even have the potential to reach the father's current earnings due to the lower tier he started on. More generally, two-tiered bargaining turns core union principles like equal pay for equal work upside down. As Chaison (2008) described, it creates a "*reverse economic revolution* where workers' wages become lower than those of the previous generation" [italics in original] (4).

Like other union concessions, what started as a desperate measure continued as economic woes abated. Two-tiered bargaining began in the airline industry in the 1970s but really took off in the deep recession of 1981–82, starting with troubled manufacturing industries. Between 1981 and 1985, the share of workers covered by two-tiered collective bargaining agreements grew from 2% to 33%. This continued post-recession and mostly held at or just below the 30% rate well into the 2000s (Bell 1989; Chaison 2008). Indeed, a second wave of two-tiered plans swept grocery workers, auto parts, and again auto manufacturing in the first decade of this century and has remained a flash point in recent high-profile strikes.

Unions' Place in Social and Political Life

The decline in membership and effectiveness in collective bargaining was accompanied by a retreat of unions from civil society. There are plenty of examples during the heyday of union strength of national labor leadership rebuffing alliances with civil rights organizations and other coalition partners. But, by the 1970s, unions were on the outs with many of the New Left movements coming into the Democratic Party. Unions were not seen as a solution to many of the inequalities raised by the new social movements (Lichtenstein 2002). The increasing isolation of unions on the political left is consistent with critiques of the American labor movement as dominated by "business unionism." Here unions are mostly staid, insular, bureaucratic entities that only tend to the concerns of existing members, serving as an insurance policy for workers as opposed to an active social movement.

The growing isolation and stagnation of the labor movement prompted many analysts to call for coalitions, union outreach, and greater integration in civil society as a route for union renewal. And there were notable outreach efforts. In 1981, the AFL-CIO organized a mass mobilization, "Solidarity Day," linking labor with a broad range of social movements. And, in the 1990s, the federation's New Voice leadership made union outreach a priority. These notable developments notwithstanding, there is little evidence that outreach increased. There is no common data source on labor–civil society ties, but quantitative research on labor activism shows outreach remained rare. Community coalitions were common in only the most innovative union organizing campaigns of the 1990s, a miniscule share of all union organizing efforts (Martin 2008). Drawing on media coverage, Dixon and Martin (2012) find only about a quarter of large strike events in the

1990s involved coalition work. And when unions did reach out, it was mostly with other unions or politicians.

Ties between unions and other social movements are only the most visible indicator of the integration of labor in civil society. The integration of union members with other groups is likewise instructive. Compared to members of other types of voluntary organizations (e.g., sports, religious, professional), Cornwell and Harrison (2004) find that union members had fewer ties to organizations outside of labor. This isolation, while visible in the 1970s, increased during the steep membership declines in the 1980s and 1990s. This placed unions on the periphery of inter-organizational culture, more so than almost any other group measured in the General Social Survey. They conclude that union members increasing isolation in daily organizational life "likely signals difficulty in [unions] attaining legitimacy from the general public and other organizations" and makes them easy targets of criticism (877). Indeed, organizations whose members have few ties with other groups, especially with those groups central to civic life, are likely to be seen as representing special interests.

This is not to say that unions and union members were all disengaged. Research still shows notable impacts of unions on civic life, from increased political and civic engagement of individuals who reside in high union density areas (Zullo 2012) to the greater likelihood of union members to protest, vote, and sign petitions relative to nonmembers (Caren et al. 2011). Instead, unions and union members are farther removed from social life than they were in the heyday of union strength, and this isolation has increased in recent decades.

The Persistent Union Wage Premium

The steep decline of unions was not only accompanied by a retreat from civil society but also a persistently high union wage premium, or the difference in wages between union members and similarly situated nonunion workers. The union wage premium can be seen as both an accomplishment of collective bargaining and the degree of separation between union members and average workers. When unions are less integrated in social and political life and represent a smaller and smaller share of the workforce, the latter is more likely to be the focus as the premium can appear exorbitant and provide an easy talking point for critics.

Figure 10.2 plots union density and the union wage premium for all workers and for workers without a college degree from the 1970s to the present.

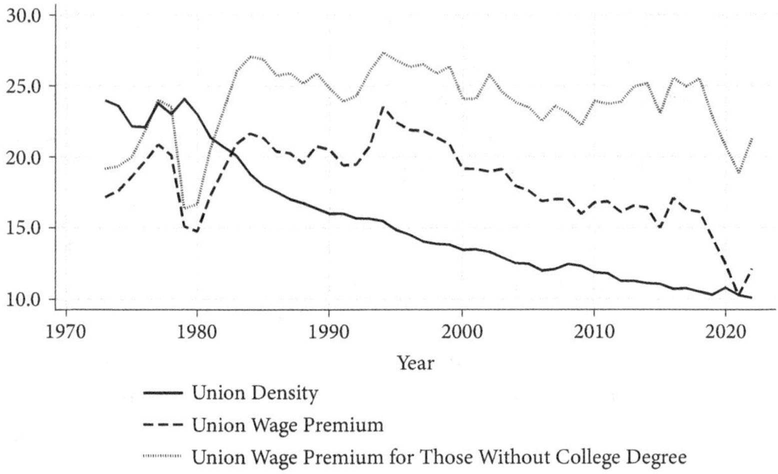

Figure 10.2 Union decline and the union wage premium

Note: Data are from Hirsch et al.'s (2024) estimates from the Current Population Survey. Union wage premium adjusted for worker/job and demographic characteristics.

The significant drop in union density in the early 1980s is followed by an increase in the union wage premium, especially for those without a college degree who earned roughly 25% more than similarly situated nonunion workers between the early 1980s and early 2000s. The union wage premium for all workers hovers around 20% during this period before decreasing in recent years.

In comparative perspective, the United States has always had a large union wage premium due in part to the decentralized nature of collective bargaining and the limited spillover of union protections to nonunion workers. That it holds, and even increases, as US unions made deep concessions in collective bargaining is surprising at first glance in that it seemingly places unions as simultaneously ineffective bargaining agents and privileged actors holding on to a labor market niche. Mostly, it speaks to the truly dismal prospects for the unorganized working class at the end of the twentieth century. Historian Jefferson Cowie (2011, 13) describes the situation in blunt terms: "The dwindling number of workers who held claim on those high-paying industrial jobs found themselves to be labor's new aristocracy—shrinking in numbers, paid beyond the imagination of the vast unorganized majority, and politically detached from those toiling in the swelling ranks of the non-unionized service sector."

Public Opinion on Labor Unions

Did the public's view of unions change as unions engaged in concessionary bargaining and grew more detached from civil society and average workers? Yes, to varying degrees. Figure 10.3 presents Gallup polling data on union approval from 1972 to 2015 compared to the average during the heyday of union strength (as I discuss in the next section, public approval of unions has seen a significant uptick after 2016). Relative to the mid-century peak of labor strength where union approval was above 68% on average, there is a long-term drop during the decline period. Approval drops substantially in the early 1980s and remains well below the postwar average, increasing briefly in the late 1990s and early 2000s before cratering at 48% during the Great Recession. Following the Great Recession, several states, including those with relatively high union density, enacted a number of restrictions on unions and collective bargaining (DiGrazia and Dixon 2020).

That union approval mostly tracks with the business cycle is consistent with statistical and ethnographic evidence showing that unions pay the price for economic decline. There is also suggestive evidence that union approval declines when the union wage premium appears exorbitant (Jarely and Kuruvilla 1994; Lopez 2004). Panagopoulus and Francia's (2008) review of polling on labor reveal other vulnerabilities during the early 1980s. In a survey a month after President Reagan's firing of striking air traffic controllers

Figure 10.3 Public approval of labor unions, 1972–2015

Note: Data from Gallup Polling (2023).

in 1981, more respondents opted to side with a large company than a union in a hypothetical strike. And while surveys during the decline period consistently show pluralities of respondents identifying unions as necessary for working people, they also show that a *majority* of respondents find unions to mostly hurt workers who do not belong to unions. Confidence in organized labor, a related question which has been asked consistently since the 1970s, likewise dips during the period of concessionary bargaining and during the Great Recession and tracks lower than approval on average.[2]

There is some evidence that union influence on general social welfare legislation dipped during this period. And labor-related ballot initiatives in the states saw a decrease in the pro-labor vote share during the 1980s and 1990s. Masters and Delaney's (2005) review of labor's political efforts during the period sums it up by noting that "labor fails at the critical test: it simply fails to inspire" (387). Unions' role as an egalitarian force and their ability to connect with broader audiences on labor and inequality-related issues both took a hit during the decline period.

A Change in Course?

In addition to steep declines in membership, unions faded as a force for equality by agreeing to deep concessions and abandoning wage uniformity, sometimes exacerbating inequalities within collective bargaining units, and by hunkering down, retreating from civil society, and seeking to protect a smaller and smaller share of unionized jobs. All this played into critiques of unions as greedy special interests. It undercut labor's moral sway and their ability to energize the public around inequality issues. These shifts in the position and practices of unions, I argue, helped make possible a broader cultural logic of acceptance to rising inequality.

Yet, recent events should at least give pause when thinking about the role of unions going forward. Over the last six years, striking and union approval have both seen an uptick. A wave of teacher strikes in 2018 secured increases in educational funding across several Republican-controlled and low union density states. Following the COVID-19 pandemic in which economic inequality and occupational privilege were laid bare, union organizing and striking surged. Indeed, workers have pushed back. In the last two years, union approval reached its highest point since the 1960s. In 2023, more than 500,000 workers participated in work stoppages, highlighted by a diverse group of workers and industries including Hollywood actors and writers, autoworkers, and educational support staff. The "hot labor summer" of 2023 is in line with 2018 for the largest share of workers participating in strikes since the 1980s (Ritchie et al. 2024).

In recent years, workers have voted to unionize at retail giants once thought unorganizable such as Amazon and Starbucks. Even more surprising, Starbucks appears to be moving forward with negotiations with the union (first contracts often take years as employers simply refuse to bargain and face few repercussions). New groups of workers have turned to unions, including undergraduate students working on college campuses, video game developers, and digital media professionals. After cratering in the 1980s and 1990s, the success rate for unions in NLRB elections has increased dramatically. And a growing share of nonunion workers indicate they would vote for a union in their workplace (Kochan et al. 2023). The new labor activism signals a rupture from the moribund character of the decline period.

Can unions capitalize on this moment and regain their moral sway? Can they shake Americans' seeming indifference to rising inequality? To do this they would need to demonstrate themselves as effective worker advocates who benefit most Americans, not just union members.

The Case for Optimism

Recent work on inequality attitudes suggests an avenue for unions. First, there is some evidence that increases in inequality have led to increased support for unions (Newman and Kane 2017). More generally, there seems to be an appetite for private sector solutions to inequality, of which unions could play an important part. Lindh and McCall (2022) argue that the comparatively greater acceptance of inequality in the United States may be biased in part by researchers' focus on government intervention as the sole solution. When asked whether the government should reduce income differences through raising taxes on the wealthy or by providing assistance to the poor, a majority of Americans routinely say no. Yet, support for redistribution is higher when respondents are asked if major companies should act to reduce pay disparities. Large majorities of survey respondents have consistently found executives to be overpaid and workers underpaid. This coupled with a majority of Americans expressing distrust in big business suggests a much greater willingness to address inequality through the private sector. Lindh and McCall's (2022) call to "bring the market in" to understanding popular responses to inequality places the pay-setting practices of corporations, including collective bargaining, as a more popular and potentially feasible route for addressing inequality than government intervention.

But unions would also need to do better at the bargaining table and in the community than they did during the period of deep decline. This is happening to a degree. Two-tiered bargaining, which gained a foothold in labor relations in the 1980s, is drawing pushback from workers and unions. Strikes and threatened strikes by auto workers and delivery drivers successfully eliminated two-tiered wage plans in major collective bargaining contracts. The success of the autoworkers "Stand Up Strike," which ratcheted up pressure by strategically targeting plants over time to gain leverage in negotiations, has spurred new organizing campaigns across nonunion auto plants in the Southern United States. Recent strikes have taken on a more public character and have addressed a wide range of issues beyond pay, from health and safety to racial justice (Kochan et al. 2023). For example, striking educational support staff in Los Angeles were joined by teachers in solidarity and parents in support in a strike explicitly framed around economic inequality (Lee and Cowan 2023).

The wave of teacher strikes in 2018 is notable in that they succeeded in unlikely places—Republican-controlled states with restrictions on public sector collective bargaining and bans on public employee strikes—and that they were widely popular. Hertel-Fernandez and colleagues' study (2021) finds that greater exposure to the teacher strikes increased support not only for the walkouts but also for teacher and union rights, and for the labor movement more generally. The authors find suggestive evidence that the support for the strikes was shaped by teachers conveying what they and their unions were doing to fight for children, communities, and educational funding. That is, they articulated labor's contribution to the public good. This is consistent with recent efforts to explicitly link union and community aims when negotiating contracts. So-called *Bargaining for the Common Good* campaigns work to build labor–community partnerships far in advance of any labor action (McCartin et al. 2020).

These efforts are an about face from the hunkering down and protectionism of prior decades. Failed strikes, concessions that challenge the very idea of unionism, and a retreat from civil society have been replaced, in part, by emboldened workers and unions, meaningful gains and community partnerships, and soaring union approval.

The Case for Skepticism

The key challenge for the labor movement is scaling up their recent successes. Indeed, the labor activism of the last six-to-eight years has not reversed or even halted union decline, though the decrease in union density has slowed. Part of this is because union organizing drives through the NLRB reach only a tiny share of the nonunion workforce every year (less than a tenth of a percent). Many of the high-profile union wins have been in small bargaining units. Union elections in multi-establishment employers such as retail and fast-food chains proceed one small unit at a time. Take the previously mentioned campaign to organize workers at Starbucks coffee shops. It stands out in that it has spread across stores rapidly, more than 300 stores across 40 states over the last 3 years. While no doubt impressive, union organizing activity at these establishments has involved only about 8,000 workers to date. Even if unions did scale up current organizing and reverse some of their losses in union density, the impact of unions on wages and earnings inequality may be reduced relative to their twentieth-century peak in that current organizing efforts are targeting workers with lower bargaining power, limiting what unions can do (Kristal 2023).

The last major surge in private sector unionization also benefited from favorable labor law in the creation of the National Labor Relations Act (NLRA), and state actors who explicitly encouraged unionization and collective bargaining. As the NLRA has failed to meet the challenges posed by contemporary work arrangements, unions have pushed for a variety of labor law reforms with little success. Despite the pro-labor stances taken by the Biden administration, no legislative remedy is on the horizon. The most recent attempt, The Protecting the Right to Organize Act, stalled in the US Senate, and the prospects for favorable reforms in the near term are not good.

More generally, the place of unions as a force for good is complicated by the contested nature of the social good itself. Public opinion is polarized across a host of social and political issues. This includes inequality, which is increasingly interpreted through a partisan lens (Waight and Goldstein 2019). The ability of unions to capture the public imagination on inequality is arguably more difficult during deeply polarized times. Unions will need significant help, and a bit of luck, to scale up their demands and reach a larger share of the public on inequality.

Conclusion

As inequality has skyrocketed since the 1980s, Americans have expressed little appetite for redistribution and, at least in some ways, have become more comfortable with inequality (Mijs 2021). Building on stratification research on unions and wage inequality, I suggested specific ways in which union practices during the depths of union decline in the 1980s and 1990s contributed to this process. Above and beyond the sheer loss of union members, unions' survival strategies during the decline period—from concessionary and two-tiered bargaining to the abandonment of principles of wage uniformity—and their increasing isolation in social and political life undermined unions' image as an egalitarian force and their ability to connect with the nonunion public on inequality. Unions lost their moral sway.

As union decline has continued, albeit at a slower rate in recent years, something interesting has happened: workers and unions have pushed back. Unions have won meaningful gains, forged community partnerships, and union approval has soared. Scaling up these recent union gains and articulating a critique of inequality that resonates with the broader public, not to mention that *moves* the broader public, will be incredibly difficult. That said, the new labor activism of the last six years marks a clear break from past practice and places unions squarely in the discussion.

Notes

1. The precise effects of unions and union decline on inequality attitudes are difficult to pin down. High quality surveys began to include questions about economic inequality in the late 1960s, but the bulk of evidence comes from the 1980s and onward as inequality was not considered a major social issue during mid-twentieth century. At the same time, many surveys stopped regularly asking questions about union membership following the 1980s as unions shrunk in size and influence. Waight and Goldstein's (2019) study of the divergence between public perceptions and actual levels of inequality is notable in that it includes a measure of union membership from the 1970s through the early 2000s. They find that while union members are typically more likely to perceive inequality than nonmembers (depending on the survey year), changes in the effect of union membership on inequality perception over time cannot account for the increasing mismatch between public perceptions and economic realities.
2. There is no similarly consistent polling on union member satisfaction. Fiorito et al. (1988) find bread-and-butter gains and positive union–member relations to be significant drivers of satisfaction—both of which faced challenges in the 1980s and 1990s. Union members in the Gallup surveys on confidence in organized labor show larger drops in confidence in the 1980s than the general public but exhibit higher confidence overall.

References

Bell, L. 1989. "Union Concessions in the 1980s." *Federal Reserve Bank of New York Quarterly Review* 14 (2): pp. 44–58.

Berman, E. Popp. 2022. *Thinking Like an Economist: How Efficiency Replaced Equality in Public Policy*. Princeton, NJ: Princeton University Press.

Bivens, J., and J. Kandra. 2023. "CEO Pay Slightly Declined in 2022." Economic Policy Institute, September 21. https://www.epi.org/publication/ceo-pay-in-2022/#full-report.

Bluestone, B., and B. Harrison. 1988. *The Great U-Turn: Corporate Restructuring and the Polarizing of America*. New York: Basic Books.

Brady, D., R.S. Baker, and R. Finnigan. 2013. "When Unionization Disappears: State-Level Unionization and Working Poverty in the United States." *American Sociological Review* 78 (5): pp. 872–896. https://doi.org/10.1177/0003122413501859.

Caren, N., R.A. Ghoshal, and V. Ribas. 2011. "A Social Movement Generation: Cohort and Period Trends in Protest Attendance and Petition Signing." *American Sociological Review* 76 (1): pp. 125–151. https://doi.org/10.1177/0003122410395369.

Chaison, G. 2008. "Two-Tiered Wage Settlements and the Legitimacy of American Unions." Proceedings of the 13th World Congress of the International Industrial Relations Association. Sydney, Australia.

Chaison, G., and B. Bigelow. 2002. *Unions and Legitimacy*. Ithaca, NY: Cornell University Press.

Clawson, D., and M. Clawson. 1999. "What Has Happened to the US Labor Movement? Union Decline and Renewal." *Annual Review of Sociology* 25: pp. 95–119.

Congressional Research Service. 2021. "State Minimum Wage Ballot Measures: In Brief." https://sgp.fas.org/crs/misc/R44706.pdf.

Cornwell, B., and J.A. Harrison. 2004. "Union Members and Voluntary Associations: Membership Overlap as a Case of Organizational Embeddedness." *American Sociological Review* 69 (6): pp. 862–881. https://doi.org/10.1177/000312240406900606.

Cowie, J. 2011. *Stayin' Alive: The 1970s and the Last Days of the Working Class*. New York: New Press.

DiGrazia, J., and M. Dixon. 2020. "The Conservative Upsurge and Labor Policy in the States." *Work and Occupations* 47 (4): pp. 439–465. https://doi.org/10.1177/0730888419876970.

Dixon, M. 2020. *Heartland Blues: Labor Rights in the Industrial Midwest*. New York: Oxford University Press.

Dixon, M., and A.W. Martin. 2012. "We Can't Win This on Our Own: Unions, Firms, and Mobilization of External Allies in Labor Disputes." *American Sociological Review* 77 (6): pp. 946–969. https://doi.org/10.1177/0003122412460649.

Farber, H.S., D. Herbst, I. Kuziemko, and S. Naidu. 2018. "Unions and Inequality over the Twentieth Century: New Evidence from Survey Data." National Bureau of Economic Research Working Paper. https://doi.org/10.3386/w24587.

Farber, H.S., and B. Western. 2001. "Accounting for the Decline of Unions in the Private Sector, 1973–1998." *Journal of Labor Research* 22: pp. 459–486.

Feigenbaum, J., A. Hertel-Fernandez, and V. Williamson. 2018. "From the Bargaining Table to the Ballot Box: Political Effects of Right to Work Laws." National Bureau of Economic Research Working Paper 24259.

Fiorito, J., D.G. Gallagher, and C.V. Fukami. 1988. "Satisfaction with Union Representation." *ILR Review* 41 (2): pp. 294–307. https://doi.org/10.1177/001979398804100210.

Galbraith, J.K. 1958. *The Affluent Society*. Cambridge, MA: Houghton Mifflin.

Gallup. 2023. "Labor Unions, Historical Trends." https://news.gallup.com/poll/12751/labor-unions.aspx#:~:text=In%202022%2C%2071%25%20of%20Americans,75%25%20in%201953%20and%201957.

Godard, J. 2009. "The Exceptional Decline of the American Labor Movement." *Industrial and Labor Relations Review* 63: 82–108.

Greenhouse, S. 2008. *The Big Squeeze: Tough Times for the American Worker*. New York: Anchor.

Hertel-Fernandez, A., S. Naidu, and A. Reich. 2021. "Schooled by Strikes? The Effects of Large-Scale Labor Unrest on Mass Attitudes Toward the Labor Movement." *Perspectives on Politics* 19 (1): pp. 73–91. https://doi.org/10.1017/S1537592720001279.

Hirsch, B.T., D.A. Macpherson, and W.E. Even. 2024. "Union Membership and Coverage Database from the Current Population Survey." https://unionstats.com/.

Isaac, L.W. 2023. "Turning Points in U.S. Labor History, Political Culture, and the Current Upsurge in Labor Militancy." *Work and Occupations* 50 (3): pp. 359–367. https://doi.org/10.1177/07308884231162944.

Jacobs, D., and J.C. Dirlam. 2016. "Political and Economic Stratification: Power Resources and Income Inequality in the United States." *American Journal of Sociology* 122 (2): pp. 469–500. https://doi.org/10.1086/687744.

Jarley, P., and S. Kuruvilla. 1994. "American Trade Unions and Public Approval: Can Unions Please All of the People All of the Time?" *Journal of Labor Research* 25 (2): pp. 97–116.

Kerrissey, J., and E. Schofer. 2013. "Union Membership and Political Participation in the United States." *Social Forces* 91: pp. 895–928. https://doi.org/10.1093/sf/sos187.

Kimeldorf, H. 2013. "Worker Replacement Costs and Unionization: Origins of the U.S. Labor Movement." *American Sociological Review* 78: pp. 1033–1062.

Kochan, T.A. 2000. "Building a New Social Contract at Work: A Call to Action." *Perspectives on Work* 4 (1): pp. 3–12.

Kochan, T.A., J.R. Fine, K. Bronfenbrenner, S. Naidu, J. Barnes, Y. Diaz-Linhart, J. Kallas, J. Kim, A. Minster, D. Tong, P. Townsend, and D. Twiss. 2023. "An Overview of US Workers' Current Organizing Efforts and Collective Actions." *Work and Occupations* 50 (3): pp. 335–350. https://doi.org/10.1177/07308884231168793.

Kristal, T. 2023. "What Can Unions Do? An Impact Estimate for an Increase in the US Private-Sector Unionization Rate on Workers' Earnings." *Work and Occupations* 50 (3): pp. 400–411. https://doi.org/10.1177/07308884231162933.

Lee, K., and J. Cowan. 2023. "Los Angeles School Workers Are on Strike, and Parents Say They Get It." *New York Times*, March 22: https://www.nytimes.com/2023/03/22/us/la-schools-strike.html.

Lichtenstein, N. 2002. *State of the Union*. Princeton, NJ: Princeton University Press.

Lindh, A., and L. McCall. 2022. "Bringing the Market In: An Expanded Framework for Understanding Popular Responses to Economic Inequality." *Socio-Economic Review* 21 (2): pp. 1035–1055. https://doi.org/10.1093/ser/mwac018.

Lopez, S. 2004. *Re-Organizing the Rust Belt*. Berkeley: University of California Press.

Martin, A.W. 2008. "The Institutional Logic of Union Organizing and the Effectiveness of Social Movement Repertoires." *American Journal of Sociology* 113: pp. 1067–1103.

Martin, A.W., and M. Dixon. 2010. "Changing to Win? Resistance, Threat and the Role of Unions in Strikes, 1984–2002." *American Journal of Sociology* 116: pp. 93–129.

Masters, M.F., and J.T. Delaney. 2005. "Organized Labor's Political Scorecard." *Journal of Labor Research* 26 (3): pp. 365–392.

McCall, L. 2013. *The Undeserving Rich: American Beliefs About Inequality, Opportunity, and Redistribution*. New York: Cambridge University Press.

McCartin, J.A., M. Sneiderman, and M. BP-Weeks. 2020. "Combustible Convergence: Bargaining for the Common Good and the #RedforEd Uprisings of 2018." *Labor Studies Journal 45* (1): pp. 97–113. https://doi.org/10.1177/0160449X20901643.

Mijs, J.J.B. 2021. "The Paradox of Inequality: Income Inequality and Belief in Meritocracy Go Hand in Hand." *Socio-Economic Review* 19: pp. 7–35. https://doi.org/10.1093/ser/mwy051.

Morris, M., and B. Western. 1999. "Inequality in Earnings the Close of the Twentieth Century." *Annual Review of Sociology* 25: pp. 623–657. https://doi.org/10.1146/annurev.soc.25.1.623.

Mudge, S.L. 2018. *Leftism Reinvented: Western Parties from Socialism to Neoliberalism*. Cambridge, MA: Harvard University Press.

Newman, B.J., and J.V. Kane. 2017. "Economic Inequality and Public Support for Organized Labor." *Political Research Quarterly* 70 (4): pp. 918–932. https://doi.org/10.1177/1065912917719501.

Page, B., L. Bartels, and J. Seawright. 2013. "Democracy and the Policy Preferences of Wealthy Americans." *Perspectives on Politics* 11: pp. 51–73.

Panagopoulos, C., and P.L. Francia. 2008. "The Polls—Trends: Labor Unions in the United States." *Public Opinion Quarterly* 72: pp. 134–159. https://doi.org/10.1093/poq/nfn002.

Pontusson, J. 2013. "Unionization, Inequality and Redistribution." *British Journal of Industrial Relations* 51 (4): pp. 797–825. https://doi.org/10.1111/bjir.12045.

Ritchie, K., J. Kallas, and D.K. Iyer. 2024. "Labor Action Tracker: Annual Report 2023." Industrial and Labor Relations School, Cornell University & LER School, University of Illinois. https://www.ilr.cornell.edu/faculty-andresearch/labor-action-tracker-2023.

Rosenfeld, J. 2006. "Desperate Measures: Strikes and Wages in Post-Accord America." *Social Forces* 85: pp. 235–265. https://doi.org/10.1353/sof.2006.0140.

Rosenfeld, J. 2014. *What Unions No Longer Do*. Cambridge, MA: Harvard University Press.

Rubin, B. 1986. "Class Struggle American Style: Unions, Strikes and Wages." *American Sociological Review* 51 (5): pp. 618–633. https://doi.org/10.2307/2095488.

Saez, E., and G. Zucman. 2020. "Trends in US Income and Wealth Inequality: Revising After the Revisionists." National Bureau of Economic Research Working Paper 27921. October. https://doi.org/10.3386/w27921. http://www.nber.org/papers/w27921.

Stepan-Norris, J., and J. Kerrissey. 2023. *Union Booms and Busts: The Ongoing Fight over the U.S. Labor Movement*. New York: Oxford University Press.

Shin, T. 2014. "Explaining Pay Disparities Between Top Executives and Nonexecutive Employees: A Relative Bargaining Power Approach." *Social Forces* 92 (4): pp. 1339–1372. https://doi.org/10.1093/sf/sou004.

Tope, D., and D. Jacobs. 2009. "The Politics of Union Decline: The Contingent Determinants of Union Recognition Elections and Victories." *American Sociological Review* 74 (5): pp. 842–864. https://doi.org/10.1177/000312240907400508.

VanHeuvelen, T. 2018. "Moral Economies or Hidden Talents? A Longitudinal Analysis of Union Decline and Wage Inequality, 1973–2015." *Social Forces* 97: pp. 495–530. https://doi.org/10.1093/sf/soy045.

VanHeuvelen, T. 2023. "The Right to Work and American Inequality." *American Sociological Review* 88 (5): pp. 810–843. https://doi.org/10.1177/00031224231197630.

VanHeuvelen, T., and D. Brady. 2021. "Labor Unions and American Poverty." *ILR Review* 75 (4): pp. 891–917. https://doi.org/10.1177/00197939211014855.

Voss, K., and R. Sherman. 2000. "Breaking the Iron Law of Oligarchy: Union Revitalization in the American Labor Movement." *American Journal of Sociology* 106 (2): pp. 303–349. https://doi.org/10.1086/316963.

Waight, H., and A. Goldstein. 2019. "Decline of the Sociological Imagination? Social Change and Perceptions of Economic Polarization in the United States, 1966–2009." Paper presented at the American Sociological Association Meetings. August. New York.

Western, B., and J. Rosenfeld. 2011. "Unions, Norms, and the Rise in U.S. Wage Inequality." *American Sociological Review* 76 (4): pp. 513–537. https://doi.org/10.1177/0003122411414817.

Windham, L. 2017. *Knocking on Labor's Door*. Chapel Hill: University of North Carolina Press.

Zullo, R. 2012. "Organized Labor's Civic Niche." *Nonprofit and Voluntary Sector Quarterly* 42 (4): pp. 781–802.

Chapter 11
Acceptance of Inequality and the American Dream

Robert C. Hauhart

From each according to cos ability, to each according to cos needs.
—Gender neutral restatement of Karl Marx's
declaration in Critique of the Gotha Program (1875, 388)
Twin Oaks Community, Louisa, Virginia (established 1967)

Our era is not the first, nor will it likely be the last, to express concern and unhappiness with respect to the divisions that beset us, including inequality. McMahon (2023), telling the history of equality (not inequality), makes this clear in 500 pages. In 1967, eight Americans left the lives they were leading in urban Detroit and moved to a small farm in Louisa, Virginia. Twin Oaks' founders had read *Walden Two* (1948), a novel by the psychologist B.F. Skinner, and were attempting to put its program for living into practice. A principal feature of the new lifestyle involved complete *sharing*, thereby eliminating the inequalities evident in mainstream US society, whether based on gender, age, religion, sexual orientation, physical ability, former status, educational attainment, or specialized training.

Kat Kinkade (1973), one of the original eight, summarized the aspirations, practices, and experiences in *A Walden Two Experiment: The First Five Years of Twin Oaks Community*. The community was poor and often teetered on the edge of collapse for reasons both economic and social. A core of the Twin Oaks system was, and remains, a labor credit system in which members are required to work on behalf of the community an equal number of hours per week. Its purpose is part of the radical income-sharing ethos that undergirds the Twin Oaks value system. As it turns out, though, equality is an elusive goal, even for the most die-hard communard. As Kinkade (1994) described her own departure in 1972 (to establish a sister community, East

Robert C. Hauhart, *Acceptance of Inequality and the American Dream*. In: *The Social Acceptance of Inequality*. Edited by: Francesco Duina and Luca Storti, Oxford University Press. © Oxford University Press (2025). DOI: 10.1093/oso/9780197814499.003.0011

Wind, in Tecumseh, Missouri), "I had reached a place where I could not think of anything to do at Twin Oaks. The days stretched ahead wearily and gray" (80).

By summer 1976, when I spent ten weeks living there while studying Twin Oaks, the community had grown to a fluctuating population of sixty-plus adults and a handful of children. Many of the community structures that were created in the first five years remained in place. Yet, turnover was quite high. One observer found that the labor credit system and the forms of nonspecialized work available at Twin Oaks were "among the principal reasons people state for leaving" (Kuhlmann 2005, 129; see also, Kanter 1972) Moreover, there were schisms among those who stayed, with obvious cliques and even separate "branches."[1] There were tensions regarding living space, with some members still living two to a room involuntarily; tensions over work quota; and open questions about community values. The community decided to engage in an intensive, six-week period of self-examination that ultimately came to be called "the Process." At the end of the tension-filled meetings, members left, including two I drove to the Richmond, VA, Amtrak station. There were debates about equality and fairness, and as Kathleen Kinkade (1994) concluded, rough equality may just not be enough to sustain humans.[2] Socialist utopianism is not, and never has been, the prevailing American ethos. Arguably, the constellation of values embodied in what we call the American Dream constitutes our collective aspirations and forms our national myth. Its content, structure, and influence exempts us from caring about inequality.

> Oh Lord, won't you buy me a Mercedes Benz?
>
> —Janis Joplin, Michael McClure, and Bob Neuwirth "Mercedes Benz" (Released 1971 on the album *Pearl* by Columbia Records)

> The American dream is the opium of the people.
>
> —Reframing of Karl Marx's well-known statement that "Religion is the opium of the people." *Contribution to the Critique of Hegel's Philosophy of Right* (1844)

What is the American Dream? As the most common understanding of the American Dream posits, "if you work hard and play by the rules you should be given a chance to go as far as your God-given abilities will take you" (Former President Bill Clinton, in a speech to the Democratic Leadership Council in 1993, quoted in Hochschild 1995, 18). Yet, Clinton's succinct summation of the dream belies its many intricacies. As Hochschild (1995) explains, perhaps the American Dream is best understood as a "bundle of shared . . . tenets about achieving success" (18). This, too, doesn't quite add up to a full meaning, Hochschild contends, for we still need to answer: Who should pursue success, by what means, to what end, and why should the pursuit of success even matter? The answers, generally, are that the dream is a universal one applicable to all Americans; that success may be sought in many endeavors, through many means, but that while seeking success is encouraged, it is not foreordained. Moreover, while success is not promised, presumably the opportunity to pursue success is a promise enshrined in the American way of life and its founding documents. Thus, the pursuit of success—rather than simply achieving success—is understood by Americans as possessing inherent virtue that needs no other justification (Hochschild 1995, 15–24.) Still, this leaves the personal goal of achieving success at the heart of our national myth; it says nothing about helping others. We don't ask that God provide a Mercedes-Benz to anyone else, as the song reflects. The success ethic, as the American Dream is sometimes called, embodies a goal so vital and strong that it shapes all our institutions, thereby informing their institutional logic (see this volume's Introduction).

Marx's reframed quotation at the head of this section hints at this deeper meaning about myth and ideology: Neither religion nor the American Dream are symbols that reflect the sacred, ideal, moral authority of society as a whole; rather, they both should be seen as features of "the ideology of the ruling class, [that is] a means of maintaining solidarity under conditions of exploitation" (Milner 1994, 21). Thus, for it to be properly understood, one needs to examine the effect the American Dream has on individuals in the context of modern institutions. Helpful studies abound, such as Armstrong and Hamilton's (2013) study of undergraduate women at a large, Midwestern, public university, where the women matriculate in a competitive environment and vie, as best they can, for institutional rewards and erotic prospects. In the ensuing competition, scant thought is given to anyone else unless—like parents (Hamilton 2016)—they can facilitate success in the individualistic scramble for advantage and status.

Moreover, if we valorize and worship success, and assume that it is universally attainable with the right amount of hard work, we are then authorized to lament and condemn failure, and impugn those who succumb to it. Historically, those who have been unproductive, living vagabond and socially "useless" lives, have been marginalized and stigmatized (Isenberg

2016, xv). Commonly called "waste people" or "white trash" in our colonial history (Isenberg 2016, xv), their status in society has been linguistically documented by a robust sequence of denigrating labels. The sequential euphemisms we conjure up to name those whose loser status we wish to reference reifies unequal status: lubbers, rubbish, clay-eaters, crackers, rednecks, and trailer trash, among them (Isenberg 2016, 2). These pejorative labels reinforce our willingness to "other" these members of our society: Those whom we describe in such terms are "not like us" and, correspondingly, beneath our concern. After all, with a little bit more effort, these losers could be like us since this is the "land of opportunity," a rhetorical construction that did not exist until the late nineteenth century (Brooks 2013, 7). Like many a nice sounding phrase, "the land of opportunity" functions more as a nostalgic, sentimentalized balm and smoke screen than as a guide to informed understanding.

> The poor will always be with us.
>
> —Professor Steven A. Vago (1937–2010)
> Chair, Department of Sociology
> St. Louis University (St. Louis, MO, US)
> In a graduate class, 1974

Expressions of concern about the existence of poverty, and inequality more generally, have a long-standing history. Steven Vago's blunt statement regarding poverty merely echoes the Bible.[3] Though he made the statement fifty years ago, it seems still supported by the available facts. Although it seems rather unnecessary to document the obvious, it is academically de rigueur to do so.

In the mid-nineteenth century, Friedrich Engels, son of a wealthy German owner of textile mills, was dispatched to Manchester, England, by his father to participate in "commercial training" in one of the mills in which Engels's father had invested (Marcus 1974, 88). Once he arrived, he did work at the mill, but "[M]ost of all, however, he undertook to investigate Manchester on his own"[4] (Engels 1845). He recorded his observations in a now famous book. In a chapter titled "The Great Towns," Engels describes the lives of the working poor beginning with London and ending with Manchester. Engels (1845) notes that in Manchester three rows of houses line the south bank of the Irk River, which is very steep. Covered passages lead from the main street into a number of courts, at the entrance of which typically stands "a privy without a door, so dirty that the inhabitants can pass into and out of the court only by passing through foul pools of stagnant urine and excrement" (49). Below the court, Engels (1845) reports there exist several tanneries "which fill the whole neighbourhood with the stench of animal putrefaction" (49). The Irk itself is described as a "narrow, coal-black, foul-smelling stream, full of debris and refuse," so that in dry weather "a long string of the most disgusting, blackish-green, slime pools are left standing" (Engels 1845, 49). Yet, not far away, he reports that "the upper bourgeoisie . . . [live in] villas with gardens . . . or on the breezy heights . . . in fine, comfortable homes, passed once every half or quarter hour by omnibuses going into the city" (Engels 1845, 46). There is much more of the same. Acceptance of extreme inequality in nineteenth-century England was robustly present and obvious (Figure 11.1 offers a modern example).

Although Engels's observations were from another country, reports from the nineteenth-century industrial era in the United States showed little difference. A famous account, although rambling and rather chaotically organized, is Jacob Riis's *How the Other Half Lives* (1890). Riis did not

Figure 11.1 Sewage and garbage in Mashimoni, Kibera (Nairobi, Kenya), 2010
Source: Christy Gilmore, The Advocacy Project. Free for Use, Creative Commons.

write nor publish his account until forty-five years after Engels's book, but he did point to historical notices of horrid conditions in the United States, including descriptions from the early and mid-nineteenth century. One writer quoted by Riis, Mary Lamb, summarized the "era of aqueduct building," that is, 1835–45, in New York City as consisting of already depleted and overcrowded housing that made the city "a general asylum for vagrants" (Riis 1890, 11). A report issued by a voluntary organization noted many blocks filled with "crowded rear tenements in filthy yards, dark, damp basements, leaking garrets, shops, outhouses and stables converted into dwellings, though scarcely fit to shelter brutes, are habitations of our fellow-beings" (Riis 1890, 11). Forty-five years later, Riis describes many tenement living quarters little differently. However, perhaps more evocative and poignant are stories of the homeless, who cannot even afford tenement life: "[Nothing] . . . can dam the stream of homelessness . . . where the very name of home is a mockery. . . . Crowded out of the tenements to shift for himself . . . he meets there the host of . . . runaways from every State in the Union" (Riis 1890, 111). "Whence this army of homeless boys? . . . likely he went away because he was hungry. Some are orphans, . . . or in effect thrown upon the world when their parents were 'sent up' to the island or to Sing Sing, . . . to be shunned until growth and dirt and the hardships of the street, that make old early [age them out of childhood]" (Riis 2010, 113–14). Explaining the source of his title, Riis (1890) states, "one half of the world does not know how the other half lives" (5). Yet, as he further observes, "It did not know because it did not care. The half that was on top cared little for the struggles, and less for the fate of those who were underneath" (1890, 5). This is a crucial recognition: Something in society enables, even authorizes, the better off to ignore the less fortunate, whether those "less equal," or the truly impoverished.

> American history and popular culture are replete with demonstrations of the connection between failure and sin. . . . Devaluing losers allows people to maintain their belief that the world is fundamentally just . . . .
>
> —Jennifer L. Hochschild, *Facing Up to the American Dream* (1995, 30–31)

Thus, we are forced to answer why it is that society did not care about the poor and homeless, particularly those whose money, influence, and power might be able to influence change. As Czitrom patiently explains, there existed then (and arguably exists now) a distinction held between the deserving and the undeserving poor (Yochelson and Czitrom 2007, 116; see also, Schmitt 2010, 12–13). Riis himself insisted that "drawing a sharp line between the pauper and the 'honestly poor'" was both a moral and socially necessary task. Indeed, Riis—foreshadowing nearly a century and a half of attitudes to the poor in the United States—contended "it all comes down to character in the end" (quoted without full citation in Yochelson and Czitrom 2007, 116).

As Duina and Storti argue in their introduction to this volume, there are four logics that can be used to support the acceptance of inequality. Institutional supports are one; attitudes toward the less fortunate are among the ideological notions that further buttress this acceptance. As Isenberg (2016) observes, "Rationalizing economic inequality has been an unconscious part of the national credo; poverty has been naturalized, often seen as something beyond human control" (xvi). So, while it is common for inequality to exist, making those who suffer it having themselves partly or wholly responsible for their circumstances enables acceptance. This permits those higher in society to look down upon those below them and generally treat them with contempt. Isenberg (2016) has written more than 400 pages documenting the specific configurations of this phenomena since the first colonists stepped ashore on the Eastern seaboard.

As Isenberg (2016, 1) observes, the history we write and the stories we tell about our country take the form of "how land and liberty were won" and "how ordinary folks seized opportunity," risked their lives in a perilous transatlantic crossing in the early seventeenth century and built a new nation out of nothing. This notion of our heritage, a cornerstone of the "hallowed American dream" (Isenberg 2016, 1), is then updated to fit each succeeding era. In the immediate post–World War II era, there was general prosperity fueled by the return of capital in the service of war production to the domestic market amidst pent-up demand. As myriad accounts attest, perhaps more Americans than ever were living the American Dream (Hauhart 2016, 93). Installment buying, beginning in the 1920s, had infiltrated most sectors of the American class system, and arguably drove the nation toward an inclusive consumer culture that made the outward appearance of equality a seeming reality (Hauhart 2016, 93–96). Still, it was not difficult to find widespread poverty in the United States.

Perhaps the best known of these reports was Michael Harrington's *The Other America* (1962). Harrington (1962, 1) wrote:

> There is a familiar America. . . . It has the highest mass standard of living the world has ever known. . . . [yet] there existed another America. In it dwelt somewhere between 40,000,000 and 50,000,000 citizens of the land. They were poor.

Harrington (1962, 21) went on to describe who it was he found poor:

> The workers in the economic underworld are concentrated among the urban section of the more than 16,000,000 Americans denied coverage by the Minimum Wage Law of 1961. They are domestic workers, hotel employees, bus boys, and dishwashers, and some of the people working in small retail stores. . . . This sector of the economy has proved itself immune to progress.

While it is no longer true that the occupations Harrington itemizes are not subject to minimum wage laws, it is true that these occupations still employ workers at the bottom of the US labor market and leaves them poor. Harrington found, too, that rural workers were among the poor: migrant workers, often subject to piece rate wages, living in shacks where there was often no heat in the southern states or the Central Valley of California (Harrington 1962, 51).

Harrington's book was so popular that it was periodically republished. Yet, routinely, Harrington found little to celebrate. In the 1969 unrevised edition of *The Other America*, Harrington (1969) wrote in a new introduction: "In the Seventies the poor may become invisible again" noting that "tens of millions" will still be living in poverty on the country's 200th anniversary (in 1976) (xi). In 1984, while new editions of *The Other America* were being reissued, Harrington found it necessary to pen another book on the poor, *The New American Poverty*. As he observed in the first line on the first page, "The poor are still there" (Harrington 1984, 1).

In the wake of Harrington's death in 1989, there was no shortage of other writers available to take up commentary on the continuing existence of poverty in the United States. Shortly after the millennium, Barbara Ehrenreich (2001) published *Nickel and Dimed*, her report questioning how anyone in the United States could live on the wages available to the unskilled, in her case by trying to do so. In 1998, Ehrenreich (2001) begins by waitressing in Key West, Florida, hoping to earn US$7 an hour, which she figures will permit her to rent lodging for US$500–600 per month, an amount which "pretty much confines [her] to flophouses and trailer homes" with "no air-conditioning, no screens, no fans, [and] no television" (11–12). Ultimately, Ehrenreich fails to survive on low wages waitressing in Florida. To the same effect, Ehrenreich (2001) rents a cheap motel apartment in Maine for US$120 per week and begins cleaning for a maid service, where her thirty minutes guaranteed for lunch turns into a "five-minute pit stop at a convenience store, if that" (77). While none of her co-workers are apparently sleeping in their cars, she recounts a litany of actual misery from them: trying to come up with fifty cents to pay a road toll; seeking free dental care for a painfully impacted wisdom tooth; the day four cleaners discover that cleaning pads were not put in their buckets, and they cannot—together—come up with $2 to buy some (Ehrenreich 2001, 80). Ehrenreich's experiences in Minneapolis working at a Walmart for $7 an hour turned out little different: She pays $245 a week for a motel room until she moves to a $179 a week room, both of which are too expensive. Her solution is a second job, hopefully making $8 an hour, but things don't work out quickly enough at the second motel, and she is forced to move into a more expensive Comfort Inn, her "moment of final defeat" (Ehrenreich 2001, 172). She cannot live on the wages of the unskilled.

Not long after, David Shipler published his own exhaustive study, *The Working Poor: Invisible in America* (2005). Shipler (2005), like most who would follow him, felt obligated to pay obeisance to Harrington's opus (6, 8–9) but argued—as many more would have occasion to do—that "the gap between rich and poor has only widened" (6) leaving, in his estimation, "a median net worth of $833,600 among the top 10% [of US households] and just $7,900 for the bottom 20%" (6).

While Shipler recited the obligatory statistics, his 300-plus pages principally consist of hard-luck stories about ordinary Americans who work but are still mired in poverty. To open any page is to be thrust into a gritty life among people beset with problems—personal, health-related, financial, you name it.

> Christie did a job . . . [the] economy could not do without. Every morning she drove her battered '86 Volkswagen from her apartment in public housing to . . . the child-care center . . . where she spent the day watching over little children. . . . For those valuable services, she received a check for about $330 every two weeks. She could not afford to put her own two children in the daycare. . . . [Christie] suffered from stress and high blood pressure.

> She had no bank account . . . she always fell behind on her bills and was peppered with late fees. Her low income entitled her to food stamps . . . but whenever she got a little pay raise, the government . . . reduced the benefits, . . . She was trapped on the treadmill of welfare reform. (Shipler 2005, 39–40)

In the end, Shipler faces one of the recurrent realities of the inequality gap in the United States: there is little political will to change the situation. As he remarks, "*If* hospitals, schools, housing authorities, police departments, and welfare offices, and other critical institutions were . . ." (Shipler 2005, 286 [emphasis added); "*If* people with family incomes under $25,000 had . . . *If* large numbers cast ballots . . ." [emphasis added] (Shipler 2005, 287). Acknowledging none of these things ever happened, Shipler then offers a list of prescriptions for reconfiguring the national budget, changing hiring and business practices, rewriting the income tax code, legislating new welfare law, and altering individual consumer and lifestyle practices, a common and essentially futile recipe for reducing inequality and eradicating poverty since there simply is no political will to do anything. As Silva (2013, 2019) more recently records, nothing much has changed for the contemporary working class.

> This program . . . is a total commitment by this President, and this Congress, and this nation, to pursue victory over the most ancient of mankind's enemies.
>
> —President Lyndon Johnson, March 16, 1964, declaring "unconditional war on poverty" (Johnson 1964)

While poverty's trajectory over the centuries may perhaps be fairly described as linear, the political trajectory of poverty solutions is anything but linear. Until the twentieth century, poverty was not identified as a societal problem that required government handling. Rather, poverty was seen as an individual problem, often treated as the result of characterological or moral weakness (Schmitt 2010, 12–13). While President Lyndon Johnson succeeded in persuading Congress (and most of the nation) to embrace his War on Poverty, and received plaudits from many unexpected sources (Goodwin 1976, 189–90), his deft legislative victory did not eradicate poverty, then or now (see Figure 11.2 for a vivid illustration).[5] Moreover, the demand to

Figure 11.2 Homeless woman (US), n.d.
Source: Creative Commons, public domain (n.d.).

achieve an end to poverty in the United States after 1964 sounds very much like those calls to arms made prior to passage of the Economic Opportunity Act (EOA). For all its ambitious ideals, the Act suffered from stifling bureaucratic oversight and chaotic disarray leading to neglect, all fostered by the federal government's "one million employees . . . involving dozens of institutions," all of which in one way or another had responsibility for Great Society benefits (Goodwin 1976, 288). The consequence was that a number of federal programs failed to effectively carry out their mission to alleviate poverty and/or suffered from political opposition. This was most evident in those community action programs which attempted to unite job training under the auspices of management from within the affected communities, as in the case of Mobilization for Youth (Lilly et al. 2015, 90–92).

One of the effects the EOA did create was an opening for a continuing focus on the need to alleviate poverty. Indeed, so large was this opening that Robert F. Kennedy stepped in to fill the space, making poverty the signature defining issue of his political career. He did so within a politically fraught period when domestic politics was overshadowed by the nation's immersion in concerns arising from Johnson's management of the war in Vietnam

(Schmitt 2010, 190). Kennedy routinely toured parts of the country mired in poverty, finding—among other examples—a tenant farmer in upstate Allegany County, New York, living in a spare, dirt-floored shack in 1967 (Schmitt 2010, 190). Yet, while Kennedy mobilized a significant number of Americans to listen to his antipoverty messages and to support his nascent political campaign for the presidency, his death by assassination foreclosed any possibility for the change his efforts and his campaign may have held. Equally to the point, analysts have questioned whether his antipoverty policy and legislative proposals, which failed to find to support, as well as "[his experiments in public–private partnerships], would have solved the poverty problem" (Schmitt 2010, 224).

In retrospect, it is apparent that poverty in America was not solved by either the EOA or Robert Kennedy's short-lived political activism. Michael Harrington, whose eloquent and powerful writing was one source of the inspiration that drove John F. Kennedy and then Lyndon Johnson to initiate the federal government's interest in tackling poverty, took up the challenge with renewed vigor during President Ronald Reagan's first term. Yet, Harrington's advocacy for policy solutions in the 1980s gained little contemporary practical support. As one example, Harrington supported reforms recommended by the then director of the Congressional Budget Office to include extending Medicaid to all poor families (Harrington 1984, 247–48). It was not until passage of the Affordable Care Act (2010), and modified regulations thereto, that a limited version of this aspiration was legislatively achieved. As Harrington (1984, 6) readily conceded at the time, there were as many poor Americans in 1982—long after Johnson's War on Poverty—as there were in 1965.

Where there's a right, there's a remedy.

—Hon. Stanley A. Sporkin (1932–2020)
United States District Judge
District for the District of Columbia
In open court, 1995

Judge Sporkin's declaration in open court in 1995 was not tantamount to finding some enforceable guarantee in the US Constitution, federal laws, or federal regulations that could be used to better the lives of poor people. Rather, Sporkin's statement is one most often used by members of the judiciary as a prelude to finding there is no legal right, whether to compel actual equality in income/wealth or to compel inclusion in opportunities within US society. This is because the United States operates under a capitalist economic system. Its dictates are incorporated in every institution of society, from our educational system to our home and personal lives to our laws. In this latter context, US employment law has been characterized as "at will" employment since 1877 when Horace Gray Wood, an attorney, defined the essence of the employment relationship as "an indefinite hiring and is determinable at the will of either party, and in this respect there is no distinction between domestic and other servants" (1877, 272, quoted in Rothstein et al. 2010, 1). This is the beginning of the legal theory called "freedom of contract." The "at will" doctrine has been subject to widespread criticism and emendation over ensuing decades, but as Rothstein et al. (2010, 4) are quick to observe, while "[B]y the end of the 1980's, virtually every state had adopted *one or more exceptions* to the at-will rule," they did so while quietly acknowledging the general rule's continuing viability. The upshot is, as everyone seems to understand, an American (or someone who lives in the United States) is not entitled to a particular job, or even any job at all. Legally, one has no inherent right, or entitlement, to any particular level of benefit, emolument, or yearly income in the United States. True, some employer prerogatives are limited under existing US law, but principally in negative ways, such as laws prohibiting employers from engaging in certain discriminatory practices. Yet, there is little requiring the vast army of private employers to equalize wages and benefits short of a unionization agreement (Rothstein et al. 2010, 5–6). Rather, inequality is once again allowed to prevail.

> Everybody sees themselves walkin' around with no one else.
>
> —Bob Dylan
> "Talkin' World War III Blues"
> *The Freewheelin' Bob Dylan* (Columbia Records. Released May 27, 1963)

The absence of any compulsory requirement to employ or reward Americans supports an individualistic ethos, a prominent feature of the American way of life and American character. One of the most notable early observers of the phenomenon was a well-known visitor from France who toured the early United States in 1831, Alexis de Tocqueville. Tocqueville's discussion of individualism in *Democracy in America* (1961; two volumes) amounts to more than 150 pages depending on how one counts his meditations on the subject (Hauhart 2016, 17).

Ironically, Tocqueville identifies the "passion for equality" he found among Americans as the wellspring from which individualism arose (1961, vol. 2, 113–70). He states the point succinctly: "I have shown how it is that in ages of equality every man seeks his opinions within himself. I am now about to show how it is that, in the same ages, all his feelings turned toward himself alone" (Tocqueville 1961, vol. 2, 118). Tocqueville characterizes individualism as consisting of a "mature and calm feeling" that arises from an individual's recognition that he is distinguishable from the mass of humanity, thereby distancing himself from the multitudes and even from family and friends (1961, vol. 2, 118). As a practical matter, Tocqueville described Americans as psychologically achieving this state of mind by creating a small circle of close friends upon whom one builds a life, leaving society to itself. In commenting on the strength of individualism, Tocqueville (1961, vol. 2) noted that,

> Amongst democratic nations new families are constantly springing up, others are constantly falling away, and all that remain change their condition. . . . Those who went before are soon forgotten; of those who will come after no one has any idea: the interest of man is confined to those in close propinquity to himself. (119–20)

This tendency becomes more common and more powerful, in Tocqueville's (1961, vol. 2) judgment, as more equal conditions emerge in society:

> [As] the number of persons increases who . . . have nevertheless acquired or reach sufficient education and fortune to satisfy their own wants [individualism flourishes]. They owe nothing to any man; they expect nothing from any man; they acquire the habit of always considering themselves as standing alone, and they are apt to imagine their whole destiny is in their hands. (120)

Thus, Tocqueville sees democratic ideals and conditions of a certain level of achieved equality as isolating the individual "entirely within the solitude of his own heart" (1961, vol. 2, 120). As Philip Slater (1990, 8–9) argued, however, subordination of the individual to the welfare of the group has been the fate of mankind from time immemorial and the aggrandizement of the individual at the expense of community permits each and every one of us to simply ignore and neglect any obligation or responsibility we have to our fellow human beings. Indeed, the American way of life is heavily invested in denying interdependence and promoting individualism, as Tocqueville recognized long ago. As Slater (1990) recites, "[W]e seek a private home, a private means of transportation, a private garden, a private laundry, self-service stores, and do-it-yourself skills of every kind" (11). Slater (1990) sums up his reflections as Bob Dylan does by noting, "The American, in fact, never thinks of other Americans at all—his most characteristic trait is that he imagines himself to be alone on the continent" (126). The upshot is that inequality, even extreme poverty, does not bother us.

Tocqueville believed that there were several antidotes that would keep American individualism from descending into atomized, isolated willfulness. First, he observed that the impulse to govern one's own affairs would produce an enlightened self-interest that would create an impetus to cooperate. Thus, it is often necessary for many persons to unite to accomplish large projects that involve shared goals for everyone's benefit, as in building the interstate highway system (Tocqueville 1961, vol. 2, 124–31). In this context, though, idealistic social goals such as reducing inequality or eradicating poverty tie a rather nebulous endpoint to controversial means. Income redistribution, for example, is conceived of as a zero-sum game: Giving more to the less well-off is perceived as having hard-earned resources taken away from oneself, a policy that is a nonstarter for individualistic Americans. Since acquisition of more income, wealth, and status are the rewards held out by the American Dream, giving them away is understandably anathema. Moreover, altruism is not a motivation that is ideologically compatible with the principal myth undergirding American culture, where rewards are supposed to flow from one's hard work. As Slater (1990) remarks, little is more typical of our society than our "exaggerated moral commitment to striving and personal achievement" and "the need to triumph over others" (128). Since individual achievement, upward mobility, and financial success are the core of the American Dream, what room is there for battling inequality?

Someone told me there's a girl out there
With love in her eyes and flowers in her hair

—Jimmy Page and Robert Plant. "Going to California."
Released November 8, 1971, for the album *Led Zeppelin IV*
(Atlantic Records, SD 7208)

The best is always yet to come. That's what they explained to me.
—Bob Dylan. "If Dogs Run Free," on the album *New Morning*, Columbia Records (KC 30290, released October 21, 1970)

Look out, kid, they keep it all hid.
—Bob Dylan, "Subterranean Homesick Blues" from the LP *Bringing It All Back Home*[6] (Columbia CS-9128, released March 22, 1965)

As Arlie Russell Hochschild (2016) recognized, the American Dream myth also embodies a "right way of feeling" (140). The dream emphasizes that one should feel "hopeful, energetic, focused, mobilized" (140) with an understanding that progress, a concept close to the dream's core, is implicitly promised, if one only believes and commits oneself to the hard work necessary to achieve its fruition. Hochschild (2012) notes in one of her earlier books that social occasions exist in a context of pre-approved and sanctioned feeling states. A funeral, for example, is a setting in which those attending generally sense that it "is the right time and right place to feel grief and not much else" (Hochschild 2012, 63). Those whose emotions do not coincide with the time, place, and manner expected—and which they commonly expect of themselves—experience the dissonance of the misfit. Having imbibed the optimistic elixir that is part and parcel of the American Dream and worked one's fingers to the bone to achieve it, one is hardly prepared to be charitable to those who do not likewise honor its tenets. The upshot is that one is virtually required to accept the legitimacy of our institutions and the legitimacy of the race to achieve the American Dream embedded in them. Hence, the diminished American Dream that many experience does not automatically, nor even necessarily, translate into empathy for the poor. Rather, the American Dream is exclusively about the individual narcissistically succeeding in a cutthroat world. Since many will fail economically, a key ingredient of the American Dream is its underlying thread of buoyant optimism and hope, sometimes embodied in substituted dreams, as in the Led Zeppelin lyrics quoted above, or ridiculed in the Bob Dylan lyrics from "If Dogs Run Free," or the cynical lyrics from Bob Dylan's "Subterranean Homesick Blues." But, as Tocqueville and others have reminded us, even the substitute dreams with any power are individualistic dreams. Dreaming of equality has little appeal.

Why can't we all be brothers?
Why can't we live in peace?

But the hands of the have-nots
Keep falling out of reach.

—"Black Day in July" by Gordon Lightfoot, released on the LP *Did She Mention My Name?* (United Artists, January 1968)

In the ideal democracy of mythical Greece, one group of people would not have more influence on government than any others. In such an enlightened system, "the young student, unemployed construction worker, retired homemaker, or small business owner" (Callero 2018, 204) would possess as much influence and sovereign autonomy as the wealthy, major corporations, and the leaders of prestigious institutions. Americans know this is not the case, but knowing something is not akin to feeling something. As Callero (2018) observes, the effect is that "the typical citizen feels incapable of changing the system" (204). In the midst of frustrated feelings shared by many others, the Occupy movement was born on September 17, 2011, when several hundred people—soon to be joined by as many as 30,000—gathered at Zuccotti Park near Wall Street and at rallies around the United States. This nationwide protest of the inequality gap between the 1% (those who control the enormously disproportionate percentage of wealth in the United States) and the 99% (those who possess so much less) made a powerful statement. It was a heady time and produced a compelling slogan that coalesced into a demand to reduce inequality. Yet, as Callero (2018) recites, by the time he wrote, "the protesters . . . have disbanded and the occupiers of Zuccotti Park have been dispersed" (205). Isenberg (2016), commenting on the normal expectation that this would be the outcome, reminds us,

> [The class basis of our society] is only occasionally shaken up, as when the Occupy Wall Street movement of recent years shone an embarrassing light on the financial sector and the grotesque separation between 1 percent and the 99 percent. And then the media giants find new crises and the nation's inherited disregard for class reboots, as the subject recedes into the background again (3).

Scholars then return to documenting inequality. Sasha Abramsky (2013) concedes, "A half-century after Harrington wrote *The Other America*, poverty remains in many ways as deep and as intangible as ever" (323). To borrow from the title of Sanford Schram's (2015) account of the post-Occupy era, it was "the return of ordinary capitalism." Or, as two social scientists pithily summed things up, it was again a country in which millions were "living on almost nothing"—no more than $2.00 a day (Edin and Schaefer 2015). Echoing Harrington's 1984 acknowledgment of continuing American inequality, Jennifer Silva's (2013) account is titled, *We're Still Here.*

James Truslow Adams (1931) held out great hope that the American Dream would lead to a society in which every man or woman could lead a life "better and richer and fuller" (317), it has not worked out that way. As Darrin McMahon (2023), historian of equality wrote just last year, "In gated compounds and private planes, the super-rich live 'cordoned lives,' foreign to all but themselves" (415). Another of our recent investigators of poverty acknowledges we haven't made much progress in reducing the percentage of Americans below the poverty line between 1970 and 2019 (Desmond 2023, 24). Yet, like many a reformer before him, Matthew Desmond, a determined optimist-activist and ardent social policy wonk, dutifully dusts off his policy tools and sets to work urging the adoption of ameliorative practices. Yet, he does so in a vacuum. Slater, writing in 1970, noted that "Poverty programs put very little money into the hands of the poor because middle-class hands are so much more gifted at grasping money—they know better where it is, how to apply for it, how to divert it, how to concentrate it" (1990, 97). Armstrong and Hamilton (2013) observing ambitious, competitive white college women, document the same.

Unencumbered by a single reference to the now defunct Occupy movement, which should be treated as a cautionary tale, Desmond (2023, 24) expresses outrage and indignation that the wealthiest country in the world permits as much as 10% of our people to live in desperate poverty. Still, his understandable anger does nothing to inspire him to undertake the hard, political work necessary to either galvanize another popular movement nor to directly motivate those in our governing bodies to support change. As Slater wrote, "We can make war on poverty but shrink from the extensive changes required to stop breeding it" (1990, 17). Warming to his theme, Slater predicts our current situation: "the structure of our society—its massive inequalities, overwhelming corporate power, and the chronic exploitation of the consumer by our professions, industry and government—has not changed. It will take more than enthusiasm to bring about that" (1990, 93). The consequence is that we are left with our individualistic American Dreams, which are not focused on remaking American society to alleviate inequality but rather are in place to insulate ourselves from loss while at the same time keeping opportunities for ourselves.

Notes

1. Some of the story behind the development of "branch" homesteads at Twin Oaks is told in Komar (1989, 40–48).
2. Turnover is a critical factor for evaluating the Twin Oaks Community. This is because, while many people come, many leave. Komar (1989, 78–9) notes that at the time she was at Twin Oaks (1979–82), the community had about 70 members, but since its founding there had been 325 unique members. Today, Twin Oaks describes itself as "made up of about 70 adult members and 15 children" and states the community "is currently looking for new members" (Twin Oaks n.d.). In short, the attractions of equality appear to pale over time (see also, "Why They Dissolve—Problems of Short-Lived Communes [and] Problems of Long-Lived Communes" in Kanter 1973, 443–544).
3. Deuteronomy 15:11 states, "The poor will never cease to be in the land," but quickly commands people to give to the poor freely.
4. Although he also benefited by the guidance from "an illiterate Irish factory girl"—Mary Burns—whom he lived with, of a sort, for the rest of her life (Marcus 1974, 98–100).
5. As Michael Harrington asked in 1984 when discussing the EOA (1964), "why is it . . . poverty . . . has become more entrenched than when the War on Poverty began?" (15).
6. Recorded on January 14, 1965, and released as a single by Columbia Records, catalog number 43242, on March 8, 1965.

References

Abramsky, S. 2013. *The American Way of Poverty: How the Other Half Still Lives.* New York: Nation Books.

Adams, J. Truslow. 1931. *The Epic of America.* Reprint 1933. Garden City: Garden City Books.

Armstrong, E.A., and L.T. Hamilton. 2013. *Paying for the Party: How College Maintains Inequality.* Cambridge, MA: Harvard University Press.

Brooks, J. 2013. *Why We Left: Untold Stories and Songs of America's First Immigrants.* Minneapolis: University of Minnesota Press.

Callero, P.L. 2018. *The Myth of Individualism.* Lanham, MD: Rowman and Littlefield.

Desmond, M. 2023. *Poverty, by America.* New York: Crown.

Dylan, B. 1970. "If Dogs Run Free." *New Morning.* Columbia Records, KC-30290.

Dylan, B. 1965. "Subterranean Homesick Blues." *Bringing It All Back Home.* Columbia Records, CS-9128.

Dylan, B. 1963. "Talkin' World War III Blues." *The Freewheelin' Bob Dylan.* Columbia Records, CS-8786.

Edin, K.J., and H.L. Schaefer. 2015. *$2.00 a Day: Living on Almost Nothing in America.* Boston: Houghton Mifflin Harcourt.

Ehrenreich, B. 2001. *Nickel and Dimed: On (Not) Getting By in America.* New York: Henry Holt and Company.

Engels, F. 1845. *The Condition of the Working Class in England in 1844.* Translated by F. Kelley Wischnewetzy, 1892. London: George Allen and Unwin.

Goodwin, D. Kearns. 1976. *Lyndon Johnson and the American Dream.* Reprint 1991. New York: St. Martin's Press.

Hamilton, L.T. 2016. *Parenting to a Degree.* Chicago: University of Chicago Press.

Harrington, M. 1984. *The New American Poverty.* New York: Penguin Books.

Harrington, M. 1962. *The Other America: Poverty in the United States.* New York: Macmillan Company.

Harrington, M. 1969. *The Other America: Poverty in the United States.* Unrevised ed. New York: The Macmillan Company.

Hauhart, R.C. 2016. *Seeking the American Dream: A Sociological Inquiry.* New York: Palgrave Macmillan.

Hochschild, A. Russell. 2012. *The Managed Heart.* 3rd ed. Berkeley: University of California Press.

Hochschild, A. Russell. 2016. *Strangers in Their Own Land.* New York: The New Press.

Hochschild, J.L. 1995. *Facing Up to the American Dream: Race, Class, and the Soul of the Nation.* Princeton, NJ: Princeton University Press.

Isenberg, N. 2016. *White Trash: The 400-Year Untold History of Class in America.* New York: Viking.

Johnson, L. 1964. "Special Message to the Congress Proposing a Nationwide War on the Sources of Poverty." March 16. *The American Presidency Project.* University of California, Santa Barbara. https://www.presidency.ucsb.edu/documents/special-message-the-congress-proposing-nationwide-war-the-sources-poverty.

Joplin, J., M. McClure, and B. Neuwirth. 1971. "Mercedez Benz." *Pearl.* Columbia Records.

Kanter, R.M. 1972. *Commitment and Community.* Cambridge, MA: Harvard University Press.

Kanter, R.M. 1973. *Communes: Creating and Managing the Collective Life.* New York: Harper and Row.

Kinkade, K. 1994. *Is It Utopia Yet? An Insider's View of Twin Oaks Community in Its 26th Year.* Louisa, VA: Twin Oaks Publishing.

Kinkade, K. 1973. *A Walden Two Experiment: The First Five Years of Twin Oaks Community.* New York: William Morrow and Company.

Komar, I. 1989. *Living the Dream: A Documentary Study of Twin Oaks Community.* Louisa, VA: Twin Oaks Publishing.

Kuhlmann, H. 2005. *Living Walden Two: B. B. Skinner's Behaviorist Utopia and Experimental Communities.* Urbana: University of Illinois Press.

Lightfoot, G. 1968. "Black Day in July." *Did She Mention My Name?* United Artists.

Lilly, J.R., F.T. Cullen, and R.A. Ball. 2015. *Criminological Theory: Contexts and Consequences.* Los Angeles: Sage.

Marcus, S. 1974. *Engels, Manchester, and the Working Class.* New York: Random House.

Marx, K. 1844. "Contribution to the Critique of Hegel's *Philosophy of Right.*" In *The Marx-Engels Reader*, edited by R.C. Tucker, pp. 11–23. 1972. New York: W.W. Norton & Company.

Marx, K. 1875. "Critique of the Gotha Program." In *The Marx-Engels Reader*, edited by R.C. Tucker, pp. 383–398. 1972. New York: W.W. Norton & Company.

McMahon, D.M. 2023. *Equality: The History of an Elusive Idea.* New York: Basic Books.

Milner, M., Jr. 1994. *Status and Sacredness: A General Theory of Status Relations and an Analysis of Indian Culture.* Oxford: Oxford University Press.

Page, J., and R. Plant. 1971. "Going to California." *Led Zeppelin IV.* Atlantic Records, SD 7208.

Riis, J. 1890. *How the Other Half Lives.* Edited by H.R. Diner, 2010. New York: W.W. Norton and Company.

Rothstein, M.A., C.B. Craver, E.P. Schroeder, and E.W. Shoben. 2010. *Employment Law.* St. Paul: West/Thompson Reuters.

Schmitt, E.R. 2010. *President of the Other America: Robert Kennedy and the Politics of Poverty.* Amherst: University of Massachusetts Press.

Schram, S.F. 2015. *The Return of Ordinary Capitalism: Neoliberalism, Precarity, Occupy.* Oxford: Oxford University Press.

Silva, J. 2013. *Coming Up Short: Working Class Adulthood in an Age of Uncertainty.* New York: Oxford University Press.

Silva, J. 2019. *We're Still Here: Pain and Politics in the Heart of America.* New York: Oxford University Press.

Shipler, D.K. 2005. *The Working Poor: Invisible in America.* New York: Vintage.
Skinner, B.F. 1948. *Walden Two.* New York: The Macmillan Company.
Slater, P. 1990. *The Pursuit of Loneliness.* 3rd ed. Boston: Beacon Press.
Tocqueville, A. de. 1961. *Democracy in America.* 2 vols. New York: Schocken Books.
Twin Oaks Community. n.d. "Welcome to the Twin Oaks Community." https://www.twinoaks.org/about-twinoaks-community/welcome.
Yochelson, B., and D. Czitrom. 2007. *Rediscovering Jacob Riis.* New York: The New Press.

PART IV
GROUP AND ETHNIC LOGICS

Chapter 12
Acceptance of Inequality in the Social Democratic Welfare State
Income Differences, Welfare Chauvinism, and Populism in Sweden

Arvid Lindh

Introduction

What inequalities are accepted, and by whom, in a polity marked by the institutional logic of a social democratic welfare state?* And to what extent might public acceptance of inequality challenge this societal model? This chapter focuses on Sweden, a country historically known as the archetype of such a model, renowned for its broad-based welfare state and universal social rights that extensively reduce the level of economic inequality (Esping-Andersen 1990; Korpi and Palme 1998; Rothstein 1998). Rather than being a divisive object among the public, it has been suggested that this institutional context has fostered strong ideological consensus around the welfare state and its various functions.

Despite the decline of the political hegemony of the Swedish Social Democratic Party movement (Oskarson and Demker 2015), cutbacks in core social insurance programs (Bäckman and Nelson 2017), privatization reforms within the welfare service sector (Svallfors 2016), and sharp increases in economic inequality in recent decades (Bengtsson 2020; Huber and Stephens 2024), leading scholars have even pointed to an apparent uptick in public support for the Swedish welfare state, particularly among the traditionally more critical higher echelons of the class structure:

> In an ironic twist of fate, market-emulating reforms of the welfare state and the changed political rhetoric of the political right-of-center completed the

Arvid Lindh, *Acceptance of Inequality in the Social Democratic Welfare State*. In: *The Social Acceptance of Inequality*. Edited by: Francesco Duina and Luca Storti, Oxford University Press. © Oxford University Press (2025).
DOI: 10.1093/oso/9780197814499.003.0012

> full ideological integration of the middle class into the welfare state. The electoral base for any resistance against a high-tax high-spending, collective welfare state now looks completely eroded. While the Social Democratic party suffers, the Social Democratic welfare state thrives. (Svallfors 2011, 15; also cited in Rothstein and Steinmo 2013, 102)

This chapter challenges the prevailing image that sociopolitical divisions related to the Swedish welfare state are negligible. It identifies income differences and welfare chauvinism as two central dimensions of inequality acceptance that could be socially and politically divisive (also) within the institutional context of a social democratic welfare state.

This study draws on previous research suggesting that income equalization and government redistribution encounter considerable resistance, not least in Sweden, primarily among the more economically advantaged segments of the managerial and business professional middle classes (Lindh et al. 2021; Lindh and McCall 2020). Moreover, a growing international literature suggests that exclusionary conceptions of social rights and welfare deservingness are relatively widespread, especially among the less advantaged working classes (Häusermann and Kriesi 2015; Lindh et al. 2021). These exclusionary attitudes are often grounded in an "us-versus-them" group logic with ethnic/nativist overtones that target immigrants and other minorities (Eick 2024; Kymlicka and Banting 2006; Van Oorschot et al. 2017). Such views often intertwine with concerns about welfare abuse and perceived overuse of social benefits (Häusermann and Kriesi 2015).

The chapter also theoretically incorporates and empirically examines whether and how acceptance of inequality might interlace with populism as a significant force in contemporary politics and society. Populist attitudes encompass a belief in "the pure people" as an imagined community with shared interests and values, engaged in a moral struggle against supposedly "corrupt elites" (Mudde and Rovira Kaltwasser 2018; Rooduijn 2019). This chapter adopts the starting point that the association between populist sentiments and acceptance of inequality should be analyzed from a multidimensional perspective. On the one hand, populist attitudes may tie in with critical conceptions of the undeserving rich and concern for those toward the economic bottom, translating into opposition to large income differences and support for redistribution from the rich to the less fortunate. On the other hand, populist attitudes may tie in with nativist conceptions of the "people," manifesting in chauvinistic attitudes toward the social rights and welfare deservingness of immigrants and other minorities. The study focuses, in particular, on the latter version of right-wing populism, seen as a form of "anti-system politics" (Hopkin 2020), which contradicts the institutional logic of the social democratic welfare state (Greve 2019; Hooijer and King 2021; Rovira Kaltwasser and Zanotti 2021).

Against this background, the chapter sets out to examine how approval of income differences, welfare chauvinism, and populist attitudes, respectively, are related and differ between social classes and between voters of mainstream and non-mainstream Left and Right parties. The study is based on original high-quality Swedish survey data collected in 2019, 2020, and 2022, consisting of three pooled cross-sections from random samples of the Swedish population aged 18–85 years, totaling 5,333 respondents.

Theory and Previous Research

The most distinguishing feature of a social democratic welfare state is arguably its universalistic character (Korpi and Palme 1998; Rothstein 1998). In essence, built on broadly based tax systems, it "aims to provide all people in society, regardless of their background, with a set of general social rights to certain kinds of service and economic support. Such programmes are not targeted on specific vulnerable groups or distinct minorities in society but cater to 'all' or very large segments of the population" (Rothstein and Steinmo 2013, 88).

This institutional logic is reflected in public opinion on the Swedish welfare state. In an international survey where respondents were asked to choose between three fixed alternatives regarding what the primary purpose of the welfare state is, 70% of Swedish respondents chose "to provide a safety net when people become, ill, old or unemployed" and 21% chose "to support people to get better education and new jobs." Only 9% answered "to redistribute money from the rich to the poor" (Buseyemer et al. 2018).

Similarly, national surveys on welfare state attitudes consistently show that most Swedes support generous government-led social spending and insurance programs, and they prefer tax-financed and publicly provided social services over private alternatives (Edlund and Lindh 2013; Goossen et al. in press; Svallfors 2011). However, while Swedes are fundamentally positive toward the welfare state and support its core social security and service functions, this does not preclude the possibility of divisions over other aspects of who should receive what, when, and how. This study focuses on income equalization and welfare chauvinism as two key areas where public opinion may diverge on such issues.

Approval of Income Differences

The proper scope of income disparities and government income redistribution has long been a central political issue and source of conflict in advanced economies (Huber and Stephens 2024). In Sweden, more than in most other countries, these welfare state-related issues have dominated political discourse for decades (Edlund and Lindh 2015; Oskarson and Demker 2015; Rydgren and van der Meiden 2019). The Social Democrats held government power continuously between 1936 and 1976, during which much of the welfare state was developed. While the Social Democrats remain the largest party in Sweden, attracting around 30% of the votes and thus, frequently in government (they were in government during the entirety of this study), they have been challenged by the Moderate Party (Conservatives) as the main government alternative for the last thirty plus years.

These two parties have mainly competed on socioeconomic issues, with the Moderate Party advocating for lower taxes and economic liberalization/privatization. This political platform has been supported by highly organized employment organizations and associated think tanks that have promoted free-market ideology and the positive aspects of income disparities as a deliberate effort to counterbalance the political discourse and alleged previous ideological hegemony of Social Democracy and the organized labor movement (Blyth 2002; Svallfors 2016).

As noted above, most Swedes think the main function of the welfare state is to provide social security for the majority, rather than being a vehicle for redistributing resources from the rich to the poor. However, this does not detract from the fact that the Swedish welfare state system has significant redistributive consequences, making incomes, living conditions, and life chances more equally distributed between social classes (Korpi and Palme 1998; Rothstein 1998).

Public opinion is divided, however, on how far-reaching and redistributively ambitious the welfare state should be in this respect. Previous studies on both Sweden and other countries show that the economically advantaged middle-class segments, such as managers and business professionals, technical professionals, and employers, who may not materially benefit from such policy, are more likely to oppose government redistribution and income equalization than the working classes (Lindh et al. 2021; Lindh and McCall 2020).

Welfare Chauvinism

Like most rich democracies, the Swedish political landscape is undergoing significant change and electoral realignment. In tandem with structural economic shifts that include a shrinking share of production workers, the Social Democrats have come to downplay their class-based redistributive ambitions with the welfare state (Oskarson and Demker 2015). Instead, to attract the growing middle classes, particularly sociocultural professionals, they have come to prioritize the welfare state's social insurance and social investment functions, similar to trends seen in other countries (Gingrich and Häusermann 2015). This has decreased ideological polarization between the Social Democrats and the Moderate Party, creating room for working-class realignment (Oskarson and Demker 2015; for similar trends in other European countries, see Evans and Tilley 2017; Oesch and Rennwald 2018).

In Sweden, support for the non-mainstream (radical) Right party, the Sweden Democrats, has sharply increased in recent national elections, largely by taking votes from both the Social Democrats and the Moderate Party (Jylhä et al. 2019; Rydgren and van der Maiden 2019). In the 2022 general election, the Sweden Democrats became the second-largest party, surpassing the Moderate Party. In Sweden, as in many other countries, non-mainstream (radical) Right voters are characterized by negative attitudes toward immigration/immigrants and are overrepresented among the working classes (Rydgren 2013; Oskarson and Demker 2015; Oesch and Rennwald 2018).

Zooming in on welfare state policy, a growing international literature stresses the heightened salience of ideological disputes over inclusionary versus exclusionary conceptions of social rights and the deservingness of welfare benefits. The inclusivist side believes that welfare recipients are deserving and promotes broad-based social inclusion via universalist welfare policies. In contrast, the exclusivist side believes that many welfare recipients are undeserving, and that immigrants and other minorities should not have equal access to the same welfare benefits as natives (Eick 2024;

Häusermann and Kriesi 2015; Kymlicka and Banting 2006; Van Oorschot et al. 2017). These exclusionary attitudes are often closely associated with concerns about welfare abuse and perceived overuse by recipients of social benefits (Häusermann and Kriesi 2015).

While historical survey data to track longitudinal trends in welfare chauvinism and deservingness are scarce in Sweden, available evidence indicates that these issues have become more ideologically charged and divisive in recent years (Eger 2010; Goossen et al. in press). Also, these attitudes tend to be connected to social class: Those in the less economically advantaged and educated working classes tend to be more socially exclusivist than those in the more materially advantaged and highly educated middle classes. Among the middle classes, sociocultural professionals tend to stand out as the most inclusivist, embracing universalist principles of social rights and welfare provision, owing to a combination of the high educational requirements and egalitarian work values inherent to such jobs (Bengtsson et al. 2013; Häusermann and Kriesi 2015; Lindh et al. 2021). In addition, recent international studies suggest that supporters of non-mainstream (radical) Right parties display more chauvinistic attitudes than voters of other parties (Busemeyer et al. 2022; Enggist and Häusermann 2024).

Populism

The study of populism through the lens of public opinion is a fairly recent research field (Akkerman et al. 2014; Castanho Silva et al. 2020). Most of this literature defines populism as a set of beliefs advocating the moral superiority of the people in a struggle against corrupt elites who are out of touch, fail to represent, and might even work against the common will of the people (Mudde and Rovira Kaltwasser 2018; Rooduijn 2019). Populist attitudes correlate with institutional distrust and perceived political inefficacy, tapping into a broad sense of societal unresponsiveness (Rooduijn 2019). Such perceptions of not having a sufficient and equal voice in society have a marked socioeconomic gradient, reflecting how those located in the working classes have fewer individual power resources and are further distanced from leading positions and centers of power in society (Evans and Tilley 2017; Lindh and McCall 2020; Rennwald and Pontusson 2022).

Extant research suggests that populism is rarely a potent *stand-alone* political force, but that it may be successfully combined with thick core ideologies, where "right-wing exclusionary versions of populism usually rely on nativism to depict a narrow ethnic understanding of who the members of 'the pure people' are, whereas left-wing inclusionary types of populism normally rely on socialism to advance a definition of 'the pure people' that embraces the socioeconomic underdog" (Mudde and Rovira Kaltwasser 2018, 1669–70).

During the welfare state's expansion in the last century, the Social Democrats used the concept of "the People's Home" (*Folkhemmet*) as a symbol for the Swedish welfare state's broad reach and inclusive character, aiming to cater to all citizens' needs from the cradle to the grave (Elgenius and Rydgren 2024). If also incorporating the anti-elitism component of populism, this raises expectations that populist attitudes may be associated with lower acceptance of income differences and potentially also support for non-mainstream Left parties that strive to shift the institutional status quo in a direction that empowers the masses at the expense of economic elites (Mudde and Rovira Kaltwasser 2018; Rooduijn 2019).

Still, most previous research indicates that the right-wing version of populism is more prevalent in Sweden (Jylhä et al. 2019; Oskarson and Demker 2015; Rydgren and van der Maiden 2019) and most of northern Europe (Hopkin 2020; Oesch and Rennwald 2018; Rydgren 2013). Some suggest that this is directly related to the scope of the welfare state: "[I]n those contexts where the welfare state is more consolidated and generous, there is fertile soil for the appearance of exclusionary populists who promise to return to an idealized image of the past characterized by ethnic homogeneity, social cohesion and generous welfare policies" (Rovira Kaltwasser et al. 2021, 48). In the Swedish case, the Sweden Democrats have indeed tried to repurpose "the People's Home" concept, instead using it to invoke collective nostalgia for an allegedly more prosperous and socially cohesive past, where supposedly deserving natives are seen as threatened by immigration and multiculturalism (Elgenius and Rydgren 2024).

Summarizing Expectations

Based on the preceding theoretical discussion and literature review, Table 12.1 summarizes the expectations regarding how social class and political partisanship might relate to approval of income differences, welfare chauvinism, and populist attitudes. While we do not have space to discuss

Table 12.1 Attitude expectations by social class and political partisanship

Attitude	Social class		Political partisanship	
	Sociocultural professionals	**Managers and business profs**	**Mainstream Left**	**Mainstream Right**
Income differences	Mixed	High	Mixed	High
Welfare chauvinism	Low	Mixed	Low	Mixed
Populism	Low	Low	Low	Low
	Service workers	**Production workers**	**Nonmainstream Left**	**Nonmainstream Right**
Income differences	Low	Low	Low	Mixed
Welfare chauvinism	Mixed	High	Low	High
Populism	High	High	Mixed	High

each case in detail, "High" and "Low" denote cases where theoretical arguments and previous empirical research provide clear guidance. The labels should be understood in relative terms, i.e., as expected attitudes compared to the population average. The label "Mixed" indicates that theory and previous research are less clear-cut about what to expect, suggesting that attitudes might be "intermediate" compared to the categories for which expectations are clear.

Using an employment-based approach, this chapter concentrates on four social classes that are particularly relevant for understanding contemporary class politics due to their sizes, as well as their distinguished political attitudes and behaviors (Häusermann and Kriesi 2015; Lindh and McCall 2020; Oesch and Rennwald 2018). Covering the working classes, the focus is on *production workers* (e.g., truck drivers, machine operators, mechanics) and *service workers* (e.g., cleaners, healthcare assistants, shop assistants). To cover the middle classes, the focus is on *sociocultural professionals* (e.g., teachers, nurses, social workers) and *managers and business professionals* (e.g., accountants, administrators, managers). (Together, these four classes include 68.1% of the respondents in our data set.)

Concerning political partisanship, besides categorizing voters based on a distinction between Left and Right parties, the study also distinguishes between mainstream and non-mainstream parties. The latter is defined as never been part of the ruling national government.

Data, Measures, and Analytical Strategy

In an extension of the Swedish branch of the International Social Survey Programme (ISSP), original new data on attitudes toward income inequality, welfare chauvinism, and populist attitudes were gathered for this study, alongside information about the class location, voting behavior, and sociodemographics of respondents. The data set is based on random samples of the Swedish population aged 18–85 years, comprising a total of 5,333 respondents across three separate rounds/years of data collection (i.e., pooled cross-sections, not an individual-level panel).

The initial round of data collection was conducted in the late fall of 2019, just before the outbreak of the COVID-19 pandemic, and it had a response rate of 34%. The subsequent waves of the survey were fielded in the fall of 2020 (response rate 40%) and the spring of 2022 (response rate 35%). During the third round of data collection, most public restrictions related to the pandemic had been lifted. Other disruptive events also took place during the study window, including the "energy crises" and associated high inflation, as well as the Russian invasion of Ukraine.

Despite these rather turbulent times, attitudes remained mostly stable throughout the study. The main change observed was that the average level of populist attitudes decreased in the wake of the pandemic (i.e., the average scores are substantively lower in 2020 and 2022 than in 2019), which seemingly parallels the upswing in political and institutional trust observed in Sweden and other countries during the pandemic (Esaiasson et al. 2021). However, additional analyses suggest that associations between populist attitudes and the other key variables were mostly stable throughout the study window. Therefore, the survey year/round only figures as a control variable in the main analysis.

Attitudes

Table 12.2 presents responses for 12 survey statements all using the same 5-point Likert-type response scale ranging from "Strongly agree" to "Strongly disagree" (full question wordings are provided in the table). These items are organized into three different dimensions, with four items per dimension.

To measure attitudes toward *income differences*, four items from the ISSP Social Inequality module are used. These items are combined into an additive index, scaled from 0 to 10, where a higher score implies more approval of income differences. Constructing an index is methodologically warranted

Table 12.2 Attitude indicators with the distribution of responses for each statement (row percentages)

To what degree to you agree or disagree with the following statements?	Strongly agree	Agree	Neither agree nor disagree	Disagree	Strongly disagree
Income differences					
a) Large differences in income are necessary for Sweden's prosperity.	2	7	29	36	26
b) Differences in income in Sweden are too large.	27	43	20	8	3
c) It is the responsibility of the government to reduce the differences in income between people with high incomes and those with low incomes.	21	41	22	11	5
d) It is the responsibility of private companies to reduce the differences in pay between their employees with high pay and those with low pay.	14	41	28	12	6
Welfare chauvinism					
e) Native Swedes should come before immigrants when it comes to jobs, housing, and benefits.	11	16	25	22	27
f) The government is spending too much funds on helping immigrants.	18	12	24	18	17
g) Most unemployed people do not really try to find a job.	3	12	28	32	25
h) Many people manage to obtain benefits and services to which they are not entitled.	15	36	24	16	10
Populism					
i) There is a conflict between the people and those in power in Sweden.	9	34	35	18	4
j) Politicians do not care about what ordinary people think.	11	28	29	26	6
k) Business leaders make their money at the expense of ordinary people.	9	28	34	22	7
l) I rather rely on the experiences of ordinary people than the opinions of experts.	5	17	34	28	15

Note: Items (b), (c), (d) are reversely phrased, implying that stronger disagreement signals stronger approval of income differences. All numbers are rounded to the nearest full percentage point.
Source: ISSP (2019, 2020, 2022).

due to substantial inter-item correlations and a satisfactory Cronbach's alpha at 0.74. From the response distributions of the individual items in the table (and the response distribution of the composite index, see Appendix Figure 12A), it is clear that a large majority of Swedes want to reduce income differences. For instance, 70% of the respondents strongly agree or agree that "income differences in Sweden are too large," and the mean index score is 3.33, notably below the midpoint of the scale (5.0). Yet, a significant number of Swedes accept or even view inequality positively, with 21% scoring 5.0 or higher on the index (see Appendix Figure 12A).

To measure *welfare chauvinism*, two items (e and f) on social rights and spending on immigrants are used (taken from Lindh et al. 2021), together with two items (g and h) commonly used to assess the perceived deservingness of welfare recipients. For instance, 25% strongly agree or agree that "native Swedes should come before immigrants when it comes to jobs, housing, and benefits," while 49% strongly disagree or disagree with this statement. Even though each item captures somewhat different aspects, their combination into an index is justified by substantial inter-item correlations and a satisfactory Cronbach's alpha (0.84). The index is scaled from 0 to 10, where a higher score implies more welfare chauvinism. The modal response is the midpoint of the index (for full response distribution, see Appendix Figure 12A). The mean value is 4.63, but 41.6% of respondents score above the midpoint of the scale. Public opinion on these issues is thus highly diverse (the standard deviation is 2.57) and more so than for acceptance of income inequality (mean of 3.33; standard deviation of 1.97).

Four items (i–l) were used to gauge *populist attitudes*. A limitation of most existing populist attitude scales is that they are restricted to relations between politicians and the people (Jungkunz et al. 2021). In addition to covering politicians (j), new items were therefore designed for this study, covering perceived conflicts between the people and business leaders (k) as well as experts (l), while also including a more general statement (i). Apart from the item covering experts, respondents are more likely to strongly agree or agree than to disagree or strongly disagree with these statements. Combining these four items into a composite index is methodologically supported (Cronbach's Alpha 0.76), where a higher score indicates more populist attitudes. The modal response is the midpoint on the scale, with a relatively normal distribution around it (see Appendix Figure 12A).

Social Class

As common in the research field, the study uses the Oesch class schema (see, Oesch and Rennwald 2018; see also, Häusermann and Kriesi 2015; Lindh and McCall 2020), which allocates respondents to a social class based on their individual occupation and employment relationship (employee, self-employed, or employer). Individuals who are currently without a paid job are sorted based on their most recent employment/occupation, and those who have never worked for pay are assigned to a social class based on their partner's occupation/employment relationship, if any.

The class schema identifies three *horizontal* "work logics" among employees: technical, organizational, and interpersonal, which differ in the type of skills required and the setting of the work process. Interpersonal jobs are oriented to the client and often operate outside hierarchical lines of command, while the organizational work logic is oriented toward fiscal efficiency and serving bureaucratic functions. Technical work is largely set by technical production parameters, with varying degrees of work autonomy depending on the level of skill requirements.

Combining a vertical distinction between more versus less advantaged employment relations with the three horizontal work logics results in six different class positions among employees. Covering the working classes: *production workers* (12.3% of the sample; e.g., truck drivers, machine operators, mechanics), *service workers* (17.4%; e.g., cleaners, healthcare assistants, shop assistants), and *clerical workers* (6.2%; e.g., clerks, receptionists, secretaries). Covering the middle classes: *technical professionals* (12.7%; e.g., architects, engineers, technicians), *sociocultural professionals* (18.1%; e.g., teachers, nurses, social workers), and *managers and business professionals* (20.3%; e.g., accountants, administrators, managers). In addition, *employers* (4.4%) and the *self-employed* (8.6%) are included as separate categories. While all eight social classes are included in the regression analysis, the results section focuses on the attitudes of production workers, service workers, sociocultural professionals, and managers/business professionals. These four class categories together account for 68.1% of the sample. Full regression models, including estimates for all eight classes, are available in Appendix Table 12A.

Political Partisanship

Political partisanship is covered with self-reported party voted for in the last (2018) general election preceding the time of the survey. In addition to categorizing voters based on a distinction between Left and Right parties, the study also distinguishes between mainstream and non-mainstream parties. A non-mainstream party is defined as one that has never been part of the ruling national government (Left Party and Sweden Democrats). All other parties, which have recently participated in a ruling coalition, are categorized as mainstream (Centre Party, Christian Democrats, Green Party, Moderate Party, Liberals, and Social Democrats). This gives the following four categories: Mainstream Left (Social Democrats, 31.8% of the sample), Non-Mainstream Left (Left Party, 9.2%), Mainstream Right (Christian Democrats, Liberals, Moderate Party, 30.7%), and Non-Mainstream Right (Sweden Democrats, 12.4%). The Green Party and the Centre Party are categorized into a fifth, residual, category (15.9%) because they are not straightforwardly placed in any other category. This residual category is also included in the regression model (see Appendix Table 12A) but is not further discussed or displayed in the main figure containing predicted attitudes.

Multivariate Regression Analysis

The study is based on multivariate ordinary least-square regression models with robust standard errors, using multiple imputation techniques to handle partial missing data (20 imputations by survey round, employing the "mi" command in Stata 17). The presented results are derived from six regression models, with two models for each attitude dimension/index.

In the first multivariate regression model for each attitude, social class is included as the main covariate while also controlling for labor market status (currently in paid work/not currently in paid work), the sector of employment (public, private), gender (man, woman), age group (18–35, 36–49, 50–64, 65–85), and place of residence (countryside, small town, medium city or suburb, large city). In addition, participants were asked to self-identify with up to two ethnic/national groups from which a dichotomous measure of ethnicity (only Swedish/including other than Swedish) was constructed.

(The number of observations is too sparse to measure ethnicity reliably in more detail.) Survey year/round (2019, 2020, 2022) is also controlled for.

Education and income are not controlled for because many consider these factors endogenous to social class or argue they should be seen as mediators of the relationship between social class and attitudes. Since the aim of this chapter is not to tease apart the precise mechanisms linking class location to attitudes, these additional (and potentially endogenous) indicators of the respondents' class location are not included in the analysis.

Political partisanship is added as an independent variable in a second multivariate regression model for each attitude index. The decision to treat partisanship as an independent variable does not stem from a simplistic assumption that there is a unidirectional causal relationship between these variables. However, given that in our dataset, partisanship is measured by the party voted for in the last general national election (which took place in the fall of 2018), and considering that the act of voting predates the attitude responses in the survey, partisanship is treated as the independent variable predicting attitudes.

Empirical Results

Associations Between Attitudes

An informative first step is to examine the associations between the three attitude dimensions. Given that approval of income differences and welfare chauvinism are theorized as two forms of inequality acceptance, we may expect them to be positively associated. This is confirmed by the data, which shows a positive correlation (Pearson's R, 0.316). However, the moderate strength of this correlation indicates that these two attitude dimensions are not only conceptually distinct but also empirically so.

When also considering populist attitudes, a more complex picture emerges: These attitudes are *negatively* correlated with approval of income differences (Pearson's R, −0.216) but *positively* correlated with welfare chauvinism (Pearson's R, 0.442). This supports our theoretical premise that the association between acceptance of inequality and populism is complex, capable of taking both egalitarian and inegalitarian forms, depending on which dimension of inequality is in focus. Notably, the positive relationship between populist attitudes and welfare chauvinism is stronger than the negative relationship between populist attitudes and approval of income differences.

To shed further light on these two forms of inequality acceptance and their relationship to populism, the next step is to examine how these attitudes differ by social class and political partisanship through multivariate regression analysis.

How Attitudes Differ by Social Class

Figure 12.1 shows predicted values for each attitude index by the four social classes in focus, based on the first set of regression models (see Models A–C1 in Appendix Table 12A). Starting with attitudes to income differences, the left panel shows that managers and business professionals (marked with a diamond) are the most accepting of the four classes, with a predicted value of 3.82 (95% CI: 3.69–3.95). This is followed by sociocultural professionals (circle), whose predicted approval level is 3.33 (95% CI: 3.18–3.48). In addition, the acceptance levels among service workers (box, point estimate: 2.85;

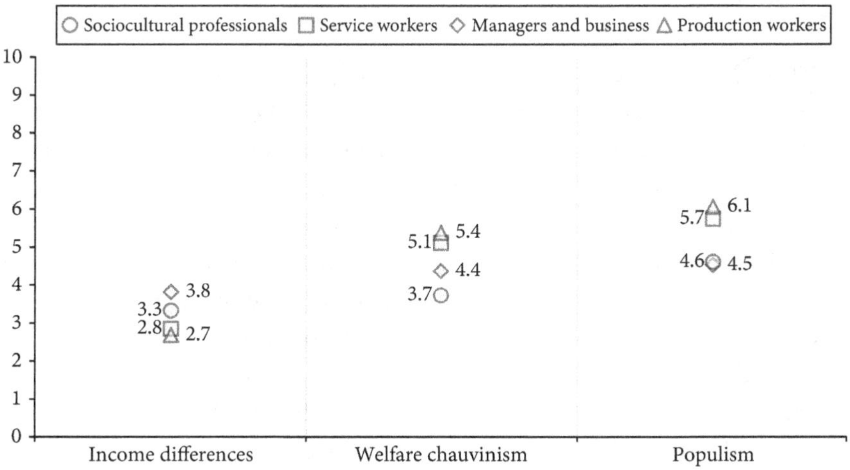

Figure 12.1 Predicted levels of approval of income differences, welfare chauvinism, and populist attitudes (each on a 0–10 scale), by social class

Notes: Based on Models A–C1 in Appendix Table 12A, using multiple imputation OLS regression with robust standard errors, including controls for labor market status, sector of employment, gender, age, place of residence, ethnicity, and survey round. All values are rounded to one decimal place.
Source: Swedish ISSP (2019, 2020, 2022).

95% CI: 2.72–2.98) and production workers (triangle, point estimate: 2.68; 95% CI: 2.52–2.84) are roughly similar but significantly lower than those of the two middle-class categories.

The magnitude of these class divides in approval of income differences depends to some extent on the perspective taken. On the one hand, considering that the scales vary between 0 and 10, the estimated 1.14 scale-step difference between manual workers and managers/business professionals might seem relatively small. On the other hand, the standard deviation on the index is 1.97, implying that the difference is still more than half of a standard deviation unit in the dependent variable. Thus, while the approval of income differences is relatively low overall, this is far from a consensual issue. Individuals more economically rewarded in the labor market are more inclined to accept or even favor existing income differences than those in less advantaged class positions.

Turning to welfare chauvinism, the middle panel of Figure 12.1 demonstrates that production workers are the most exclusionary, with a predicted average score of 5.38 (95% CI: 5.15–5.60), followed by serviced workers at 5.11 (95% CI: 4.93–5.30). The predicted values are significantly lower for managers/business professionals (point estimate: 4.37; 95% CI: 4.19–4.54) and, even more so, for sociocultural professionals (point estimate: 3.73; 95% CI: 3.53–3.92).

These results fit with expectations, although there was theoretical uncertainty regarding what to expect from service workers. The results suggest that the interpersonal work practices characterizing many jobs of service workers do not seem to dampen the level of welfare chauvinism compared to production workers. This contrasts with the particularly low welfare chauvinism observed among sociocultural professionals, suggesting that educational resources and job requirements may be more important than interpersonal work relations per se in preventing welfare chauvinism. The predicted attitude difference between sociocultural professionals and production workers is 1.65 scale points, corresponding to about two-thirds of a standard deviation unit in the dependent variable.

Populist attitudes are covered in the right panel of the figure. Production workers (point estimate: 6.06; 95% CI: 5.90–6.22) are predicted to score slightly higher than service workers (point estimate: 5.74; 95% CI: 5.59–5.90). Moreover, sociocultural professionals (point estimate: 4.62; 95% CI: 4.47–4.76) and managers/business professionals (point estimate: 4.53;

95% CI: 4.40–4.66) have markedly lower populist attitudes than the working classes. The predicted attitude gap between managers/business professionals and production workers is 1.21 scale points, corresponding to almost two-thirds of a standard deviation unit in the dependent variable.

To summarize, although approval of income differences and welfare chauvinism are *positively* related at the individual level, these two attitude dimensions are *negatively* correlated at the level of social class; those in the working classes are more opposed to income inequality but express more chauvinistic attitudes than the middle classes. In addition, the working classes tend to hold more populist attitudes than the middle classes. These multidimensional cross-cutting patterns are fundamental for understanding the increasingly complex relationship between social class and political behavior in contemporary welfare states (Evans and Tilley 2017; Häusermann and Kriesi 2015; Lindh and McCall 2020; Oesch and Rennwald 2018).

How Attitudes Relate to Political Partisanship

Figure 12.2 presents predicted attitudes by partisan vote choice, holding social class, and demographic covariates at their means (for full regression estimates, see Appendix Table 12A, Models A–C2). Approval of income differences is covered in the left panel, revealing a difference of about 1.62 scale points between more approving mainstream Right voters (marked with a diamond, point estimate: 4.31; 95% CI: 4.21–4.42) and less approving mainstream Left voters (box, point estimate: 2.69; 95% CI: 2.60–2.78). Non-mainstream Right voters (triangle, point estimate: 3.85; 95% CI: 3.68–4.03) are somewhat less approving of income differences than their mainstream Right counterparts, but the difference is relatively small. As expected, non-mainstream Left voters (circle, point estimate: 1.72; 95% CI: 1.58–1.86) are the least approving of income inequality.

Approval of income differences thus has a twofold character among the electorate: There is a marked ideological divide between Left and Right voters; however, the general approval rate is not that high in absolute terms, falling below the scale's midpoint even among mainstream Right-party voters.

The middle panel of the figure reveals pronounced political divisions tied to welfare chauvinism. The attitude gap between the more inclusivist

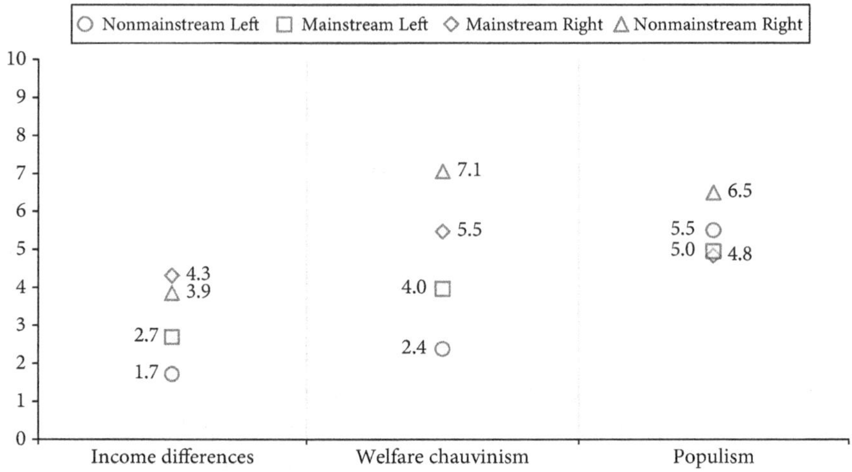

Figure 12.2 Predicted levels of approval of income differences, welfare chauvinism, and populist attitudes (each on a 0–10 scale), by partisan vote in the preceding national election

Note: Based on Models A–C2 in Appendix Table 12A, using multiple imputation OLS regression with robust standard errors, including controls for social class, labor market status, sector of employment, gender, age, place of residence, ethnicity, and survey round. All values are rounded to one decimal place.
Source: ISSP (2019, 2020, 2022).

mainstream Left voters (point estimate: 3.97; 95% CI: 3.84–4.09) and the more exclusivist mainstream Right voters (point estimate: 5.47; 95% CI: 5.36–5.59) is about the same size as the gap observed for attitudes to income differences. However, there is an additional gap of similar size between mainstream and non-mainstream Right voters, with the predicted value of the latter being as high as 7.06 (95% CI: 6.88–7.23). In addition, the Left, non-mainstream voters (point estimate: 2.38; 95% CI: 2.14–2.62) are markedly *less* chauvinistic than mainstream voters. The observed gap between Left and Right non-mainstream voters is an astonishing 4.68 scale points.

The right panel shows that populist attitudes display less variation and take a different shape across party lines. Mainstream Left (point estimate: 4.95; 95% CI: 4.85–5.06) and mainstream Right voters (point estimate: 4.84; 95% CI: 4.74–4.94) have similar attitudes, both scoring around the scale's midpoint. Instead, a more notable difference emerges between mainstream and non-mainstream voters on both sides of the Left–Right spectrum. Non-mainstream Left voters (point estimate: 5.51; 95% CI: 5.32–5.69) are slightly more populist than mainstream voters, while non-mainstream Right voters (point estimate: 6.49; 95% CI: 6.35–6.64) stand out with the most populist attitudes.

To summarize, within the political mainstream, the observed gap in acceptance of inequality between Left (less accepting) and Right (more accepting) voters is similar for approval of income differences and welfare chauvinism. Substantive gaps between mainstream and non-mainstream voters are also observed. To the Left, non-mainstream voters are generally less accepting of inequality than mainstream Left voters, particularly in relation to welfare chauvinism. To the Right, the gap in attitudes to income differences between mainstream and non-mainstream voters is relatively small, challenging the widespread assumption that non-mainstream (radical) right supporters take a moderate stance on traditional Left–Right distributive issues. In contrast, non-mainstream Right voters are characterized by much more chauvinistic conceptions of social rights and welfare (un)deservingness than mainstream Right voters. Taken together, these results indicate that welfare chauvinism/deservingness is more politically divisive than attitudes to income differences among the Swedish electorate.

Another interesting finding is that the level of populist attitudes is remarkably similar between Left and Right voters within the political mainstream. However, non-mainstream voters on both the Left and the Right exhibit more populist attitudes than their mainstream counterparts. This suggests that populism is not a central issue in mainstream party competition but rather serves as a supporting ingredient and potentially mobilizing force for non-mainstream political challengers. In this regard, non-mainstream voters to the Right tend to exhibit more populist attitudes than non-mainstream Left voters. Coupled with the previous finding that populist attitudes are more strongly linked to welfare chauvinism than to disapproval of income inequality, this indicates that the exclusivist right-wing version of populism currently plays a more notable role in Swedish politics than the inclusivist left-wing version.

Conclusion

The results of this chapter challenge—and arguably warrant a reconsideration of—the predominant scholarly view that the institutional logic of the social democratic welfare state generates strong sociopolitical consensus and erases public acceptance of inequality. Contrary to this belief, the study uncovers sizeable attitudinal divisions, rooted in social class and attached to political partisanship, concerning how redistributively ambitious and socially inclusive the welfare state should be. A striking finding is that welfare chauvinism and views of deservingness are more politically divisive than issues of income inequality. While overall approval of income inequality is relatively low, the sharpest divides emerge in the exclusivist conceptions of social rights and welfare deservingness held by voters of the non-mainstream (radical) Right party, the Sweden Democrats.

Could these findings signal trouble for the future of the social democratic welfare state model? While approval of existing income differences is not uncommon among more economically advantaged middle-class segments and right-wing voters, this is unlikely to pose a critical threat as long as a supermajority keeps supporting income redistribution. In addition, as discussed in the front sections, the social democratic welfare state model is not primarily built on explicit government redistribution from the rich to the poor but rather rests on universal welfare programs that are broadly popular for providing social security for all.

Therefore, the results regarding welfare chauvinism and undeservingness are arguably more concerning, suggesting that substantial parts of the population might accept reforms that deviate from the universalist principles of these social security programs. A pressing question for future research is whether conflicts over inclusivist vs. exclusivist conceptions of social rights and welfare deservingness may become a central battleground in Swedish welfare politics in the years ahead. If so, this could mark a potentially game-changing shift away from the universalist principles that have long underpinned the social democratic welfare state model for which Sweden has been internationally known.

Appendix

Table 12A OLS regression models covering approval of income differences, welfare chauvinism, and populist attitudes (each on a 0–10 scale) by social class, partisan vote in the preceding national election, and sociodemographic controls

	Income differences		Welfare chauvinism		Populism	
	A1	A2	B1	B2	C1	C2
Social class						
Employer	1.490***	1.006***	−0.993***	−1.262***	−1.725***	−1.551***
Self-employed	0.682***	0.379**	−0.680***	−0.756***	−1.003***	−0.853***
Managers and business	1.136***	0.790***	−1.012***	−1.066***	−1.531***	−1.290***
Technical professional	0.877***	0.651***	−0.887***	−0.952***	−1.184***	−1.054***
Sociocultural professional	0.647***	0.536***	−1.651***	−1.364***	−1.446***	−1.214***
Clerical worker	0.400**	0.216	−0.510*	−0.444*	−0.609***	−0.418**
Service worker	0.170	0.058	−0.266	−0.266	−0.317**	−0.252*
Production worker (ref.)	0	0	0	0	0	0
Partisanship						
Other		0.362***		−0.495***		−0.409***
Non-mainstream Right		1.162***		3.090***		1.541***
Mainstream Right		1.621***		1.506***		−0.113
Non-mainstream Left		−0.972***		−1.587***		0.554***
Mainstream Left (ref.)		0		0		0
Labor market status						
Currently in paid work	−0.032	−0.016	0.041	0.041	−0.311***	−0.217**
Not in paid work (ref.)	0	0	0	0	0	0
Sector of employment						
Public sector	−0.444***	−0.305***	−0.204*	−0.071	0.010	−0.013
Private sector (ref.)	0	0	0	0	0	0
Gender						
Woman	−0.582***	−0.468***	−0.400***	−0.111	−0.099	0.021
Man (ref.)	0	0	0	0	0	0
Age						
65-85	−0.165	−0.222*	0.765***	0.605***	0.228*	0.259*
50-64	0.178	0.064	0.476***	0.144	0.205*	0.134
36-49	0.098	0.031	0.193	0.039	0.048	0.042
18-35 (ref.)	0	0	0	0	0	0

Continued

Table 12A *Continued*

	Income differences		Welfare chauvinism		Populism	
	A1	A2	B1	B2	C1	C2
Place of residence						
Countryside	−0.038	−0.044	0.497***	0.395***	0.426***	0.365***
Small town	−0.027	−0.076	0.399***	0.305**	0.221**	0.211**
Medium city or suburb	0.187*	0.043	0.497***	0.253*	0.067	0.074
Large city (ref.)	0	0	0	0	0	0
Ethnicity						
Incl. other than Swedish	−0.079	0.039	−0.258*	−0.099	0.354***	0.352***
Only Swedish (ref.)	0	0	0	0	0	0
Survey round						
2022	−0.064	−0.001	−0.108	−0.055	−0.470***	−0.477***
2020	0.204**	0.208**	0.086	0.073	−0.428***	−0.438***
2019 (ref.)	0	0	0	0	0	0
Constant	3.121***	2.647***	4.913***	4.208***	6.209***	5.838***
R-square	0.111	0.284	0.090	0.351	0.130	0.210
N observations	5.333	5.333	5.333	5.333	5.333	5.333

Unstandardized regression coefficients. *** $p < 0.001$, ** $p < 0.01$, * $p < 0.05$. All estimates are rounded to three decimal places.
Based on multiple imputations (20 imputations by survey round), using robust standard errors.
Source: ISSP, 2019, 2020, 2022.

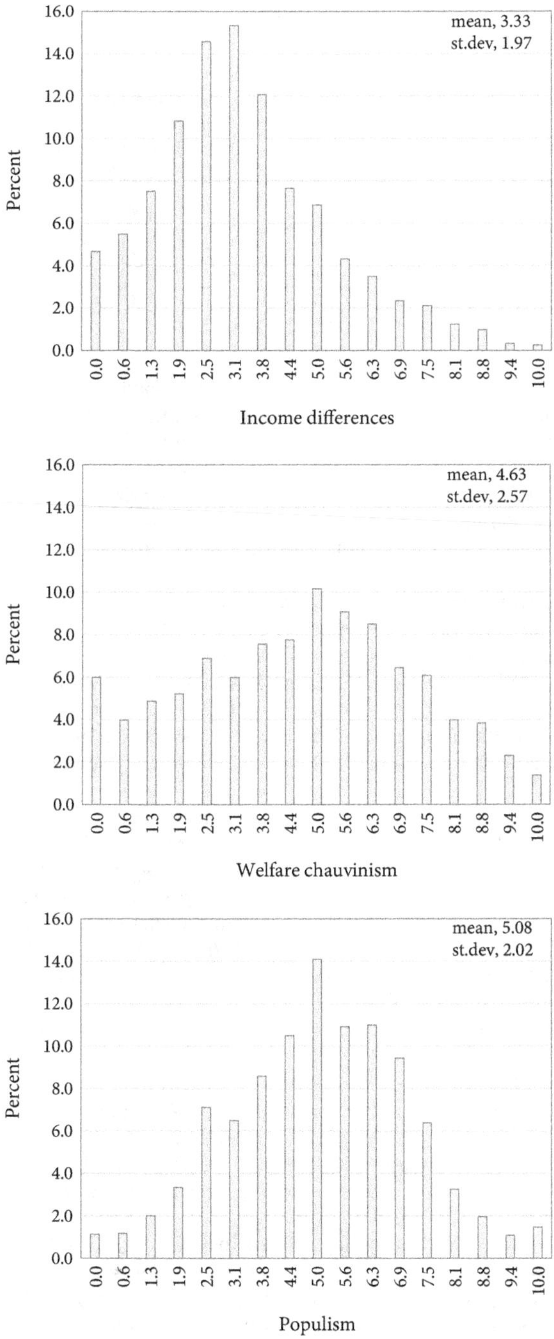

Figure 12A Distribution of indices covering approval of income differences, welfare chauvinism, and populist attitudes, respectively (all on 0–10 scales)

Source: ISSP (2019, 2020, 2022).

Note

* I am grateful for comments from John Campbell, Francesco Duina, Ann-Zofie Duvander, Cassandra Engeman, Tomas Korpi, Henning Lohmann, and Luca Storti, as well as from presentations at the book volume workshop, the biannual conference of the Swedish Sociological Association, and at the Social Policy unit of the Swedish Institute for Social Research. This work was supported by the Swedish Research Council for Health, Working Life and Welfare under Grant No. 2017-00079.

References

Akkerman, A., C. Mudde, and A. Zaslove, 2014. "How Populist Are the People? Measuring Populist Attitudes in Voters." *Comparative Political Studies* 47 (9): pp. 1324–1353.

Bäckman, O., and K. Nelson. 2017. "The Egalitarian Paradise?" In *The Routledge Handbook of Scandinavian Politics*, edited by P. Nedergaard and A. Wivel, pp. 25–35. London: Routledge.

Bengtsson, E. 2020. *Världens jämlikaste land?* Lund: Arkiv förlag.

Bengtsson, M., T. Berglund, and M. Oskarson. 2013. "Class and Ideological Orientations Revisited: An Exploration of Class-Based Mechanisms." *British Journal of Sociology* 64 (4): pp. 691–716.

Blyth, M. 2002. *Great Transformations: Economic Ideas and Institutional Change in the Twentieth Century*. Cambridge: Cambridge University Press.

Busemeyer, M.R., J. Garritzmann, E. Neimanns, and R. Nezi. 2018. "Investing in Education in Europe: Attitudes, Politics and Policies (INVEDUC)." GESIS Data Archive, Cologne. ZA6961 Data file Version 1.0.0. https://doi.org/10.4232/1.13140.

Busemeyer, M.R., P. Rathgeb, and A.H. Sahm. 2022. "Authoritarian Values and the Welfare State: The Social Policy Preferences of Radical Right Voters." *West European Politics* 45 (1): pp. 77–101.

Castanho Silva, B., S. Jungkunz, M. Helbing, and L. Littvay. 2020. "An Empirical Comparison of Seven Populist Attitudes Scales." *Political Research Quarterly* 73 (2): pp. 409–424.

Edlund, J., and A. Lindh. 2015. "The Democratic Class Struggle Revisited: The Welfare State, Social Cohesion and Political Conflict." *Acta Sociologica* 58 (4): pp. 311–328.

Edlund, J., and A. Lindh. 2013. "Institutional Trust and Welfare State Support: On the Role of Trust in Market Institutions." *Journal of Public Policy* 33 (3): pp. 295–317.

Eger, M.A. 2010. "Even in Sweden: The Effect of Immigration on Support for Welfare State Spending." *European Sociological Review* 26 (2): pp. 203–217.

Eick, G.M. 2024. *Welfare Chauvinism in Europe*. Cheltenham, UK: Edward Elgar Publishing.

Elgenius, G., and J. Rydgren. 2024. "The Politics of Ethnic Nationalism, Nostalgia and Anti-Immigrant Framing: The Trajectory of the Sweden Democrats 1989–2022." In *Migration and Nationalism*, edited by L. Lessard-Phillips, A. Papoutsi, N. Sigona, and P. Ziss, pp. 114–135. Cheltenham, UK: Edward Elgar Publishing.

Enggist, M., and S. Häusermann. 2024. "Partisan Preference Divides Regarding Welfare Chauvinism and Welfare Populism—Appealing Only to Radical Right Voters or Beyond?" *Journal of European Social Policy* 34 (2): pp. 142–158.

Esaiasson, P., J. Sohlberg, M. Ghersetti, and B. Johansson. 2021. "How the Coronavirus Crisis Affects Citizen Trust in Institutions and in Unknown Others: Evidence from 'the Swedish Experiment.'" *European Journal of Political Research* 60 (3): pp. 748–760.

Esping-Andersen, G. 1990. *The Three Worlds of Welfare Capitalism*. Princeton, NJ: Princeton University Press.

Evans, G., and J. Tilley. 2017. *The New Politics of Class: The Political Exclusion of the British Working Class*. Oxford: Oxford University Press.

Gingrich, J., and S. Häusermann. 2015. "The Decline of the Working-Class Vote, the Reconfiguration of the Welfare Support Coalition and Consequences for the Welfare State." *Journal of European Social Policy* 25 (1): pp. 50–75.

Goossen, M., M.A. Eger, I. Johansson Sevä, and J. Kulin. In press. "Support for the Swedish Welfare State: The Role of Socioeconomic and Sociocultural Conflict in Four Decades of Public Opinion." In *A Research Agenda for the Political Sociology of Welfare*, edited by M.A. Eger. Cheltenham: Edward Elgar.

Greve, B. 2019. *Welfare, Populism and Welfare Chauvinism*. Bristol: Policy Press.

Häusermann, S., and H. Kriesi. 2015. "What Do Voters Want? Dimensions and Configurations in Individual-Level Preferences and Party Choice." In *The Politics of Advanced Capitalism*, edited by P. Beramendi, S. Häusermann, H. Kitschelt, and H. Kriesi, pp. 202–230. Cambridge: Cambridge University Press.

Hooijer, G., and D. King. 2021. "The Critics of Welfare: From Neoliberalism to Populism." In *The Oxford Handbook of the Welfare State*, 2nd ed., edited by D. Béland, S. Leibfried, K.J. Morgan, H. Obinger, and C. Person, pp. 53–70. Oxford: Oxford University Press.

Hopkin, J. 2020. *Anti-System Politics: The Crisis of Market Liberalism in Rich Democracies*. Oxford: Oxford University Press.

Huber, E., and J.D. Stephens. 2024. *Challenging Inequality: Variation Across Postindustrial Societies*. Chicago: University of Chicago Press.

International Social Survey Programme (ISSP). 2019. ISSP 2019—Ojämlikhet i Sverige. Umeå University.

International Social Survey Programme (ISSP). 2020. ISSP 2020—Åsikter om miljön. Umeå University.

International Social Survey Programme (ISSP). 2022. ISSP 2022—Åsikter om familjeliv och arbete. Umeå University.

Jungkunz, S., R.A. Fahey, and A. Hino. 2021. "How Populist Attitudes Scales Fail to Capture Support for Populists in Power." *PLoS One* 16 (12): e0261658.

Jylhä, K.M., J. Rydgren, and P. Strimling. 2019. "Radical Right-Wing Voters from Right and Left: Comparing Sweden Democrat Voters Who Previously Voted for the Conservative Party or the Social Democratic Party." *Scandinavian Political Studies* 42 (3–4): pp. 220–244.

Korpi, W., and J. Palme. 1998. "The Paradox of Redistribution and Strategies of Equality: Welfare State Institutions, Inequality, and Poverty in the Western Countries." *American Sociological Review* 63: pp. 661–687.

Kymlicka, W., and K.G. Banting. Eds. 2006. *Multiculturalism and the Welfare State: Recognition and Redistribution in Contemporary Democracies*. New York: Oxford University Press.

Lindh, A., A.B. Andersson, and B. Volker. 2021. "The Missing Link: Network Influences on Class Divides in Political Attitudes." *European Sociological Review* 37 (5): pp. 695–712.

Lindh, A., and L. McCall. 2020. "Class Position and Political Opinion in Rich Democracies." *Annual Review of Sociology*, 46, pp. 419–441.

Mudde, C., and C. Rovira Kaltwasser. 2018. "Studying Populism in Comparative Perspective: Reflections on the Contemporary and Future Research Agenda." *Comparative Political Studies* 51 (13): pp. 1667–1693.

Oesch, D., and L. Rennwald. 2018. "Electoral Competition in Europe's New Tripolar Political Space: Class Voting for the Left, Centre-Right and Radical Right." *European Journal of Political Research* 57 (4): pp. 783–807.

Oskarson, M., and M. Demker. 2015. "Room for Realignment: The Working-Class Sympathy for Sweden Democrats." *Government and Opposition* 50 (4): pp. 629–651.

Rennwald, L., and J. Pontusson. 2022. "Class Gaps in Perceptions of Political Voice: Liberal Democracies 1974–2016." *West European Politics* 45 (6): pp. 1334–1360.

Rooduijn, M. 2019. "State of the Field: How to Study Populism and Adjacent Topics? A Plea for Both More and Less Focus." *European Journal of Political Research* 58 (1): pp. 362–372.

Rothstein, B. 1998. *Just Institutions Matter: The Moral and Political Logic of the Universal Welfare State*. Cambridge: Cambridge University Press.

Rothstein, B., and S. Steinmo. 2013. "Social Democracy in Crisis? What Crisis?" In *The Crisis of Social Democracy in Europe*, edited by M. Keating and D. McCrone, pp. 87–106. Edinburgh: Edinburgh University Press.

Rovira Kaltwasser, C., and L. Zanotti. 2021. "Populism and the Welfare State." In *Handbook on Austerity, Populism and the Welfare State*, edited by B. Greve, pp. 41–53. Cheltenham, UK: Edward Elgar Publishing.

Rydgren, J. (Ed.). 2013. *Class Politics and the Radical Right*. London: Routledge.

Rydgren, J., and S. van der Meiden. 2019. "The Radical Right and the End of Swedish Exceptionalism." *European Political Science* 18 (3): pp. 439–455.

Svallfors, S. 2011. "A Bedrock of Support? Trends in Welfare State Attitudes in Sweden, 1981–2010." *Social Policy and Administration* 45 (7): pp. 806–825.

Svallfors, S. 2016. "Politics as Organised Combat—New Players and New Rules of the Game in Sweden." *New Political Economy* 21 (6): pp. 505–519.

van Oorschot, W., F. Roosma, B. Meuleman, and T. Reeskens. Eds. 2017. *The Social Legitimacy of Targeted Welfare: Attitudes to Welfare Deservingness*. Cheltenham, UK: Edward Elgar.

Chapter 13
Dignifying Economic Inequality
Authoritarian Populist Governance in India

Priya Chacko

Introduction

Inequality has been a persistent and entrenched feature of Indian society and appears to be gaining social acceptance. The World Values Survey (WVS) reveals a 20% decrease in support between 2010–14 and 2017–22 in India for the proposition that governments have more responsibility to provide than individuals. It also indicates a 40% drop in support for the assertion that incomes should be made more equal (Haerpfer et al. 2022; Inglehart et al. 2014). For both questions in the 2017–22 wave, there is minimal variation in responses between ethnic groups (castes), genders (male and female), and major religious groups (Hindus and Muslims). Only those on high incomes indicate significantly less support for both questions than other income levels. Yet, the WVS reveals a 30% decrease in support for the idea that competition is good, also with little variation in gender, ethnicity, and religion, but it showed more support for those with high incomes (Haerpfer et al. 2022; Inglehart et al. 2014). Moreover, according to a recent study, while 47% of young voters would like to be "wealth givers," and one third attributed individual responsibility for unemployment, 63% desire government jobs (Mishra et al. 2024).

This mixed and dynamic picture requires more in-depth investigation. One explanation may have to do with India's changing politics around inequality and its effects since 2014. Since 2014, there has been an actual rapid rise in inequality which, perhaps, tempers its social acceptance. This chapter does not seek prove this hypothesis. Rather, it takes the first step of showing that, while previous governments have sought, with varying degrees of success, to address economic and social disadvantage, India's

Priya Chacko, *Dignifying Economic Inequality*. In: *The Social Acceptance of Inequality*. Edited by: Francesco Duina and Luca Storti, Oxford University Press. © Oxford University Press (2025).
DOI: 10.1093/oso/9780197814499.003.0013

current government, a coalition led by the Bharatiya Janata Party (BJP), is distinctive because its authoritarian populist politics ideologically enshrines inequality and mobilizes social acceptance for it.

Specifically, the chapter aims to show that intertwined moral, market, cultural, and group logics of acceptance, supported by institutional disintermediation, underpin the BJP-led government's authoritarian populist governance. It does so through analysis of social and economic policies over the last decade, focusing particularly on its demonetization of high value currency and its social policies. "Authoritarian populist governance" refers to the use of nationalist-populist discourses and strategies that pit a Hindu "people," embodied in Prime Minister Narendra Modi, against a "corrupt" liberal-left elite and "antinational" religious minorities to legitimize and facilitate increasingly authoritarian and exclusionary policies. While the BJP government's anti-minority policies and undermining of civil liberties have been subjected to much criticism and analysis (Jaffrelot 2021), its economic policies are often viewed as producing growth and improving living standards (Bajpaee 2023). This chapter seeks to draw attention to the ways in which the government's policies have, in fact, enhanced economic inequality and have been justified and enabled by diversified repertoires of acceptance of inequalities that intersect and complement each other.

The chapter begins by detailing India's growing economic inequality, particularly since the COVID-19 pandemic. It then makes the case that this inequality is justified by intertwined moral, market, cultural, and group logics shaped by the party's Hindutva nationalist-populist ideology, neoliberal political-economic strategies, and supported by a populist institutional logic of disintermediation. In particular, a moral logic of duties, based on religious texts that justify inequality as cosmologically sanctified, forms the basis of the BJP's ethical framework. This moral logic is aligned with a market logic, emphasizing personal responsibility and minimal government support. These moral-market logics are further entangled with cultural and group logics of inequality, taking advantage of preexisting social hierarchies of gender, caste, and religion. Government policies characterized as Modi's "guarantees" emphasize market participation and involve sacrifice and hardship as the performance of duties particularly by women and lower castes. The creation of an undeserving Muslim poor is facilitated by a moral and group logic that characterizes Muslims as abandoning their duties and becoming threats to the nation. These logics of acceptance are facilitated through an authoritarian-populist institutional context of disintermediation which curtail avenues for contestation and resistance, by labeling them anti-people and corrupt. Finally, the chapter demonstrates that disintermediation and the entangled moral, market, cultural, and group logics give rise to policies that justify and enhance economic inequality.

India's Growing Inequality

India is the world's third-largest economy, and one of the fastest growing economies; however, it is also the one of the world's most unequal countries. According to the World Inequality Report 2022 (Chancel et al. 2022, 193), the top 10% of income earners in India held 57% of total national income, earning more than twenty times than the bottom 50% that hold 13% of national income. Overall, the top 1% of Indians held 22% of national income (Oxfam India 2022). Gender inequality is particularly high in India, with women's labor income share equal to 18% (Chancel et al. 2022, 19). Inequality based on caste and religion is also high, with wealth concentrated with upper caste and lower-caste Other Backward Class (OBC) Hindus. The wealth share of those at the bottom of the caste and religious hierarchy, Dalits, Adivasis, and Muslims is much lower than their household shares (Tagade and Thorat 2020).[1]

While inequality has been growing in India since the early 1980s when it began to deregulate and liberalize its economy, wealth concentration rapidly increased from the mid-2010s, particularly between 2014–15 and 2022–23 (Anand and Kumar 2023; Bharti et al. 2024). The COVID-19 pandemic and lockdown, which led to a deep recession, has worsened poverty and inequality. According to the Pew Research Center, while the number of poor in India (living on US$2 a day or less) decreased from 2011 to 2019 from 340 million to 78 million, the pandemic pushed 75 million into poverty in 2020 and shrank the middle class by 32 million (Kochhar 2021). Groups particularly affected by unemployment during the pandemic were those who are both the poorest and suffer the most discrimination—women, Dalits, Adivasis, internal migrant workers, young workers, and Muslims (Azim Premji University 2021).

India has experienced a "K-shaped" post-COVID recovery, exacerbating preexisting trends. Luxury consumption and urban consumption has spiked, benefiting from a booming stock market and rising company profits.

However, rural wages have stagnated, alongside growing reliance on agricultural employment. Poor-quality casual wage employment has risen, as have rural self-employment and unpaid family employment. These outcomes have affected Dalits, Adivasis, women, and Muslims, in particular. Muslims have experienced declining labor force participation and a dramatic drop in enrollment in higher education. A rising share of rural women are engaged in self-employment, with over half of these women working in unpaid employment, indicating high levels of household distress (Ahmed et al. 2024; Azim Premji University 2023; Roy 2023; Verma 2024; *The Wire* 2023a).

Rising inequality has been recognized as a problem by many state and national governments in India. In 1993, the Janata Party–led National Front government introduced caste-based reservation (positive discrimination) policies in government jobs for OBCs. The Congress Party–led United Progressive Alliance government (2004–14) further extended reservation for OBCs to higher education institutions in 2006 and formed commissions and committees to report on Muslim disadvantage. It was also pushed by civil society movements and the Supreme Court to ameliorate the effects of economic liberalization and deregulation through the introduction of rights-based social policies like the Right to Food Act, the Right to Education Act, and the Mahatma Gandhi National Rural Employment Guarantee Act (MGNREGA) (Ali 2010; Chacko 2018, 2019a). Seeking to address Muslim disadvantage, state governments in the states of Karnataka, Kerala, Tamil Nadu, and West Bengal led by the Congress, the Communist Party, and regional parties, like the Telugu Desam Party, introduced religion-based reservation policies (Jaffrelot and Kalaiyarasan 2023). These policies had mixed outcomes due to poor implementation, inadequate policy designs and a lack of supportive public goods like good quality health and education; nonetheless, they have been shown to have had some impact on addressing gross inequalities (Chiriyankandath et al. 2019).

Logics of Acceptance for Economic Inequality: Moral-Market Logics

The BJP has long rejected caste and religion-based reservation policies and minority rights, though it has tactically supported some policies for electoral advantage. The BJP subscribes to an organicist nationalist-populism, Hindutva (Hinduness), which identifies India and the ideal Indian with the upper caste, middle-class Hindu practices and behavior of its "founding fathers" (Jaffrelot 1996). While Hindus nominally form 80% of India's population, they are divided by region, language, sect, and caste. Emerging in the early twentieth century and shaped by earlier Hindu reform movements, Hindutva combines European organicist nationalism; Italian fascism; German and British orientalist notions of India as an ancient, degraded civilization; and concepts derived from Vedic era (1500–500 BCE) texts. Hindutva naturalizes social hierarchy and, therefore, inequality by portraying the national body as the "Virat Purusha" (Cosmic Man), a concept taken from Vedic texts (Basu 2020, 32; Bhatt 2001; Marzia 2000). The Hindutva movement or "Sangh Parivar" (family) of organizations—the BJP, Rashtriya Swayamsevak Sangh (National Volunteers Association (RSS), and Vishwa Hindu Parishad (World Hindu Council)—has a paternalistic, Hindu upper-caste supremacist mission, aimed at inculcating a sense of "one nation, one culture, one people" among Indians. It aims to produce upper caste behavior in oppressed castes and tribes; co-opt Sikhs, Jains, and Buddhists (as adherents to Indian religions) to the Hindu fold; and subordinate Muslim and Christian minorities whose loyalty is deemed suspect due to their adherence to "foreign" religions. It has long also utilized a populist discursive strategy (Laclau 2005) to undermine secular and liberal-left "elites" who promote a politics of equality. These "elites" are said to be influenced by foreign ideologies, deemed to be corrupt, and accused of pandering to minorities for support and votes at the expense of the Hindu "people."

The BJP was a part of coalition governments in the 1980s and 1990s and led the National Democratic Alliance government (NDA) from 1998 to 2004. The NDA was re-elected in 2014 and again in 2019. While its ideological commitment to organicist nationalism has remained consistent, the party's approach to politics and economics has varied with the pressures of coalition politics, the interests of its changing electoral support base, and its status as an opposition party or a party in power. For instance, as its base diversified from small traders and farmers to the urban middle classes in the late 1990s, the BJP largely abandoned anti-economic liberalization policies and embraced neoliberal policies oriented toward trade and markets (Chacko 2019b). After being re-elected to power in 2014, the BJP-led national government in India has fashioned an authoritarian populist project underpinned, it is argued here, by intertwined moral, market, cultural, and group logics shaped by the party's Hindu nationalist-populist politics, its neoliberal political-economic strategies, and supported by institutional disintermediation. These logics, which are elaborated in this, and the next, section, have underpinned India's growing authoritarianism and social and economic policies, worsening and justifying economic inequality.

Moral Logics: Duties over Rights

Moral logics justify inequality based on adherence to overarching ethical principles. As articulated by Prime Minister Modi, the BJP's ethical framework rests on a conception of "duties" over "rights." In 2022, during an event celebrating seventy-five years of India's independence, hosted by a controversial Hindu sect, the Brahma Kumaris, which promotes patriarchal and upper-caste Hindu social norms, Modi (2022) asserted that a "malaise has afflicted our society, our nation and all of us. It is that we turned away from our duties and did not give them primacy . . . neglecting one's duties completely has played a huge role in keeping India vulnerable" and urged the cultivation of a "spirit of sacrifice and duty." The notion of duties, often translated as *dharma*, derives from Hindu religious texts in which they are associated with social order, religious conduct, social boundaries, and the caste system. When brought into politics as an ethical framework *dharma* has had different interpretations.

For instance, the notion of *swadharma* (own duty), in traditional readings of texts, such as the *Bhagavad Gita*, identifies duty with the varna caste hierarchical order and considers this just and righteous even though it institutionalizes inequality. Caste is a social system originating in the fourfold varna classification in Vedic-era texts which grants symbolic and material rights and privileges based on membership of particular castes. Varna consists of Brahmins (priests and scholars), Kshatriyas (the rulers and warriors), Vaishyas (agriculturalists and merchants), and Shudras (laborers who serve the other higher castes), with numerous subcastes or "jatis" within these categories, and Dalits and Adivasis positioned as outsiders to the system. As the anti-caste leader B.R. Ambedkar observed, these privileges are "graded": "it places these communities in a graded order one above the other in social status. Each caste takes its pride and its consolation in the fact that in the scale of castes it is above some other caste" (Ambedkar 2014).

The anti-colonial leader Mohandas Gandhi reconfigured *swadharma* as a "conservative equality," wherein equality is rooted in self-sacrifice. He rejected the idea of inalienable or abstract rights and instead made rights dependent on the duty of self-sacrifice toward both friends and enemies (Skaria 2016, 159). This was because, whereas rights are passive and could be given and taken by states, duties resided with individuals who, therefore, had inalienable sovereignty and a moral responsibility to actively perform their citizenship of the world (Devji 2012, 190). Gandhi's conservative equality sought to maintain varna as a social system but subvert its social hierarchy, something that Ambedkar (2014) pointed out was impossible.

The notion of duties in Hindutva politics is shaped by its organicist nationalism, which promotes "terrestrial homogeneity" and "cosmogenic inequity" (Basu 2020, 32), meaning that individuals and the state uphold a hierarchical social order to produce harmony by performing "selfless service to the nation" (Golwalkar 1968, 48). According to this moral logic, inequalities are seen as natural and as derived from differentiated duties and "Citizenship shall be defined by selfless service and sacrifice, not by individual rights and interests" (Basu 2020, 32). Discussing the Hindutva ideologue Deendayal Upadhyaya, whose philosophy of "integral humanism" has been adopted by the BJP, his RSS biographer, C.P. Bhishikar (2014, 202) wrote: "Even though slogans of equality are raised in the modern world, the concept of equality has to be accepted with discretion." "Considerable bitterness," Bhishikar argued, "could be avoided" by adopting "the idea of equality as conceived by Hindu thinkers" according to which "if men have different qualities and different kinds of duties allotted to them according to their qualities or aptitudes, all duties are equally dignified. This is called *swadharma*, and there is an unequivocal assurance that to follow *swadharma* is itself equivalent to the worship of God."

Moral-Market Logics: Duties as Personal Responsibility

The BJP's authoritarian populist politics articulates a moral logic of duties over rights with a market logic associated with personal responsibility. This is the idea that citizens should engage with the market rather than rely on the state. This is deemed to be the best means of self-sufficiency and efficient, non-corrupt resource allocation. The melding of markets and morals is not unique to the BJP; it is a key feature of neoliberal thought and practice. The foundational neoliberal thought of Friedrich Hayek and ordoliberals like Wilhelm Röpke combined ideals of market rationality with conservative moralism which valorized traditional social hierarchies of gender, race, and class, and authority structures (Whyte 2019). For Hayek, conservative morals and markets epitomized the value of freedom because they had spontaneously evolved. The inequality produced by market competition and the upholding of traditional hierarchies was, therefore, necessary for political freedom (Brown 2019, 96). In the implementation of neoliberal policies, conservative morals have helped to enforce the market reform of the state and the household by emphasizing the inculcation of personal responsibility in individuals, legitimizing the inequalities produced by markets, and facilitating privatized social reproduction (Chacko 2023). Behavioral science research has also found a link between neoliberal beliefs about meritocracy and economic freedom and acceptance of social hierarchy at both the individual and societal levels (Bettache et al. 2020).

Neoliberalism as a development discourse propagated by international institutions, such as the World Bank, has influenced Indian political leaders and bureaucrats. Neoliberal concepts like good governance and austerity, are melded with Indian philosophies to justify inequality (Chacko 2023). In a 2010 speech, when he was chief minister of Gujarat, Modi (2010) equated good governance with "self-discipline" and "making people responsible" but tied it to lessons from ancient Hindu texts, noting "good governance cannot be apolitical" but must be a part of a political program. In India, "'Suraj' (Good Governance) or 'Sushashan' (good administration) is not new to us as we Indians have been hearing the concept of 'Ram Rajya' since our childhood days . . . the concept of Ram Rajya and the advice given by Lord Krishan to Arjuna in Gita is only about good governance." He hailed the "changing role of the government from being a provider to facilitator through the 'private-public partnership model and public-citizen partnership models'" and identified good governance as "our weapon in the fight against fissiparous tendencies, both within and without, to destablise the country." As Ambedkar (2014, 127–28) pointed out, however, governance in these texts is concerned with the maintenance of the inequality of the caste order through the performance of prescribed duties.

The defense of economic inequality based on the need for a social hierarchy is apparent in recent comments by Indian leaders. Modi's (quoted in Mukul 2024) conception of development is anti-political; it is influenced by his organicist Hindutva ideology and mirrors the varna social order: "For me, it should be the money of the capitalist, the brain of management and the sweat of hard workers. And, only then, development takes place . . . I see all three as a family." Asked to comment on India's growing income inequality, Modi (quoted in Mukul 2024) replied that the choice was between everyone being poor and income inequality. "Wealth creators," he said, should be respected, "Some will come, they will bring those who are below. Those who will come a little higher, they will pull up others. So there is a process." Modi's appointee as chair of the Finance Commission, neoliberal economist Arvind Panagariya, who is not a proponent of Hindutva, nonetheless deploys a complementary economic logic for inequality acceptance, arguing that "in a developing country, fighting poverty trumps the pursuit of equality. Poverty reduction, in turn, requires wealth creation" (Panagariya 2024). Moreover, "inequality elicits little opprobrium from the masses," he argues, because they care more about poverty and immediate social context.

Cultural and Group Logics of Acceptance for Economic Inequality

Moral-market logics of acceptance of economic inequality have combined with cultural and group-based logics of acceptance to shape the government's social and economic policies in ways that target and impact particular groups such as women, lower castes, and Muslims, taking advantage of existing social inequalities.

Sacrificing Women

Women, for instance, have been assiduously cultivated as voters and economic contributors by Modi. Traditional gender norms are common in India and facilitate gender inequality. A recent Pew survey, for example, found that 87% of respondents agreed that wives should obey their husbands, while 80% agreed that men have more rights to jobs than women in times of job scarcity (Pew Research Center 2022). Female labor force participation in India is particularly low and has fallen as the economy has grown. This has been attributed to deficient state services such as piped water, healthcare, and education, and gendered social norms which mean that women are responsible for the unpaid work in their households and communities, which increases without adequate state services (Chatterjee and Sircar 2021; Costagliola 2021; Singh and Pattanaik 2020).

Instead of addressing these structural issues, however, the BJP-led government has reinforced these social norms, deploying a moral-market logic of acceptance, to define women primarily in relation to their familial duties, while additionally appealing to them to be productive workers for the nation. Modi frequently refers to women as mothers, sisters, and daughters in his speeches and cites "women's empowerment" as a priority for his government. He has targeted women with welfare "gifts" that are designed to encourage market participation and precarious forms of home-based entrepreneurship (Chacko 2020; Dutta 2024; Qureshi 2015).

Caste Pride

While the philosophy of *swadharma* associated with the textual varna caste order is the basis for the BJP's moral logic for the acceptance of economic inequality, caste discrimination is also a pervasive practice in Indian society, crossing religious lines, and is reproduced through endogamy, religious and ritual practices, and educational and social networks. Caste presents a dilemma for the organicist nationalism of Hindutva because it is a source of stratification and disunity. Hindutva's founders, leaders, and core supporters are predominantly upper caste, and upper caste social norms related to Brahminical cosmology provide its foundation. This presents a barrier to attracting a broad cross-caste electoral base. Some Hindutva leaders have sought to defend caste hierarchies as natural or divert blame onto British colonizers or Islamic invaders for distorting it from an ancient merit-based system into a system of rigid hierarchy. More commonly, they promote notions of caste equality through self-improvement and caste pride, however, which reduce caste to a depoliticized cultural or occupational preference while obscuring and reinforcing its symbolic and material hierarchical essence (Barua and Vasanthakumar 2024; Natrajan 2022).

Undeserving Muslims

Muslims are the poorest religious group in India with the lowest levels of asset ownership and consumption. Research has shown that even upper-caste Muslims (the all-pervasive caste system is also practiced by non-Hindus) have incomes that are lower than Hindu OBCs. This reflects their lower educational levels and employment in the informal sector and low and declining rates of intergenerational mobility (Asher et al. 2022; Jha and Kishore 2023). The 2006 Sachar Committee report commissioned by the previous Congress government to study the social, economic, and educational status of Muslims found that the community suffers significant social and institutional discrimination and marginalization with underrepresentation in the bureaucracy, a lack of access to public services, good quality education, housing discrimination, and segregation (PMHLC 2006). Later studies have confirmed the persistence of these findings, with Muslims faring worse in several indicators, such as education, than Dalits and Adivasis (Adukia et al. 2022; Jaffrelot and Kalaiyarasan 2023).

Muslim marginalization and discrimination have historical roots, with the migration of Muslim elites to Pakistan after the partition of British India and the divisive legacies of partition violence, particularly in Northern India. However, Muslim marginalization and discrimination have intensified since the election of the BJP government in 2014. In Hindutva organicist nationalism, the *swadharma* (or duty of Indians) is complete religious and territorial identification with the "land of the Hindus" (Savarkar 1969, 111). This means that Indians who subscribe to other religions like Islam or Christianity cease to perform their duties—"their love is divided," wrote the Hindutva ideologue V.D. Savarkar (1969, 113) in his founding text—and become potential "antinational" threats who are undeserving of state aid. This serves the purpose of creating a diversion from the caste conflicts that divide Hindus, building intra-group cohesion against an externalized enemy (Shani 2007). In its election campaigns, the BJP has long invoked the "appeasement" of Muslims by opposition parties and the threat posed by Muslims to the Hindu poor. For instance, the Ranganath Misra Commission recommendation in 2010 to introduce reservations for Muslims and Christians (many of whom also suffer from disadvantage) in government jobs and educational institutions was resisted by Hindu nationalist organizations as "antinational," "appeasement," and "vote-bank" politics that would result in reducing the share of reservation for Hindu OBCs leading to "civil war" and conversions of low caste Hindus to Islam and Christianity (Rahman 2010).[2]

Facilitating Logics of Acceptance for Economic Inequality: Populist Institutional Disintermediation

Institutional disintermediation supports logics of acceptance for inequality curtailing avenues for contestation. Modi, as a populist leader exercising his duties, has sought to portray himself as a representative of God who embodied the common people and was sent to rescue the poor and restore India's (Hindu) civilizational greatness (Bajpaee 2023; Modi 2019; *News 18* 2024). Those who access welfare programs are termed *labharthis* (beneficiaries), and these private goods are presented as personally delivered by Modi, sometimes as "gifts" or "guarantees" of a better life. Welfare schemes are directly linked with Modi through the "Pradhan Mantri" (Prime Minister) prefix, his image adorns food ration bags and COVID vaccination certificates, and he refers to shops selling subsidized medicine as "Modi's medicine shops" (Modi 2023). Such "gifts" of everyday household goods are designed to establish intimacy and kinship while invoking gratitude from recipients (Martelli and Jaffrelot 2023, 1153). Modi's "guarantees" are meant to reassure those who have not received benefits that their time will come (Modi 2024). This "politics of *vishwas* [trust]," as Sircar (2020) notes, "engenders the centralisation of power." In his 2010 speech, Modi (2010) privileged "performance accountability" over "procedural accountability." While the latter involves "transparency," he argued, the former involves "people's participation" and "collective thinking" through technological initiatives like an online grievance system "that helps common people to meet me and seek redressal of their grievances once a month."

This populist authority structure has also led to the delegitimization of intermediary institutions that are meant to ameliorate social and economic inequality. Using a populist corrupt elite/beleaguered people discourse, Modi (2010) has claimed that instruments of procedural accountability like the Right to Information (RTI) Act, "more often used by middlemen and vested interests to harass administration rather than by the genuine and needy," would be made redundant. Likewise, invoking a populist conception of corrupt elites, he (2010) questioned the role of "non-state actors such as NGOs, and voluntary agencies and activists," noting that, though international funding agencies and nongovernmental organizations (NGOs) think good governance results from civil society activities, political parties were more important. In 2015, the government accused prominent NGOs of "using foreign funds for anti-national activities" (GOI 2015). The RTI Act was introduced in 2005 as the result of a grassroots rural protest movement that began in the 1990s to address the economic inequality resulting from the underpayment of wages on government projects and the diversion of government expenditure. While the aim of the Act was furthering economic equality, it also aligned with the neoliberal good governance agenda in which state transparency was necessary for markets to flourish (Sharma 2013). Under the Modi regime, amendments to the RTI Act have undermined the aim of improving economic equality. The BJP government has diminished the independence of the commissioners and introduced a new data protection law that limits access to information in the name of privacy. These changes have increased the number of RTI rejections based on the right to privacy even when the information requested pertains to issues like the expenditure of public funds and inaction against corrupt officials (Bhalla 2023; Gandhi 2022).

Withholding data related to poverty and inequality and the co-optation of independent institutions also function as modes of populist institutional disintermediation, particularly since 2014, when the Modi government was elected, there has been a decline in both the availability and quality of economic data (Bharti et al. 2024). The withholding of economic data enables the delegitimization of news unfavorable to the government while preventing accurate analysis from intermediary institutions. India's highest court, the Supreme Court, under the BJP regime, has increasingly become an executive court, characterized by judicial evasion, whereby cases are delayed in ways that benefit the executive; the adoption of the language and moral logic of the executive; and basing judgments on "sealed covers," i.e., secret documents not made public or provided to petitioners (Bhatia 2023).

Logics and Acceptance in Social and Economic Policies

Logics of acceptance have been mobilized in social and economic policies that are touted as fair even though they impose hardship and result in inequalities. The implementation of these inequality-enhancing policies has been facilitated by institutional disintermediation and existing social hierarchies, exacerbating economic inequality.

Demonetization

On November 8, 2016, the Modi government enacted its demonetization policy, which invalidated the 500 and 1,000 rupee notes (86% of the currency in circulation). The policy was justified using a moral logic of duties, which was communicated through a populist discourse wherein "the people" are personified by Modi and pitted against corrupt elites and threatening minorities. Modi uses a populist political style to invoke emotional and religious-cultural intimacy with individuals, in a strategy of "mimesis" (Martelli and Jaffrelot 2023), which seeks to mirror everyday language and behavior, reducing the distance between the leader and led. Modi's populist mimesis, through its constant invocation of Hindu rituals and precepts, both naturalizes the conflation of India with Hindus and seeks to generate acceptance of policies that cause hardship. "I feel as much pain as you do," he (Modi 2016a) told listeners to his radio program, *Mann Ki Baat*. "But when a task is taken up with a noble objective, to realize a lofty intent, with a clear conscience, the countrymen stay firm courageously amidst all these trials and tribulations" (Modi 2016a). Demonetization was depicted by Modi as a "wonderful chance to serve our mother India and to take our country to new economic heights," a "historic rite of purification," as an "ongoing 'Yagna' [individual ritual sacrifice] against corruption [implicitly of elites], terrorism [implicitly by Muslims] & black money" and a "Mahayagya [prolonged ritual sacrifice for society] against black money and corruption" (Modi 2016a, 2016b; PTI News Agency 2016).

Demonetization was facilitated through an institutional context of disintermediation, with little consultation with government agencies or the Reserve Bank of India. The policy was announced revealed in a Gazette notification, announced by Modi in a speech and passed with an ordinance, which allowed the government to avoid parliamentary debate (Chacko 2018, 18). The coercive and sudden nature of demonetization was justified as necessary by government advisor and RSS leader S. Gurumurthy as an enforcement of duties: "[n]othing happens in India through persuasion which is why determined action by the government is justified"

(Kanwal 2016). After being touted as a remedy for corruption and terrorism, demonetization was promoted as a way to produce market efficiency by formalizing India's economy and to stop worker exploitation through the adoption of digital transactions and payment systems (Chacko 2018, 19). The government put the onus on individuals, in particular, young people, to lead this "*maha abhiyan* [great mission]" for a "cashless society" by teaching shopkeepers, the poor, and "ten families" how to make digital payments (Modi 2016b). Demonetization also served to grow local financial technology companies, like Paytm, which was promoted as a national provider. Following demonetization, Modi (2016a) announced a number of "gifts," such as lotteries with winnings deposited into bank accounts accessible only through digital payments.

The policy is widely regarded as a failure, since 90% of the currency was returned to banks through various types of money laundering. Despite evidence of some redistributive effects due to money laundering, a voluminous body of research has detailed the widespread and uneven forms of hardship caused by demonetization particularly to poor woman and the rural poor who experienced lower incomes, less work, and greater reliance on informal borrowing (Chanda and Cook 2022; Fouillet et al. 2021). Only 17% of rural areas, 27% of semi-urban areas, and 56% of metropolitan urban areas had access to ATMs, and many rural areas lacked a digital payments infrastructure (Fouillet et al. 2021). Paytm rapidly expanded into rural areas, benefiting from light government regulation which enabled the proliferation of online fraud (Dasgupta 2024). Housing segregation in areas with poor access to amenities meant that lower-caste Muslims and Dalits had particular challenges in accessing ATMs and digital payments. When this concern was pointed out by a Muslim leader, Asaduddin Owaisi, it was dismissed by government officials as "divisive" and dishonest, highlighting Muslims' status as an undeserving poor (Jagannathan et al. 2018, 974). As a Muslim worker in the scrap metal trade put it: "We cannot protest. If we protest, the government tells us, go to Pakistan. Why are you people there in India?" (Jagannathan et al. 2018, 980). Studies have shown that digitalization during demonetization led to a loss of control of household finances among women, exposing money hidden from abusive husbands (Guérin et al. 2017, 49). Dalits reported a lack of access to credit due to their caste status in the aftermath of demonetization and having to work for months without wages (Jagannathan et al. 2018, 977).

Demonetization was immediately challenged in courts by numerous petitioners who raised concerns about procedure, proportionality, and constitutionality. The Supreme Court appointed a five-judge bench, which after six years of delays, on January 2, 2023, ruled in favor of the government based on secret documents that were provided to the court after the hearing was completed. The majority judgment dismissed the hardships suffered by citizens by observing that if "a few individuals suffer severe hardship, that cannot be helped . . . individual interests must yield to the larger interests of the community or the country as indeed every noble cause claims its martyr" (Supreme Court of India 2023, 216).

Social Policy

The government's approach to welfare has been minimal, compensatory, and aimed at facilitating market participation in the absence of universal public goods and good quality employment (Chacko 2019b, 2020; Roy 2019). This "new welfarism" (Anand et al. 2020) has largely consisted of subsidies for the purchase of goods from the private sector like toilets, bank accounts, cooking gas, and insurance, as well as bank accounts and microcredit to facilitate financial inclusion and entrepreneurship, rather than spending on universal public goods like health and education. This approach has been presented as superior to previous programs, which were marked by elite corruption. Yet, their limited nature means considerable onus is placed on personal duty to pursue "empowerment" through market participation. This is consistent with Hindutva's emphasis on *swadharma* for the upholding of social order rather than social transformation. As expressed by the Home Minister, Amit Shah: "we have given gas connections, power connections and it's up to them to pay their bills. We have made toilets for them but they have to maintain them. . . . What we did was to provide help to upgrade their lives—this is empowerment. This triggered aspirations too" (quoted in Mathew et al. 2022).

In line with its focus on poverty reduction rather than inequality, a government discussion paper has sought to create a national multidimensional poverty index measuring health, education, and access to private goods like sanitation and cooking gas as indicators, to claim that 248 million Indians have been pulled out of poverty. Aside from using problematic methodology involving data projections, the paper eschews previous methods of calculating poverty estimates using consumption expenditure data, which, though collected in 2017–18, was withheld on the basis that it was poor in quality. Leaked data from this survey revealed that consumption among the poor had fallen, suggesting an increase in poverty after demonetization (Sinha 2024).

Consistent with populist strategies of disintermediation, the use of direct benefit transfers (DBTs) for the provision of cash transfers and subsidies for the purchase of private goods enables "techno-patrimonialism." The provision of welfare benefits is linked to Modi as the beneficent leader and is said to have ended "leakages" (the siphoning off resources to middlemen), facilitated greater monitoring via a digital public infrastructure (through, for instance, apps, GPS mapping, biometric monitoring, and digital dashboards), and enabled "faceless" governance for fairer outcomes (Aiyar 2023; *The Wire* 2023b). Studies have shown, however, that significant exclusions have arisen due to India's digitized and financialized welfare system and other practices of disintermediation. For instance, the DBT system has resulted in exclusions of poor households due to network, equipment, authentication, and biometric failures. One survey found that during the COVID pandemic, 40% of households faced such issues when trying to withdraw welfare payments (Gupta et al. 2022). Another survey revealed that incomplete coverage of the national bank account scheme, unlinked biometric numbers, and lack of access to banks and ATMs meant that many did not receive cash transfers (Guérin et al. 2021b). Moreover, under the DBT system, recipients are partially reimbursed for the purchase of private goods which disadvantages those with low incomes (Gupta 2022).

Moreover, despite its claims of "faceless" governance, digital public infrastructure still relies on NGOs to enroll recipients into schemes, like the biometric identity program, Aadhar, which is necessary for accessing welfare schemes, using various community identification documents. Poor internal migrant workers, in particular, struggle to provide the documents, worsening preexisting exclusions (Baxi 2019). The government's hostility to transnational NGOs has resulted in major organizations like Save the Children and Oxfam, and thousands of Indian NGOs, losing access to foreign funding since Modi's election in 2014. They are alleged to have violated the Foreign Contribution (Regulation) Act, which was further tightened in 2020 (Chander 2022). These NGOs performed critical service delivery and relief work, filling gaps in government services, and provided thousands of jobs.

During the COVID pandemic, these additional regulations led to delays in the distribution of essential medical aid like oxygen concentrators (Kotecha 2021).

The COVID pandemic lockdown was accompanied by limited increases in social spending for healthcare and welfare, which left the public health system underprepared and India's largely informal workforce without adequate incomes for many months. Instead, the government's COVID welfare package included an increased amount of food rations, several free cooking gas refills, small cash transfers, and an expansion of the MGNREGA workfare scheme. This approach to social policy provided partial and temporary relief contributing to growing economic inequalities. For instance, a World Bank report, which was withdrawn following government pressure, found the use of toilets in rural India has declined from 87% in 2018–19 to 75% in 2020–21, particularly among Dalits and Adivasis, for reasons of cost, poor infrastructural support, and water supply (Barman 2023). The lack of affordability of gas cylinders means that the exclusive use of cooking gas over polluting biomass remains low in poor rural households (Chindarkar et al. 2021). Despite its expansion during COVID, the MGNREGA remained underfunded, providing less than two weeks of work per household (Narayanan et al. 2022). The national health insurance scheme is likewise underresourced with a high rate of rejections for health insurance claims (Barnagarwala 2024). The limited nature of additional social protection provided during the pandemic, moreover, meant that many turned to emergency loans from microfinance institutions (MFIs) leading to significant increases in consumer debt. Despite being largely publicly funded, MFIs prioritized their financial stability over borrowers' capacities, exerting pressure to repay loans, including through technology-enabled credit scoring. This led to loan defaults, or alternatively, household sacrifices that included reducing food consumption and selling assets and means of production, and depression and suicide (Guérin, Guermond et al. 2021; Guérin, Joseph, et al. 2021).

During the pandemic, lower-caste women, in particular, faced challenges such as a lack of access to menstrual products (which were omitted from the list of essential products) (Babbar 2024), economic abuse (Chowbey 2023), and higher rates of domestic violence (Krishnakumar and Verma 2021). The share of women working in agriculture, self-employment, and as unpaid helpers increased significantly, regardless of education levels (Dhamija and Chawla 2023). Rather than addressing these issues, however,

Modi's speeches praised women's sacrifices in distributing COVID relief and sanitation. He also encouraged female entrepreneurship through the manufacturing of masks while cutting spending on gender-related programs (Kapoor and Sinha 2021; Modi 2020). While the government has reported an increase in expenditure on gender-based interventions from 5% in 2023–24 to 6.5% in 2024–25, the proportional allocation for schemes that have proven welfare and income benefits for women like MGNREGA and sanitation have stagnated or decreased while allocations have increased for schemes that have ambiguous benefits for women, such as subsidies for the purchases of houses and new entrepreneurship schemes like the National Rural Livelihoods Mission (McNabb 2023; Rana 2024).

Consistent with its logics and institutional strategies of inequality acceptance, Modi has sought to obscure caste as an ongoing instrument of social oppression by rhetorically replacing the fourfold varna system in his speeches with the "four major castes" of women, youth, farmers, and poor families, whom he claims to be rescuing through his schemes by making them "empowered" market actors who will contribute to national empowerment (Modi 2023). These strategies obscure the role of caste in facilitating economic inequality in markets by, for instance, enabling opportunity hoarding for upper castes and lower-caste exclusion and occupational ranking (Mosse 2018). Government policies reflect these attempts to obscure caste-based oppression. Social spending on Dalits and Advasis has consistently declined (Mohan 2024; Teltumbde 2020, xix, xxxviii). At the same time, contemporary government documents draw on notions of caste pride to reinforce caste-based practices, recommending drawing on "mythological insights" about "caste equality" to promote a "sense of sacrifice, empathy and humility to serve the needs of other people" (Government of India 2019, 44). Entrepreneurship initiatives related to traditional caste occupations, like the Swachhta Udyami Yojana and the Sanitary Mart, have also been introduced. These provide low-interest loans to Dalits to build cleaning-based businesses, entrenching caste and its links to ritual purity (Gudavarthy and Vijay 2020, 475).

While overt welfare chauvinism, whereby group logics lead to welfare exclusion, is not evident in India, the treatment of Muslims as an undeserving poor has manifested in other areas of social policy. For example, BJP leaders have blamed Muslim educational disadvantage on the low quality of Muslim institutions (madrasas), which they claim only teach religion (which is not the case) (Saikia 2020). The BJP government in

Assam has derecognized madrasas as educational providers and demolished madrasas accused of having "jihadi" (violent Islamist extremist) links (The Hindu Bureau 2022; Sitlhou 2021). The BJP state government in Uttar Pradesh ended the payment of honorariums to madrasa teachers employed to teach nonreligious subjects. A high court in Uttar Pradesh recently struck down the Madrasa Act, claiming a violation of constitutional secularism, potentially threatening the employment of thousands of teachers and the education of millions of students (Rashid 2024; Sharma and Das 2024). Adopting the government's rhetoric, the high court suggested that Muslim unemployment was due to deficient madrasa religion-based education (Rashid 2024). Moreover, in northern Indian states, like Madhya Pradesh, Uttar Pradesh, and Haryana, BJP governments have exacerbated Muslim income and housing insecurity through the demolition of the houses of Muslims accused of involvement in protests against the discriminatory Citizenship Amendment Act, and by encouraging economic boycotts of Muslim businesses and Muslim workers (Lalwani 2022; Raj 2023).

Conclusion

Inequality has been a persistent and entrenched feature of Indian society. This chapter has argued that whereas previous governments have sought, with varying degrees of success, to address the economic and social disadvantage faced by Muslims, women, Dalits, and Adivasis through a rhetorical commitment to equality and state intervention in the forms of policies like reservation for oppressed castes, India's current government is distinctive because it ideologically enshrines inequality and mobilizes social acceptance for inequality through institutional disintermediation and its economic and social policies.

Aside from the survey data mentioned at the beginning of the chapter, the BJP's repeated election victories, ethnographic studies, voter surveys, and news reports indicate the rhetorical and institutional strategies the government has adopted to foster social acceptance of inequality appear to have been somewhat effective, though this needs more in-depth research. News reports indicated support among the poor for demonetization based on the punishment it promised the rich and Modi's good intentions (Jha 2021). They also provide evidence of trust in Modi among the poor to eventually deliver employment and welfare goods (Menon 2021; MN 2020). Voter surveys revealed limited damage to Modi's popularity during the COVID pandemic, and ethnographic studies report rising anti-Muslim sentiment (Mathur 2023; Mukherjee 2020; Sinha and Priyam 2023).

The outcome of India's 2024 national election, however, suggests that the effects of inequality-enhancing policies will eventually diminish this acceptance. While the government was re-elected, the BJP lost its majority, losing support in key states among lower-caste voters and women (Deshpande 2024). Post-election surveys indicate that the key issues for voters were inflation and unemployment, and that personal financial conditions, which the majority of respondents felt had deteriorated, influenced voting choices (Alam 2024). Moreover, the opposition alliance made growing inequality—namely wealth concentration and the government's potential revocation of caste-based affirmative action—a major aspect of its election campaign. The rise of social acceptance for inequality, therefore, may ultimately portend a more profound rejection of a politics of inequality once the effects are apparent. While this chapter has not sought to prove a connection between the apparent fluctuations in social acceptance of inequality and the rise of a politics of inequality, their emergence in same period suggests the need for greater investigation.

Notes

1. "Caste" is a dynamic social institution with economic, political, and cultural elements. "Tribes" in an Indian context are also known as Adivasis (original inhabitants) or Scheduled Tribes and refer to those who originally resided in forest and mountain regions. Along with Dalits (downtrodden) or Scheduled Castes, Adivasis were considered to be apart from and therefore at the bottom of the caste-based social order. "Other Backward Class" is a term used in the Constitution to refer to mid- and lower-caste Hindus.
2. The transfer of resources from poor Hindus to Muslims by the opposition was a prominent theme in the BJP's 2024 election campaign.

References

Adukia A., S. Asher, K. Jha, P. Novosad, and B. Tan. 2022. "Residential Segregation and Unequal Access to Local Public Services in India: Evidence from 1.5 m Neighborhoods." Indian Statistical Institute, Delhi Centre. https://www.isid.ac.in/~epu/acegd2022/papers/Sam_Asher.pdf.

Ahmed A., S. Sharma, and J. Dash. 2024. "Insight: World-Beating Growth? Not for India's Rural Majority." *Reuters*, January 31. https://www.reuters.com/world/india/world-beating-growth-not-indias-rural-majority-2024-01-31/.

Aiyar, Y. 2023. "Citizen vs Labharthi? Interrogating the Contours of India's Emergent Welfare State." *The India Forum*, December 5. https://www.theindiaforum.in/public-policy/citizen-vs-labharthi.

Alam, S. 2024. "CSDS-Lokniti Post-Poll Survey: Personal Financial Conditions Played Key Role in Voting Choice." *The Hindu*, June 6. https://www.thehindu.com/elections/csds-lokniti-post-poll-survey-personal-financial-conditions-played-key-role-in-voting-choice/article68255516.ece.

Ali, A. 2010. "The Sachar Committee Report and Multiculturalism in India: Questions of Group Equality and the Public Sphere." In *Religion, Community and Development: Changing Contours of Politics and Policy in India*, edited by G. Mahajan and S.S. Jodhka, pp. 77–94. New Delhi: Routledge.

Ambedkar, B.R. 2014. *Annihilation of Caste: The Annotated Critical Edition*. New York: Verso Books.

Anand, A., V. Dimble, and A. Subramanian. 2020. "New Welfarism of Modi Govt Represents Distinctive Approach to Redistribution and Inclusion." *Indian Express*, December 22. https://indianexpress.com/article/opinion/columns/national-family-health-survey-new-welfarism-of-indias-right-7114104/.

Anand, I., and R. Kumar. 2023. "The Sky and the Stratosphere: Wealth Concentration in India During the Last (Lost) Decade." *The Review of Income and Wealth*. https://doi.org/10.1111/roiw.12661.

Asher, S., P. Novosad, and C. Rafkin. 2022. "Intergenerational Mobility in India: New Measures and Estimates Across Time and Social Groups." G2LM LIC Working Paper No. 66.

Azim Premji University. 2021. *State of Working India 2021: One Year of COVID-19*. Bengaluru: Centre for Sustainable Employment, Azim Premji University.

Azim Premji University. 2023. *State of Working India: Social and Labour Market Outcomes*. Bengaluru: Centre for Sustainable Employment, Azim Premji University.

Babbar, K. 2024. "How India's COVID Lockdowns Impacted Menstrual Health." *The Wire*, February 5. https://thewire.in/health/how-indias-covid-lockdowns-impacted-menstrual-health.

Bajpaee, C. 2023. "Modi's India Has Become Less Liberal but Better Governed." *The World Today*, December 1. Chatham House. https://www.chathamhouse.org/publications/the-world-today/2023-12/modis-india-has-become-less-liberal-better-governed.

Barman, S.R. 2023. "World Bank Papers Show 'Most Concerning' Decline in Toilet Usage. Withdrawn 'Under Pressure' Later." *The Print*, December 1. https://theprint.in/india/governance/world-bank-papers-show-most-concerning-decline-in-toilet-usage-withdrawn-under-pressure-later/1866108/.

Barnagarwala, T. 2024. "Modi Government's Insurance Scheme Pushes Hospitals into Debt—Threatening Patient Admissions." *Scroll.in*, March 11. https://scroll.in/article/1064819/modi-governments-insurance-scheme-pushes-hospitals-into-debt-threatening-patient-admissions.

Barua, A., and V. Vasanthakumar. 2024. "Renaming Caste, Retaining Privilege." *The India Forum*, June 15. https://www.theindiaforum.in/caste/renaming-caste-retaining-privilege.

Basu, A. 2020. *Hindutva as Political Monotheism*. Durham, NC: Duke University Press.

Baxi, P. 2019. "Technologies of Disintermediation in a Mediated State: Civil Society Organisations and India's Aadhaar Project." *South Asia* 42 (3): pp. 554–571.

Bettache, K., C.-Y. Chiu, and P. Beattie. 2020. "The Merciless Mind in a Dog-Eat-Dog Society: Neoliberalism and the Indifference to Social Inequality." *Current Opinion in Behavioral Sciences* 34: pp. 217–222.

Bhalla, V. 2023. "How Modi Government Is Using Data Privacy as an Excuse to Cripple the Right to Information." *Scroll.in*, August 2. https://scroll.in/article/1053514/how-modi-government-is-using-privacy-as-an-excuse-to-cripple-the-right-to-information.

Bharti, N.K., L. Chancel, T. Piketty, and A. Somanchi. 2024. "Income and Wealth Inequality in India, 1922–2023: The Rise of the Billionaire Raj." World Inequality Lab Working Paper 2024/09.

Bhatia, G. 2023. *Unsealed Covers: A Decade of the Constitution, the Courts and the State*. New York: HarperCollins.

Bhatt, C. 2001. *Hindu Nationalism: Origins, Ideologies and Modern Myths*. Oxford: Berg.

Bhishikar, C. P. 2014. *Pandit Deendayal Upadhyaya, Ideology and Perception: Volume 5—Concept of the Rashtra*. 2nd ed. New Delhi: Suruchi Prakashan.

Brown, W. 2019. *In the Ruins of Neoliberalism: The Rise of Anti-Democratic Politics in the West.* New York: Columbia University Press.

Chacko, P. 2023. "Disciplining India: Paternalism, Neo-Liberalism and Hindutva Civilizationalism." *International Affairs* 99 (2): pp. 551–565.

Chacko, P. 2019a. Emerging Regimes of Market Citizenship: The Politics of Social Policy in Contemporary India. In *Changing Contexts and Shifting Roles of the Indian State: New Perspectives on Development Dynamics,* edited by A.P. D'Costa and A. Chakraborty, pp. 39–55. Singapore: Springer.

Chacko, P. 2020. "Gender and Authoritarian Populism: Empowerment, Protection, and the Politics of Resentful Aspiration in India." *Critical Asian Studies* 52 (2): pp. 204–225.

Chacko, P. 2019b. "Marketizing Hindutva: The State, Society, and Markets in Hindu Nationalism." *Modern Asian Studies* 53 (2): pp. 377–410.

Chacko, P. 2018. "The Right Turn in India: Authoritarianism, Populism and Neoliberalisation." *Journal of Contemporary Asia* 48 (4): pp. 541–565.

Chancel, L., T. Piketty, E. Saez, and G. Zucman. 2022. *World Inequality Report 2022.* World Inequality Lab. https://wir2022.wid.world/.

Chanda, A., and C.J. Cook. 2022 "Was India's Demonetization Redistributive? Insights from Satellites and Surveys. *Journal of Macroeconomics* 73: 103438.

Chander, M. 2022. "An Arbitrary Crackdown on Foreign Donations Cripples NGOs at a Time When India Needs Them Most." *Article 14,* January 22. https://article-14.com/post/an-arbitrary-crackdown-on-foreign-donations-cripples-ngos-at-a-time-when-india-needs-them-most-61f20bac480a9.

Chatterjee, D., and N. Sircar. 2021. "Why Is Female Labour Force Participation So Low in India?" *Urbanisation* 6 (1_suppl): pp. S40–S57.

Chindarkar, N., A. Jain, and S. Mani. 2021. "Examining the Willingness-to-Pay for Exclusive Use of LPG for Cooking Among Rural Households in India." *Energy Policy* 150: 112107.

Chiriyankandath, J., D. Maoirano, J. Manor, and L. Tillin. 2019. *The Politics of Poverty Reduction in India: The UPA Government, 2004 to 2014.* Hyderabad: Orient BlackSwan.

Chowbey, P. 2023. "India: How COVID Enabled New Forms of Economic Abuse of Women." *The Conversation,* November 24. https://theconversation.com/india-how-covid-enabled-new-forms-of-economic-abuse-of-women-212822.

Costagliola, A. 2021. "Labor Participation and Gender Inequalities in India: Traditional Gender Norms in India and the Decline in the Labor Force Participation Rate (LFPR)." *Indian Journal of Labour Economics* 64 (3): pp. 531–542.

Dasgupta, D. 2024. "India's Fintech Star Paytm Totters After Being Hauled Up for Lapses, Prompting Industry Concerns." *The Straits Times,* February 19. https://www.straitstimes.com/asia/south-asia/india-s-fintech-star-paytm-totters-after-being-hauled-up-for-lapses-prompting-industry-concerns.

Deshpande, R. 2024. "CSDS-Lokniti Post-Poll Survey: BJP's Sustained Loss in Women's Vote." *The Hindu,* June 9. https://www.thehindu.com/elections/lok-sabha/csds-lokniti-post-poll-survey-bjps-sustained-loss-in-womens-vote/article68260486.ece.

Devji, F. 2012. *The Impossible Indian: Gandhi and the Temptation of Violence.* London: Hurst & Co.

Dhamija, D., and A. Chawla. 2023. *Decoding Women's Labour Force Participation in 2021–22: What the Periodic Labour Force Survey Shows.* Centre for Data & Economic Analysis. March 20. https://ceda.ashoka.edu.in/decoding-womens-labour-force-participation-in-2021-22-what-the-periodic-labour-force-survey-shows/.

Dutta, S. 2024. "PM Modi's Women's Day 'Gift': Rs 100 Cut in Domestic LPG Prices." *Times of India,* March 8. https://timesofindia.indiatimes.com/business/india-business/pm-modis-womens-day-gift-rs-100-cut-in-domestic-lpg-prices/articleshow/108334195.cms.

Fouillet, C., I. Guérin, and J.-M. Servet. 2021. "Demonetization and Digitalization: The Indian Government's Hidden Agenda." *Telecommunications Policy* 45 (2): p. 102079.

Gandhi, S. 2022. "How a Flawed Interpretation of the RTI Act Is Being Used to Protect Corrupt Officials." *Scroll.in*, September 19. https://scroll.in/article/1031322/how-a-flawed-interpretation-of-the-rti-act-is-being-used-to-protect-corrupt-officials.

Golwalkar, M.S. 1968. *Bunch of Thoughts*. Bangalore: Vikrama Prakashana.

Government of India (GOI). 2019. *Economic Survey 2018–2019*. New Delhi: Government of India.

Government of India (GOI). 2015. *NGOs Using Foreign Funds for Anti-National Activities*. http://pib.nic.in/newsite/PrintRelease.aspx?relid=116430.

Gudavarthy, A., and G. Vijay. 2020. "Social Policy and Political Mobilization in India: Producing Hierarchical Fraternity and Polarized Differences." *Development and Change* 51 (2): pp. 463–484.

Guérin, I., V. Guermond, N. Joseph, N. Natarajan, and G. Venkatasubramanian. 2021. "COVID-19 and the Unequalizing Infrastructures of Financial Inclusion in Tamil Nadu." *Development and Change* 52 (4): pp. 927–951.

Guérin I, N. Joseph, and G. Venkatasubramanian. 2021. "How India's Financial Inclusion Infrastructure Failed During the Pandemic." *The Wire*, June 23. https://thewire.in/economy/how-indias-financial-inclusion-infrastructure-failed-during-the-pandemic.

Guérin, I., Y. Lanos, S. Michiels, and C.J. Nordman. 2017. "Insights on Demonetisation from Rural Tamil Nadu: Understanding Social Networks and Social Protection." *Economic and Political Weekly* 52 (52): pp. 44–53.

Gupta, A., I. Ghosh, and S. Hussain. 2022. "What Two New Surveys Say About the State of DBT's Last Mile Woes." *The Wire*, April 7. https://thewire.in/economy/two-surveys-dbt-schemes-last-mile-woes.

Gupta, V. 2022. "Since 2016, PMUY Beneficiaries Consuming Less LPG Than Non-Ujjwala Consumers: RTI Data." *The Wire*, October 5. https://thewire.in/government/pm-ujjwala-scheme-beneficiaries-consuming-less-lpg-rti-data.

Haerpfer, C., R. Inglehart, A. Moreno, C. Welzel, K. Kizilova, J. Diez-Medrano, M. Lagos, P. Norris, E. Ponarin, and B. Puranen. Eds. 2022. World Values Survey: Round Seven—Country-Pooled Datafile Version 6.0. Madrid, Spain & Vienna, Austria: JD Systems Institute & WVSA Secretariat. https://doi.org/0.14281/18241.24.

The Hindu Bureau. 2022. "Probe Madrasa Demolition: Assam Congress to NCM." *The Hindu*, September 6. https://www.thehindu.com/news/national/other-states/assam-madrasa-demolition-congress-writes-to-national-commission-for-minorities-seeks-probe/article65856048.ece.

Inglehart, R., C. Haerpfer, A. Moreno, C. Welzel, K. Kizilova, J. Diez-Medrano, M. Lagos, P. Norris, E. Ponarin, B. Puranen, et al. Eds. 2014. World Values Survey: Round Six—Country-Pooled Datafile Version. www.worldvaluessurvey.org/WVSDocumentationWV6.jsp. Madrid: JD Systems Institute.

Jaffrelot, C. 1996. *Hindu Nationalist Movement and Indian Politics: 1925 to the 1990s*. London: Hurst and Co.

Jaffrelot, C. 2021. *Modi's India: Hindu Nationalism and the Rise of Ethnic Democracy*. Princeton, NJ: Princeton University Press.

Jaffrelot, C., and A. Kalaiyarasan. 2023. "Indian Muslims: Varieties of Discriminations and What Affirmative Action Can Do." In *Handbook on Economics of Discrimination and Affirmative Action*, edited by A. Deshpande, pp. 543–564. Singapore: Springer.

Jagannathan, S., P. Packirisamy, and J. Joseph. 2018. "Worlds of Demonetisation and Delegitimising the Grief of the Marginal." *Journal of Marketing Management* 34 (11–12): pp. 965–988.

Jha, A., and R. Kishore. 2023. "Muslims Are the Poorest Religious Group in India." *Hindustan Times*, June 30. https://www.hindustantimes.com/india-news/muslims-in-india-the-

poorest-religious-group-with-high-inequality-and-limited-opportunities-data-analysis-reveals-101688097160955.html.
Jha. P. 2021. "5 years of Demonetisation: Understanding the Political Impact of Note Ban." *Hindustan Times*, November 8. https://www.hindustantimes.com/india-news/five-years-of-demonetisation-understanding-the-political-impact-of-note-ban-101636310630497.html.
Kanwal, R. 2016. "New Rs 2,000 Notes to Be Phased Out Within 5 Years, Says RSS Ideologue Gurumurthy." *India Today*, December 12. https://www.indiatoday.in/india/story/2000-notes-new-currency-phased-out-rss-demonetisation-note-ban-357084-2016-12-12.
Kapoor, A., and H. Sinha. 2021. "View: Assessing India's Gender Budget." *Economic Times*, February 14. https://economictimes.indiatimes.com/news/economy/policy/view-assessing-indias-gender-budget/articleshow/80906668.cms?utm_source=contentofinterest&utm_medium=text&utm_campaign=cppst.
Kochar, R. 2021. "In the Pandemic, India's Middle Class Shrinks and Poverty Spreads While China Sees Smaller Changes." Pew Research Center, March 18. https://www.pewresearch.org/short-reads/2021/03/18/in-the-pandemic-indias-middle-class-shrinks-and-poverty-spreads-while-china-sees-smaller-changes/.
Kotecha, S. 2021. "India Covid: How Law Stops NGOs Distributing Essential Aid." *BBC*, May 13. https://www.bbc.com/news/world-asia-india-57095591.
Krishnakumar, A., and S. Verma. 2021. "Understanding Domestic Violence in India During COVID-19: A Routine Activity Approach." *Asian Journal of Criminology* 16 (1): pp. 19–35.
Laclau, E. 2005. *On Populist Reason*. London: Verso.
Lalwani, V. 2022. "In a Riot-Torn MP Town, Hindus Organise an Economic Boycott of Muslims." *Article 14*, April 29. https://article-14.com/post/in-a-riot-torn-mp-town-hindus-organise-an-economic-boycott-of-muslims-626b0b188f64b.
Martelli, J.-T., and C. Jaffrelot. 2023. "Do Populist Leaders Mimic the Language of Ordinary Citizens? Evidence from India." *Political Psychology* 44 (5): pp. 1141–1160.
Marzia, C. 2000. "Hindutva's Foreign Tie-Up in the 1930s: Archival Evidence." *Economic and Political Weekly* 35 (4): pp. 218–228.
Mathew, L., P.V. Iyer, and R.K. Jha. 2022. "Amit Shah Interview: 'Anger Comes Out When People Do Not Have Confidence in Leadership . . . But People Have Confidence in PM Modi.'" *Indian Express*, March 1. https://indianexpress.com/elections/amit-shah-interview-uttar-pradesh-elections-pm-modi-bjp-7794992/.
Mathur, V. 2023. "'Modi'-fied Beliefs: Assessing Cognitive Dissonance in Populist Voting Behaviour in India." *South Asia: Journal of South Asian Studies* 46 (5): pp. 1–21.
McNabb, M. 2023. "Garuda Aerospace Accelerates IPO in Wake of 'Namo Drone Didi' Initiative." *Drone Life*, December 4. https://dronelife.com/2023/12/04/garuda-aerospace-accelerates-ipo-in-wake-of-namo-drone-didi-initiative/.
Menon, A. 2021. "Data Reveals the One Factor Causing Ups & Downs in Modi's Ratings." *The Quint*, May 28. https://www.thequint.com/news/politics/pm-narendra-modi-approval-rating-coronavirus-morning-consult-cvoter.
Mishra, J., S. Kumar, S. Shastri, and S. Palshikar. 2024. "Is Unemployment a Major Factor in Shaping the Vote Choice of the Youth?" *The Hindu*, March 27. https://www.thehindu.com/news/national/is-unemployment-a-major-factor-in-shaping-the-vote-choice-of-the-youth/article67995800.ece.
MN, P. 2020. "Travels Through the Hindi Belt: Bihar's Unemployed Keep Faith in Modi, Mainly Due to Lack of Credible Opposition." *Firstpost*, October 10. https://www.firstpost.com/politics/travels-through-the-hindi-belt-bihars-unemployed-keep-faith-in-narendra-modi-largely-due-to-absence-of-credible-opposition-face-6365131.html.
Modi, N. 2016a. "English Rendering of PM's 'Mann Ki Baat' Address on All India Radio." *PMINDIA*, November 27. http://www.pmindia.gov.in/en/news_updates/pms-mann-ki-baat-address-on-all-india-radio/?comment=disable.

Modi, N. 2016b. "English Rendering of PM's 'Mann Ki Baat' Address on All India Radio." *PMINDIA*, December 25. https://www.pmindia.gov.in/en/news_updates/pms-mann-ki-baat-address-on-all-india-radio-2/.

Modi, N. 2024. "PM Modi Live: Public Meeting in Parbhani, Maharashtra: Lok Sabha Election 2024." *YouTube*, April 20. 37:30. https://www.youtube.com/watch?v=QTBrK__pTxg.

Modi, N. 2022. "PM's Address at the Launch of 'Azadi Ke Amrit Mahotsav se Swarnim Bharat Ke Ore' Programme." *PMINDIA*, January 20. https://www.pmindia.gov.in/en/news_updates/pm-delivers-the-keynote-address-at-the-national-launch-ceremony-of-azadi-ke-amrit-mahotsav-se-swarnim-bharat-ke-ore/.

Modi, N. 2023. "PM's Address During His Interaction with Beneficiaries of Viksit Bharat Sankalp Yatra." *PMINDIA*, November 30. https://www.pmindia.gov.in/en/news_updates/pms-address-during-his-interaction-with-beneficiaries-of-viksit-bharat-sankalp-yatra/.

Modi, N. 2020. "PM's Address in the 14th Episode of 'Mann Ki Baat 2.0.'" *PMINDIA*, July 26. https://www.pmindia.gov.in/en/news_updates/pms-address-in-the-14th-episode-of-mann-ki-baat-2-0/.

Modi, N. 2010. "Shri Narendra Modi's Keynote Address at the 'Suraj Sankalp' National Convention." *Narendra Modi*, June 5. https://www.narendramodi.in/"suraj-sankalp"-national-convention-keynote-address-by-hon'ble-cm-2679.

Modi, N. 2019. "Swachh Bharat Mission Has Benefited the Poor and the Women Most: PM Modi." *Narendra Modi*, September 25. https://www.narendramodi.in/text-of-pm-modi-s-speech-at-goalkeepers-global-goal-award-2019-546603.

Mohan, D. 2024. "Interim Union Budget Follows Tradition of Modi Government's Apathy Towards Most Vulnerable." *The Wire*, February 1. https://thewire.in/economy/interim-union-budget-follows-tradition-of-modi-governments-apathy-towards-most-vulnerable.

Mosse, D. 2018. "Caste and Development: Contemporary Perspectives on a Structure of Discrimination and Advantage." *World Development* 110: pp. 422–436.

Mukherjee, S. 2020. "Hungry, with No Money, Yet Rural India Backs Modi Govt in COVID War: Study." *Business Standard*, August 1. https://www.business-standard.com/article/current-affairs/hungry-with-no-money-yet-rural-india-backs-modi-govt-in-covid-war-study-120081001107_1.html.

Mukul, S. 2024. "I Worry for Wealth Creators' Wealth Like I Do for Labourers' Sweat, Says PM Modi." *India Today*, May 16. https://www.indiatoday.in/elections/lok-sabha/story/pm-modi-exclusive-interview-bjp-on-capitalists-workers-sweat-labourers-all-combine-to-bring-development-says-pm-modi-2540084-2024-05-16.

Narayanan, S., C. Oldiges, and S. Saha. 2022. "Does Workfare Work? India's Employment Guarantee During COVID-19." *Journal of International Development* 34 (1): pp. 82–108.

Natrajan, B. 2022. "Racialization and Ethnicization: Hindutva Hegemony and Caste." *Ethnic and Racial Studies* 45 (2): pp. 298–318.

News 18. 2024. "Whatever I'm Doing Is Inspired by a Divine Power, God Has Sent Me to Do This Work: PM Modi." *News 18*, https://www.news18.com/elections/whatever-im-doing-is-inspired-by-a-divine-power-god-has-sent-me-to-do-this-work-pm-modi-8870459.html.

Oxfam India. 2022. *Inequality Kills: India Supplement 2022*. New Delhi: Oxfam India.

Panagariya, A. 2024. "Don't Lose Sleep over Inequality." *Times of India*, April 1. http://timesofindia.indiatimes.com/articleshow/108951692.cms?pcode=462&_gl=1*10rih2z*_ga*YW1wLXQ4QTRoUmxMM0dmSE02YzFQY1phMGc.&utm_source=contentofinterest&utm_medium=text&utm_campaign=cppst_prime.

Pew Research Center. 2022. "How Indians View Gender Roles in Families and Society." March 2. https://www.pewresearch.org/religion/2022/03/02/how-indians-view-gender-roles-in-families-and-society/#in-india-men-a-little-more-likely-than-women-to-have-conservative-views-on-gender.

Prime Minister's High-Level Committee (PMHLC). 2006. *Social, Economic and Educational Status of the Muslim Community of India: A Report*. New Delhi: Government of India.

PTI News Agency. 2016. "Demonetisation: Rahul, Mamata Attack PM; 'Yagna' Against Graft, Says Modi." *Indian Express*, December 9. http://indianexpress.com/article/india/demonetisation-rahul-mamata-attack-pm-yagna-against-graft-says-modi-4417144/.

Qureshi, S. 2015. "Modi to Gift Women Insurance Scheme This Raksha Bandhan." *India Today*, September 4. http://indiatoday.intoday.in/story/narendra-modi-to-gift-women-insurance-scheme-this-raksha-bandhan/1/460260.html.

Rahman, S.A. 2010. "Hindu Fundamentalists to Oppose Job Quota Proposals." *The National News*, January 20. https://www.thenationalnews.com/world/asia/hindu-fundamentalists-to-oppose-job-quota-proposals-1.543198.

Raj, K. 2023. "Indian Muslims in Haryana Face Calls for Economic Boycott After Violence." *Al Jazeera*, August 12. https://www.aljazeera.com/news/2023/8/12/muslims-in-haryana-face-calls-for-economic-boycott-after-violence-in-nuh.

Rana, T. 2024. "Why This Year's Interim Gender Budget Is Riddled with Ambiguity." *Behan Box*, February 6. https://behanbox.com/2024/02/06/why-this-years-interim-gender-budget-is-riddled-with-ambiguity/.

Rashid, O. 2024. "Over 10,000 Teachers and 26 Lakh Students Left in Lurch with UP Madrasa Act Struck Down." *The Wire*, March 24. https://thewire.in/education/uttar-pradesh-madrasa-act-allahabad-high-court.

Roy, R. 2019. "A Tale of Two Disenchantments." *Business Standard*, August 1. https://www.business-standard.com/article/opinion/a-tale-of-two-disenchantments-119030500024_1.html.

Roy, T. 2023. "Unpaid Labour on the Rise, Muslims Not Looking for Work: What the PLFS Data Reveals." *The Wire*, October 16. https://thewire.in/economy/unpaid-labour-on-the-rise-muslims-not-looking-for-work-what-the-plfs-data-reveals.

Saikia, A. 2020. "Assam Says It Banned Madrassas and Sanskrit Schools to Secularise Education. Critics Say Look Closer." *Scroll.in*, December 17. https://scroll.in/article/981434/assam-says-it-banned-madrassas-and-sanskrit-schools-to-secularise-education-critics-say-look-closer.

Savarkar, V.D. 1969. *Essentials of Hindutva*. Bombay: Veer Savarkar Prakashan.

Shani, O. 2007. *Communalism, Caste and Hindu Nationalism: The Violence in Gujarat*. Cambridge: Cambridge University Press.

Sharma, A. 2013. "State Transparency After the Neoliberal Turn: The Politics, Limits, and Paradoxes of India's Right to Information Law." *PoLAR: Political and Legal Anthropology Review* 36 (2): pp. 308–325.

Sharma, S., and K.N. Das. 2024. "Thousands of Indian Teachers Set to Lose Jobs as Muslim School Funding Ends." *Reuters*, January 11. https://www.reuters.com/world/india/indian-state-cuts-pay-some-teachers-muslim-religious-schools-2024-01-11/.

Singh, P., and F. Pattanaik. 2020. "Unfolding Unpaid Domestic Work in India: Women's Constraints, Choices, and Career." *Palgrave Communications* 6 (1): p. 111.

Sinha, A., and M. Priyam. 2023. "'Willing' Ethnic-Nationalists, Diffusion, and Resentment in India: A Micro-Foundational Account." *Modern Asian Studies* 57 (3): pp. 1027–1058.

Sinha, D. 2024. "The Multidimensional Poverty Index Is Not All-Encompassing." *The Wire*, January 24. https://thewire.in/economy/the-multidimensional-poverty-index-is-not-all-encompassing.

Sircar, N. 2020. "The Politics of Vishwas: Political Mobilization in the 2019 National Election." *Contemporary South Asia* 28 (2): pp. 178–194.

Sitlhou, M. 2021. "In Assam, Ban on State-Run Madrassas May Force Girls to Drop Out." *Al Jazeera*, March 11. https://www.aljazeera.com/features/2021/3/11/shut-down-of-madrasas-in-indias-assam-could-see-girls-drop-out.

Skaria, A. 2016. *Unconditional Equality: Gandhi's Religion of Resistance*. Minneapolis: University of Minnesota Press.

Supreme Court of India. 2023. In the Supreme Court of India Civil/Criminal Appellate/Original Jurisdiction, Writ Petition (Civil) No. 906 of 2016; 2 January 2023,

Vivek Narayan Sharma versus Union of India. https://main.sci.gov.in/supremecourt/2016/37662/37662_2016_3_1501_40708_Judgement_02-Jan-2023.pdf.
Tagade, N., and S. Thorat. 2020. "Intergroup Inequality in Wealth Ownership in Rural India: Caste, Tribe and Religion." *Journal of Social Inclusion Studies* 6 (2): pp. 117–132.
Teltumbde, A. 2020. Introduction to the Revised Edition. In *Hindutva and Dalits: Perspectives for Understanding Communal Praxis*, edited by A. Teltumbde, pp. xiii–xl. New Delhi: Sage.
Verma, P. 2024. "CMIE Data Points to Rising Unemployment Among the Youth." *Financial Express*, January 10. https://www.financialexpress.com/jobs-career/cmie-data-points-to-rising-unemployment-among-the-youth-3360188/.
Whyte, J. 2019. *Morals of the Market: Human Rights and the Rise of Neoliberalism*. London: Verso.
The Wire. 2023a. "Muslims' Enrolment in Higher Education Less Than SCs, STs; UP Worst, Kerala Lone Outlier." *The Wire*, May 30. https://thewire.in/education/muslims-enrolment-in-higher-education-less-than-scs-sts-up-worst-kerala-lone-outlier.
The Wire. 2023b. "Questioned on Minorities, Jaishankar Says 'Show Me Discrimination.' The Facts He Can See." *The Wire*, September 29. https://thewire.in/government/questioned-on-minorities-jaishankar-says-show-me-discrimination-the-facts-he-can-see.

Chapter 14
Redressing Structural Inequalities of Displaced Women and Girls in Latin America's Protracted Crises

Pía Riggirozzi

Introduction

In the last several decades, increasing inequalities across the Global South have been accelerated by political, economic, social, health, and climate crises in a wide range of countries. Consequently, Latin America, the most unequal region in the world, has seen a significant number of people falling into cycles of vulnerabilities, poverty, and dispossessions, with millions embarking on migration trails, some more dangerous than others.

While shocks from some (global) crises may be inevitable, what should not be unavoidable are policies and systems of protection, nationally and regionally, that address and reduce vulnerabilities and inequalities. Most inequalities and vulnerabilities, including those caused by failed political and protection systems, are seen in what became south–south migration corridors. In effect, Latin America faces one of the largest mass migrations worldwide. By 2024, nearly 8 million refugees and migrants have left Venezuela; 84% of whom fled to the Latin American region. In Central America, the number of asylum seekers and refugees traveling northward, particularly from El Salvador, Guatemala, and Honduras, has grown rapidly since 2016 by almost 60%, due to a combination of gang violence, poverty, and the increasing impact of droughts on farmers, which forced thousands to leave their places. Half of the displaced are women and girls, who carry their path dependency to transit and destination countries, where they face further systemic vulnerability compounded by unequal access to rights, services, and social protection.

Pía Riggirozzi, *Redressing Structural Inequalities of Displaced Women and Girls in Latin America's Protracted Crises*. In: *The Social Acceptance of Inequality*. Edited by: Francesco Duina and Luca Storti, Oxford University Press.
 DOI: 10.1093/oso/9780197814499.003.0014

This chapter assesses structural inequalities leading to protracted crises in Latin America and how the effects are gendered. It argues that the salience of (forced) migration is a marker of structural inequities that are gendered, and that the politics of protection and social norms risk defaulting to logics of gender-blindness and even neglect, reproducing further inequalities that tend to be socially legitimized and rarely contested.

Following the framework proposed in this volume, this chapter focuses on intersecting inequalities that affect forced migrant women and that reproduce what are identified as "group logic inequalities," which in this case are manifested in arbitrary hierarchical distinctions between groups where some are deemed either inferior in the social hierarchy, or not deserving, or are simply neglected. This logic often intersects with other dimensions, including gender, migration status, and poverty, which perpetuates conditions of group inequality.

In the context of displacement, governments and nongovernmental organizations supporting humanitarian action may implement policies that are ostensibly neutral but fail to account for the specific needs and vulnerabilities faced by displaced women and girls. These gender-blind policies effectively position women and girls in further situations of vulnerability and precarity, perpetuating their marginalization. In light of this, the chapter also proposes that a new approach to share responsibility, suggesting that regional governance is needed in order to redress gender inequalities and to support adequate, fair, sustainable, and gender-responsive governance and societies.

Inequality in Latin America

The unequal distribution of income, wealth, and opportunities in Latin America has significantly hindered the development of cohesive societies and robust democracies. During most of the first two decades of this century, solid economic growth rates in Latin America helped improve social indicators (Lopez-Calva and Lustig 2010). However, gains have stagnated since 2015, when growth started to falter with the end of the commodity boom (Feierherd et al. 2023). Furthermore, despite significant efforts in social policy to address poverty and inequality through post-neoliberal welfare strategies, these efforts have not succeeded in redefining the structural determinants of inequality. Instead, they have created tensions between socioeconomic and ecological spheres, which undermine inclusive citizenship and democracy (Riggirozzi 2020).

Inequality in Latin America is a persistent and pervasive issue that significantly affects social mobility, perpetuating a cycle of poverty and limiting opportunities for economic advancement and inclusive development (Alvaredo et al. 2024). The economic divide is stark: The World Inequality Report stated that the poorest 50% of the population earns a mere 10% of the total income, while the wealthiest 10% take home 55% (see Arreaza Coll 2023). According to the CAF Development Bank's report (2022), *RED 2022: Inherited Inequities*, this inequality perpetuates itself because human capital, which includes education and health, asset accumulation such as property and investments, and labor opportunities, strongly favors wealthy families. This is the inequality trap that impedes social mobility—that is, a break with those conditions that reproduce poverty and inequality in Latin American nations and across generations.

This has been the core of a recent debate about inequality of opportunity, a concept that has been developed by Ferreira and Gignoux (2008) since the mid-2000s, and that refers to the unequal distribution of life chances among individuals, which is determined by circumstances beyond their control, such as their family background, place of birth, gender, ethnicity, and social class. For example, a recent study led by Brunori et al. (2023) examines the significant role of "inherited" factors in contributing to current income inequality in Latin American countries. It highlights that a substantial portion of income inequality, ranging from 44% in Argentina to 62% in Guatemala (Brunori et al. 2023, 31), stems from factors such as being born in low-income areas, belonging to ethnic minorities, and having parents with limited education or low-paying jobs. The study also points out that in countries with histories of slavery or oppression of Indigenous peoples, these inherited factors significantly hinder social mobility. Similarly, the study notes that geography also plays a crucial role in inequality. Although 80% of the population in Latin America lives in cities, rural dynamics, particularly the low productivity of small farms, contribute significantly to income inequality. Ultimately, the findings underscore the variable nature of inequality in the region, showing how it is influenced by factors that affect its transmission across generations, hence the complexity of approaches to address it.

While this debate about (the lack of or truncated) opportunities leading to the perpetuation of inequalities makes a clear case for inherited background conditions, family networks, and societal biases that may prevent social mobility and escape from the poverty and inequality trap, this analysis of determinants of persistent inequality has been criticized for being overly focused on individual- and family-level skills reproducing self-perpetuating cycles of social disparities. This is problematic because such an approach overlooks structural barriers, including power relations, that inhibit equality of opportunities and conditions for living independently in and contributing to society. In other words, individuals' capabilities and social mobility opportunities are part and parcel of a social order that may manifest and reproduce itself through a complex interplay of various factors that contribute to (the reproduction of) inequality, many of which are more difficult to quantify but are crucial in shaping social and economic outcomes. For example, Anderson (2015), Piketty (2014), and Stiglitz (2012) argue for a comprehensive approach to understanding inequality, one that transcends the individualistic and/or family path–dependent focus on capabilities and income to emphasize the importance of recognizing factors that include cultural capital, certifications, status, social class, citizenship, ethnicity, gender, and other individual attributes such as height, weight, physical appearance, skin color, and neuro and physical divergency. These factors influence the construction of stereotypes and prejudice that structure various types of inequalities and inequities, discriminatory policies, economic systems, and social norms that advantage certain groups over others. Furthermore, these types of social and normative constructions not only affect and inhibit the social acceptance, integration, and social mobility of disadvantaged groups but also shape and reproduce relations of domination and what is identified here as group inequalities.

What this discussion suggests is that, while inequality is related to access to opportunities, and to a large extent access to economic survival, this is just one aspect of the broader experience of individuals and groups for whom inequality is also the result of how they are perceived and accepted in and as part of society. All of this points to relational explanations in the scope of other spheres linked to daily and social life in which subjects interact and the unequal relations they may be subject to.

This relational aspect of inequality highlights how individuals and groups in society are immersed in socioeconomic, political, social, and cultural relations. For example, in everyday relationships and practices, discrimination and prejudice may operate based on value judgments rooted in customs, traditions, myths, beliefs, and perceptions that affect not only social notions of entitlement, belonging, and deservingness for some (and not others) but also the formation of identities based on racial, gender, national, and other prejudices. Consequently, a group logic of inequality manifests where inequalities are deemed justified and normalized reflecting perceived and manifested unequal standing of groups in relation to each other within society. In contexts of forced migration and displacement, particularly in relation to women and girls in displacement, migration management practices by governments and social constructions often reflect hierarchical distinctions and biases against this specific group, perpetuating gendered inequality as a result. In other words, a group logic of inequalities in this case manifests in gender-blind policies and practices that systematically disadvantage displaced women and girls in contexts of transit and settlement. Furthermore, social (political and economic) relations in these scenarios lead to social segmentation and inequalities, cementing power relations that are gendered. Often, despite efforts to address inequality, resistance to change from those benefiting from the status quo further entrenches these patterns.

The next section builds from these notions to examine how migration and inequality intersect and reproduce gendered harms affecting opportunities for migrant women and girls in Latin America to rebuild lives and communities.

Situating Gender Inequalities and Opportunities in the Context of Forced Migration

The potential role of migration for development has been recognized in the 2030 Agenda for Sustainable Development with a specific target in Sustainable Development Goal 10.7, although it remains silent on broader contributions of migration to development outcomes, let alone to reduce inequalities and further gender inequalities.

Over the past two decades, global instability has increased and with it more people have been forced to flee their homes. By 2023, a staggering 110 million individuals had been displaced worldwide, according to the United Nations High Commissioner for Refugees (UNHCR), mainly due to conflict, climate shocks, and economic turmoil.

Within the Americas, these changes are largely propelled by persistent inequalities, including economic insecurity, political turmoil, poverty, and violence, forcing many individuals to consider migration as their most viable option for seeking new opportunities and even survival. For example, in the last decade alone, El Salvador, Guatemala, and Honduras have seen the number of asylum seekers and refugees moving northward grow rapidly because of insecurity, human rights violations, poverty, and inequality. Globally, the number of asylum seekers and refugees from El Salvador, Guatemala, and Honduras had reached over 687,000 by mid-2023. Conditions in Venezuela have led almost 8 million to leave their country for Colombia, Brazil, Ecuador, and the Caribbean since 2014. Women represent around 30% of the total of Central American migrants to Mexico and 50% of Venezuelan migration to Brazil and Colombia.

Displacement often emerges as an alternative to enhance the living conditions of individuals and their families, especially women facing vulnerable circumstances. Conflict and wars are determinants of forced migration but so are economic challenges, political unrest, poverty, and gender violence, which stand out as primary drivers compelling people to seek refuge outside their countries, particularly for women and girls. For many women and girls, conditions in their home country are intolerable and leave them with no reasonable alternative other than to flee the country because of direct threat or the prospects of physical insecurity, because of the loss of shelter and livelihood, or because their ability to care for themselves and their families is radically undermined.

In stark contrast to the prosperity of previous decades, and despite being home to the world's largest oil reserves, economic chaos, the decay of state infrastructure, and intense social and political conflict meant that, by 2020, Venezuela had become the poorest economy in the region (Cheatham and Roy 2023), and that, by 2024, nearly 8 million people had fled the country. Half of them are women and girls (HRW n.d.). This is a crisis with a distinctive gendered feature, not only because of the magnitude of displaced women and girls but also because this exodus has seen thousands of pregnant women fleeing for reasons of practical necessity including fear of losing their babies or their own lives if they remained to give birth in their own country. According to Amnesty International (2018), maternal mortality increased by 65% in Venezuela between 2015 and 2016, a regression of twenty-five years due to the lack of medicine, such as anticoagulants, painkillers, and antibiotics; and the lack of basic medical tools, equipment, and medical personnel. That context prompted many women to flee.

Migration provoked by the lack of food, adequate healthcare in the home country, lack of access to adequate education for children, or violence, particularly gender-based violence (GBV), is forced and is gendered. A study about health inequalities of migrant women and adolescent girls in Latin America shows that out of 2,012 Venezuelan migrant women and girls interviewed in Manaus and Boa Vista, Brazil, 54% highlighted reasons related to difficulties in obtaining food and hunger as reasons for fleeing, 38% stressed access to health treatments, and 28% cited GBV reasons (Do Carmo Leal et al. 2024).

In Central America, extortion and GBV have also meant that many women and mothers with their children faced no other option but to leave. According to Mejia-Mantilla and González Rubio (2024), migration flows from the north of Central America (El Salvador, Guatemala, Honduras, and Nicaragua), follow a regional trend that has intensified over the past ten years. Around 3.8 million people from these countries were living in the United States in 2021 (Meija-Mantilla and González Rubio 2024). Flight from violent contexts may be motivated both by generalized fear of death or injury and by women's fears of vulnerability to sexual violence or fears as mothers caring for their children. Or women may be compelled to flee by the urgent need to secure minimally decent living conditions for themselves and their children, for example, healthcare and education opportunities. As women are often primary caregivers, in situations of extreme poverty or environmental disasters, there are often gendered social expectations that delegate the role of seeking new opportunities to support their families to them (Cintra et al. 2023; Lines et al. 2024).

Feminist work in migration studies has underscored the nuanced and often invisible gender-specific challenges that women and girls face in relation to migration, including biased power relations and harmful practices in their home countries. Situations of early marriage, female genital mutilation, social stigma, GBV, and poverty not only affect the autonomy and well-being of women and girls but also are in themselves drivers of migration (Menjivar and Walsh 2017; Tastsoglou et al. 2021).

The increased attention on the gendered makeup and motivations of migration also increased the focus on the risks that women and girls face on the move, particularly in relation to sexual abuse, violence, trafficking, and labor exploitation. Crossing borders can also be biased and affected by institutional violence, institutional and interpersonal forms of discrimination, arbitrary decisions, and treatment. For example, at Mexico's southern border, where migrants from Central and South America traveled on foot to avoid border controls, Médecins Sans Frontières (2020) reported that police and gangs, often in collaboration with one another, were alleged to be perpetrators of sexual and gendered violations.

This bleak situation is manifest in the hundreds of thousands that have crossed the Darién Gap into Panama. This is one of the most dangerous crossings in the world, where border crossers have reported being victims of robberies, assaults, and sexual violence. These large numbers primarily represent Venezuelan migrants who initially settled in countries such as Colombia, Ecuador, Peru, and Chile, and who, due to low wages, inflation, and job shortages in those countries, were now undertaking the perilous journey to reach the US border. Médicins Sans Frontières reported treating over 100 cases of sexual violence in the first five months of 2022 alone, not to mention the ones that go unreported. Sadly, gender-specific challenges that women and girls face in displacement are often concealed and unreported.

The circumstances and conditions of displacement may themselves generate threats to the sexual and reproductive health of women and girls. The Pan American Health Organization reported that female forced migrants are particularly exposed to risks of exploitation, sexual violence, and risky sexual behavior for survival, leading to increasing numbers of unwanted pregnancies, sexually transmitted infections, maternal death, and precarity in general (PAHO 2019). In addition to the dangerous journeys, many women and girls suffer inadequate access to food and water, and experience exhausting walks and traumatic situations during and as a consequence of modalities and duration of travel. Furthermore, choices that women and girls (are forced to) make in order to respond to, and cope with, risks faced during displacement may bring about new risks to their health, well-being, and dignity more broadly. For instance, women may (be/feel forced to) exchange sex for food, protection, or transport while in displacement (Angulo-Pasel 2018). Some migrants may also be subject to labor exploitation (Bastia and Piper 2019; Delgado Weiss 2013).

Finally, diverse migration statuses also affect and shape access to rights, and migration governance, including decisions over migration policy adopted by any one country will affect the number of people forced to take alternative, dangerous, and irregular routes, exposing them to further abuse and exploitation and to the strengthening of organized activities of gangsters, *polleros*, and *trocheros* (smugglers).

These factors, coupled with the denial of rights, discriminatory practices, and anti-migrant sentiments, determine gender inequalities, exacerbate vulnerabilities, and complicate not only the migration experience but also opportunities for women and girls in displacement to integrate in society, act autonomously, and achieve rights, goals, and equitable lives in society.

Upon arrival and settlement, women face multiple forms of inequality and discrimination; they have the most precarious and lowest-paid jobs; they suffer exploitation, abuse, and systemic violence; they do most of the unpaid domestic and care work; they have less access to education and healthcare; they are underrepresented in all spheres of political and economic power; and they are often excluded from decision-making. OXFAM (2024) reveals a dreary scenario where hunger, extreme economic inequalities related to labor exploitation, and various hardships characterize the daily lives of a large part of the world's population and are aggravated based on gender, and particularly affecting migrant women.

However, migrant populations are often not prioritized by social policies or social protection systems. Destination countries present difficulties in both labor inclusion, such as seeking decent employment, and social inclusion, including access to housing, healthcare, and education. Irregular migration status and manifestations of xenophobia, nationalism, and racism also impact the well-being of migrants, further complicating their situation.

Latin America's Progressive Migration Policies Are Insufficient to Address Inequality

Prior to the Venezuelan crisis, Latin America developed a distinctive approach to migration governance, emphasizing social entitlements like the portability of social security, labor mobility rights, and migrant human rights (Acosta Arcarazo and Freier 2015). Latin American migration and asylum frameworks are widely recognized as "progressive," "open," and "human rights-based" (Brumat and Finn 2021; Brumat and Freier 2020; Hammoud-Gallego and Freier 2023; Zapata and Wenderoth 2021). Experts have praised the region for its sustained and generous asylum policies since adopting the 1951 UNHCR Refugee Convention and its 1967 Protocol. The region's advanced understanding of refugeehood is reflected in the expanded definition within the 1984 Cartagena Declaration, inspired by mass displacements during the Central American civil wars of the 1980s (Cantor et al. 2015).

The Cartagena Declaration broadened the definition of a refugee to include those whose lives and liberties are threatened by various circumstances, without requiring a subjective fear of threat. An objective situation, such as an armed conflict, suffices for international protection under this regional framework (Cintra et al. 2023).

Countries like El Salvador, Guatemala, Nicaragua, and Panama have included protection for migrant women fleeing sexual violence, generalized violence, GBV, security threats, and human rights violations in their refugee laws. These provisions extend beyond the original 1951 Refugee Convention and 1967 Protocol, though dissemination of information on how to apply for refuge remains insufficient.

Latin America has significantly reshaped the international norms on refugee status, influencing humanitarian and regional cooperation in response to rights violations and refugee conditions. The Inter-American Human Rights System and regional integration processes have established jurisprudence to protect migrants, asylum seekers, and refugees. Agreements recognize the vulnerability of migrants and guarantee rights such as non-refoulement and due process in refugee status determination (CIDH 2015).

The Montevideo Consensus (2013) and the Brazilian Declaration and Plan of Action (2014) highlight these regional commitments, recognizing the integration of human rights jurisprudence with international refugee instruments. The Brazil Plan of Action also emphasized eradicating statelessness and improving cooperation on migration and asylum, including social integration and protection for vulnerable groups like children and survivors of sexual violence and GBV. The Regional Safe Spaces Network was created to ensure access to protection services for individuals at risk (UNHCR 2018).

Latin America's regional frameworks aim to secure human rights and meet the Sustainable Development Goals. The Mesoamerican Comprehensive Development Plan, for instance, seeks to make migration safe and address its root causes in Mexico and Central America (ECLAC 2021). The Comprehensive Regional Protection and Solutions Framework in Central

America and Mexico exemplifies regional cooperation for managing forced displacement, aligning with UNHCR's Global Compact on Refugees.

Despite these frameworks, implementation on the ground has been inconsistent. While Latin America's migration policies are progressive in principle, national policies often fall short in practice. Migration governance has focused more on management and securitization than on rights-based approaches (Lavenex and Piper 2019; Riggirozzi et al. 2023). Regional and national frameworks have also failed to address gender-specific drivers of migration and provide gender-responsive services for displaced women and girls.

Displaced women and girls who cross borders in search of refuge and well-being confront further challenges. Migration statuses work in practice to obstruct access to, and exercise of rights—both by blocking access to services and by obstructing conditions of reasonable security from exposure to sexual exploitation, assault, and violence. Challenges may reflect generalized conditions—municipal, provincial, or national governments in the places of temporary abode may lack capacity or will to provide the necessary protection—or more specific issues—insecure accommodation, lack of sensitivity to gender or culture in provision of health services, limited access to official employment (often related to lack of childcare), and local hostility to necessary fleers. Recent reports acknowledge that xenophobia is spiking, and Amnesty International (2022) highlights the continuing failure in places like Colombia and Peru, significant receivers of Venezuelan migrants, "to provide adequate protection for the women, who often face physical and sexual violence at home, but also exploitation at work, including being co-opted into sexual exploitation," noting that in spite "of high levels of under-reporting, GBV cases rose 71% between 2018 and 2021 in Colombia." A poll conducted by Gallup in 2016 and 2019 shows a sharp decline in migrant acceptance in Latin America, particularly in nations hosting Venezuelans (Esipova et al. 2020).

Feminist scholars of migration in particular have drawn attention to the problematic gender bias of protection in regional and international frameworks and practices. For example, Hennebry and Petrozziello (2019) claim that migration governance has historically been "gender-blind," as international commitments ignore the realities of movement and the gendered risks that women experience during migration. There is, they charge, a lack of gender responsiveness even in recent commitments such as the 2018 Migration and Refugee Compacts. Similarly, Sahraoui and Tyszler (2021) and

Freedman et al. (2022) have explored gender-blindness in current migration policies and practices, highlighting its effects on GBV and trauma (23). Others have claimed that there is a neglect of gendered specificities in the implementation of humanitarian programs in Latin America, all of which not only neglect gender-specific needs and rights but also reproduce gender inequalities (Riggirozzi et al. 2023). Furthermore, in the realm of humanitarian aid, a common concern is that gender-blindness in forced migration manifests as a lack of implementation of gender-sensitive programs and actions (Freedman 2010) that not only significantly impact on the effectiveness and sustainability of the aid provided but also reproduce disparities. That is, as Riggirozzi et al. (2023) argue, humanitarianism may alleviate the physical suffering of displaced women, prioritizing their immediate necessities, such as food, shelter, and medical attention. However, such a narrow focus may overlook the underlying factors contributing to the creation of such suffering, the contextual factors, or the effects of programs that empower but do not create conditions of autonomy. Such programs may support self-governance but sideline discussions and actions to redress both social, political, and economic relations of dependency and domination. They cannot address the systemic causes behind the harms that result from a humanitarian insistence on maintaining a needs-led program with a focus on emergency response and a nonpolitical stance.

A significant factor is that border towns, critical spaces of arrival and first settlement, often face preexisting conditions of uneven development, poverty, and economic inequalities. Local populations already struggling to have their needs and rights met by underresourced services, now must also struggle to respond to the needs and rights of migrants. This context not only exacerbates existing social and economic inequalities but also increases animosity against migrants. The lack of adequate housing, healthcare, education, and employment opportunities creates a harsh environment for newcomers. Already vulnerable because of their migration journey, they now often face social rejection, stereotyping, discrimination, and further barriers to integration. In such a context, discrimination, for instance, not only directly affects protection and health-seeking behavior but also contributes to a range of other negative outcomes such as interpersonal violence, stigma, and psychological distress. In many cases, precarious and informal work conditions further perpetuate poverty and inequality, constraining choices and leading to homelessness, transactional/survival sex, labor, and sexual exploitation.

These issues are exacerbated by misogynistic views and stereotypes that portray women in general, and migrant women and girls in particular, as hypersexual or promiscuous. These views and stereotypes lead to the acceptance of unequal standings in society as migrants are judged for being women, for being migrant, and for being a "moral risk." Furthermore, these constructs may be reproduced through social and cultural norms, attitudes, and the media, leading to discrimination and the objectification and dehumanization of (migrant) women who may lack the resources or support networks to report, defend themselves, or seek justice. Overall, in these kinds of scenarios, groups of migrants, and in our case, migrant women and girls, are affected by (unfair, harmful, and exclusionary) social notions and constructions of (un)deservedness based on migratory status, racial, gender, national, and other biases that create hierarchical distinctions between collectivities, i.e., between those who are seen as superior and deserving, and those who are seen as inferior and not deserving (of rights, economic opportunities, and social entitlement).

Gendering Responsibility for the Protection of Forced Migrant Women and Girls

Who holds the responsibility for respecting, protecting, and fulfilling the rights of women and girls in displacement? What role, if any, do regional organizations play in supporting governments to address the challenges and risks faced by migrants, especially forced migrants, and particularly women and girls in displacement?

These questions underscore the need for nuanced understandings both of gender inequalities and of group and gender inequalities as well as policies and systems of protection in place to redress such inequalities. Such efforts demand responsibilities of various actors, at different levels of governance. In addressing gender inequalities, particularly concerning women and girls in displacement, it is essential to recognize that responsibilities intersect with the specific challenges and inequalities faced by migrant women and girls throughout their journeys and in their places of abode.

In Latin America, inequalities refer not only to access to opportunities and resources that can break cycles of deprivation and exclusion, including those perpetuated across generations, but also to changing conditions that reproduce situations of vulnerability and unequal power relations due to discriminatory and abusive practices. Women and girls in displacement are often subject to domination due to dispossession and a lack of opportunities to exercise their lives independently and autonomously in the places of their choice. Redressing inequalities thus demands investment in distributional policies to enhance access to income, education, housing, and health, as well as to uphold equality of social status and reverse conditions that reproduce domination and abuse.

Ensuring safe passage and providing initial protection must address these gender-specific risks. This includes prioritizing safe routes that consider women and girls' safety concerns and offering gender-sensitive accommodations and support services at initial protection sites and places of first refuge. Gender inequalities can exacerbate women's vulnerability to exploitation and violence during transit and settlement. Ensuring safe mobility entails not only protecting women from abuses like human trafficking but also addressing underlying gender inequalities that make them more susceptible to harm. Providing settled protection must prioritize addressing these inequalities by creating conditions that support women's economic empowerment, education, and participation in decision-making processes (Cintra et al. 2023).

National responsibilities related to providing protection include safeguarding women and girls' safety and dignity in shelters, preventing exposure to risks of sexual assault and other harms, and providing adequate, gender- and age-appropriate, and culturally specific health services (Riggirozzi et al. 2023). This also involves creating conditions for women and girls to make autonomous and safe decisions about where and when to leave and live. These responsibilities are often affected not just by distributional costs and resources but also by social constructions of migrants, and forced migrants in particular, as risks (i.e., security risks and moral risks) reproducing biases and undermining opportunities for inclusion and mobility. States often leverage their sovereign prerogative, including political and economic (mis)calculations, to control the entry and rights of noncitizens and to pledge "security" of their populations for political ends, often undermining the social standing and opportunities of migrants.

Policies can address the needs and rights of migrant women and girls through legal and bureaucratic as well as social policies, welfare-oriented policies, and awareness campaigns to change attitudes against migrants and the acceptance of discriminatory and exclusionary outcomes.

Regional organizations hold significant potential in shaping collaborative, rights-based, and equitable approaches to migration, as well as supporting states developing effective strategies that address the intersecting vulnerabilities faced by migrant women and girls (Riggirozzi and Ryan 2022). Regional organizations can leverage their networks, including financial coordination with development banks and aid agencies, to support protection and welfare programs in compliance with the Cartagena Declaration, the Global Compact on Refugees, and international development commitments. The transnational and transboundary nature of displacement and protection highlights the importance of regional governance in coordinating policies and implementing programs that respond to these needs and rights in main traveling routes that connect states and border areas, as well as in places of permanent or temporary abode.

Conclusion

This chapter assessed structural inequalities embedded in protracted crises in Latin America and highlighted how these effects are gendered. It focused on the salience of forced migration as a marker of structural inequities and emphasized the need to redress politics of protection and social norms that reproduce socially legitimized and rarely contested inequalities. In this context, the chapter explored intersecting inequalities that affect forced migrant women, which default into logics of gender-blindness and are identified here as "group logic inequalities." These are manifested in arbitrary hierarchical distinctions between groups where dimensions including gender, migration status, and poverty perpetuate conditions of group inequality, in this case affecting forced migrant women and girls in Latin America.

This is a pressing case since the region has been facing what is the largest and unprecedented mass migration due to political, economic, and humanitarian crises in Venezuela. But sadly, the logics of group, gender-blind inequalities identified in this chapter are seen across the globe. Here, it was argued that in the context of displacement, governments and nongovernmental organizations supporting humanitarian action may implement policies that are ostensibly neutral but fail to account for the specific needs and vulnerabilities faced by displaced women and girls. These policy dynamics are heightened by social biases and power relations based on misconceived notions of "social deservedness" and social attitudes that reinforce situations of vulnerability and precarity, perpetuating harms and marginalization of migrant women and girls. In light of this, the chapter also proposed that a new approach to share responsibility and regional governance is needed to redress gender inequalities and support adequate, fair, sustainable, and gender-responsive governance and societies.

National responsibilities in providing protection include ensuring the safety and dignity of women and girls in shelters, preventing exposure to sexual assault, and offering adequate health services tailored to gender, age, and cultural specifics. However, these responsibilities are often undermined by social constructions of migrants as security and moral risks, which perpetuate biases and hinder their inclusion and mobility. States frequently leverage their sovereign prerogatives to control noncitizens' entry and rights, ostensibly pledging "security" for their populations, which often undermines the social standing and opportunities of migrants.

The transnational nature of displacement underscores the importance of regional governance in coordinating policies and implementing programs that respond to migrants' needs and rights. Effective regional collaboration can address these challenges in major traveling routes and border areas as well as in places of temporary or permanent settlement. This approach requires a concerted effort to change societal attitudes and norms regarding migrants and refugees, shaping collaborative, rights-based, and equitable approaches to migration and supporting states in developing effective strategies to address the intersecting vulnerabilities faced by migrant women and girls.

Grounding and institutionalizing national and regional commitments, programs, and policies to change conditions that justify and maintain economic and social inequalities and gender-based disparities within society demand a reconsideration of how "state sovereignty" and transnational responsibility are exercised. This includes border management and decisions about who has access to rights, what responsibilities are owed to forced migrants and refugees, and who deserves fair and equal treatment in society.

References

Acosta Arcarazo, D., and L.F. Freier. 2015. "Turning the Immigration Policy Paradox Upside Down? Populist Liberalism and Discursive Gaps in South America." *International Migration Review* 49 (3): pp. 659–696.

Alvaredo, F., F. Bourguignon, F. Ferreira, and N. Lustig. 2024. "Inequality Bands: Seventy-Five Years of Measuring Income Inequality in Latin America." CEPR Discussion Paper 18852. https://cepr.org/publications/dp18852.

Amnesty International. 2022. "Constant Violence and Absent Governments: The Twofold Lack of Protection Faced by Venezuelan Refugees." July 22. https://www.amnesty.org/en/latest/news/2022/07/twofold-lack-faced-by-venezuelan-refugees/.

Amnesty International. 2018. "Fleeing the Country to Give Birth: The Exodus of Pregnant Venezuelan Women." May 6. https://www.amnesty.org/en/latest/news/2018/05/huir-para-ver-la-luz-el-exodo-de-las-embarazadas-venezolanas/.

Anderson, T. 2015. "¿Por qué importa la desigualdad? Del economicismo a la integridad social" [Why Does Inequality Matter? From Economism to Social Integrity]. *Revista Mexicana de Ciencias Políticas y Sociales* 60 (223): pp. 191–207.

Angulo-Pasel, C. 2018. "The Journey of Central American Women Migrants: Engendering the Mobile Commons." *Mobilities* 13 (6): pp. 894–909.

Arreaza Coll, A. 2023. "Latin America's Inequality Is Taking a Toll on Governance." *Americas Quarterly*, February 8. https://www.americasquarterly.org/article/latin-americas-inequality-is-taking-a-toll-on-governance/.

Bastia, T., and N. Piper. 2019. "Women Migrants in the Global Economy: A Global Overview (and Regional Perspectives)." *Gender and Development* 27 (1): pp. 15–30.

Brumat, L., and V. Finn. 2021. "Mobility and Citizenship During Pandemics: The Multilevel Political Responses in South America." *Partecipazione e conflitto* 14 (1): pp. 322–340.

Brumat, L., and F. Freier. 2020. "South American *De Jure* and *De Facto* Refugee Protection: Lessons from the South." ASILE Project, Belgium, Forum on the new EU Pact on Migration and Asylum in light of the UNGCR. October 26. https://www.asileproject.eu/south-american-de-jure-and-de-facto-refugee-protection/.

Brunori, P., F. Ferreira, and G. Neidhöfer. 2023. "Inequality of Opportunity and Intergenerational Persistence in Latin America." *Latin America and Caribbean Inequality Review* Working Paper No. 109. https://eprints.lse.ac.uk/120555/1/LACIR_WP_109.pdf.

Cantor, D., L. Freier, and J.P. Gauci. 2015. "Introduction: A Paradigm Shift in Latin American Immigration and Asylum Law and Policy?" In *A Liberal Tide? Immigration and Asylum Law and Policy in Latin America*, edited by J.C. Cantor, J.P. Gauci, and L.F. Freier, pp. 1–10. London: School of Advanced Study, University of London.

Cheatham, A., and D. Roy. 2023. "Venezuela: The Rise and Fall of a Petrostate." Council on Foreign Relations, December 22. https://www.cfr.org/backgrounder/venezuela-crisis.

Cintra, N., D. Owen, and P. Riggirozzi. 2023. *Displacement, Human Rights, and Sexual and Reproductive Health: Conceptualizing Gender Protection Gaps in Latin America*. Bristol: Bristol University Press.

Development Bank of Latin America (CAF). 2022. *Inherited Inequalities: The Role of Skills, Employment, and Wealth in the Opportunities of New Generations*. Caracas, VE: Corporación Andina de Fomento. https://www.caf.com/media/4663355/red2022-english-version.pdf.

Do Carmo Leal, M., T. Dutra Gomes de Carvalho, Y. Ramos Portella Santos, R. Suely Bacuri de Queiroz, P.A. Morelli Fonseca, C. Landmann Szwarcwald, and P. Riggirozzi. 2024. "Migration Process of Venezuelan Women to Brazil: Living Conditions and Use of Health Services in Manaus and Boa Vista, 2018–2021." *BMC Public Health* 24 (1051). https://doi.org/10.1186/s12889-024-18109-5.

Economic Commission for Latin American and the Caribbean (ECLAC). 2021. *Comprehensive Development Plan*. https://repositorio.cepal.org/server/api/core/bitstreams/731c11c0-8099-4a63-9861-a4a7f32031b9/content.

Esipova, N., J. Ray, and A. Pugliese. 2020. "World Grows Less Accepting of Migrants." *Gallup*, September 23. https://news.gallup.com/poll/320678/world-grows-less-accepting-migrants.aspx.

Ferreira, F.H., and J. Gignoux. 2008. "The Measurement of Inequality of Opportunity: Theory and an Application in Latin America." Policy Research Work Paper No. 4659. The World

Bank Development Research Group Poverty Team. https://documents1.worldbank.org/curated/es/712171468154764908/pdf/WPS4659.pdf.

Feierherd, G., P. Larroulet, W. Long, and N. Lustig. 2023. "The Pink Tide and Income Inequality in Latin America." *Latin American Politics and Society* 65 (2): 110–144. 10.1017/lap.2022.47.

Freedman J. 2010. "Mainstreaming Gender in Refugee Protection." *Cambridge Review of International Affairs* 23 (4): pp. 589–607

Freedman, J., N. Sahraoui, and E. Tyszler. 2022. "Asylum, Racism, and the Structural Production of Sexual Violence Against Racialised Women in Exile in Paris." *Social Sciences* 11 (10): p. 426.

Hammoud-Gallego, O., and L. Freier. 2023. "Symbolic Refugee Protection: Explaining Latin America's Liberal Refugee Laws." *American Political Science Review* 117 (2): pp. 454–473. https://doi.org/10.1017/S000305542200082X.

Hennebry, J.L., and A.J. Petrozziello. 2019. "Closing the Gap? Gender and the Global Compacts for Migration and Refugees." *International Migration* 57 (6): pp. 115–138. https://onlinelibrary.wiley.com/doi/epdf/10.1111/imig.12640.

Human Rights Watch (HRW). n.d. "Venezuela: Events of 2023." Human Rights Watch. https://www.hrw.org/world-report/2024/country-chapters/venezuela.

Inter-American Commission on Human Rights (CIDH). 2015. *Human Rights of Migrants, Refugees, Stateless Persons, Victims of Trafficking in Persons, and Internally Displaced Persons: Norms and Standards of the Inter-American Human Rights System.* OEA/Ser.L/V/II. Doc. 46/15. http://www.oas.org/en/iachr/reports/pdfs/humanmobility.pdf.

Lavenex, S., and N. Piper. 2019. "Regional Migration Governance: Perspectives from Above and from Below." In *The Dynamics of Regional Migration Governance*, edited by A. Geddes, M.V. Espinoza, L. Hadj Abdou, and L. Brumat, pp. 15–35. Cheltenham, UK: Edward Elgar.

Lines, T., B. Curcio, J. Grugel, and N. Cintra. 2024. "Visual Narratives of Care and Reproduction in Forced Migration: Women Displaced from Venezuela to Brazil." *Bulletin of Latin American Research*. https://doi.org/10.1111/blar.13579.

Lopez-Calva, L.F., and N. Lustig. 2010. *Declining Inequality in Latin America: A Decade of Progress?* Washington, DC: Brookings Institution Press.

Médicins Sans Frontières. 2020. "Report: No Way Out—The Humanitarian Crisis for Migrants and Asylum Seekers Trapped Between the United States, Mexico and the Northern Triangle of Central America." February 11. https://www.msf.org/report-no-way-out-central-american-migration.

Meija-Mantilla, C., and S. González Rubio. 2024. "A Journey Through Borders: Understanding Migration in Central America." *World Bank Blogs*, January 18. https://blogs.worldbank.org/en/latinamerica/understanding-migration-central-america.

Menjívar, C., and S.D. Walsh. 2017. "The Architecture of Feminicide: The State, Inequalities, and Everyday Gender Violence in Honduras." *Latin American Research Review* 52 (2): pp. 221–240.

OXFAM. 2024. *Desigualdad S.A* [Inequality S.A]. https://oi-files-d8-prod.s3.eu-west-2.amazonaws.com/s3fs-public/2024-01/Davos%202024%20Report%20-%20Spanish.pdf.

Pan American Health Organization (PAHO). 2019. "Gender Equality in Addressing the Causes and Consequences of the Health of Migrant Women." Technical Report. https://www.paho.org/hq/index.php?option=com_docman&view=download&slug=international-women-day-2019-technical-note-eng&Itemid=270&lang=en.

Piketty, T. 2014. *Capital in the Twenty-First Century.* Translated by A. Goldhammer. Cambridge, MA: Belknap Press.

Riggirozzi, P. 2020. "Social Policy, Inequalities and the Battle of Rights in Latin America." *Development and Change* 51: pp. 506–522.

Riggirozzi, P., and M. Ryan. 2022. "The Credibility of Regional Policymaking: Insights from South America." *Globalizations* 19 (4): pp. 604–619.

Riggirozzi, P., N. Cintra, J. Grugel, G. Garcia Garcia, and Z. Carvalho Lamy. 2023. "Securitisation, Humanitarian Responses and the Erosion of Everyday Rights of Displaced Venezuelan Women in Brazil." *Journal of Ethnic and Migration Studies* 49 (15): pp. 3755–3773.

Sahraoui, N., and E. Tyszler. 2021. "Tracing Colonial Maternalism Within the Gendered Morals of Humanitarianism: Experiences of Migrant Women at the Moroccan-Spanish Border." *Frontiers in Human Dynamics* 3: pp. 642326.

Stiglitz, J. 2012. *El precio de la disgualdad* [The Price of Inequality]. Madrid: Taurus.

Tastsoglou, E., S. Petrinioti, and C. Karagiannopoulou. 2021. "The Gender-Based Violence and Precarity Nexus: Asylum-Seeking Women in the Eastern Mediterranean." *Frontiers in Human Dynamics* 3 (27). https://doi.org/10.3389/fhumd.2021.660682.

United Nations High Commissioner for Refugees (UNHCR). 2018. "The Regional Safe Spaces Network in the Americas: Lessons Learned and Toolkit." https://www.acnur.org/media/regional-safe-spaces-network-americas-lessons-learned-and-toolkit.

Zapata, G.P., and V. Tapia Wenderoth. 2021. "Progressive Legislation but Lukewarm Policies: The Brazilian Response to Venezuelan Displacement." *International Migration* 60 (1): pp. 132–151. https://doi.org/10.1111/imig.12902.

Chapter 15
Conclusion
From Acceptance Toward a More Equal World?

Francesco Duina and Luca Storti

The preceding chapters allowed us to grasp, with a good amount of empirical support, the four logics of acceptance/approval as they manifest in specific contexts. In this Conclusion, we leverage those insights to three ends. First, we reflect on how the logics function as mechanisms for the endurance and replication of economic as well as other kinds of inequalities. Second, we put forth ideas for possible initiatives for the reduction of those inequalities. Third, we identify promising new venues for empirical research.

The Logics as Mechanisms for the Endurance and Replication of Inequalities

We saw that the logics function as conceptual frameworks through which actors, in various positions of advantage or disadvantage, interpret and find acceptable economic inequalities. The logics are hence in the first instance subjective and can be investigated starting from the actors that subscribe to them. Yet, they are not "located" merely "in" those actors: They have intersubjective origins and evolve independently of any one person or group. They are transmitted, and partly modified, through the dynamics of action and interaction that occur in specific social contexts over time and space. The logics have a predominantly cultural nature. At the same time, their relevance extends well beyond the cultural sphere: They shape processes that are primarily economic and social in character. This perspective is consistent with long-standing research on the role of culture in structuring durable inequalities (Lamont et al. 2014; Tilly 1998; Valentino and Vaisey 2022; see also the Introduction in this volume).

Francesco Duina and Luca Storti, *Conclusion*. In: *The Social Acceptance of Inequality*.
Edited by: Francesco Duina and Luca Storti, Oxford University Press. © Oxford University Press (2025).
DOI: 10.1093/oso/9780197814499.003.0015

Our initial framework and the subsequent empirical chapters added further specifications. First, actors might differ in how intentionally and consciously they adopt these logics. Second, actors may vary in the enthusiasm or intensity with which they adopt any one logic or a combination of them. Third, while each logic is self-standing, it can combine with others to further reinforce the acceptance of economic inequalities. These combinations are diverse and varied, just like the mechanisms that underpin them. As such, they require empirical investigations to be understood and clarified, and this is best done in specific contexts. The chapters turned in most cases to countries for analysis: These are macro-scale territorial aggregates often characterized by internal heterogeneity, but they still function as one of the primary political, cultural, and institutional environments in which the logics are embedded. Accordingly, we paid attention to the multitude of factors that drive or support the logics, and to the connections between economic and other kinds of inequalities.

We wrote in the Introduction that any given work in the fairly extensive research on the acceptance of inequalities tends to focus on a single logic, typically in a single setting and in relation to a homogeneous set of actors. While valuable, such efforts hence preclude the possibility of a sustained, analytically cohesive comparative assessment of those logics as a variety of actors—including those in disadvantaged positions—employ them in multiple settings. One of the main contributions of our volume has therefore been not only to put forth a number of propositions (such as those just stated) that apply to all logics, while also recognizing the substantive differences between the logics, but also to reconstruct how the four logics can combine in different ways across specific contexts while adopting various nuances that still produce what we may call coherent "knowledge systems" that support the status quo and lead to the acceptance, and even approval, of inequalities.

In this section, we accordingly reflect on each logic and how—based on the findings from the preceding chapters—we see it combine with elements of other logics to generate powerful and multifaceted narratives of acceptance. This is perhaps one of the most distinctive insights emerging from the analyses in the chapters, and certainly one of the most relevant if our concern is to grasp how inequalities are produced and maintained. Our observations are by necessity not exhaustive but, rather, focused on some of the conceptually clearest—"ideal-typical," to return to Weber's language—combinations.

Consider first market and economic logics. We saw that adherence to these logics has strong instrumental and utilitarian traits. Typically, these rely on the belief that the market is an efficient mechanism for the allocation of resources and that inequalities, which it inevitably produces, must therefore be tolerated as negative externalities given all the efficiencies that market economies offer (Chapter 2). Yet, we also learned that market and economic logics can intersect with moral logics rather quickly (Chapter 2). Actors can view inequalities as desirable because they result from the application of different talents or dispositions that markets are able to recognize and reward more efficiently than other methods of resource allocation. Inequalities are therefore not only acceptable in a practical sense but also because they are fair. Indeed, at an even higher level of moral abstraction, the possibility of unequal outcomes may be seen as serving as a sort of glue for social integration: Individuals, after all, are willing to participate in society in part because of the rewards they can obtain (Chapter 7).

And here elements of cultural and institutional logics can therefore also find their way into the thinking process. One subscribes to market and economic logics partly because they appear to be in line with existing organizational arrangements or shared interpretations and representations that are valid and should not be disturbed (Chapter 10), or that are in the process of emerging with considerable momentum as a society evolves (Chapter 9). Calculations of practical benefits are in this manner matched with assessments of what sustains the social order. In all these cases, it is easy to see how the elements of logics thus combined can exert a remarkable hold on those who subscribe to them.

In contrast to market and economic logics, moral logics are in their purest form reliant on abstract values. As such, they are often unrelated to calculations of practical impacts on society. At the same time, it would be reasonable to expect them to vary across contexts, since ethical principles are often specific to local realities. But an important takeaway from our chapters suggests something different worth noting before reflecting on how these logics may interact with elements of other logics. As we move across models of capitalism, i.e., countries with uncoordinated market economies, those with coordinated market economies, and Asian capitalisms (Hall and Soskice 2001), similar moral narratives emerge supportive of economic inequalities. These include principles such as individual responsibility, meritocracy, the primacy of freedom over equality, and respect for free individual choices. They are the pillars of neoliberal ideology, present even in places that support a strong sense of collectivity, such as some Eastern Asian countries (Chapter 6; see also, Huat 1998), where they can combine with expectations of citizens' contributions toward social cohesion and the status quo.

At the same time, the chapters also highlighted the presence of potentially contradictory strands or conceptual tensions between certain elements of these moral logics. For instance, merit is often used to justify unequal outcomes. The same can be said of one's right to intergenerational wealth by way of, for instance, inheritances. Both can be seen as fair—in a moral sense—mechanisms for the creation and reproduction of inequalities. But, at their core, they are fairly antagonistic: Inheriting has little or perhaps nothing to do with merit. One result of this is that we saw actors working hard to smooth out these tensions, so as to use the most important strands for the acceptance of inequalities. In this example, those who inherit wealth seek (with more or less success, depending on their own intersectional positionalities) ways to instill merit in the process by, among other things, appealing to the idea of the intergenerational self (Chapter 8). The result is a more compelling logic of acceptance.

The chapters showed that these moral logics can combine with elements of other logics. Those from group logics seem especially relevant. Returning for a moment to the concept of the intergenerational self, we see, for instance, the reliance on relationships with family, kinship, and strong friendships. One extends oneself into an exclusive and elevated group which is deemed entitled to the advantages in question. Moral judgments, hence, flow into the worthiness of certain collectivities to which one belongs. Importantly, these groups can be very large, such as entire castes or religious communities (Chapter 13). Such combinations give moral reasonings of acceptance further appeal and legitimacy.

Our chapters suggest that moral logics can also combine with cultural and institutional logics. In the case of China, for instance, the widespread acceptance of economic inequalities based on a high level of institutional trust in the state also relies on moral notions of hard work (Chapter 9): If inequalities exist, they must be fair because they must reflect the broader will of the state. Abstract moral notions thus intersect with institutional variables. Of course, here the question of cognitive biases presents itself (Chapter 7): Those invested in the legitimacy of the status quo are less likely to see inequalities in the first place and thus are more likely to accept them when they are observed. More broadly put, several of our chapters emphasize how cognitive biases—about institutional realities and levels of inequalities—influence the adoption of single or combined logics.

Several chapters shed valuable light on cultural and institutional logics. As noted, the guiding principle of those logics is that inequalities "make sense" given existing interpretations, representations, and organizational arrangements. The latter are of course transmitted and socially acquired. It appears, therefore, that cultural and institutional logics unfold their potential when structures stabilize and persist over time: The logics require, and then further support, a certain continuity. The empirical evidence in the chapters confirms this (see, for example, Chapter 11 on the American Dream). However, our contributors also point to important moments of change which instigate the spread and adoption of new or existing elements of those logics.

In China, for example, a unique (re)configuration of market economy and socialist institutional structures (Nee and Opper 2012) has contributed to a reduction in absolute poverty, a sharp rise in economic inequalities, and a high level of acceptance of the new status quo still based on a perceived continuity between outcomes and the political system (Chapter 9). As a second example, in the Nordic countries, a combination of local and global economic changes accompanied by demographic shifts have made some resources, such as public funding for welfare programs, scarcer while also heightening concerns for the long-term viability of those societies (Chapters 5 and 12). This has prompted articulations of new or at least revised cultural and institutional logics whereby differences in otherwise historically egalitarian societies are now to be accepted when it comes to, for instance, access to welfare funds and levels of wealth. Not surprisingly, elements of group and ethnic logics have here come into play—contributing to what scholars have more broadly described as historical moments of continuing but also disruptive change in which different social orders reconfigure (for the idea of change as reconfiguration of preexisting social orders, see Boudon 1986; Stark 2009, xv).

The main driver of group and ethnic logics is a sense of belonging that we can define as oppositional. Processes of constructing collective identities are based on two complementary dynamics: the identification of a "we" and the opposition toward the "others" (Jenkins 1996; Remotti 2012; Sciolla 1983). In the case of group and ethnic logic, the second dynamic is predominant over the first. This, our chapters help us see, makes group and ethnic logics flexible. There are multiple communities, or multiple types of "others," that can be identified (or, more precisely put, constructed or imagined) in order to build oppositional relationships that solidify hierarchies among different social groups (Anderson 1983). In Chapter 5, for instance, the "others" are "foreign investors" in Finland. These are seen as potentially dangerous because they can distort the economic assets and power relations of the country. In India (Chapter 13), they include Muslims and anyone who departs from the prescribed vision of the country as Hindu and, as such, hierarchically organized and reliant on everyone's commitment to that order. In Scandinavian countries (Chapter 12), a social resentment is growing, with immigrants increasingly being identified as scapegoats for the perceived risk of losing once-guaranteed public services. Consequently, there is a rising demand for restricting immigrant access to welfare—a disposition labeled as welfare chauvinism.

This helps us see how group and ethnic logics can interact with elements of the other logics and, as with the other logics, it is perhaps in these combinations that they provide the most useful material for the acceptance of inequalities. Again, in the case of India (Chapter 13), we observed them at work with cultural and institutional and market and economic logics that invoke a mixture of populist and authoritarian policies with neoliberal principles. In Latin America (Chapter 14), the acceptance of female migrants as unequal is predicated on group differentiation that is itself reliant on broader cultural and institutional contexts in those countries that have naturalized asymmetric relationships when it comes to women and migrants. Simply put, creating a "lower" group of migrant women that is less deserving is consistent with existing attitudes and policies.

These intersections among the four logics enhance their abilities to support and reproduce the acceptance of economic inequalities and, with those, other kinds of inequalities that interact with economic ones, such as those related to religion, gender, status, or class. Certainly, each logic has its own impact. The acceptance of inequalities based on economic logic hinders the demand for policies aimed at reducing inequalities. Moral logics, on the other hand, lend normative support narratives that justify inequalities. Cultural and institutional logics foster a sort of cognitive conformity that orients people to the existing order and hampers alternative possibilities. Group and ethnic logics promote, in turn, the maintenance of privileges for certain groups over others, who have fewer resources to overturn the existing order. But one of our main points is that these logics are seldom at play on their own. They are active in specific contexts, where they take on particular articulations that are embraced by actors in various positions. And there they combine with elements of the other logics to further solidify and likely amplify the presence of economic and other kinds of inequalities. Table 15.1 summarizes the following points.

Table 15.1 The four logics and the acceptance of inequalities

Logics	Core features	Observed combinations with other logics	Support and reproduction of inequalities
Market and Economic	Instrumental and utilitarian disposition	Inequalities emerging from the market can also be seen as fair (moral logics) and in line with existing organizational arrangements/shared interpretations (cultural and institutional logics)	Reducing the demand for policies addressing inequalities
Moral	Abstract values	Moral judgments are also influenced by the perceived worthiness of the collectivities to which one belongs (group logics) and intersect with institutional variables (cultural and institutional logics)	Normative support for narratives justifying inequalities
Cultural and Institutional	Sense-making according to interpretations, representations, and organizational arrangements	The sense-making of inequalities based on shared interpretations and representations can also be mediated by the collectivities to which one belongs (group and ethnic logics)	Cognitive conformity supporting the existing order and hampering alternative possibilities
Group and Ethnic	Oppositional belonging	Hierarchical relationships between different groups can support identity or even authoritarian policies, which can coexist with certain neoliberal principles (cultural and institutional and market and economic logics)	Promoting the maintenance of privileges for certain groups over others

Initiatives for the Reduction of Inequalities

We stated at the outset that a motivating factor for this volume was our concern with growing economic inequalities in the world. We join many others in deeming many of the existing inequalities harmful to social cohesion, the fulfillment of human potentials, the well-being of vast segments of the world's population, the environment, the fate of democracy, and more (Killewald et al. 2017; Krugman 2007; Milner 2021).

But we, of course, do not intend to suggest that we oppose every single case of inequality. One of the takeaways from our chapters is in fact the presentation of evidence suggesting that contextual considerations matter a great deal. Growing inequalities in India, for instance, are the result of tens of millions of people leaving absolute poverty behind—something hardly dismissible as altogether undesirable. By contrast, wealthy Americans becoming even better off, while the American Dream becomes truly just a dream for most, is certainly less appealing. Whether more inequality in historically egalitarian Nordic countries should be categorically opposed seems, in turn, debatable. There is also truth to the notion, associated with market and economic logics, that the promise of greater wealth is a genuinely motivating factor for most people in ways that can create positive outcomes for others as well. The same may be said for cultural and institutional systems that are supportive of some unequal outcomes, and for the fact that changing those systems can sometimes generate widespread negative consequences.

With this said, there are, of course, plenty of reasons to worry about the extent of the existing inequalities—from the presence of entrenched barriers to opportunities to the promotion of ineffective policies—and to wonder what steps might be taken toward their amelioration. In our review of the literature in the Introduction, we pointed to an extensive body of work on the topic. We do not aim to delve deeply into this discussion: It is not the volume's primary objective. At the same time, our chapters provide us with insights that lend themselves to certain ideas. We highlight some of the most relevant here.

Our main focus is on three types of interventions addressing the logics themselves. Those logics support inequalities. We saw in the various chapters, however, that they may rely on inaccurate or biased processes. If so, it seems reasonable to suggest that efforts be made to redress or even challenge those logics. Doing so could decrease the acceptance of inequalities that they generate, or at least help not to take existing inequalities for granted and natural.

To start, some of our contributors highlighted that those who subscribe to those logics have incorrect understandings of the actual inequalities in the world. For instance, those who believe in meritocracy in the first place are less likely to perceive existing inequalities accurately: They see less of them (Chapter 7). As a result, while already predisposed to not consider inequalities a problem (given their beliefs in meritocracy), the selection bias in perception further decreases the chances that they will worry about them. We also learned that those who have limited exposure to lower-income and lower-wealth realities are less likely to think those realities exist or are significant (Chapter 4).

It follows that think tanks and government agencies interested in correcting this tendency could invest in producing high quality data and campaigns designed to disseminate relevant information widely in media outlets, publications, and other venues. Those who are inclined not to see the existing inequalities would have more contact points with reliable information and empirical material. We recognize that exposure to the data may on its own not change people's minds, as social scientists have argued for a long time (Hoschild and Einstein 1993). But we also know that how them data is presented can make a big difference for how it is received and processed: If put forth in narrative form as part of a story, for instance, it may be better received (Krause and Rucker 2020). Attention should therefore go to ensure the most effective communication strategies.

Second, we learned that actors tend to accept inequalities because they see them in line, or consistent, with supposed cultural and institutional arrangements that, in fact, may not be as they are assumed to be. This has less to do with perceptions of inequalities as such, and more with assessments about the world around those inequalities. Thus, we read that Americans are fine with inequalities because they see them, after all, as the natural result of the American Dream—which, it turns out, is increasingly a myth not reflective of current levels of intergenerational mobility and life chances (Chapter 11). In the case of China, a large number of Chinese look favorably on inequalities because they assume they are somehow reflective of a capable and well-intentioned (i.e., trustworthy) government (Chapter 9). Their assessment of the Chinese state can certainly be questioned. In cases like these, it follows that acceptance of inequality would diminish greatly if the working assumptions about the broader world are challenged.

Specific circumstances would dictate how such challenges could be mounted. But they would likely rely on informational campaigns, sustained data dissemination efforts, and other such initiatives undertaken by domestic or external actors. This is precisely what Riggirozzi proposes in Chapter 14 when envisioning a transformative role for regional organizations in Latin America in mobilizing networks and financial resources to increase, among other things, awareness of the plight of female migrants—whose inequalities are otherwise accepted partly because key actors fail to see them as derivative of particular intersections and instead bundle them with a more generic understanding of what migrants experience.

A third point of intervention would address the expectations present in specific articulations of the four logics—especially market and economic ones—which lead actors to accept inequalities. In Chapter 3, for instance, we read that people working in hedge funds, venture capital, and technology startups are quite comfortable with inequalities in part because they believe in the benefits their industries generate for the economic well-being of citizens, pension funds, and philanthropic activities. But whether these are correct assessments is an open question. In Chapter 5, we see that Finnish legislators have proposed wealth tax reforms that would widen inequalities domestically as desirable because, supposedly, those reforms would encourage wealthy Finns to invest domestically and keep away harmful foreign investors who do not have Finland's best interest at heart. The argument, however, is clearly reliant on several suppositions—which may or may not be true—around what wealthy Finns might do, what the impact of their actions might be, and whether, in fact, this would prevent foreigners from investing in the country.

It would be useful to identify those expectations, make them explicit, and assess them. It would thus seem constructive to undertake empirical analyses to test these expectations and make the resulting findings publicly available in simple language accessible to those who hold on to the logics but also those inclined to challenge them. Here, too, we recognize that the presentation of facts alone can only do so much. For instance, plenty has been written about the limitations of trickle-down economics around tax cuts for the rich, which serves as a frequent expectation in market and economic logics (Hope and Limberg 2022). Yet, the idea has become a myth that is difficult to debunk (Campbell forthcoming). But our suggested point of intervention departs from challenging those logics in a general sense. We think more success can be encountered when elements of those logics are invoked at times implicitly in particular moments and places, as, for instance, shown in Chapters 3 and 5. Unveiling those elements as specific actors employ them implicitly and bringing awareness to them could have value, especially when accompanied by empirical counterarguments. Hence, our point of intervention calls again for finely tuned approaches targeting specific moments and places.

We have so far made suggestions centered on the inherent shortcomings of the logics themselves. Our chapters, however, also put forth ideas and empirical material that could prove useful for the design of policies aimed more directly at the reduction of some of the most significant levels or dimensions of inequalities. Consider the findings around the extent to which wealth, supported precisely by the logics of acceptance, tends to reproduce itself and activate what are sometimes called St. Matthew effects: The rich get richer, and conversely, those who are not rich will stagnate or have less and less going forward and into future generations (Storti and Dagnes 2021). This is often not only a matter of economic class but also of race, gender, and more broadly socioeconomic status. Intergenerational inequalities continue while barriers to entry into the elite classes get increasingly difficult to penetrate. We learned about this in the case of those who inherit wealth in the United Kingdom (Chapter 8), financial and tech elites in the United States (Chapter 3), the upper castes in India (Chapter 13), and high-income, educated males in countries across the globe (Chapter 2).

What do these chapters suggest? The logics of acceptance operate in (and lend support to) entrenched systems of self-sustaining inequalities that are exclusive: Those who are in reap the benefits of further wealth, while those who are out continue to be excluded. It follows that simply spreading more opportunities and enabling markets to reallocate resources—while potentially useful—will likely not prove sufficient to change matters. Automatic corrections relying on market dynamics will not be sufficient. Something else is required. Transferring some wealth from the top to the bottom of social hierarchies might yield some results. The prioritization of fiscal interventions on income should accordingly be considered (Guillaud et al. 2020). We note that the conservative turn that began in the 1980s has reduced the progressivity of income taxes, though this process has unfolded differently across various contexts (Lierse 2022). In Europe, the progressivity of income tax has persisted much longer; whereas in the United States, it has been significantly reduced. This trend is widely regarded as one of the main causes of the increase in economic inequalities. A promising lever would therefore be the increased progressivity of taxation of income.

Such a move, however, would not single-handedly solve the problem: The postindustrial, globalized, and highly financialized economy has made wealth accumulation partly independent of income dynamics (Keister 2018; Killewald et al. 2017). Thus, it would also seem essential to consider increasing wealth taxation and developing methods to identify hidden wealth (Harrington 2016; Scheuer and Slemrod 2021; Zucman 2015). This calls for innovative policies and coordination among countries. It will of course be challenging to achieve because many countries, not just so-called tax havens, compete by creating advantageous fiscal frameworks to attract foreign capital, resulting in fiscal dumping. But efforts in this direction could bear significant fruit in attractive ways that might gain wide support. They may be balanced by tax-reducing measures, such as tax exemptions for companies for profits reinvested in innovative, environmentally sustainable initiatives, as well as by measures that support business practices that, while still aiming for profit, promote less hierarchical organizational and decision-making processes (Sobering 2022).

Thus, our chapters also suggest that attention go to policies that prevent the consolidation of inequalities in the first place. Those promoting equal opportunities, regardless of individuals' social backgrounds (Keister and Southgate 2022; McCall 2016), come immediately to mind. These include a broad spectrum of initiatives that span from equal access to the school system and higher education to active initiatives to succeed in unstable labor markets. They are primarily social policies that constitute the main pillars of welfare systems and that, it seems to us, should be pursued with conviction.

New Venues for Empirical Research

We stated in the Introduction that once the logics of acceptance emerge and consolidate, they can be considered—to use Durkheim's terminology—as social facts that are cultural in nature. At the same time, we saw—in line with Weberian sociology—that actors appropriate and use these logics in ways that are not purely passive: They create and recreate articulations of these logics. Our approach is not eclectic but follows a well-established attempt to combine cultural (and structural) factors with agency. Actors operate in constraints and opportunities that are more or less binding, but they retain initiative and latitude. Consequently, we believe that future research on this topic should empirically turn to the schema of the four logics spanning both macro and micro levels of analysis (Hedström and Bearman 2009).

We do not adopt an organicist or consensualistic view of society, imagining that logics tend to spread in a homogeneous and undifferentiated manner. We have already indicated this when discussing the intensity and enthusiasm with which logics are adhered to. Future research should delve into these aspects more deeply. The embeddedness of these logics within social groups should be further investigated through situated comparative studies. Who adopts these logics and in what combinations?

One option is to keep the territorial context fixed and compare social classes to observe whether the logics correlate with class variables. Preliminary examples of this type of research include examining the logics behind significant issues like tax progressivity and redistribution, whose importance we have already highlighted (Atria 2023). From our perspective, in fact, low enthusiasm toward progressivity suggests a preference for existing economic inequalities. For instance, what logic underlies the resistance to accepting tax progressivity among the elites, middle classes, or lower classes? Additionally, within a given social class or specific social group, such as the elite, other variables—such as gender, generational affiliation, and access to different schools (Carranza et al. 2024)—should be tested for their relevance.

Another option would see scholars identify empirical puzzles—e.g., correlations contradicting expectations, "common sense or the predictions of established theory" (Gambetta n.d., 1; Swedberg 2014, 149)—that need exploration.[1] For example, what logics lead some members of the elite to take positions that appear contrary to their interests, considering economic inequality unacceptable and urging redistributive political measures? On the other hand, what combinations of logics do individuals belonging to the lower class adopt in their support for and acceptance of inequalities, despite being disadvantaged? Or why, in highly disadvantaged urban areas, do we often see more acceptance of inequalities than in areas with moderate well-being?

Reversing perspectives, we could keep class belonging or other similar variables constant and compare different territories to see how diverse combinations of logics might emerge. This approach would allow us to estimate the weight and relevance of contextual variables in shaping these logics. Such research could be quantitative or qualitative, similar to multi-sited field ethnographies. Contextual variables to observe might include the economic structure of production (e.g., the prevalence of traditional or innovative activities), demographic variables (e.g., a population's distribution by age and the presence of immigrants), political arrangements (e.g., stable or conflicting government coalitions), macroeconomic institutions and systems of economic organization (e.g., the different models of capitalism) (Granovetter 2017, 2), and the preexisting levels of economic inequalities.

An additional value of such a research project would be that it would allow for the accumulation of knowledge and a repertoire of mechanisms that can be useful for diachronic comparative investigations. Through diachronic comparisons, conducted at different points in time within a defined territory, it might be possible to understand if and how the logics change in relation to more or less radical and abrupt changes occurring in a circumscribed context, which itself may be rather local or extensive and beyond national boundaries.

When it comes to techniques for empirical analysis, we think—as the chapters themselves have shown convincingly—that there is no reason to express an a priori preference for qualitative or quantitative ones. Each type has its advantages. Moreover, there are, in fact, strong grounds to recognize the value of combining qualitative and quantitative methods for one main reason: Quantitative analyses of data from large databases can help identify correlations between variables, but these must be supplemented by in-depth case studies if we wish to obtain a deeper sense of how people think. Put differently, employing both techniques could serve as an effective way to identify macro-empirical regularities and grasp the micro-mechanisms that can explain them. On this front, we point here to the strength of two non-standard techniques, often used to combine micro and macro perspectives so as to capture the dynamics of interaction within structures of interdependence (Squazzoni et al. 2014). These are experiments and simulation analyses (Gërxhani and Miller 2022; Squazzoni et al. 2014). Both have proven effective in research on economic inequalities and could find valid applications in the empirical study of the logics of acceptance.

Regardless of the style and type of empirical investigations, we believe that a great deal remains to be discovered about the logics of acceptance. We hope that our volume offered a sustained and useful effort in that direction and look forward to seeing what future studies will reveal.

Note

1. We point here to the work of Abbot (2004) and Becker (2008) as valuable references for how to identify promising research questions in given fields of inquiry.

References

Abbott, A.D. 2004. *Methods of Discovery: Heuristics for the Social Sciences*. New York: W.W. Norton & Company.

Anderson, B. 1983. *Imagined Communities: Reflections on the Origin and Spread of Nationalism*. London: Verso.

Atria, J. 2023. "No Taxation Without Efficiency? Elite Perceptions of Redistribution and Progressivity in Chile." *Journal of Latin American Studies* 55 (1): pp. 103–128.

Becker, H.S. 2008. *Tricks of the Trade: How to Think About Your Research While You're Doing It*. Chicago: University of Chicago Press.

Boudon, R. 1986. *Theories of Social Change: A Critical Appraisal*. Los Angeles: University of California Press.

Campbell, J.L. Forthcoming. *Pay Up! Conservative Myths About Tax Cuts for the Rich . . . And Why They're Wrong*. New York: Cambridge University Press.

Carranza, R., D. Contreras, and G. Otero. 2024. "What Makes Elites More or Less Egalitarian? Variations in Attitudes Towards Inequality Within the Economic, Political and Cultural Elites in Chile." *Socio-Economic Review* 22 (3): pp. 1141–1167. https://doi.org/10.1093/ser/mwae008.

Gambetta, D. n.d. "Empirical Puzzles for Teaching and Research." https://www.nuffield.ox.ac.uk/people/sites/gambetta-research/.

Gërxhani, K., and L. Miller. 2022. "Experimental Sociology." In *Handbook of Sociological Science*, edited by K. Gërxhani, N. D. de Graaf, and W. Raub, pp. 309–323. Cheltenham, UK: Edward Elgar Publishing.

Granovetter, M. 2017. *Society and Economy: Framework and Principles*. Cambridge, MA: Harvard University Press.

Guillaud, E., M. Olckers, and M. Zemmour. 2020. "Four Levers of Redistribution: The Impact of Tax and Transfer Systems on Inequality Reduction." *Review of Income and Wealth* 66 (2): pp. 444–466.

Hall, P.A., and D. Soskice. Eds. 2001. *Varieties of Capitalism: The Institutional Foundations of Comparative Advantage*. Oxford: Oxford University Press.

Harrington, B. 2016. *Capital Without Borders: Wealth Managers and the One Percent*. Cambridge, MA: Harvard University Press.

Hedström, P., and P.S. Bearman. Eds. 2009. *The Oxford Handbook of Analytical Sociology*. Oxford: Oxford University Press.

Hochschild, J., and K. Einstein. 1993. *Do Facts Matter? Information and Misinformation in American Politics*. Norman: Oklahoma University Press.

Hope, D., and J. Limberg. 2022. "The Economic Consequences of Major Tax Cuts for the Rich." *Socio-Economic Review* 20 (2): pp. 539–559.

Huat, C.B. 1998. Asian Values: Restraining the Logic of Capitalism? *Social Semiotics* 8 (2–3): pp. 215–226.

Jenkins, R. 1996. *Social Identity*. New York: Routledge.

Keister, L.A. 2018. "Income and Wealth Are Not Highly Correlated: Here Is Why and What It Means." *Work in Progress*, October 29. http://www.wipsociology.org/2018/10/29/income-and-wealth-are-not-highly-correlated-here-is-why-and-what-it-means/.

Keister, L.A., and D.E. Southgate. 2022. *Inequality: A Contemporary Approach to Race, Class, and Gender*. New York: Cambridge University Press.

Killewald, A., F.T. Pfeffer, and J.N. Schachner. 2017. "Wealth Inequality and Accumulation." *Annual Review of Sociology* 43 (1): pp. 379–404.

Krause, R.J., and D.D. Rucker. 2020. "Strategic Storytelling: When Narratives Help Versus Hurt the Persuasive Power of Facts." *Personality and Social Psychology Bulletin* 46 (2): pp. 216–227.

Krugman, P. 2007. *The Conscience of a Liberal*. New York: W.W. Norton.

Lamont, M., S. Beljean, and M. Clair. 2014. "What Is Missing? Cultural Processes and Causal Pathways to Inequality." *Socio-Economic Review* 12 (3): pp. 573–608.

Lierse, H. 2022. "Globalization and the Societal Consensus of Wealth Tax Cuts." *Journal of European Public Policy* 29 (5): pp. 748–766.

McCall, L. 2016. "Political and Policy Responses to Problems of Inequality and Opportunity: Past, Present, and Future." In *The Dynamics of Opportunity in America: Evidence and Perspectives*, edited by H. Braun and I. Kirsh, pp. 415–442. Berlin: Cham, Springer International.

Milner, H.V. 2021. "Is Global Capitalism Compatible with Democracy? Inequality, Insecurity, and Interdependence." *International Studies Quarterly* 65 (4): pp. 1097–1110.

Nee, V., and S. Opper. 2012. *Capitalism from Below: Markets and Institutional Change in China*. Cambridge, MA: Harvard University Press.

Remotti, F. 2012. *Contro l' Identità*. Roma-Bari: Laterza.

Scheuer, F., and J. Slemrod. 2021. "Taxing Our Wealth." *Journal of Economic Perspectives* 35 (1): pp. 207–230.

Sciolla, L. 1983. *Identità: Percorsi di Analisi in Sociologia*. Torino: Rosenberg & Sellier.

Sobering, K. 2022. *The People's Hotel: Working for Justice in Argentina*. Durham, NC: Duke University Press.

Squazzoni, F., W. Jager, and B. Edmonds. 2014. "Social Simulation in the Social Sciences: A Brief Overview." *Social Science Computer Review* 32 (3): pp. 279–294.

Stark, D. 2009. *The Sense of Dissonance*. Princeton, NJ: Princeton University Press.

Storti, L., and J. Dagnes. 2021. "The Super-Rich: Origin, Reproduction, and Social Acceptance." *Sociologica* 15 (2): pp. 5–23.

Swedberg, R. 2014. *The Art of Social Theory*. Princeton, NJ: Princeton University Press.

Tilly, C. 1998. *Durable Inequality*. Los Angeles: University of California Press.

Valentino, L., and S. Vaisey. 2022. "Culture and Durable Inequality." *Annual Review of Sociology* 48: pp. 109–129.

Zucman, G. 2015. *The Hidden Wealth of Nations: The Scourge of Tax Havens*. Chicago: University of Chicago Press.

Index

For the benefit of digital users, indexed terms that span two pages (e.g., 52–53) may, on occasion, appear on only one of those pages.